NORWAY	1940	ARCTIC	1941–3
SPARTIVENTO	1940	NORTH AFRICA	1942
ATLANTIC	1941–3	BARENTS SEA	1942
BISMARCK ACTION	1941	SALERNO	1943
MEDITERRANEAN	1941	BISCAY	1943
MALTA CONVOYS	1941	NORTH CAPE	1943

Above: *Sheffield* was the first major warship to abandon traditional brass in exchange for stainless steel, an experiment it was hoped would eliminate the daily polishing of easily tarnished brass. The cruiser's bell was a gift from Hadfield Ltd, and all other brightwork was of brilliant steel. *Sheffield* would subsequently always be the 'Shiny Sheff' or simply 'Old Shiny'.

Below: HMS *Sheffield* in October 1937, when she joined the fleet at Rosyth.

HMS SHEFFIELD

The Life and Times of 'Old Shiny'

RONALD BASSETT

NAVAL INSTITUTE PRESS

Published and distributed in the United States of America by the
Naval Institute Press, Annapolis, Maryland 21402

Library of Congress Catalog Card No. 88-61703

ISBN 0-87021-434-9

© Ronald Bassett, 1988

Designed and edited by DAG Publications Ltd. Designed by
David Gibbons; edited by Michael Boxall, layout by Anthony A.
Evans; typeset by Typesetters (Birmingham) Ltd., camerawork
by M&E Reproductions, North Fambridge, Essex; printed and
bound in Great Britain by The Bath Press, Avon.

Jacket illustration: HMS *Sheffield* in late 1942; a painting by
Geoff Shaw.

The illustrations in this book have been collected from many
sources, and vary in quality owing to the variety of circumstances
under which they were taken and preserved. As a result, certain
of the illustrations are not of the standard to be expected from the
best of today's equipment, materials and techniques. They are
nevertheless included for their inherent information value, to
provide an authentic visual coverage of the subject.

GENERAL ARRANGEMENT, TOWN CLASS CRUISERS, AS BUILT

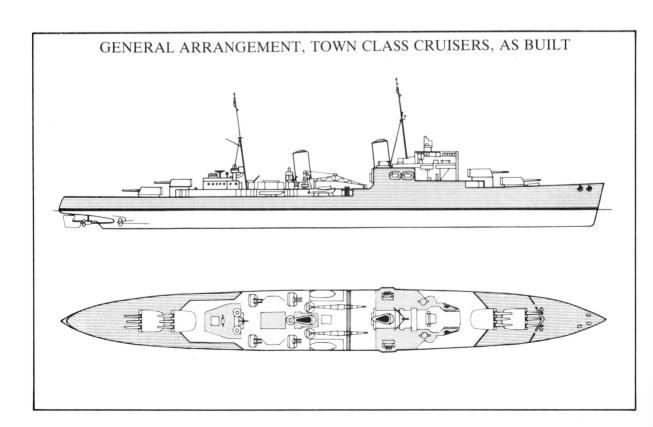

Contents

Preface

HMS SHEFFIELD was one of the most distinguished warships to serve throughout the Second World War and, indeed, for twenty-two years after. The story of her life was originally planned by Lieutenant-Commander Hubert Treseder, RN, who had been her Air Defence Officer, then Damage Control Officer, and finally her First Lieutenant. He began by faithfully copying every entry in *Sheffield*'s logs from August 1937, when she was accepted from the builder, to September 1967, when she was towed to the breaker's yard. In 1968 he contacted hundreds of ex-members of *Sheffield*'s crews, asking for their memoirs, photographs, diaries and letters relating to their service in the ship, and from these he formulated a preparatory chronological outline. Unfortunately, before a typescript suitable for publication could be embarked upon, Treseder died.

The material he had accumulated was left in the care of Captain Kenneth Harkness, CBE, DSC, RN (Rtd), who had commanded *Sheffield* during 1945 and 1946. Subsequently, in the hope that something could be salvaged from Treseder's preliminary work, Harkness consulted the Naval Historical Branch of the Ministry of Defence; it was possible, he considered, that another author of suitable qualification might be persuaded to adopt the project and carry it through to completion. Agreeing, the present author made a fresh start in August 1983, and although Treseder's material amounted to little more than a ship's log embel-lished by anecdotes from her crews, I have no hesitation in conceding that all the wearying spadework of foundation research was Treseder's. He provided the thread; I knitted it.

In addition to Hubert Treseder and, of course, the very many officers and men who contributed material – some of whom are mentioned in the narrative – I owe a special debt of gratitude to Captain Harkness, without whose persistence this chronicle would never have been started; to Mr Timothy Nixon, assigned the copyright of the Treseder papers, and finally for the immense help and cheerful encouragement of Commander Michael Wilson and Miss Muriel Thirkettle of the Naval Historical Branch of the Ministry of Defence – who, in response to my frequent silly questions, never gave me a silly answer. Michael Wilson, of course, is a distinguished author in his own right.

All that is written here is true. Most is drawn from the experiences of those who took part, and much has never before been published. There is only one person in these pages for whom I cannot vouch with hand on heart. He is Bungy Williams, who symbolizes the British lower deck rating in every warship and every theatre during the war. If Bungy Williams did not serve in *Sheffield*, he served in another cruiser, or perhaps a destroyer, or anything, and if he did not say what I have written, it must have been Bogey Knight, or Tug Wilson, or Pincher Martin.

Ronald Bassett

Genesis

HMS *SHEFFIELD* was one of a class of ten light cruisers laid down for the Royal Navy between 1934 and 1936 in answer to the new *Mogami* class of Japan and the *Brooklyn* class of the USA. The British warships, with a designed speed of 32 knots, would have a displacement of almost 10,000 tons and carry twelve 6-inch guns in four triple turrets, eight 4-inch guns in twin mountings, and lighter calibre AA weaponry in addition to six deck-mounted torpedo tubes. Their Japanese and American rivals all mounted heavier armament, but the Director of Naval Construction had advised against following suit and, indeed, in due course the *Mogami* and *Brooklyn* designs were both found to be attempting too much within the limitations imposed by light cruiser dimensions.

The first of the British ships, building on the Clyde and Tyneside respectively, were named *Polyphemus* and *Minotaur*, and if normal practice was being followed the remaining vessels would probably have been *Bacchante*, *Argonaut*, *Ariadne*, *Amphitrite*, *Spartiate*, *Europa*, *Endymion* and *Theseus*.

There was no official explanation for a sudden departure from tradition; one suggestion was that lower deck sailors were incapable of correctly pronouncing these mythological names, but it seems more likely their abandonment was part of a pallid attempt to generate local interest in the new ships at a time of widespread resentment towards expenditure on the armed services. Before completion, *Polyphemus* and *Minotaur* were renamed *Southampton* and *Newcastle*. The others were to be *Sheffield*, *Glasgow*, *Birmingham*, *Manchester*, *Liverpool*, *Gloucester*, *Belfast* and *Edinburgh*. The *Town*-class cruisers were arguably the best known during the war – a compromising but well-balanced design based on proven principles and exploiting the best features of the earlier *Leander*s and *Amphion*s. One of them, *Sheffield*, became almost certainly the most famous cruiser in the history of modern sea warfare.

The Admiralty was still uneasy about the new ships' main armament, which was undeniably lighter than that of foreign counterparts, and in 1935 decided to 'stretch' the last two hulls building – *Belfast* and *Edinburgh* – by 22 feet, adding a thousand tons, so that they could accommodate sixteen 6-inch guns in four quadruple turrets. However, following trials with the new gun mounting at Shoeburyness during February 1936, the DNC had to concede that, for four-gun turrets to function satisfactorily, the entire design of the ship must go back to the drawing-board; it was not enough simply to tack on 22 feet of length.

There was, however, no time for replanning. Germany, having already produced three 'pocket battleships' and laid down two further and even better vessels, had re-introduced conscription. The Italians were bombing Abyssinian tribesmen; the League of Nations was totally discredited. Spain was on the brink of civil war. Nobody knew what the Japanese were up to, but it was sure to be sinister, and the USA, under Franklin D. Roosevelt, recovering from the evils of prohibition but not yet having clawed free of the depression, wished to know nothing about anything except re-establishing the dollar and cultivating the Hollywood bonanza. The rest of the world could go to hell.

Belfast and *Edinburgh*, lengthened, received the same main armament as others of the class, but with twelve instead of eight 4-inch guns. Despite being built largely in order to keep pace with other navies, all the *Town*s would serve with distinction during the Second World War, and although in profile they presented a somewhat massy target, high standards of peacetime construction allowed them to absorb heavy punishment, and neither the *Brooklyn* nor the *Mogami* cruisers possessed their seagoing qualities.

The *Town*s could bring six guns to bear on a target ahead or astern, and twelve on either beam, and wartime experience was to show that fire control and armour were just as important as the number of guns.

1

'May God bless all who sail in her . . .'

THERE was news from Spain of a revolt against the Republican government, a matter of small concern yet. The Abyssinian slaughter had ended as Emperor Haile Selassie fled his country and Mussolini proclaimed the birth of a new Roman Empire. In Soviet Russia a series of purge trials had liquidated more than half the Red Army's senior officers, and German troops had occupied the demilitarized Rhineland.

In New York Max Schmeling had knocked out the young Negro Joe Louis in twelve rounds, and the huge airship *Hindenburg* was flying the first regular transatlantic passenger flights. The Berlin Olympic Games were only a month away. In the cinemas Garbo, Coleman and Cagney ruled; recent releases included Korda's *Things to Come* and Chaplin's *Modern Times*. Amy Johnson was a national heroine and Sir Oswald Mosley had raised the British Union of Fascists. In Trenton State Prison, USA, Bruno Hauptmann had died in the electric chair for the alleged kidnapping and murder of the Lindbergh baby, and in Manchester, England, a man was fined £4 for being drunk on one of the new Belisha pedestrian crossings.

The first Hawker Hurricane fighter had just been delivered to the Royal Air Force, and the Air Ministry had placed an order for 310 Supermarine Spitfires. The black homburg hat, now an 'Anthony Eden', was replacing the bowler for the smart executive, but twenty years after the Somme disabled ex-servicemen still stood at kerbsides, caps in hand. Most of the great names were no more; French, Haig, Allenby, Lawrence of Arabia – all had gone. Only four months earlier, Admiral Earl Beatty had died after attending the funeral of old King George and, shortly before, that of Admiral Lord Jellicoe.

There was shocked discussion of an alleged attempt on the life of the new King as he was riding in state up Constitution Hill by one George Andrew McMahon, who had flourished a pistol wrapped in a newspaper. Only a discreet few in Britain yet knew of the King's deepening involvement with the twice-married American, Mrs Wallis Simpson; none guessed he had only five months to reign.

On 23 July, in Newcastle-upon-Tyne, rain had fallen with monotonous persistence all day, stippling the gun-metal surface of the river, filling the gutters and soaking the soot-blackened brickwork of congested yards, foundries, wharfs and engine sheds on both sides of the waterway. In the Scotswood Road and City Road, shining with wetness, workpeople with shoulders hunched waited for the swaying trams that would take them eastward to Hebburn or westward to Blaydon. There was a pervading, inescapable smell of wet coal-dust and chimney smoke.

In Vickers-Armstrong's yard at Walker the red-and-white bunting that draped the planking of a launching platform hung heavily sodden. For several days past workmen had been white-washing kerbstones and walls, pulling weeds from the crane-tracks and filling pot-holes with gravel, and since early morning anxious faces had peered at the sky. Now the tenacious rain had penetrated the whitewash to the grime beneath and the pot-holes again brimmed with black water.

At five in the evening the first of the seven thousand ticket-holding guests were arriving – first the ordinary folk in their Sunday and funeral clothes, wives and families of the yard's workmen anxious to be early and so miss nothing, many with treasured hats confined to paper bags until the last moment. There followed the foremen, junior managers and office staff in suits made to measure and feigning nonchalance, then the brass band from the Company's works in Barrow and a visiting party of German schoolboys. The bored-looking reporter from the Newcastle *Journal* pushed his bicycle clips into a damp pocket and sucked on a Gold Flake.

The last accessible shelter from the rain had been appropriated by the guard and band of the RNVR Tyne Division in their pipe-clayed caps, belts and gaiters, with the two groups of bandsmen eyeing each other distantly. The hired limousines were arriving with their distinguished passengers – local councillors and their wives with marcelled hair and dressed à la Ascot, the Lord Mayors of both Newcastle and Sheffield, each with retinue, the Vicar of Walker and a coterie of confused choirboys. Three tugs were idling on the Hebburn side of the river, with just sufficient way to hold them against the current, while at the head of the slipway the Union Flag, the White Ensign and the Vickers-Armstrong house flag were hoisted, to hang limply against their masts.

At 5.30 p.m., however, the rain suddenly ceased. There followed a few moments of uncertainty, and then the drenched, open space around the red-and-white platform began to fill with people anxious for a place. Polished boots sank unnoticed into puddles, hats emerged from paper bags, hair was patted and ties straightened. Shipyard apprentices raced to climb nearby cranes, and a party of men, each carrying a heavy hammer, filed in solemn step down into the dock and disappeared from sight. The bandsmen from Barrow gazed at the clouds because they had done this all before, and the guard of the RNVR Tyne Division shuffled self-consciously into straight lines hoping that nobody was watching who lived in our street. The Chairman, accompanied by several ladies and a knot of directors emerged from the yard office building, where they had been taking tea. Sir Charles frowned up at the sky, the directors frowned up at the sky, and hundreds of guests and employees dutifully followed suit.

The bandmaster from Barrow lifted his baton, but the introduction to *HMS Pinafore* was marred by a series of

bugle notes from the direction of the shipyard gate. Sir Charles removed his hat in anticipation and a black Daimler whispered through the puddles and halted. From it stepped Her Royal Highness the Duchess of Kent, that beautiful and serene lady who, as Princess Marina of Greece, had married George, Duke of Kent, two years before, to capture the affection of the British public as probably no foreign princess had done since Alexandra of Denmark.

Polite clapping, then cheers, came from the crowd, and the band from Barrow at last burst into brassy melody. The Duchess, ritually presented with a bouquet of dark-red roses, was shaking hands, smiling, nodding. Cameras flashed and councillors' wives curtsied, the Chairman beamed and the naval guard crashed to attention. The reporter from the *Journal* licked his pencil. Always get *names*, his editor insisted. And he would telephone London. It would be too late for the evening papers but he might get a column inch or two in the national dailies. There could be a tenner in it, all told, if he could use the shipyard telephone and if the *Chronicle* man didn't get to it first.

The warship launching ceremony was a well-rehearsed one in this yard and others on the river; generations of Tynesiders had built warships for the world. The choir chanted Psalm 107, of 'they who in this Ship, now and hereafter, shall commit their lives unto the perils of the deep'. The crowd needed no hymn sheets to help them sing 'Eternal Father, Strong to Save.' Exactly six months earlier they had voiced the same as an identical, sister hull had been named *Newcastle* in this very yard, and watched it slide slowly into the cold river. The blueprint had been three years in gestation, but it was hailed as the best for a 6-inch gunned cruiser to come from the Director of Naval Construction since the War. It was hardly surprising; only a handful of light cruisers had been put into the water in fifteen years.

And those years had not been the most harmonious for the Royal Navy, for the shipyards of Newcastle or for Britain. They had seen the General Strike and massive unemployment, widespread bankruptcy, demoralization and hunger, with men selling apples or matches at street corners or chalking pictures on the pavement to achieve a few coppers. Faced with a savage reduction in pay, the Atlantic Fleet had mutinied in 1931, and even dockyard workers such as these, who wore their Sunday clothes on a Thursday to watch a warship launching – among the most skilled of artisans – had queued for soup and bread at Salvation Army kitchens.

Now, God willing, the worst was past. There were ships to build and brass to be earned. The toffs could have their

Left: *Sheffield* was launched on 23 July 1936 by HRH Princess Marina, Duchess of Kent, attended by Commander Sir Charles Craven, Chairman of Vickers-Armstrong Ltd, from the Walker yard on the Tyne.

Imperial Airways and their weekends in Deauville. For working folk there was wireless in the home – the BBC and Radio Luxemburg – talking films and Newcastle United, the permanent wave, Woodbines, Weights, six pints on Saturday after the game, a lay-in on Sunday and a spare rib of beef with parsnips and Bisto gravy . . .

Mind, 'appen there were many on Tyneside less fortunate than the men of Vickers-Armstrong. Down river, two years before, the great Palmer's yard had been closed down, and Jarrow was still a ghost town of shuffling unemployed, means tests, pawned wedding rings, malnutrition and simmering desperation. Was not the age of Dickens long past? Very soon two hundred men of Jarrow, the fittest chosen from thousands of willing, would begin a march of 300 miles to London, carrying a petition to Parliament, to be shrugged off by Baldwin's government, disowned by both Labour Party and TUC, and condemned as 'mob pressure' by the Conservative Party.

Under the long hull the slipway chocks had been hammered free. It was 6.20 p.m. 'I name this ship *Sheffield*. May God bless all who sail in her –'

The bottle of champagne splintered whitely against the high stem painted in the Admiralty's specified 507A Grey. The crowd cheered again, anxious now to sidle towards the gate; there would be long queues for the trams and there could be more rain yet. The tugs' syrens whoop-whooped

as slowly, very slowly, the great hull began to move down the slipway towards the river.

Very many warships of the past had carried the names of counties, towns and seaports, and it was mildly surprising that none before had borne the name of the Yorkshire city of steel. The omission had at last been corrected, and Sheffield's leading citizens had no intention of allowing the occasion to pass unnoticed. After all, ten *Town*-class cruisers meant only ten selected names, of which Sheffield was one – and tha' knows what that means, lad, eh?

For a beginning, 'We feel that the Ladies of Sheffield', the Lord Mayor announced, 'would appreciate the opportunity of being associated with this historic occasion, and present for the use of the cruiser a silken Union Jack and a silken White Ensign.

'In order to make the appeal as widespread and representative as possible, donations of 6d and upwards will be welcomed, and it is suggested that £1.1s.0d. be fixed as the maximum individual gift.'

Sixpence, in July 1936, was perhaps a lot to expect as a minimum contribution. Sixpence (2½p) would buy freshly fried fish and chips for two, wrapped, with vinegar and salt thrown in, or a front seat at the Astoria for two hours of Paul Muni or George Raft, with a news reel and a Mickey Mouse. In Woolworth's, the Queen of every High Street, a wide miscellany of articles at sixpence were available to

Sheffield ladies – a pair of 'French suede' gloves or rayon stockings, stick-on rubber soles for worn shoes, lipstick or a bottle of Californian Poppy perfume, a string of synthetic pearls or eight ounces of good toffee. Sixpence would pay a man's tram fare to work for a week (he would walk home) or buy eight pounds of potatoes – so there would have been few sixpences from the working shop girls and factory women. Even so, the flags were presented to the Commander Superintendent three days before the launching, and would remain in HMS *Sheffield* for the next twenty-seven years.

The publicity value of contributing gifts to the first warship named after the city, however, was not overlooked in City Hall, by the Cutlers' Company and the boardrooms of a dozen other local organizations, most of which, it must be observed, showed a marked preference for having their names associated with the ship's officers than with her lower deck. There was a magnificent silver centre-piece for the Captain's cabin and another for the Wardroom, silver tankards, cigarette boxes and ash trays for both Gunroom and Warrant Officers' messes, a silver cigar box for the Captain and another for the Wardroom, a set of old Sheffield Plate coasters which would not have gone to the ratings' galley, and a number of paintings. Mind you, the ratings were not entirely ignored; they received dominoes, draughts and eight dartboards complete with darts. Only the two local football clubs, Sheffield Wednesday and Sheffield United, regarded the ship's ratings deserving of anything better than a few shillings' worth of table games. They jointly presented a silver challenge cup for inter-divisional football.

One unique gift to *Sheffield*, however, was the ship's bell. The warship was the first of her name and the first vessel to be launched by the Duchess of Kent. Because of her affiliation, stainless steel had replaced the traditional brass of centuries. Now she would be the first to install a bell of ERA/CR steel, cast in the East Hecla foundry of Hadfields Ltd, to a pattern lent by Mears & Steinbank, bell-founders of Whitechapel, London, who also tuned the finished casting when completed. The bell weighed 2½ hundredweights.

'We are not bell-founders,' Sir Robert Hadfield told his annual general meeting, 'but this bell has been completely manufactured within our own works, apart from the chasing of the coat of arms, from electrically melted ERA/CR steel. The casting was flawless and its surface was brought to a mirror finish in our own shops. It is the first and only bell to be made in this type of steel.'

Hadfield's ERA steel had capped armour-piercing shells for a quarter of a century and 'perforated Krupp Cemented Armour Plate of the Latest Type from 12 inches to 15 inches' during the previous war, but elsewhere in *Sheffield* many fixtures normally of brass were of stainless steel – handrails, staghorns, boat fittings, ladder trims – not, as

was suggested, because of the ship's name but simply as an experiment with a material that did not tarnish so quickly. Even so, within weeks, *Sheffield* had been nicknamed 'Shiny Sheff'.

Specialist officers, key ratings and the ship's first commanding officer, Captain W. P. Mark-Wardlaw, DSO, began standing by the ship, in the Naval Yard at Walker, as early as July 1936, a full year before her acceptance trials. They had the advantage of observing the progress of *Newcastle* (ex-*Minotaur*) which was building in the same yard and about three months advanced, so a number of the normally inevitable installation problems could be foreseen and avoided. On 20 August 1937 *Sheffield*, still the property of Vickers-Armstrong and flying the company's house flag in addition to the Red Ensign, slipped from her Tyneside berth for five days of trials in the North Sea. The day was fine and bright, a tangy breeze whipping the tops from a long swell as the cruiser cleared the estuary and heeled tentatively, turning northward into her first sea. On bridge and in engine-room it was impossible, now, for *Sheffield*'s naval personnel not to speculate as to whether this was going to be the ship in which they would serve during the coming war – for there was no reasonable doubt remaining that war in Europe must come soon. Franco's Nationalist armies were steadily devouring Spain, and the bombing of Madrid, Bilbao, Valencia, and the obliteration of Guernica had shown the world the devastating potential of air power. Both Germany and Italy had sent squadrons, tanks and other matériel to aid Franco's Fascists, and the Rome-Berlin Axis had been consolidated. The Japanese had signed the anti-Comintern pact and launched her armies into open war with China. The League of Nations looked the other way. Six months before, Hitler had boasted in the Munich Hofbrauhaus: 'We have become once again a world power.'

'During our 24-hour full-power trial,' recalled Lieutenant-Commander G. Blundell, one of the naval steaming party, 'we steamed flat out between the entrance of the Tyne and the Forth. One of the sea trials was to throw the engines at full speed ahead, about 34½ knots, to full astern. I went down to the main engine room to witness this manoeuvre, and I shall never forget the sight of the Engine Room Artificers on the controls, shutting off the ahead throttles and opening the astern throttles as fast as they could.'

It was as if, driving a powerful car at high speed, one suddenly hammered the gear lever into reverse – assuming that to be possible – only *Sheffield* was a ship of 10,000 tons.

'The whole engine-room shuddered – shook like a leaf – fit to bring the main steam pipes down on us. It was frightening.'

Blundell did not know, then, that the drastic test had cracked the 'A' bracket of the ship's starboard inner screw, and that specialist welders would be brought from Sweden to repair the damage.

On 25 August the ship, under the command of a civilian Tyne pilot, was pounding southward towards the home estuary at 32 knots, a bone in her teeth and her funnels streaming. To Blundell, the watchkeeping naval officer, the shoreline to starboard seemed uncomfortably close, and he suggested to Williamson, the pilot, that he might ease to seaward, but Williamson, with years of experience limited to slow-plodding freighters, was enjoying the rare experience, and shook his head. 'Oh, no, Mister – but if you don't like it, you take the ship.' Blundell shrugged, aware of the rebuke, and held his peace. The ship, after all, wasn't the Navy's yet, and presumably Williamson knew what he was doing.

Williamson, however, did not. *Sheffield*'s massive bow wave was generating a tidal bore that collided with the shore, raced along it with devastating speed, and exploded over the two old-fashioned breakwaters at Cullercoats. An elderly lady, Mary Graham of Newcastle, was swept into the sea accompanied by her deck-chair – fortunately to be quickly rescued – and dozens of basking holidaymakers on the sands were drenched.

If there were to be local recriminations, *Sheffield* was not to know, for the first entry was being written into the ship's log:

Wednesday, 25th August 1937.
1700: Hoisted White Ensign, and accepted HMS SHEF-FIELD from Messrs. Vickers-Armstrong Ltd., off Tyne entrance. Captain W. P. Mark-Wardlaw, DSO, Royal Navy, assumed command – with navigating party for passage to Chatham.
First turn of the screws, all debts paid.

Sheffield was a Chatham ship, to be serviced by that depot and manned from Chatham Barracks throughout her naval life. Chatham ships and men were regarded by those of the other two port divisions – Devonport and Portsmouth – as being lax and inefficient. There was never any real

evidence for such a claim, but it may have derived from the fact that Chatham, the smallest of the three dockyards, did not accommodate or provide crews for the larger and inevitably more rigidly disciplined warships – battleships, battle-cruisers and aircraft carriers – and were more accustomed to the comparatively relaxed routine of light cruisers and destroyers.

All three depots, however, were cheerless and dilapidated establishments dating from the beginning of the century, that had been neglected by successive Boards of Admiralty, who maintained that expenditure was unjustified because the barracks were soon to be demolished and rebuilt. They never were. Most men in barracks, unless they were natives of the locality, hungered for a draft to a sea-going ship, and, when it came, prayed that it did not mean a long and barren foreign commission during which so many became simply bovine time-servers, wishing away the months that separated them from their home-coming. As *Sheffield* sounded her way through fog to a buoy at Sheerness and, on the following day, entered the North Lock at Chatham, there would have been several hundred lower-deck men in the barracks with bags packed and hammocks lashed, speculating on their drafting instruction. Some of the older ratings wore 1914–18 medal ribbons; they could talk about Beatty's Battle-Cruiser Squadron and the German High Seas Fleet. This would be their last commission before retirement on pension. Many others had enlisted for seven or twelve years to escape the poverty and degradation of unemployment, only to find that there was poverty and degradation in the Royal Navy. In the barracks canteen they listened to the news on the BBC's National and Regional programmes. The Spanish war continued and Japanese naval forces had begun blockading Chinese ports; troops had landed at Woosung, north of Shanghai. The search continued for the missing Lockheed *Electra* aircraft flown by Miss Amelia Earhart and her navigator Fred Noonan,

Opposite page: In August 1937 *Sheffield*, completed, and in her flat grey coat of Admiralty 507A, with Red Ensign flying, leaves the Tyne to begin five days of engine trials in the North Sea.

Right: Working up to 34½ knots – about 2 knots better than her designed speed. Returning to the Tyne, *Sheffield*'s powerful bow wave generated a swell that collided with the shore and swept an elderly lady and her deck-chair off the pier at Cullercoats. She was rescued from the sea unharmed.

Below: Clear of the river, the bridge orders full power, and Chief Stoker Tom Bolton watches his gauges as the new engines draw a deep breath.

Below right: At 1700 on 25 August 1937 the Red Ensign was lowered and the White Ensign hoisted. *Sheffield* had been accepted into the Royal Navy.

which had vanished off New Guinea. Most important to the men with their pints of Taylor-Walker bitter was the news that the Welshman Tommy Farr, in New York, had satisfactorily completed his training for his World Heavyweight Championship fight against Joe Louis, in two days' time. The long-weekend leave men had gone; they would be back by the first train on Monday, swollen-eyed and hoping that the new ship's messdeck radio would be functioning clear and loudly for the fight broadcast during the early hours of Tuesday morning.

Dry-docked, provisions were trickling aboard followed by the junior officers of the Gunroom and the first of the draft from RNB. The wardroom's wines and spirits arrived from Messrs Saccone & Speed and the men's rum in wicker-covered jars from the dockyard's bonded warehouse. It was at this time, too, recalled Leading Stores Assistant Clay, that the ship was fitted with radar, then known as RDF – the first operational version. 'It was the grandfather of air-warning equipments, Type 79X. Captain Mark-Wardlaw later cleared lower deck and warned us that strangers would be inquisitive about the outlandish gear at out masthead, and we were to say nothing about it. This was a joke, because only a handful of officers and ratings knew anything about it anyway.'

Stores and ammunition were taken aboard at Sheerness and, with many of those new to the decks and passageways of a warship still unable to find their way from the gunroom or the Boys' mess to the cable deck without finding themselves in the paint store or the seamen's bathroom, *Sheffield* began three weeks of intensive working-up trials.

She was not a stately or handsome warship and, indeed, the dumpy bridge structure and an unsightly gap between the raked funnels presented an almost mercantile profile, but she was to prove more seaworthy than her American and Japanese counterparts, and a steady gun platform. Both armour and speed were only moderate, but neither could have been improved without reducing the other, and *Sheffield* and several of her class sisters would later absorb damage that might have been fatal to a less balanced design. In short, the *Town*s were good value for money.

A great deal was to be done during the few weeks of working-up to a state of efficiency before joining the Home Fleet. There were more evolutions at speed, communications circuits to be tested, turret drill, magazine drill, the Walrus amphibian to be launched, recovered and launched again to carry out mock attacks for the benefit of the 4-inch HA crews and pom-poms. Sea-boats were lowered and hoisted, manually and by power, torpedo tubes traversed, ammunition hoists exercised and guns loaded repeatedly until every unnecessary movement had been eliminated and the seamen gunners and Marines functioned like automata. On the flag-deck the signalmen

Right: The first Walrus, L2180, is hoisted in. She was later to be named 'Terror of Trondheim', her partner 'Spotter of Spartivento'.

Below: *Sheffield* as she joined the Fleet at Rosyth in October 1937. Twin raked funnels and a piled-up midships structure gave her and her sisters a slightly alien profile, but she would acquit herself well on active service against both enemy attacks and extreme weather.

hoisted streams of bunting, flashed messages and sema-
phored imaginary orders to non-existent flotillas, while
the Main Wireless Office, the Auxiliary Office, the 3rd
and the Bridge Wireless Office, connected by internal
Morse lines, exchanged blood-chilling enemy reports, rapid manoeuvring signals and it's tot time and don't forget
you owe me sippers, Bogey. The midshipmen and seamen
boys discovered that sea service did not mean the end of
physical jerks at 0630, and unwary lubbers were persuaded
to descend to the boiler room to request a bucket of revs
or a pint of green oil for the starboard lamp. The Chief
Stoker, concentrating on maintaining 400 pounds/square
inch boiler pressure, was seldom amused.

At a time when warship captains were not noted for
their tolerance, Mark-Wardlaw, *Sheffield*'s first commanding officer, was considered a gentleman. 'I have heard him
described by some as an old woman,' Blundell, the Torpedo Officer, remembered, 'but they mistook his innate
kindliness. The ship's company liked him because he was
always courteous to every man whatever his rank, and he
treated everyone with the same good manners as he would
his own relations or superiors. I have always found that
pays off with the men; they see through a prig or a pimp,
or a poseur or a bragger, but Mark-Wardlaw was none of
those.'

Blundell was to be grateful for his captain's good nature
when things went wrong during *Sheffield*'s first double
broadside torpedo exercise off Portland. This entailed
firing one broadside of three torpedoes at the target from
one mounting, and then the cruiser performing a high-speed
U-turn to fire another triple salvo from her other side.

'It was just before sunset, and fog was setting in,' Blundell
recalled. 'The target was an RFA oiler. The sight operator
reported "on target" and, checking my own control sight, I
fired the three port torpedoes. Visibility by now was very
poor, but as the ship completed her turn the operator sang
out that he was again on target. As the margin for the second broadside was short, I took a hasty look, saw the dim
shape of the target and gave the order to fire. Alas, in the
dim light we had let go the second broadside at a merchant
ship *nowhere near the target!*'

Three torpedoes, the cost of which was more than a
Lieutenant-Commander's pay for a lifetime, were vanishing
in the direction of the Channel Islands, another three had
already been swallowed up by the darkness eastward. It
must, Blundell choked, mean at least a court-martial.

'Feeling the deck sinking beneath my feet I went to the
bridge to report my humiliation. The sea mist was setting
in and the light gone – but I shall never forget Mark-
Wardlaw's response. He simply shrugged. "That's all right,
Torps. Give me the course and distance to pick up the first
broadside, then go down to the chart-room, work out the
course and distance to get us where your second broadside
should end up." He grinned. "Don't worry – we'll recover
the lot." And we did. We picked up the first three torpedoes
and hoisted them inboard, then turned to the new estimated
course, steamed about nine miles, and came slap on top of
the second three, all in complete darkness and thick fog.
You can imagine my relief – and I shall never forget the
Captain's confidence and support at a moment which was
very dark for me.'

It was the beginning of a relationship that was to endure

Left: In Chatham dockyard
during September 1937,
the cruiser's personnel,
provisions and war stores
were taken aboard. The
Torpedo Officer, Blundell,
and his men greet their
first 21in torpedo . . .

for the warship's entire life. 'She was, without a doubt, the happiest ship I served in during the whole of my service,' confirmed L/SA Clay, 'and that was twenty-seven years.' Chief Stoker Tom Bolton, the first rating to join *Sheffield* in mid-1936, when she was only a hull on the slipway, confirmed, 'I had a premonition that this was to be the best ship that the RN could boast of – and she was.'

Working-up trials in the Channel continued well into October with the ship anchoring nightly in Portland Harbour, Weymouth Bay or Tor Bay, and, if she was not yet an efficient fighting unit, *Sheffield*'s machinery was functioning smoothly and her company had settled into their watchkeeping routine. There was evening Tombola in the canteen flat and a Crown & Anchor school in the stokers' bathroom. The days were getting chillier, with darkness falling as the Second Dog watch-keepers closed up; the holidaymakers and the girls had gone from Torquay and Weymouth, the esplanade booths were shuttered and the festival lights removed. The Channel was a leaden grey.

Still, it had been a good summer. Tommy Farr had failed to defeat Louis, but he had fought gamely, and now the new football season was a month old. A large percentage of the ship's company were natives of the Home Counties and supported, albeit at a distance, London's four First Division clubs, Arsenal, Chelsea, Charlton and Brentford. They could listen to match results on the messdeck loudspeakers, or to the dance music of Carol Gibbons, Jack Payne and Henry Hall if it was not too frequently interrupted by the shriek of a bosun's pipe.

There was speculation – but only superficial because information was sparse – on the build-up of those foreign navies that might threaten world peace. The Japanese were least considered; they were far distant Orientals who manufactured cheap tin toys and whose warships had superstructures like pagodas that would collapse at the first salvo. Italian ships had a certain Latin elegance and were reputedly fast, but they were built for the sun-drenched Mediterranean, and Mussolini's comic opera sailors would suffer sudden colonic convulsions if they ever ventured into the heaving green Atlantic.

The Germans, however, were something different. The Great War experience had shown that they built very good ships indeed. They had already floated three big armoured cruisers, *Deutschland, Admiral Graf Spee* and *Admiral Scheer*, which other envious nations had dubbed 'pocket battleships', had launched two battle-cruisers – *Scharnhorst* and *Gneisnau* – and had five further heavy cruisers building. The Royal Navy possessed nothing that could both outrun and outgun these ships except three elderly battle-cruisers, and nothing whatsoever to match the two battleships, destined to be *Bismarck* and *Tirpitz*, being constructed in Hamburg and Wilhelmshaven.

Such a building programme suggested to the Admiralty that the German Navy was preparing for a surface strategy based on commerce raiding by cruisers and armed auxiliaries. Certainly there could be no repetition of the 1914–18 U-boat campaign that had almost defeated Britain. Since 1920 the Royal Navy had been developing a submarine detection device and had established an Anti-Submarine Branch in 1922. Within ten years all post-war destroyers had had Asdic equipment installed, and an anti-submarine school, HMS *Osprey*, had been located at Portland. In any future war the submarines would meet their come-uppance. The First Sea Lord, Admiral of the Fleet Lord Chatfield, assessed Asdic as being 80 per cent successful. 'Our methods are so efficient', he declared, 'that we shall need fewer destroyers in the North Sea and Mediterranean.' Air attacks on shipping, he believed, were unlikely, but, 'even one AA gun in a merchant ship' would compel an aircraft to fly so high that the chances of destroying the ship were 'very small'.

Sheffield, then, with eight 4-inch AA guns and eight 2-pounder pom-poms, not to mention two quadruple 0.5-inch guns, was totally safe from enemy aircraft.

Permission had been given for the cruiser to be taken as near as possible to the city of Sheffield so that she could receive visitors and also send a representative party from the ship to the city. It would be a valuable public relations gesture, good for recruiting, and would cost little, especially as the *Sheffield Telegraph* had offered to provide an excursion train for the naval contingent. At first light on Tuesday 12 October 1937, following two days and a night of intensive exercising, *Sheffield* departed Portland for Immingham, on Humberside, to secure in Timber Pool at 1000 on the following day.

The ship's company, ordered into No. 2 blue suits, were mildly bewildered when, on Friday, a distinguished company from the city of Sheffield climbed the brow to the quarterdeck – the Lady Mayoress, the Master and Mistress Cutler, the Deputy Lord Mayor and the Bishop of Sheffield, the Chief Constable and the Town Clerk, aldermen, councillors, members of the Chamber of Commerce. They stared about them with proprietory interest as a Royal Marine guard presented arms, then stubbed their toes on ring-bolts and their shins on coamings as the Captain and Commander led them below for refreshment. Earlier, the forward messes had been scoured for natives of Sheffield, and four had been found – a Signalman, a Telegraphist, a Stoker and a Marine – who were now thrust forward to be introduced to their Lord Mayor and were astonished to discover that she was a woman, Mrs. A. E. Longden. 'I trust', she said, 'that the fine example of service, which I know you will uphold to the full, will long be associated with the honoured name which we both bear.' They nodded politely, anxious to get changed back into overalls; it was nearly tot-time.

On Saturday, Sunday and Monday the ship was open to the public and, it was anticipated by younger crew members, there would be hundreds of nubile young females climbing ladders and revealing thighs or, alternatively, descending ladders and revealing bosoms, and all needing a helping hand from a gallant sailor. In the event a total of more than 22,000, including several trainloads from Sheffield, came aboard the cruiser. And it was on Saturday that 200 ratings volunteered to travel by the *Telegraph*'s train to Sheffield, accompanied by two officers – Lieutenant-Commanders Hopkins and Blundell – to ensure that they did indeed get to Sheffield. Everyone alighted at Wadsley Bridge Halt, the nearest station to the Hillsborough ground of Sheffield Wednesday, who were to play their local rivals, United, that afternoon; the sailors were to see the game as the clubs' guests before being received by the City.

'When we arrived at the station,' Blundell said, 'there was what we thought was a "funny party", dressed in fancy clothes, standing on the platform. This turned out to be the Mayor, Aldermen and Civic Henchmen in their seventeenth-century rig, while a police band waited in the road to lead the ratings, who, it was expected, would march to the football ground.'

A car, however, had been provided for the officers. Blundell consulted Hopkins, and then smilingly declined. The two officers, he said, prefered to march with their men.

It was a democratic gesture that met with everyone's approval; it showed just how naval officers shared every demand made on their ratings. 'The real reason', Blundell confessed, 'was that we were quite certain the men would disperse into the pubs on the route, and few would get to the ground at all unless we remained with them.' Led by

the police band and five mounted constables, the mildly embarrassed officers and men from *Sheffield* were marched off to the strains of 'Sons of the Sea' and 'The Fleet's in Port Again', and on reaching Hillsborough were paraded around the ground as 30,000 spectators cheered, before being released. It is probable that the crowd would have applauded anything that moved, but the sailors were beginning to ask who was supposed to be entertaining whom.

Wednesday defeated United by a single goal, which hardly mattered because the men had little regard for either; they had come primarily for the beer, but had tasted none yet. Anticipation rose as opening time approached, but plummetted again when, transported into the city centre by several coaches, the contingent was divided, half having tea at the Brightside & Carbrook Co-op and the others at Stephenson's Exchange Restaurant. The men's faces were becoming increasingly wooden, but they remained polite.

The next stage of Sheffield's entertainment itinerary was a film showing of *Captains Courageous* at the Central Picture House, where a segregated block of two hundred seats had been reserved. To the sailors, Freddie Batholomew was a stroppy little OD and Spencer Tracy should have kicked his arse. But the period of trial was ending and reward was in sight – the Lord Mayor's dance at the Town Hall, exclusively for *Sheffield*'s men, for whom two hundred partners had been provided. It was one of those opportunities, matie, that present themselves only once in a commission, and it would have to be fully exploited before the *Telegraph*'s special train left Victoria at five minutes past midnight.

Right: Guests of the City of Sheffield, 250 sailors and marines, with two officers, had arrived by train, but were surprised to find that they were expected to march to Sheffield Wednesday's football ground behind a police band, then parade around the pitch to crowd cheers before taking their seats for the Derby match against Sheffield United.

Far right: Saturday night, 16 October 1937, was 'Nautical Night at Sheffield Town Hall,' said the *Daily Mirror*, 'where officers and men from HMS *Sheffield* – on a visit to the city – were entertained at a dance. Two hundred Sheffield girls acted as hostesses.' They had all been carefully screened by the Town Clerk and a committee of Sheffield ladies.

Below: Special trains brought citizens of Sheffield to inspect the warship, moored at Immingham – 2,200 on the first day, 13,000 on the second, 7,000 on the third.

The Watch Committee, however, had already decided that the provision of two hundred innocent Sheffield virgins for the entertainment of licentious sailors could result in a municipally sponsored orgy as heinous as the Rape of the Sabines. Besides, had not Lady Nancy Astor, Member of Parliament for the naval base of Devonport, suggested that all sailors returning from foreign service should wear a yellow armlet to indicate that they *might* have a venereal disease?

'Two hundred Sheffield girls', the *Telegraph* announced, 'have been specially chosen to be dancing partners for the sailors from HMS *Sheffield* who will visit the city. The Town Clerk, aided by Employment Exchange officials, approached local employers, and through them suitable girls were invited to attend the dance for the sailors at the Town Hall. The task of picking the girls was not easy. They had to have an evening dress, be good dancers, good-lookers and be *good girls . . .*'

Blundell's report was that of an officer and a gentleman. 'I must say that the dance organized for the men was rather a flop, because the girls for partners were selected by a committee of Sheffield ladies, no doubt for their virtue rather than those qualities which would appeal more to the sailor . . .'

Able Seaman Bungy Williams was neither an officer nor a gentleman, and expressed himself more explicitly. 'My party had her soddin' knees welded together, mate. *Welded*. Look at them fingers. Yer'd think they'd been clenched in a six-inch hydraulic shell rammer . . .'

Sheffield joined the Fleet, then lying at Rosyth, on 20 October. The ship's log merely records *Off Bass Rock, Firth of Forth. 1614: moored off Rosyth*. Her sister ships, *Southampton* and *Newcastle*, had already joined, while *Glasgow*, completed only fifteen days after *Sheffield*, had suffered the embarrassment of running aground in Weymouth Bay, a location more scrupulously charted than almost any other in the world. Her navigator would be shuddering in anticipation of the ribaldry to be endured when the ship did arrive in the Forth.

There now began, however, the new cruisers' period of assimilation with a Home Fleet which, at that time, included the battleships *Nelson* and *Rodney* and the older 'R'-class ships *Royal Oak, Ramillies, Revenge* and *Resolution*. Squadron exercises meant manoeuvring by flags, by light, by wireless, in line ahead, line astern and line abreast, by divisions and by sub-divisions. It did not seem remarkable that almost all training revolved around fleet actions; nobody seemed very interested in the dull subject of mercantile convoying, and the Fleet's programme for 1937 culminated in a Night Coast Defence Exercise before dispersal for Christmas and New Year leave. *Sheffield* secured alongside in Chatham.

As the first leave party left the ship on 15 December, newspapers were shouting the news of Japanese air attacks on British and American gunboats in Chinese waters, resulting in USS *Panay* being sunk at anchor. Nanking had fallen and allegedly 200,000 people had been slaughtered.

China, however, was far distant.

2

'Total Germany repeat
Total Germany'

THE year 1938 was the last full year of peace, the last in which there survived any real hope that a major European war could be avoided. There was no talk of conscription yet, and the British public were not very interested in foreign affairs; the country was still an island, and cinema audiences could watch, smugly satisfied, the Navy's battleships wallowing majestically with their massive guns and fluttering ensigns. The kingdom was surely secure from lesser breeds, despite the lack-lustre premiership of Neville Chamberlain and his equally undistinguished cabinet.

Britain was emerging from the years of depression; many people, particularly in the midlands and south-east, were experiencing a slowly growing affluence. If they did not talk about the possibility of war, perhaps it would go away. Four hundred thousand cars a year were rolling off the production lines in Oxford, Birmingham and Coventry. There was television, as yet enjoyed by only a few hundred families, but most homes boasted a wireless. The shopgirl and the dejected housewife took refuge from their daily drudgery in the darkness of the cinema every week for ninepence, and their menfolk on the terraces of a football club. There were still unemployed – nearly two million of them, one worker in three – concentrated most heavily in the north-east, Lancashire, Ulster and South Wales, the areas of old heavy industry, mining and ship-building. An unemployed married man with four children drew a weekly benefit of 23s.6d., which meant bread and margarine, the cheapest of fish or minced meat, tea with condensed milk.

The King, on the throne for only a year, was still a stranger to his people. He was a shy man who, as Duke of York, had never been exposed to public gaze nor sought the company of that high-living set so loved by his abdicated brother. George was decent, conscientious and tradition-al, and the people noted that he had served in the Royal Navy. The British always approved of their royal males serving at sea. Although only one in five thousand had ever trodden a ship's deck, and the vast majority's knowledge of the sea did not extend beyond the mud at Southend or a few days at Blackpool, the British were convinced that they were a hardy, seafaring race. Of the peak-faced sixteen-year-olds who presented themselves for enlistment in the Navy's Boy's Service, one in four could not swim

and many had never seen a swimming-pool. True, during sixteen or eighteen months in HMS *Ganges*, Shotley, an ample, well-balanced diet filled out their ribs, and the dis-cipline and training of those months produced confident young men ready for anything, but when most of the graduates of both *Ganges* and *Britannia* complied with their first drafting order they were also about to have their first meeting with the real sea.

In mid-January 1938 the Home Fleet assembled off Port-land for the Mediterranean Spring Cruise. The Admiral, Second-in-Command, Vice-Admiral Tom Calvert, decided to hoist his flag in the new cruiser *Sheffield* and conduct the fleet exercises on passage in the absence of the CinC.

Between the wars it was customary for the Home Fleet to join forces with the Mediterranean Fleet at Gibraltar and carry out intensive combined exercises for about two months. For the home ships' crews it was a welcome avoid-ance of the worst weeks of English weather in exchange for the sunny Mediterranean, Gibraltar and Algeciras, visits to Toulon, Tangier and Mers-el-Kebir, perhaps even Malta. When thousands of sailors poured ashore from the two fleets moored in Grand Harbour and Sliema Creek they would be greeted by prostitutes who had travelled from France, Spain, Italy and Greece for just this great occasion, and six months' production of *Blue Label* bottled beer would be consumed in one week.

More usefully, the combined Spring Cruise offered opportunities not only for large-scale war games and a punishing series of inter-Fleet sporting confrontations, but also for parading the world's most powerful concentration of warships in Europe's shop window.

This was particularly important in view of the activities of the Spanish Nationalist naval forces under Vice-Admiral Francisco Moreno, which were blockading Loyalist-held ports. When the Home Fleet reached Gibraltar on 25 January it was learned that the Dutch freighter *Hannah* had been torpedoed and sunk during the previous week, six miles south-east of Cape San Antonio, presumably by a German or Italian submarine. The British ship *Clonlara* also reported an attack by an unidentified submarine, which she evaded, and *Thorpness* had been bombed at Tarragona with two British seamen killed, seven wounded and five missing. Earlier, in 1937, the destroyer *Hunter* had been mined, with eight killed, and *Havock* was narrowly missed by a torpedo (subsequently discovered to have been fired by the Italian submarine *Iride*).

It was undeniable that British freighters were blockade-running with highly profitable war contraband, largely from Russian Black Sea ports, and the Nationalists were understandably intent on stopping them. The merchantmen were supposedly safe from interference unless and until they entered Spanish territorial waters, which international law defined as three miles from the coast. The Nationalists, however, had unilaterally declared a six-mile territorial limit, and it was this that usually involved the British in confrontation.

Among the British vessels already detached to 'supervise by sea all approaches to Spanish ports', *Hood* had trained her guns in the direction of the Nationalist warships *Almirante Cervera* and *Galena*. When the German pocket battleship *Deutschland* shelled the town of Almeria, killing nineteen people to avenge bombs dropped on her by two aircraft, the international situation had become very tense; with so many ostensibly non-involved countries supporting and supplying one side or the other, a flash-point had been reached which could so easily generate a general European war. In the House of Commons the the government was being bitterly attacked by the Labour opposition for 'failing to give protection to British merchant ships on their lawful business' – a somewhat fragile argument. In Cabinet, the Foreign Secretary, Anthony Eden, had suggested the sinking of the Spanish Nationalist heavy cruiser *Canarias*, but it was finally decided merely to intensify operations against the commerce-raiding submarines, known to be predominantly Italian, by the thirty-six Asdic-equipped destroyers deployed in the western Mediterranean and Malta Channel. The destruction of only one submarine, it was considered, would be an effective deterrent.

This was the climate into which the Home Fleet, led

by *Sheffield*, steamed during late January 1938, but under firm orders to avoid any confrontation with Spanish, Italian or German forces – which, it must be said, were equally anxious to keep a respectful distance. The British ships had come to exercise, and the martinet Tom Calvert intended that they should, without pause.

'The Admiral was a tiger', recalled *Sheffield*'s navigating officer, Masterman, 'and there was no respite by day or night until the first Saturday afternoon, when we were in the smooth and sunny waters off Cape Saint-Vincent. The Midshipman of the Watch had told me that the Admiral was sunning himself in his bridge chair, but I was roused from my doze in the charthouse when I heard his sepulchral, ominous voice: "Tell the Paymaster-Commander I should like to see him on the bridge, at once."

Immediately, of course, everyone in the vicinity had their heads down, counting the rivets. Minutes lapsed before a sleepy-eyed Paymaster-Commander stumbled up the ladder. He glanced at me, whispering, "What's up?" I could only sympathize. "Mischief," I whispered back.

The Admiral lifted his head. "Ah – Paymaster Commander. How many fire extinguishers have we on board?"

The statistic was not one that the Paymaster had committed to memory, and it was a long descent to the Office flat on the maindeck aft. The Supply CPO, who had the keys to the relevant filing cabinet, had to be roused from sleep in his mess and then a frantic search made through the lists of stores taken aboard at the fitting-out berth in Newcastle. Canvas, cap ribbons, catapult lubricant, Carley floats, cocoa, condensers, contraceptives, copper wire, cotton waste, cordite hoppers, CO_2 equipment . . .

The Paymaster regained the bridge, drained of breath and sweating, to make his report to an Admiral who appeared to have forgotten the enquiry but merely enquired, "Why are Supply and Secretariat officers always in such poor physical condition?" '

Gibraltar was a delight, however brief, for the sailors from an England deep in winter. In the 1930s foreign travel was far beyond the resources of ordinary people, and the wealthy who did holiday abroad rarely paused in places like Gibraltar or Malta; they gathered in Biarritz, Cannes, Nice and Monte Carlo. The Navy's bases were therefore fully geared to the earthier but still profitable entertainments of the sailor. Gibraltarians and Maltese knew exactly what ratings wanted – cheap alcohol, a large plateful of food (the traditional order was for steak, egg, chips and baked beans, the whole drenched with tomato sauce – but some were more discerning), and female company, although less frequently for copulation than was generally assumed or the sailor pretended. When the Fleet, or a substantial part of it, tied up alongside the jetties and the South and Detached Moles of Gibraltar Harbour, the port's streets – Main Street, Irish Town, Line Wall Road, Rosia Road and even the upper Engineer Lane – were awash with the white caps of men and officers. The men went to the bars, bazaars, cafés and cheapjack souvenir shops, the officers

Above: The City of Sheffield's gifts to the new cruiser included silver centre-pieces for the wardroom and the Captain's cabin, silver tankards, cigarette boxes, cigar boxes and ashtrays for officers and Warrant Officers, a set of antique Sheffield plate and several paintings. The ratings were given dartboards, dominoes and draughts. Chief Stoker Tom Bolton (right) was the first man to board the ship during her construction. Thirty years later he would be the last man to leave her.

to the Rock Hotel or the Bristol, or the officer's club in *Rooke*.

None of these, however, were to be enjoyed for longer than one shore leave for each part of watch. On Friday, 28 January, the combined fleets departed Gibraltar to begin exercises that would continue until 18 March. This was a period during which the warships, continuously steaming, logged almost six thousand miles with only 72 hours anchored off Tangier for the crews to draw breath.

At midday on 12 March the Welshmen among the messes were sulkily surrendering their rum to the Englishmen and Scots; Tommy Farr, confidently expected quickly to re-establish his challenge for the world heavyweight title, had been outpointed by Max Baer in New York. On that same day, at dawn, German troops had marched into Austria unopposed, and the Prime Minister, Mr. Chamberlain, had conceded that 'nothing could have arrested this action by Germany unless we and others with us had been prepared to use force to prevent it'. Britain was not, and the European time bomb had begun to tick.

On regaining Gibraltar, *Sheffield*'s men were denied a further reconnaissance of the port's delights. The ship had been detached and ordered to Chatham. Few sailors resent orders that return them home, but on this occasion *Sheffield*'s crew would gladly have accepted a few more days of exile, and they had not even seen Malta and its gloriously notorious Gut which the older hands talked about with their eyes raised ecstatically to the deckhead.

Sheffield had survived her first three months of intensive Fleet work without mishap. Red lead showed through the worn grey paint at her bows, and her hull was salt-streaked, but the welded starboard 'A' bracket had given no trouble, and all departments reported equipment and machinery working efficiently. Everyone was delighted to be rid of the daily chore of cleaning the upper deck brightwork with Brasso, except Leading Stores Assistant Clay. 'The "Staybrite" bell, handrails, guardrails, staghorns and awning stanchions – I had to enter them all in the Naval Store Trophy Account and check them at regular intervals. The ship had become known as the "Shiny Sheff".' Later she would be, simply, 'Old Shiny'.

The year moved on with the long-established rhythm of Home Fleet peacetime routine – first the Spring Cruise and the Easter leave period, the Summer Cruise to show the flag at holiday resorts around the coast, Summer leave and finally the Winter Cruise to take the training programme through to Christmas. There were regattas and tugs-of-war between the *Town*s of the 2nd Cruiser Squadron, boatwork for the Ordinary Seamen, navigation instruction for the Midshipmen and the Chaplain's optimistic confirmation classes during the dog watches. It was a fine summer, despite the ominous international trends that nobody wanted to think about, satisfaction in the forward messes at the news that the German Max Schmeling had been pulverized in New York by Joe Louis in two minutes and four seconds of the first round. 'If it had been Tommy

Farr, look,' the Welshmen promised at tot time, 'it've been *one* minute and four seconds, boyo.'

At Sheerness on 26 July the ship said farewell to a departing Captain Mark-Wardlaw before continuing into Chatham dockyard for the annual Navy Week demonstrations. It was a week during which the public in their thousands climbed over the ships, peered into gun-breeches, stumbled down ladders to sniff the galley and leave sticky finger-marks on paint and brightwork. *Sheffield*'s company were required to contribute to several displays on shore, including landing a party with a field gun, bombarding a plywood fort and repelling a noisy attack by a smoke-spilling Gloster Gladiator. In one basin a submarine was 'sunk', and lifted her stern dramatically clear of the water. In the next, in the turret of *Marshal Soult*, small boys watched in deafened awe as 15-inch dummy shells and propellants were rammed into the huge firing chambers. Yet others, gathered about a table-top model of Zeebrugge, listened to a Chief Petty Officer describing, for the thirty-seventh time that day, the story of the 1918 raid. There was a brisk trade in bric-à-brac made of teak from old warships, ice cream and teas, recruiting literature, a beer tent denied to ratings, and finally a sunset ceremony presented by the Royal Marines.

It was a tiring week for the men, but most enjoyed it. Pretty teenage girls in colourful print dresses agreed a later rendezvous which might or might not be kept, and hundreds of schoolboys resolved to join the Royal Navy as soon as they achieved 15½ years. It offered a life-style of the most desirable quality. That week Germany announced the call-up of 750,000 men for the armed services and ordered manoeuvres near the Czech border.

With a new commanding officer, Captain E. de F. Renouf, CVO, *Sheffield* remained alongside in Chatham for six weeks of refitting before steaming for Rosyth, Scapa Flow and Invergordon. On 27 August Sir John Simon, the Chancellor of the Exchequer, warned that Britain might become involved in a war over Czechoslovakia, but, more importantly, Len Hutton had scored 364 runs in the Fifth Test at the Oval against Bradman's Australians, and ice-skating was the newest fad among teenagers.

The 2nd Cruiser Squadron now consisted of *Southampton*, *Newcastle*, *Sheffield*, *Glasgow* and the 'County'-class *Cornwall*, while *Manchester* had also been commissioned and *Birmingham* and *Gloucester* were only weeks away from acceptance. *Edinburgh* and *Belfast*, the 'stretched' ships, would not be in service until the late summer of 1939. Sixteen 'Dido'-class and eleven *Fiji*-class cruisers were on the stocks; most of these would not be ready until 1940. Dockyards were racing to complete in time for the war that, now, must come. On 31 August 1938 Germany announced that the Kriegsmarine would begin manoeuvres in the North Sea in response to similar operations by the British.

The scientist, John Logie Baird, had visited *Sheffield* to see the Navy's first RDF installation. The receiver office had been situated in the after galley flat, the transmitter station on the flag-deck, to the resentment of the signals personnel, but there were no specifically trained RDF operators yet. During October and November the initial calibration was carried out by several civilian technicians and the Chief Telegraphist, White. The Walrus aircraft, manned by pilot, observer and telegraphist air gunner, was providing the target by flying many weary hours at altitudes up to 13,000 feet and landing alongside at dusk to be lifted aboard.

The air surveillance equipment was crude by later standards, but it could locate aircraft up to ninety miles away, more usually forty, record bearing and distance accurately and continuously, and distinguish between a single target and a group. The ship's company were just beginning to realize the significance of the freakish contraption on the mast they had nicknamed 'the Cuckoo'. Only a small handful outside *Sheffield* did.

Czechoslovakia had declared a state of emergency, and in London there was the sudden smell of fear. Thirty-eight million gas-masks were being distributed, trenches were being dug in parks and gardens, and ARP was no longer a joke in *Punch*. Neville Chamberlain was given an ovation at Heston airfield as he waved aloft a paper, claiming, 'I believe it is peace in our time.'

Moored in the desolate anchorage of Scapa Flow, the five ships of the 2nd Cruiser Squadron, ordered to a state of readiness since 14 September, lay under a leaden, drizzling sky. There was nothing to be seen or done ashore – a clutter of clap-trap wooden buildings and rusted corrugated iron, windswept slopes dotted with muddy sheep, a few football pitches with sagging goal-posts and too often sheeted with water, unfit for play. The only available news of current events was that afforded by BBC bulletins; sailors rarely saw newspapers unless they were brought off shore by libertymen, and there was no liberty in Scapa Flow. The films *Private Lives of Henry VIII, Sanders of the River* and *Thirty-Nine Steps* were passed from ship to ship.

God-forsaken bloody Scapa.

Then, as a gesture of belligerent readiness, all five Walrus aircraft were ordered into the air to fly a concerted 'Balbo' over the Flow. It would be a show of strength not to be ignored by the *Kirkwall Herald* and the children of Stromness Infants' School. The formation of stubby little flying-boats putter-puttered over the rain-stippled anchorage, climbed over Flotta and followed the eastern edge of Hoy northward, to collide suddenly with a 50-knot gale which nobody had forecast.

All the aircraft except *Sheffield*'s battled on over the islet of Graemsay and landed at Stromness, where all capsized and were badly damaged by the gale, but Sub-Lieutenant John Groves turned back to the squadron and brought his machine down on the Flow. Conditions, however, were too rough for recovery, and the Walrus was made fast astern of

Sheffield at the end of a grass line. She rode out the gale, complete with crew, from 1500 to 0900 the next forenoon. Sustenance was periodically passed to the bucketing aircraft in a bottle labelled 'Tonic Water' – the contents of which however, were a familiar amber colour. In the event the observer and telegraphist were too ill to be interested, so Groves drank all three rations, and was comfortably aglow when he and his aircraft were safely hoisted inboard next day, proving, he grinned, 'the firsh-clash shea-keeping qualities of the Walrush . . .'

There was hardly a ripple of concern in either ward-room or forward messes when in late October the First Lord, Alfred Duff Cooper, resigned in protest at the Munich settlement, to be replaced by Lord Stanhope. A by-election in Oxford has been won by the Conservative candidate, 31-year-old Quintin Hogg, who supported the League of Nations, re-armament, peace, democracy and unity against war; so did the Socialist candidate. Taxation had lifted the price of a bottle of Hennessy brandy to 17 shillings (85p) and better quality pipe tobacco to 11½d. (5p) per ounce.

By mid-November *Sheffield* was back in Chatham, to remain there for the rest of the year, and on 18 December the first leave party raced for the station and the train for London Bridge. This would be their last peacetime Christmas for eight years, for some simply the last Christmas of their lives.

It was a wholly volunteer navy, even if for many ratings the alternative had been unemployment and the dole queue. It was also the largest, most highly trained and experienced navy in the world, even if efficiency was frequently blunted by out-dated ritual, with enterprise discouraged by the maxim that things had been done that way since the days of sail and so must be right. The Royal Navy was among the poorer paid navies in western Europe and the British Commonwealth, and far behind the United States Navy. The quality of accommodation, food and conditions generally were acceptable. When, unavoidably, they were not, as in submarines and small vessels, modest increments were paid in compensation.

There was a wide social chasm between officers and ratings, although less of a scholastic one than officers persuaded themselves, but the estrangement was not as emphatic as in the Army. Naval officers seldom attempted genuinely to liaise with their men on anything approaching equal terms. When Blundell, *Sheffield*'s Torpedo Officer, remarked that, with regard to officers, the men could see through a prig, a pimp, a poseur or a bragger, it was tantamount to admitting that inadequate and unpopular officers did exist among his fellows; it would be remarkable if they had not. It is doubtful, however, if even the most tolerant of officers regarded his lower deck ratings as being any more culturally acceptable than a country squire might his forelock tugging tenants. It is unfortunate that widely read authors like Captain Henry Tapprell Dorling and Paymaster-Commander Lewis da Costa Ricci ('Taffrail' and 'Bartimeus' respectively) and, worst of all, Noël Coward, always portrayed ratings as poorly spoken and simple, but, when firmly led by officers who were products of Dartmouth and the public school system (even midshipmen of sixteen), capable of loyalty and devotion to duty, rather like gun-dogs. Ratings (and army rankers) never displayed gallantry, élan or audacity, which were exclusively officer qualities, but only hardihood and fortitude – which was why they were not awarded crosses or orders, merely medals.

That a major war was only eight months away was not apparent that Christmas of 1938. The shops were well-stocked for those who could afford to buy. London's Oxford Street and Regent Street were festooned with decorations, and Harrod's, Gamages and Selfridge's teemed with shoppers. Every provincial department store had its Santa Claus. There was a new phenomenon – teenaged girls shrieking hysterically and even swooning in the presence of a visiting American film actor named Robert Taylor – one swearing that she would never wash the hand that he had briefly and disinterestedly shaken.

With Christmas and New Year leaves finished, the crew of *Sheffield* turned their attention once again to the well-worn Spring programme, and by 22 January the cruiser was moored alongside in Gibraltar harbour. The European situation had not improved. Barcelona had just fallen to Franco's forces and, with Catalonia lost, 200,000 Republicans had crossed into France, to be disarmed. The Spanish war was entering its last phase. Italy had announced a fleet expansion, including the construction of battleships.

The Rock had not changed, either, in shape or character – the old Casemates, wind-swept Europa Point, the neat little Trafalgar Cemetery and the changing of the guard at the Governor's Residence. It was hardly warm enough yet for swimming from Catalan Bay or Eastern Beach, but there were the bars and bazaars, a casino and those quiet brothels in Flat Bastion Road, above Alameda Gardens, with their narrow, rickety stairs and grubby lace curtains.

But not yet. Immediately on arrival the ship's Royal Marines were ordered to participate in a mock attack on the Rock, and this following a crossing of the Bay of Biscay so rough that 'most of the newcomers, and some of the older hands, experienced that desire to crawl away and die'. Under cover of darkness the marines in two cutters were towed by the destroyer *Keith* to be released some hundreds of yards off Gibraltar's eastern shore with the hopeful intention of approaching the naval base from the blind Mediterranean side.

At 0400, as the sun rose, the marines were still pulling on their oars; the shore seemed a lot further away than a few hundred yards, they could see nothing that resembled their intended landing place, and *Keith* had disappeared.

'From then on', the *Globe & Laurel* reported, 'it was pull, pull, and then more pull'. Nobody could be certain that the shore was even that of Gibraltar; it might be Spain –

or, somebody spat, bloody Morocco. They could all clew up as slaves in the soddin' Casbah. 'We had missed the landing place, and now it meant hours and hours of rowing into a heaving sea. We pulled completely around the Rock.' The boats reached the Mole during early afternoon, the marines exhausted, blistered and famished, with rum issue past and dinner ruined. Gibraltar had survived the amphibious attack of January 1939.

A five-day visit to Lisbon was ample compensation, with a bonus for libertymen on the first night ashore in the form of a sudden fog that prevented boats from returning to the ship after about 2230. Renouf had no choice but to approve all-night leave for the stranded men, who turned back into the terraced city with no discernible display of annoyance. Such is the phlegmatism of the British sailor. Lisbon welcomed foreigners with jingling pockets, and for the foreigners Lisbon with its wines, liqueurs and easy senhoritas – even if the beer was worse than an infusion of senna pods – was better than a hammock and defaulters' muster at 0600. 'Many strange places', wrote the Royal Marines' correspondent to the *Globe & Laurel*, 'were slept in that night.' He adds smugly, 'Readers who have visited Lisbon will understand that; to those who haven't I leave it to their imagination.'

Alongside in Gibraltar again by mid-January, *Sheffield* watched the arrival of the new aircraft carrier *Ark Royal*, on her shake-down introduction to the Fleet, with Swordfish and Skua aircraft embarked. She looked both impressive and, from the marines' viewpoint, intimidating; the flight deck seemed too much like a parade-ground.

Ashore, cinema newsreels were showing the launching, on 14 February, of the German battleship *Bismarck* from the yard of Blohm und Voss in Hamburg, watched by Adolf Hitler, Goering, Goebbels, Hess, Ribbentropp, Himmler, Raeder, Keitel and Bormann. Most of those names were only vaguely familiar to the majority of *Sheffield*'s company; they would know more of them later. Indeed, they knew little of *Bismarck*. Very few of her details had been released – but for *Bismarck*, *Sheffield* and *Ark Royal* there was to be a rendezvous two years hence, that no one dreamed of. Forty-five days after *Bismarck*'s launching, the hull of her sister *Tirpitz* slid into the waters of Wilhelmshaven.

There were more important things to think about. Could Ted Drake lead Arsenal to a sixth League Championship in 1939? Could Len Harvey defeat Larry Gains for the Empire Heavyweight title? Did anyone really care if Germany's expenditure on armaments had risen to 57.9 per cent of the country's total budget? A newspaper told of a German army tank, built of plywood, being demolished in a collision with a small car. German clothing, it was claimed, was being manufactured from processed paper, and it was estimated that after six weeks of war blockade, German industry would have to run on vegetable oil.

The Home Fleet was back in home waters by mid-May, with *Sheffield* assuming the duties of guard ship off Dover for the visit of President Albert Lebrun of France to Britain during 21–24 March. On 31 March the ship was in Chatham. Twenty-year-old Able Seaman Whitmore was drafted to the ship from Chatham Barracks in April, 1939.

'I wondered, as one always does, what the ship was like, and the Captain. The Drafting Office had indicated that I was lucky to be going to the Shiny Sheff, as she was reputedly a happy ship. When I first saw her, she was alongside in the dockyard, and most noticeable were her sleek lines, more like those of a large destroyer, and also the queer lattice contraption at the masthead. I learned later that this was connected with radio direction-finding. To us matelots at that time it was something really wonderful and very hush-hush. The first few weeks were spent in dockyard hands with the usual clutter of cables, airlines and litter strewn around the upper deck.' It was unusual for sailors to want to terminate an easy-going dockyard routine, daily liberty and long weekend leave for those whose homes were within reasonable travelling distance, yet, says Whitmore, everyone seemed to have only one ambition: to get clear of the yard and bring the ship up to what she was before refit. I have never experienced enthusiasm like that from a ship's company, and it was to be the same for the whole time I was aboard *Sheffield*.'

The ship rejoined the Fleet, lying off Portland, on 4 May, and two days later fired a farewell royal salute as the King and Queen, aboard *Empress of Australia*, departed for Canada. Intelligence from Berlin indicated that Germany was planning to seek an agreement with Russia on the division of Poland, while Britain and Poland had rejected Russia's proposals for a defensive alliance. Nobody in London, Berlin, Paris or Warsaw knew – or, if they did, they were completely uninterested – that an undeclared war had exploded on the disputed Manchurian–Mongolian border. By September the Russians would suffer 9,000 casualties and the Japanese 18,000, but all attention would then be directed towards more momentous events in western Europe.

Meanwhile, the Marines of *Sheffield* and the light cruiser *Aurora* joined forces to launch an attack on the coast of Dorset, defended by the Royal Lincolnshire Regiment and watched from a distance by sailors who never did understand why grown men should want to play soldier games. 'All went well', *Globe & Laurel* later reported, lamely, 'until one of the men, doing an individual stalk, startled a cow. She tore down on No. 1 Section, and that unit of Britain's sheet anchor scattered to the winds as fast as their legs could carry them.'

The Military Training Act was approved by Parliament on 26 May, requiring all men on reaching the age of eighteen years to serve for six months in the Royal Navy, the Army or RAF, followed by three years in the reserve. (Three months later this would be superseded by the National Service Act, covering all men between eighteen and forty-five.) The regular-serving ratings, resignedly tolerating the 'Saturday Night Sailors' of the RNVR, who spent two weeks annually in a sea-going ship, did not relish a sudden flood of pimply youths with George Raft sideburns and patent-leather shoes, but there was a compensating factor. As a percentage of the pimply youths conscripted and reduced to two shillings a day might well be married, even have children, the qualifying age for the receipt of dependants' allowances was to be lowered from twenty-five to twenty years. Many young married ratings, hitherto impoverished, could secretly bless an international situation that put a handful of coppers into their pockets, and even cheerfully debate how many children they should have in order to achieve a profit.

During early June 1939 *Sheffield* moved to the Firth of Forth, where the Home Fleet was host to a visiting French squadron – the new and fast battleships *Dunkerque* and *Strasbourg* and the cruisers *Gloire*, *Montcalm* and *Georges Leygues*. Entertainments included a Fleet-size dance in the Royal Naval Canteen in Rosyth, to which, it can be assumed, the local ladies invited were rather more sporting than those in Sheffield's Town Hall. The French were

Right: In Chatham dockyard, with the destroyer *Foxhound* alongside, *Sheffield*'s junior ratings scrub decks. It is late summer 1939, and the war is only weeks away.

particularly impressed by *le Lambeth Walk* and insisted on several encores, while the British noted, for future use elsewhere, the effectiveness of a Charles Boyer accent enquiring, 'Voolay-voo don-say?'. As Bungy Williams so rightly said, 'Faint 'eart never screwed a pig.'

The Spanish Civil War was now ended; 75,000 Italian 'volunteers' and 19,000 Germans were beginning to withdraw. Germany, 'earnestly desirous of maintaining peace', had just signed non-aggression pacts with Denmark, Estonia and Latvia. In England, Butlin's holiday camp at Skegness was requisitioned to accommodate the first infusion of conscripted naval personnel.

Europe was plunging towards war with terrifying speed. 'I joined *Sheffield* at Chatham in late July', recorded Commander Charles Norris (later Vice-Admiral Sir Charles Norris) 'and found her exceptionally well organized for war.' During August the cruiser assumed the role of a German squadron in a big 'break out' exercise in the North Sea. At that time it was confidently assumed that *Sheffield* and *Rodney* were the only ships afloat equipped with RDF. 'But passing Borkum in this exercise we had a great shock. Our own RDF operators reported that another station was transmitting on roughly the same frequency band as ourselves!'

A rapid exchange of signals with the Admiralty confirmed that *Rodney* was far too distant for her transmissions to carry, and so the Navy's worst fears were confirmed; the Germans, too, had developed something that resembled RDF.

Only a few days earlier the Admiralty had warned that 'in order to increase the readiness' the larger part of the Reserve Fleet was to be commissioned and reservists and pensioners recalled to the service. The word 'mobilization', however, was not to be used. Despite the proscription, mobilization proceeded smoothly.

British and French missions had been in Moscow since 12 August to hammer out a policy for meeting the German threat militarily, but had achieved nothing by the 23rd when, in a move that electrified the world, Molotov and Ribbentrop, the foreign ministers of Russia and Germany respectively, signed a non-aggression pact. On the following day the Admiralty despatched an 'Immediate Telegram' to all relevant naval authorities declaring that the situation with Germany was 'critical'.

Sheffield had anchored in Scapa Flow for only hours on 25 August when she was ordered again to proceed to sea. The order was not entirely unwelcome; it was Friday, when at least some of the watchkeepers might normally expect to be released on weekend leave, but the privilege was worthless in Scapa Flow. There was only the old steamer *Saint Ola* daily (except Sundays) to Thurso, a dozen miles from John o' Groats and then an impossible rail journey which put all short leave prospects beyond consideration.

'D'yer hear there? Secure for sea. Close all scuttles and watertight doors. Special sea duty men close up. Ship will assume second state of readiness . . .'

The ship slipped past Long Hope into the Pentland Firth, turned to eastward and increased speed. Dusk came early in the Orkneys. A few lights glimmered on the smudge of the shoreline astern. Then they faded into blackness.

By noon on Monday 28 *Sheffield* had turned again to patrol southward, and was roughly equidistant between the Scottish and Norwegian coasts when she was ordered to proceed at speed to Bergen to embark the British military mission dejectedly homeward bound from Moscow. Renouf began to work the ship up to 25 knots.

As misty twilight fell over a North Sea, calm and empty, a large vessel was sighted astern and to westward, overtaking on a converging course. It was the German liner *Europa*, completely darkened and heading for the Skagerrak. Renouf altered course to follow, and increased speed to 29 knots, but the German, amazingly, gradually drew away in the mist. There was nothing to be gained in pursuing further, so Renouf resumed course for Bergen. He was unaware that the Admiralty had 'lost' *Europa* after she had departed New York several days earlier. It was not learned until after the war that Adolf Hitler had advanced the day for his invasion of Poland to 26 August, but on 25 August drew back, briefly alarmed by that day's Anglo-Polish mutual assistance agreement and also by Mussolini's refusal to promise Italy's involvement in a war against Britain and France. Hitler's hesitation allowed *Sheffield* to embark her passengers in Bergen on 29 August and regain Scapa Flow on the 30th.

The following day, Tuesday 31 August 1939, she was ordered again to sea. Seventy-two hours later, when war became a shuddering reality, the cruiser was in the northerly Atlantic, in position 58°43'N, 19°04'W, 200 miles due south of Iceland and slightly more north-west of Scotland.

Sheffield was on station. It was Sunday, the sun was shining, the sea calm – a fine, late summer morning with the horizon as clear as crystal. Underfoot the decks throbbed very gently, reassuringly. The messdeck cleaners had finished and many off-duty hands had already drifted below, their eyes on the clock, thinking of tot-time and the Afternoon watch to follow. In anticipation of the Prime Minister's statement at 1115, the Captain had ordered an early secure and the radio broadcast to be relayed over the messdeck loudspeakers. Mr. Chamberlain's voice was tired but controlled.

'I am speaking to you from the Cabinet room at 10 Downing Street. This morning the British Ambassador handed the German Government an official Note stating that unless we heard from them by 11 o'clock that they were prepared at once to withdraw their troops from Poland a state of war would exist between us.

I have to tell you that no such undertaking has been received, and that consequently this country is at war with Germany. You can imagine what a bitter blow it is to me that all my long struggle to win peace has failed . . .'

'From Admiralty. Most Immediate. Total Germany repeat Total Germany = 1117/3.'

3

'Secure for Sea.
Special dutymen close up!'

BY NOON the following day, 4 September, *Sheffield* was west of the Faroes Bank and heading for Scapa Flow. Young Sub-Lieutenant Colin Ross was writing his first wartime letter, in which the uncertainties and nervous excitement experienced by everyone could not be disguised.

'This must be a somewhat limited letter because of the censorship regulations. How strange it is to be writing to you in wartime. I think we all felt it had to come sooner or later, and probably sooner, but I know most of us felt rather a shock when we heard Chamberlain's speech saying war had come. We drank success to ourselves in the Gunroom and Warrant Officers' messes, and otherwise went on much as usual! Certainly it is grand to know where we stand at last, to know we tried everything, and that now we can take off our coats and get at them.

We have heard awfully little news, so don't know whether they have started any bombing yet. I hope not. Anyway, I don't think it will be worth their while in the long run.

I have celebrated the occasion by getting a streaming cold! Not very dramatic, I'm afraid. I am not allowed to tell you "the condition of officers and men", so perhaps I am not allowed to tell you whether we are cheerful; need I?'

At 1930 during the evening of that day, the second of the war, the passenger ship *Athenia* was torpedoed and sunk by *U-30* with the loss of 118 passengers, 22 of whom were American.

Anchoring in Scapa Flow on 5 September, *Sheffield* disembarked her two Walrus aircraft, which, for the next five months, were to fly anti-submarine and raider patrols from RNAS Hatson, at that time having only one runway – the road between Kirkwall and Stromness; it had to be closed to traffic during aircraft landing operations. The following day, shortly after daybreak, a single Heinkel He 111 circled high over the anchorage taking photographs, and departed unobserved. The pilot was unaware that the larger vessels below were three decoy battleships and a decoy aircraft carrier; the real targets – *Nelson, Rodney, Royal Oak, Royal Sovereign, Ramillies, Hood* and *Repulse* – were at sea, deployed to meet the threat of enemy blockade-runners. Later on the 5th, at about 1800, a second German reconnaissance Heinkel circled the Flow, this time to be sighted.

Sheffield's 4-inch gun-crews fired several salvoes, the first to be fired at the enemy by a British warship, but the aircraft flew off without appearing unduly embarrassed. The incident was not mentioned by the national newspapers, still frantically trying to come to terms with an unreal war situation. 'Burly Ted Drake', reported the *Daily Mail*, 'at his bold and thrustful best, assumed leadership of Arsenal's front line for the first time this campaign, scoring four of the five goals which made up his side's tally in their 5–2 defeat of Sunderland.'

In London, the same newspaper's columnist Charles Graves was sneering at 'no dining-car facilities in any trains; nurses; sandbags around doors but unprotected glass roofs; sandbags all along the Trocadero, where I ate my first partridge stuffed with oysters yesterday; *Dodge City* is showing at Warner's Cinema (appropriate title, what?); Keith Prowse still covered with billboards about *The Importance of Being Earnest, Sitting Pretty* and *Black & Blue* – and at the London Pavilion, *The House of Fear*; a street bag-piper wearing his Mons Star . . . I wonder, by the way, what historians will call this war? Probably the "War of the Polish Independence", unless that name has been taken already . . .'

The appointment of Winston Churchill to the War Cabinet as First Lord of the Admiralty did not, as the Press claimed, generate widespread elation throughout the Navy. There were very few serving personnel old enough to have been influenced by his performance in that same office from 1911 to 1915, while as Chancellor of the Exchequer under Stanley Baldwin he had been no friend to the Royal Navy, persistently opposing ship-building proposals and being particularly hostile towards the 8-inch 'County'-class cruisers that were, in the event, to prove superb investments. During the war years to come, there were never enough cruisers, and it is ironic that in February 1941 Churchill would seriously suggest exchanging the newly built battleship *Duke of York* for eight American 8-inch cruisers.

Churchill's principal opponents in the fierce battles over Naval Estimates during the previous two decades had, of course, been Admiral Beatty supported by Admiral Ernle (later Lord) Chatfield. The latter was indisputably the most capable naval officer of that period, but Churchill never forgave nor forgot. Chatfield became First Sea Lord in

1933 – until 1940, when Churchill dismissed him in favour of Sir Dudley Pound – a poor exchange.

This was not predictable in September 1939; the Navy adopted a wait-and-see attitude, and by common consent, eight months later, there was simply no other who could have lifted the nation from a slough of despair and defeat, then bullied and cajoled that same nation into arrogant defiance. Churchill, like his arch-enemy Adolf Hitler, never did master the complexities of naval strategy and only imperfectly understood, or chose to ignore, that warship squadrons marked on charts could not be lifted like chesspieces from one ocean to another, that they needed fuel, ammunition, provisions and water, and bases for recuperation. Battleships could not live off the land like horsemen on Lieutenant Churchill's African veldt.

Even now, there could hardly have been a man in *Sheffield*, patrolling from the Kattegat to Denmark Strait, who knew what the war was about. There was a pact with Poland, but it was clear that nothing could be done to help that country militarily. Chamberlain's declaration of war, some suggested, was just diplomatic bluff; it could all be settled at the negotiating table by the end of the week. No, said others, eyeing their grog or their midday gin, Germany had to be stopped. Perhaps the German ships would never leave their bases; the RAF would do the sinking, if there was going to be any sinking.

But the RAF's first offensive against enemy naval bases proved a fiasco. Of twenty-nine Blenheims and Wellingtons launched against Wilhelmshaven and Brunsbüttel, ten failed to find their targets and returned without dropping their bombs. One bombed the Danish town of Esbjerg, 110 miles from the intended target, and three decided to attack British warships in the North Sea before discovering their mistake. Seven were shot down by German anti-aircraft batteries.

Generally, there was an unreal quality about everything. News was scant. The only avenue of information was the BBC, broadcasting from 7 a.m. to 12.15 a.m., but reduced to a single programme, while the ships at sea, with only a peacetime complement, were subjected to a watch-and-watch-about discipline that was fatiguing. When a man came off watch he wanted little more than to snatch a meal and then sleep; there was little desire to wait for BBC news bulletins. Even in harbour, because of her unique RDF facility, *Sheffield* was invariably ordered to assume AA guard.

'On Northern Patrol', Commander Norris remembers, 'the weather was exceptionally heavy, and there were no shelters or "comforts" in those early days. We were nearly always at sea. I don't think I have ever been so tired, before or since. The whole ship's company were really fagged out by continuous cold, wet and lack of sleep. We operated a great deal from Sollum Voe, in the Shetlands, and always missed mails, fresh vegetables, etc. By the end of the year we had several cases of scurvy – difficult to believe, but true.'

But during the last week of September *Sheffield* and *Aurora* were detached to escort to safety a damaged submarine, *Spearfish*, a component of the Obrestad Line, extending from the Norwegian coast and intended to intercept enemy shipping exploiting the neutral territorial waters. The conditions were those that *Sheffield* would later meet frequently in northern operations – visibility reduced to five miles and occasionally less than one, sun and stars obscured by heavy cloud or mist. The two cruisers located *Spearfish* with difficulty, then found conditions clearing miraculously to allow German aircraft to launch attack after attack on the retreating British ships.

'It was our first dose of fairly heavy bombing – a few aircraft at a time, not more than ten, but for long periods of attack and very accurate stuff. It must have been the Germans' First XI.' The sailors watched the attacking Dorniers emerging from the distant, south-easterly cloud; many men were off-duty watchkeepers drawn to the upper deck from curiosity, until bombs began to erupt, tearing great holes in the sea and plucking dirty grey water upward. The spectators scattered and the ships' 4-inch guns crump-crumped, spilling empty brass shell cases over the decks and pock-marking the sky. The noise of the 2-pounder pom-poms was deafening.

L/SA Clay recalls that the ship's Asdic was reported out of action at this crucial time, and would remain so until Rosyth was reached; *Sheffield* was blind to any approach by enemy U-boats. 'Still, we comforted ourselves with the asumption that *Aurora* would be covering us. We did not know that *Aurora* had no Asdic at all. My brother, who was in *Aurora*, told me later that *they* were relying on *Sheffield* to screen *them*. Ignorance is indeed bliss.'

From 8 October *Sheffield* was sharing Northern Patrol duties with an assortment of old 'C', 'D' and 'E' class light cruisers, several hurriedly commissioned and manned by volunteers and Fleet Reservists, and seven armed merchant cruisers, guarding some 435 miles of sea route north from Scotland, averaging two ships south of the Faroes, four between Faroes and Iceland and four in the Denmark Strait.

Conditions were atrocious. The Commodore, 11th Cruiser Squadron, reported: 'In all ships conditions under which men are living are extremely bad . . . upper decks are permanently awash in normal Northern Patrol weather. Sleeping accommodation is quite inadequate; men, most of whom (had recently) been living in their own homes, have now to sleep on and under mess-tables; every slinging berth is occupied. Mess decks are wet and drying room facilities are very poor, with the result that watch-keepers come down from their watch as look-outs, etc. (often in northerly gales and blizzards) to great discomforts and little opportunity of drying their clothes.' The cruiser *Dragon* reported, 'Most electrical fittings exposed above the upper deck are waterlogged, one magazine practically flooded, and a sea finding its way into the main W/T office had temporarily put out of action the main transmitter.'

Aboard *Sheffield* young Colin Ross wrote home on 14

October. 'At present we are feeling a bit depressed, as we have just heard of the loss of *Royal Oak*. We have no details yet beyond the (BBC) wireless news, but it certainly did come as a nasty shock. Did I say in my last letter that I would *very* much like the Duffel Coat? It would be a grand thing to have. There have been only a limited number issued, and officers have not been lucky enough to get them. One sees the most amazing Eskimos and Arabs going about when one is at sea!'

The shortage of clothing suitable for Arctic conditions would continue throughout the war; garments like duffle coats and sea-boots had to be passed from one watch-keeper to the next, and almost all men resorted to football jerseys, towels, and the Balaclava helmets and gloves knitted by their families, the WVS and schoolchildren throughout the land, without which operations in northern seas could surely not have been sustained.

Despite the circumstances, however, the Northern Patrol was succeeding. During October 1939 seventy-three of eighty-four east-bound neutral ships were sent in for examination and seven German blockade-runners were intercepted. Of these one was sunk and one scuttled, but five were captured.

It was Renouf's practice to send his crew to action stations at 2100 every night, to test circuits, check equipment and then order Quarters Rest, when most off-watch men would seek their sleeping billets – the more fortunate in slung hammocks and the recently joined reservists and RNVR men on mess-stools and lockers, spilling over into the office flat and the officers' bathroom flat. Lighting below would be reduced to knee-height, red police lights. The decks would soon quieten to that never-ceasing throbbing hum of every living ship and the occasional, low-whispered warning over the address system – for watchkeepers at midnight and four – until six, when the shriek of a bosun's pipe

mustered defaulters and sent cooks to the galley, and men groaned in their too-brief sleep, thrust away the thought of yet another day of chilling cold and stinging wetness, numbed extremities and always the leaden weariness that dogged every hour. Would there ever again be a time when a man could lie in his warm bed on a Sunday morning – or any morning – hear distant church bells, the chatter of birds and the shrill play of children, and say to his pillow, 'Today the world must rotate without my assistance. I am going back to sleep.'?

At 2200 on Friday 20 October, in position 66°40'N, 22°08'W – just off the north-west tip of Iceland – *Sheffield* sighted a darkened freighter of about 5,000 tons which, on examination, revealed herself as the German *Gloria*, hugging the neutral coast before, presumably, her hoped-for dash across to the haven of Norwegian and then Swedish coastal waters and a safe home-coming. *Sheffield* remained close to the German throughout the night, and at dawn put aboard a prize crew under Sub-Lieutenant S. Phillips, who, recalled Vice-Admiral Norris, 'did very well indeed' in bringing the enemy ship and its arrogant crew into Kirkwall, Orkneys.

At the beginning of July the Admiralty had expected 300 Scottish women to enlist in the WRNS, but by September had achieved only 50. The number of applicants for enlistment increased at the outbreak of war but, an Admiralty spokesman announced, 'We shall be wanting still more, mainly girls with secretarial knowledge, but we need cooks and domestic workers, too. They will gradually be given work after being trained; many are already doing important work.'

Sheffield's Walrus aircraft and its pilot, Johnny Groves, had been put ashore at Hatston during early September,

Right: For the warships and auxiliaries of Northern Patrol, conditions were miserable. The weather was atrocious, temperatures bitterly cold, and no adequate clothing had been issued. Men slept anywhere, often at their action stations; here the Royal Marines of *Sheffield*'s 'X' turret sleep at their guns.

Left: Despite the demands of war, midshipmen were still required to attend instructional classes when off watch – here navigational chartwork under 'Schoolie' Jones.

and on 10 November was required to fly two Wren officers from Orkney to Shetland, where they were to organize a recruiting campaign. 'One of them', says Groves, 'was a senior WRNS officer with 1914–18 war medals, for whom the provision of a Mae West was as coals to Newcastle and the fitting of a parachute an impossibility. So, being nothing if not chivalrous, I refrained from wearing either myself.

We took off and flew in extremely murky weather, with nothing to see but grey and white-flecked waves, only a few hundred feet below, and frequent demands from my passenger, seated beside me – "Have you any idea where you are, young man?"

I confess that, after about an hour, I was beginning to have grave doubts with regard to our position. However, feigning confidence, I assured the lady that we were dead on schedule.

Suddenly the weather cleared, and there, just ahead, was Sumburgh Head. My instant relief was short-lived; the sky all around us was pock-marked with black smoke-puffs, and I realized, with a shock, that we were under fire. "What *are* they doing, young man?" asked my passenger. "Only practising, Ma'am," I told her, frantically searching for the Very pistol and a two-star identification cartridge. Satisfied by my signal-flare, the AA cruiser *Carlisle* ceased firing in our direction and turned her attention to a stray Heinkel III which had been beating up Sullom Voe when our Walrus appeared.

The only casualty of the raid was apparently one rabbit, and we landed on the water at Sullom Voe without further mishap to make fast to a buoy. A boat from *Carlisle* came alongside, and the AB coxswain, before he had a chance to observe our female passenger, exulted, "Gawd, sir – laugh! They thought you was a soddin' Jerry!" It was then necessary for me to explain apologetically to "Ma'am" that she had actually been the target of some uncomfortably accurate AA fire.

Her recruiting operation netted one cook for the WRNS, and we subsequently returned to Hatston without further

incident. However, gossip had it that the following monologue was overheard in the Kirkwall Hotel several evenings later: ". . . And then the pilot drew out a pistol; I guessed, then, that I had been right all along. He had been lost, and now thought we had arrived over Heligoland. He had decided to shoot me to prevent me falling into enemy hands – and we all know what happens to women prisoners. He was very embarrassed, when we landed, to discover that we were in Sullom Voe after all . . ."'

Following the torpedoing of *Royal Oak* in Scapa Flow, with the loss of 833 men, the anchorage had been bombed and the old battleship *Iron Duke*, now disarmed, was badly damaged.

Ordinary Seaman Frank White, awaiting a gunnery course in Portsmouth Barracks, was ordered to join *Sheffield*.

'I mustered with twenty-three others, to find that eight were bound for *Curlew*, eight for *Rodney*, and I with seven others for *Sheffield*. So off we went for Thurso and Scapa, only to find *Sheffield* gone. The powers that be said, "Right – off to the *Delhi*." Well, after a couple of Northern Patrols we were drafted off to Rosyth – and there was *Sheff* at last, on her hook. We got aboard at eleven p.m., and that night I slept with my head on a hatch-cover.'

During the following forenoon White and his fellows were mustered before the Commander and the Chief Telegraphist, and after enigmatic references to the Official Secrets Act told that they were to be the first ratings to operate the ship's RDF equipment. 'Thereafter', says White, 'we were the targets of persistent harassment by our messmates, all curious to know something about the freak gear carried up top, but not a word could we say.'

By 9 November the ship was at sea again, heading northward, and just in time for White to experience his first bad weather and *Sheffield*'s worst yet. A hundred miles north of the Faroes, on the 11th, the ship's log noted: *P.M. Very heavy squalls. Ship labouring and rolling heavily. Lost 1st Whaler . . .*

It was an understatement. 'It was terrible,' White recalls. 'Both "A" and "B" turrets were lifted clean off their mountings; the starboard davits (the whaler had disappeared) were twisted as if by some giant hand. I think every boat was damaged.' Unknown to anyone that day, *Sheffield* had also sustained damage to her keel which caused leaks in one of her fuel tanks. It was a defect that would dog her all her life.

Petrol rationing had reduced the flow of London's traffic, and by five in the evening of 23 November 1939 darkness and the blackout were approaching. The glitter of West End lights had long gone, although Gary Cooper, as *Beau Geste*, performed gallantly at the Marble Arch Pavilion, as did Lupino Lane, twice daily, in *Me and My Girl* at the Victoria Palace. The war was far distant, and did not really seem like a real war at all. Well – there were no *battles*, were there? Apparently the Merchant Navy had already lost 150 ships, and a battleship and an aircraft carrier had been torpedoed, but there seemed no justification for rationing ham, bacon, butter, eggs and sugar, particularly as the shops all had full shelves. 'It's nice to read about something else,' said the *Daily Mail*, and proceeded to describe the 'brisk breeze, a stirring of the first covering of leaves under the trees, a tang of autumn in the air and the swish of horses' hooves through the dew-drenched grass'. The first cubbing meeting of the Bramham Moor Hounds was announced.

On that evening of 23 November, Whitehall W/T received the following signal: 'From Rawalpindi. Immediate. Enemy battle-cruisers sighted.'

Gneisenau and *Scharnhorst*, ordered to distract the attention of prowling British cruisers so that home-bound German ships, including *Bremen*, could more easily slip through to sanctuary, had stumbled on one of the weaker links of Northern Patrol, the AMC *Rawalpindi*, south-east of Iceland. She did not hesitate to engage, but was quickly destroyed by the battle-cruisers' 11-inch guns before they disappeared northward.

At sea, strung between the Denmark Strait, Iceland, the Faroes and Shetland were six old light cruisers (*Caledon, Colombo, Cardiff, Ceres, Calypso* and *Delhi*), three heavier ships (*Norfolk, Suffolk* and *Newcastle*), and three more AMCs. *Sheffield* had just anchored in Loch Ewe after eleven days of punishing sea-time.

But not for long. 'We left that night,' related Able Seaman Whitmore, 'heading north at full speed and, on clearing harbour, Captain Renouf told us we were joining the search for *Gneisenau* and *Scharnhorst*.' There was not one ship of Northern Patrol qualified to engage either of the German battle-cruisers, far less both. 'Everyone was tense and excited, especially the guns' crews, who had a high opinion of their own abilities and no doubt whatsoever they could "get one in first", given the chance.'

The search, however, was abortive – as so many similar future searches for German raiders would prove. Only *Newcastle* came within fleeting sight of the enemy and prepared to fight, but they would have none of it. *Sheffield* regained Scapa Flow on 2 December after steaming 3,122 miles over seven days.

The ship's company were physically drained. They had been continuously at sea under gruelling conditions for more than three weeks; clothing and hammocks were damp, dhobeying in arrears, the messdecks neglected. Naafi stocks were depleted and all fresh provisions consumed. Many men had not stepped ashore since July, and it was now almost December. There was one thing, however, that everyone wanted more than anything else; their mail.

A cutter landed the mail Corporal at Flotta within minutes of the ship's anchoring. For certain there must be twenty bags. Probably twenty-five. It was likely, someone savoured, that the Corporal would issue mail in several instalments during the day – the pigeon-holes in the mail office were not very big. There'd be snapshots of the kids, the girl-friend's shy love, Mum's fussing and Dad's references to the Great War and how he and Kitchener had fought it. And parcels – cakes and woollens from home, new suits from Bernards and Moss Bros . . .

When the cutter came alongside the gangway it was empty, and the Corporal shook his head angrily as they stared at him. No soddin' mail, mate. It was still chasing the ship – from Scapa Flow to Invergordon, down to Rosyth, then to Loch Ewe just as *Sheffield* was returning to Scapa Flow. The Fleet Mail Office at Loch Ewe would redirect to Scapa – by which time *Sheffield* would be in the Shetlands.

But there was worse.

'D'yer hear there? Secure for sea. Fo'c'sle party to muster. Special sea duty men close up. Close all scuttles and watertight doors . . .'

It was, as Able Seaman Bungy Williams succinctly observed, bleedin' diabolical. Someone ought to write to Cassandra of the *Daily Mirror*. Renouf was uncomfortably aware how quickly a first-class crew, deprived of mail from home, could turn sour, particularly when hearty BBC voices and newspaper columnists assured the public that 'our boys are receiving your letters every day of every week, so keep writing!' The ship could not be back in harbour in less than another week, and Renouf wished that somebody who mattered in Whitehall would come to grips with the fact that servicemen would accept hardship, shortages, fight any odds, suffer atrocious food, be almost comatose from exhaustion, but they would not long tolerate being starved of their mail.

'Today', he told his crew, 'I have represented to the Vice-Admiral Commanding the Northern Patrol the urgent need of men and ship for a "spell". He fully realized the situation and told me he would energetically support my signal, which has just been sent, pointing out the necessity of at least 4 or 5 days in harbour. The mail question is extremely annoying, and the officers and ship's company have my sincere sympathy in the way things have turned

out. They may rely on me to do the utmost possible to ensure an "easy" soon, as I know I can rely on them to bear it in the interest of a common cause. I have no definite information with regard to leave, but I do not think it will be long deferred.'

For the following week *Sheffield* crossed and recrossed the Faroes Bank in bitter December temperatures. Whitmore recalls that 'In those early months we had no means of keeping ourselves or the ship warm; neither officers nor men had been issued with protective clothing. I can remember standing on the wings of the bridge with brown paper wrapped around my legs – *anything* for warmth.

We didn't see much of our messdecks, being almost continuously closed up. Below, ice would form on the bulkheads and deckheads, and on returning southward the ice would melt, making everything sodden wet and almost muddy underfoot. We tried to keep the ship clean, but it was almost impossible.'

And the Engineer Commander, Gallimore, tells of the astonishment of Captain Renouf when told that the engine-rooms were nicely warm, but the boiler-room crews had to keep their greatcoats on to keep out the cold.

On 10 December 1939, *Sheffield* docked in Wallsend, her birthplace, to carry out the repair of bad-weather damage. Since the first day of the war the ship had been at sea for two days of every three and had steamed 26,000 miles. A grateful Admiralty conceded her crew 72 hours leave for each watch. And on the 14th Renouf was relieved of his command, replaced by Captain Charles Larcom. *Sheffield*'s men were convinced that Renouf had been removed because of his insistence on respite for his crew, but were relieved to learn, some weeks later, that he had been promoted to the rank of Rear-Admiral.

The cruiser departed Wallsend on 18 December following a brief, bitter-sweet few days ashore. The newspapers were jubilant over the sinking of *Graf Spee* off Monte Video and indignant over governmental 'control mania' which threatened to ration margarine and coal. This rationing business could be taken too far. Many civilians, *Sheffield*'s men realized, lived in trance-like ignorance of war conditions and refused totally to allow their daily lives to be influenced by official pleas for economy. They were impatient with queues, travel restrictions and women bus conductors, and regarded itinerant servicemen with their kitbags as impositions on the fare-paying public.

For the next nine days, over Christmas, the ship patrolled the Iceland-Faroes gap. This was to be the worst winter for forty years, and the Navy was not equipped nor the men clothed for arctic temperatures; those manning the bridge and flagdeck, the air defence positions, the lookouts, the AA Director crews and AA gun crews were viciously exposed. Some ratings, at this time, did not possess even a pair of gloves. Conditions below decks were terrible. Bad weather had caused many of the forecastle fittings to leak, and the maindeck messes were awash with filthy, icy water. Condensation dripped continuously. Canvas covers had been made up for the leaking ventilator tops, but these were soon torn to shreds by the heavy seas.

On the evening of 24 December, a hundred miles south-east of the Icelandic coast, the ship's action alarm stiffened everyone, then flung them into frenzied movement. Water-tight doors and hatches crashed shut, passageways and ladders teemed with men climbing to gun-positions, flag-deck and director control, down to engine-room, transmitting station or magazine. Hoses were snaking along the main deck as damage control parties mustered, and on the bridge eyes were streaming, stinging, seeking another glimpse of a darkened shape reported to westward. The sea was leaden, with long rollers crested with white that flung off a mist-like spume. The sky was the colour of chocolate. Below decks, within moments, all noises had ceased save for the hum of generators and the occasional whine of turret motors as the guns traversed, sniffing for their target.

'There she is, sir – fine on the port bow.'

On the flag deck the shutters of a signal lamp clack-clacked, challenging, and from across the dark, torn water came an answering flicker of light. 'Transylvania fm Denmark Strait bnd Port A. God rest ye merry gentlemen.'

They all watched the tall-funnelled AMC as she closed, rolling and plunging her bows deep. They had all heard of *Transylvania*. She had not fought against heavy cruisers, like *Rawalpindi*, but in late October she had captured the German freighter *Bianca* and, within twenty-four hours, sunk *Poseidon*, both vessels intercepted after crossing the Atlantic in far northern latitudes. Then, in November, *Transylvania* had halted *Teneriffe*, which scuttled rather than surrender. That meant that the 17,000-ton ex-passenger liner and her Reservist crew, with a maximum speed of 15½ knots in good weather and six 6-inch guns that had been forged in the 1890s, had achieved rather more than the fine new cruiser *Sheffield*. The thought was not lost on those who were beginning to ask if *Sheffield* was the only bleedin' ship fighting the war. The cruiser men eyed the AMC's gaunt shape respectfully as she turned away south-easterly and vanished into the snow-swirling gloom.

Able Seaman Whitmore would never forget his first wartime Christmas.

'I normally manned the Torpedo 'B' light, but that night, not being required, I took shelter with four others in a sea cabin immediately below the bridge. There we lay, in a row, in oilskins and huddled together for warmth, our feet against a gangway lighting trough. Someone had obtained several of the old type filament lamps, which we hoped would help thaw our numbed limbs – but it didn't make the slightest difference. The temperature was well below zero and I have never been so cold in all my life.

When the weather eased a little, it was decided we should vote on whether the Chief Cook ought to have a go at cooking our Christmas dinner. The galley was in chaos, with cooking utensils sliding about and the big soup tureen becoming unmanageable. The alternative was to wait until we returned to Scapa. Unanimously, we voted to wait, and so on Christmas Day, closed up at defence stations, we dined on corned beef and biscuits, washed down with cocoa.'

As night fell on Christmas Day, west of the Faroes, greetings were exchanged with the Swedish ship *Kiruna*, bound for Göteborg.

'The cooks' action station', says Chief Cook Carter, 'was in the after magazine – mine, the Pom-pom ammunition supply. The action feeding routine, which required one rating from each station to collect food from the galley, to be eaten at the action station, was not resorted to if it could be avoided, as some always got more than others. The officers usually suffered. Northern Patrol was the worst for feeding. It was not unusual to lose an entire tub of soup, and have to replenish it. Cocoa and tea were available when steam could be put on, which we had to request from the Engineer Commander.

The Captain occasionally sent a messenger to the galley to complain about our smoke, so when convoying it was always useful to have a Smokey Joe in company; we could blame him.'

Scapa Flow was regained on 28 December.

Under wartime conditions a warship was required to refuel immediately on arrival; everything else had to wait. 'As we were due in Scapa Flow before noon,' the Engineer Commander, Gallimore, remembers, 'it was decided that the ship's company should have their dinner at midday and the officers in the evening. So, to release as many stokers as possible for their Christmas dinner, I called for volunteers from among the off-watch officers, including the Principal Medical Officer and the Chaplain, to tend the fuel hoses. When the oiler came alongside, her captain enquired if we'd had a mutiny on board.' Forward, the hands were sitting down to their first real food for weeks – cream of tomato soup, roast chicken with stuffing, potatoes and green peas, Christmas pudding. There were nuts, figs, dates and tangerines to follow, but few were interested, because the shriek of a bosun's pipe had been followed by the sweetest of music:

'D'yer hear there? Hands to make and mend.'

Sheffield would spend the next ten days in Scapa Flow. The ship's log for December was closed with the entry, *A calm still night saw '39 out and 1940 in.*

They would not have chosen Orkney in which to spend either Christmas or the New Year, but there were compensations – like a relaxation to four watches, which meant a full night's sleep in every four. There was mail every day, and new films on loan from the base. They watched *The Lady Vanishes* and *The Lion Has Wings* – which was the first time they had seen the RAF in action since the war began. Ashore on Flotta a Naafi beer bar and a Salvation Army canteen had been opened, a Nissen-hut cinema was promised. There was nothing else for libertymen, and no means of visiting Kirkwall or Stromness, where, allegedly, there were real houses and civilians. A chilling, damp wind stirred the gorse and stippled the surface of the vast anchorage, criss-crossed by panting drifters and motor-cutters. In the north-east corner, below the low cliffs of Gaitnip, a lonely buoy rose and fell; below it lay the sunken *Royal Oak* and the bodies of 833 officers and men. The boats that served the anchored warships avoided the vicinity of the buoy as one might avoid walking over a grave. Above, gulls wheeled and screamed.

In Long Hope Sound the old, disarmed battleship *Iron Duke*, used only for accommodation, had been damaged by bombing. She was being relieved by the geriatric and decrepit *Dunluce Castle*, once of the Union-Castle Mail Steamship Company. It was from her decks, cluttered with kitbags, hammocks and mail sacks, that incoming drafts of men from the south would be distributed among the Fleet, or retained if their ships were temporarily absent. Graffiti in her squalid latrines warned, 'It's no use standing on the seat; Dunluce's crabs can jump six feet.'

4

'Find your way to Aandalsnes tonight'

THE half-yearly promotions had been promulgated, and Sub-Lieutenant Colin Ross wrote from the Gunroom:

'I wonder if you saw in the papers that their Lordships have decided I am a Lieutenant . . . it's a very pleasant surprise. I am appointed to *Sheffield* again, but I don't know how long it will last, as I believe they are wanting people in destroyers. Also I am not sure whether I will go into the Wardroom or not, as no relief has been appointed. The Sub(E) is just on his second stripe; I rather fancy we shall both go up and leave the Pay Sub to look after the Gunroom.

The unfortunate Mids are still expected to do their exams on arrival in harbour. Bad luck for them as they don't have any spare time now, but I have no doubt the Board will be lenient . . .'

The new commanding officer, Captain Charles Larcom, had followed two men who had been held in high regard by *Sheffield*'s crew. Marke-Wardlaw had been a tolerant father-figure and Renouf was an officer with a strong sense of fair play, known to punish a technical offence by awarding the culprit several days' stoppage of leave when aware that the ship would be at sea anyway, thus satisfying both regulations and defaulter.

Larcom made a bad start. On his first day of command he made an inpromptu inspection of the ship with the First Lieutenant, and then ordered lower deck cleared.

The men filed onto the quarterdeck, many in cotton overalls and shivering in the December cold – marines, stokers, petty officers, seamen, canteen assistants. Larcom addressed them with hands behind back.

He was disappointed, he declared, to find that the ship, one of the newest cruisers in the Royal Navy, had been allowed to deteriorate into such a dirty and neglected condition. War routine was no excuse for slackness, and the ship's officers were as much to blame as the men. A ship's discipline and efficiency was based on its clean and uncluttered condition.

'I understand', he concluded, 'that this ship was known as the Shiny Sheff. Well, I'd call it something else beginning with "S".'

They stared at him, only slowly comprehending. The First Lieutenant was flushed. Didn't this Johnny-come-lately know that, except for a few hours for refuelling in Loch Ewe and Scapa Flow, *Sheffield* had been continuously at sea since 9 November, usually in arctic temperatures and atrocious seas, with decks swilling with filthy brine and the men nearly comatose through lack of sleep? 'There was an awful silence,' says AB Whitmore. 'We were simply stunned. One could *feel* the tension on the quarterdeck that day. You see, *we* all knew the reason.'

Well, officers came in all shapes. Some were gentlemen and some were pigs. As Blundell had said, long ago, the men could always see through a prig or a pimp, a poseur or a bragger. *Sheffield*'s company dispersed forward in silence. It takes all kinds, mate.

It was the mixture as before. Week followed week of thankless patrolling between Iceland in the north and the mouth of the Skagerrak to the east – weeks of heaving, slate-grey seas, snow, stinging sleet driven by gales that screamed in the rigging and threatened to tear the ensign from its halyard. During mid-January, astride the Iceland-Faroes Ridge, the weather was so ferocious that Larcom was compelled to heave-to. Bread-baking and the provision of varied, hot food was frequently impossible, and the men grew increasingly weary of corned beef, tinned herrings, baked beans, unidentifiable soup (except that it was identifiable as the same as yesterday and the day before), hard biscuit, baked beans, corned beef, tinned herrings, baked beans . . .

But young Ross, enjoying the privileges that accompany higher rank, wrote home: 'I did have a good (sleeping) billet under the chart-table, but it was a bit cramped, and I developed the habit of kicking through one end in my sleep and planting my boot in my neighbour's mouth – to which he took exception. However, I now have a more roomy one in the wheelhouse, and no complaints about my stable behaviour yet. Our mail usually goes to the wrong place first, which makes it twice as good when we do get it . . .'

Like when *Sheffield*'s dog-weary, soaked and unshaven crew anchored in Scapa Flow on 19 January, promised mail and six days in harbour. There was no mail and the ship was ordered back to sea within eighteen hours of arrival. The main deck was rancid with stale, recirculated air, and Will Hay in *Ask a Policeman* had already been screened four times. At 1030 during the forenoon of 30 January, again in that brutal Iceland-Faroes gap, teenager John Penn, Stoker 2nd Class, was flung overboard as the ship plunged into a massive trough. Larcom ordered the ship about immediately, aware that the chances of locating the lost man in the teeth of a blinding snow blizzard and a pounding sea were negligible, and thirty minutes later *Sheffield*'s log concedes:

Search not successful. 1100 resumed course and speed.

There were not a few in the forward messes who would have said, if asked, that the search might have been longer, but in the heavy seas running, the gale and sub-zero temperature, it is doubtful if even the most robust of men could have survived for more than three or four minutes. Even so, the death did nothing for the ship's morale. In war

circumstances, during which destruction by enemy action was a continuous, haunting threat, there was something obscenely unjust about a young man's death by accident.

Scapa Flow was not regained until late on 4 February, the cruiser delayed first by the heavy seas and then, incredibly, by dense fog. There was no mail awaiting the ship on Flotta, and now the men were beginning to believe that some conspiracy of ill intent had levelled every possible discomfort at *Sheffield* for reasons beyond the comprehension of seamen and stokers. Bungy Williams suggested that someone ought to write to somebody about it.

Monday 5 February was just another Scapa Flow day, of

Right: Appointed to *Sheffield* at the beginning of 1940, Captain Charles Larcom followed two men who had been held in high regard by the ship's crew, and his initial criticisms offended almost everyone. Later, however, he had the grace to apologize, and thereafter held his men's respect and loyalty.

grey skies and cold, drizzling rain, oilskinned boat crews, football pitches unfit for play, an RFA alongside and the sweet smell of fuel oil permeating the messdecks and flats. And then it would be northward again, to the sleet-shot wastes of the Iceland-Faroes gap . . .

But not this time.

'D'yer hear there? Clear lower deck. Hands to muster on the quarterdeck negative watchkeepers.'

Captain Larcom gazed down at a sea of upturned, unsympathetic faces. 'A few weeks ago,' he began, 'when taking command of this ship, I cleared lower deck.' He paused. 'I said several things, then, which I have since regretted, and for which I now apologize. I was wrong; I had no conception of the circumstances under which you had been serving – and are still serving – on Northern Patrol, and every criticism I made of this ship's condition I withdraw unreservedly.'

He half turned as if to depart, then stopped. Oh, yes – I almost forgot. There are *one hundred bags of mail* waiting for us in Rosyth. We are departing Scapa Flow today and will pick up that mail tomorrow. Then we will proceed to the Tyne for docking. The ship will be docked until the middle of next month, so –' he smiled, '– I think we can give two weeks' leave to each watch.'

'Like I said,' Bungy Williams opined as the hands dispersed, 'There's some officers that's soddin' pigs, and there's some that's gentlemen . . .'

They were all familiar with the hearty civilian acquaintance who greeted them with 'Hello – home again? You always seem to be on leave! When do you go back?' And now, in mid-March, as the ship departed Wallsend, there was not a man among them who was not a victim of the throat-choking withdrawal symptoms that terminated a home leave so more precious in wartime than in peace – home-sickness disguised by bravado and weak jokes, the young men's stories of sexual conquests, the older men's silence, the mutual feeling of resignation towards the months ahead, of crowded, noisy messdecks, indifferent food, the endless round of watchkeeping, exposure and fatigue, the demeaning hunger for that one anodyne each noon – a tot of rum.

This time, however, there was no time for lamenting. *Sheffield* was ordered to proceed direct from the Tyne to cover a convoy homeward bound from Hardanger Fiord in Norway. Within hours of losing sight of the Northumbrian coastline a vicious gale struck from SSE, and both whalers were torn away by the sea. From that moment the ship's company was seldom stood down from defence stations. There were many on board during the next three weeks who would never hereafter separate one enemy air attack from another. The logs of *Sheffield* and *Cairo*, sharing the same convoy actions, disagree widely with regard to times, positions and numbers of enemy aircraft. The Commander, Charles Norris, recalls that between 19 March

and 9 April, when German forces invaded Denmark and Norway, *Sheffield* escorted six convoys of British, French and Norwegian merchant ships between Bergen and the east coast without herself entering harbour. Late on 20 March five neutral vessels of convoy HN20 were hit by enemy bombs; one of these, the Norwegian *Svinka*, was torpedoed without warning while being towed back to harbour. Two convoys later *Sheffield* was barely a hundred miles from the Norwegian coast when her Asdic operator reported a submarine contact.

'Asdic to bridge. Reciprocating engines green one-two-oh, range two thousand and closing . . .'

The time was 2155 and darkness was almost complete, but the cruiser turned to engage with depth-charges.

'Asdic to bridge. Target bearing green oh-three-five. Extent of target three degrees, moving from left to right, range twelve hundred and closing . . .'

The ship's depth-charge facility was modest, but the amatol-packed canisters trundled off the quarterdeck rail and disappeared, twelve seconds later to lift a colossal mushroom of white water astern. The sea writhed and *Sheffield* turned. The shelves of the dry canteen, mess lockers and the stoves in the galley jettisoned their contents as the ship heeled crazily to press home a second and then a third attack before contact was reported lost. The depth-charge crew swore that a dark shape had been plainly visible in the cruiser's white, frothing wake, but action was broken off and *Sheffield* resumed course for Scapa Flow.

'We are on a pretty strenuous job now,' Lieutenant Ross recorded, 'and for the past week my quota has been 11 hours a day on the bridge, but I have now got quite into the routine of it and am feeling perfectly fit and full of beans as I have just had a really good bath – a luxury reserved for days when one is not likely to be roused from it in too much of a hurry. The most unexpected people are developing a sense of humour, and we might be a lot worse off.'

But *Sheffield* was soon going to be; a *lot* worse off.

The German six-pronged operation against Norway was set into motion on Sunday 7 April. On that day *Sheffield* was anchored in Scapa Flow. Divisions had been delayed until 1030 because of an aircraft warning, and normally shore leave would have been piped for 1315, but reports from a patrolling Sunderland suggested that an unusually large proportion of the German Navy was at sea off the coast of Norway, and leave was vetoed, The CinC's signal ordering all ships to raise steam for full speed by 2000 came as no surprise.

Sheffield weighed at 1957 and passed the Hoxa boom eighteen minutes later to assume night cruising station ahead of the battle fleet, steering north-east. There was nothing, yet, to warn of the costly and embarrassing fiasco soon to unfold.

By noon on the 9th the Fleet had made a wide northerly sweep into the teeth of a gale and was steaming southward, about sixty miles from the Norwegian coast. It was apparent that German naval formations had landed troops in Oslo, Bergen, Kristiansand, Trondheim and Narvik, but Intelligence was vague. The Admiralty prevaricated, issued orders, withdrew them, and the First Lord, Winston Churchill, was responsible for a number of confusing communications which illustrated his poor grasp of the situation. *Sheffield*, in company with *Glasgow, Manchester* and *Southampton*, was to the eastward of the battle fleet when, at 1430, the *Luftwaffe* attacked with eighty-eight Heinkel 111s and Junkers 87s.

'Then the bombers arrived', recalls AB Whitmore, 'to deliver both high-level and diving attacks. Again and again they came in; the Stukas screaming as they came to masthead level, greeted by our multiple pom-poms and point-fives. The Captain at this time was really doing his stuff, and I could see him from a wing of the bridge. He stood with legs apart, the peak of his cap shading his eyes, looking up and watching the bombs leave the high-level planes. It was hard-a-port or hard-a-starboard – as each release warranted. He kept this up for hours, with the ship zigzagging. Not one missile came inboard.'

A near miss by one stick of bombs heeled *Sheffield* alarmingly to port, and the explosive eruption almost engulfed her. Ordnance Artificer Lucas was in the Fire Control Tower above the bridge. 'Bombs fell so close to us that the flagship [*Rodney*] thought we had been hit, had already decided we should return to Scapa Flow, and now enquired if we required an escort. Captain Larcom replied: "Never touched me." ' *Sheffield* had fired 700 rounds of 4-inch shell. Three other cruisers had been damaged with two ratings in *Glasgow* killed, and a 500kg bomb had hit *Rodney* but had been stopped by the battleship's armoured deck. Only the destroyer *Gurkha*, struck by five bombs, succumbed after four hours of fighting the damage. In return, four aircraft were shot down – although the British saw only one crash and the Germans admitted nothing.

The Royal Navy, however, was learning its first hard lesson – that to operate without fighter air cover within reach of shore-based enemy bombers could be suicidal. It was a lesson to be learned less rapidly by politicians and the Chiefs of The General Staff. And there was little doubt that British warships' gunnery defence against air attack was less than adequate. Four-inch HA guns in sufficient numbers and in controlled barrages were reasonably effective against middle-altitude formations of enemy bombers which obligingly flew a straight course, but the close-range guns – the 2-pounder pom-poms and 0.5-inch machine guns were of very limited value, and it would be several years before improvements in the form of Bofors and Oerlikon guns became widely available.

During the afternoon of the 9th, *Sheffield* and *Glasgow*, accompanied by four destroyers, were detached to watch Bergen while the Fleet turned away northward again. Enormous quantities of anti-aircraft ammunition had been expended, and the CinC, Admiral Sir John Forbes, was not anxious to experience a repetition of the day's action. Incoming news of events was fragmented and frequently contradictory. Commanding officers trying to keep crews briefed from the information gleaned from signals traffic were as confused as the men by BBC bulletins, which spoke of a big naval confrontation in the North Sea, with heavy German losses. 'British and German battleships', it was announced, 'are fighting the first great sea battle of the war off the west coast of Norway.' Fleet Street reasoned that if thousands of enemy troops were being transported and put ashore at five different Norwegian locations, it was impossible that the British and German Navies were *not* fighting massive battles. 'Three separate actions were reported to have taken place . . . raging over a 400-mile line from the Skagerrak to Narvik in heavy seas.' The sailors could vouch for the heavy seas; they knew that the destroyer *Glowworm* had apparently disappeared after transmitting an incomplete enemy report, and *Renown* had exchanged long-range salvoes with *Scharnhorst* and a second unidentified German ship, but nobody knew anything of sea battles raging over 400 miles, or even of the German liner *Bremen* sunk with 1,300 men on board. As AB Bungy Williams so rightly observed: 'When yer think about it, yer don't know arf of what goes on.'

Both *Sheffield* and *Glasgow* were desperately low on fuel and AA ammunition. At dawn on Wednesday, 10 April they turned away from Bergen and at 1830 passed the Hoxa boom to anchor in Scapa Flow thirty minutes later. Oil and ammunition lighters came alongside *Sheffield* almost immediately and the mail Corporal was quickly despatched to Flotta. The Last Dog Watchmen had cleared away supper, the Officer of the Day was carrying out perfunctory Rounds, and hammocks were being slung in anticipation of a full night's slumber, when, at 2100, the action alarm bells hammered and a bugle screamed. Scapa Flow was under air attack.

Sheffield had an oiler on one side of her and an ammunition lighter on the other, while her own stocks of AA ammunition had been almost drained. 'The air was filled with every variety of fireworks,' said Ordnance Artificer Lucas, 'while we had replacement ammunition scattered everywhere as it was being transferred from the lighter to the magazines and the ready-use lockers. It was hair-raising.'

The raid by sixty aircraft was the fiercest yet mounted by the Luftwaffe against Scapa Flow, and OA Lucas knew better than most the horrific consequences of a single bomb on *Sheffield* at this time. The cruiser's remaining available 4-inch ammunition was quickly expended, and she began using her 6-inch guns as the comparatively few warships still in the anchorage and the eight-gun battery on Hoy raised a barrage that only a few of the high-flying Heinkels attempted to penetrate. Lucas cringed mentally as a bomb smashed into the water only three hundred yards from *Sheffield* and another erupted on nearby Flotta. The attack persisted for one hour and twenty minutes and cost the Luftwaffe six aircraft – four of them to AA fire, two to fighters. No ships had been damaged and the only buildings ashore of consequence to the Fleet – the mail office and the beer canteen – were unharmed, but OA Lucas debated whether his hair would go white before it all fell out. It was mildly comforting to learn from the BBC that all leave for the BEF and RAF in France had been stopped until further notice. It was about bleedin' time someone else joined in this soddin' war, mate.

On Saturday, 13 April *Sheffield* and *Glasgow*, accompanied by the 6th Flotilla of 'Tribal'-class destroyers, were sweeping the ragged Norwegian coast north of Bergen when orders were received to prepare to land a force of 350 marines and sailors at a location yet unspecified.

The ships at sea knew almost nothing of the situation ashore and even less of the confusion among the Chiefs of Staff and the Cabinet as a result of the German landings in Norway. In the event, ignorance was probably bliss. The mixed bag of fifty seamen who were detailed to accompany the 300 marines, unaware that they were likely to be met by specialist German storm-troopers fully armed and equipped for arctic warfare, struggled to piece together antique webbing pouches and buckles as their messmates guffawed, pulled on borrowed boots and tentatively worked the bolts of Lee-Enfield rifles that had not been free of grease since 1918. Ominously, the galley prepared mounds of corned beef sandwiches.

More specific orders were received on the following day, Sunday 14 April, and effectively scotched even the chaplain's optimistic plans for some sort of divine service. The 'battalion' drawn from *Sheffield* and *Glasgow* was to be landed at Namsos, a small, fiord-enclosed port ninety miles north of Trondheim, to deny it to the Germans and hold it as one of two disembarkation points (the other was Aandalsnes) for the British forces already on their way to drive the Germans out of Norway.

How many *krones*, a stoker enquired, grappling with unfamiliar gaiters, did a fur coat cost in Norway? There was a certain party in Luton who might be prepared to capitulate at the sight of a fur coat . . .

The two cruisers and five destroyers entered Folden Fiord at 1940 after driving off an inquisitive Heinkel floatplane. The landing operation was clearly no secret, and now speed was essential. *Matabele* came alongside *Sheffield* and, wrote an unnamed correspondent to the *Globe & Laurel*:

'The men literally came direct from manning the AA guns to jump into the destroyer; the transfer of the battalion, complete with stores, took only 13 minutes. We then steamed at high speed for about 15 miles up the fiord, where the companies were landed.'

Namsos was in darkness. 'We were all tense and expectant as we went in,' recalls OA Lucas, 'and wondering what sort of reception we were going to get. Fortunately we had beaten the Germans to it, and outposts quickly occupied strategic positions around the town. The Headquarters Staff, which included me, moved into the local school. Our force of Royal Marines, seamen and stokers, equipped with rifles, pistols and four museum-piece machine-guns, were ashore to hold this small port at all costs pending the arrival of "the military". We kept well out of sight, as the town was under almost constant surveillance by enemy aircraft which circled overhead at very low altitudes; the temptation to fire at them was almost overwhelming, but had we done so they would have immediately bombed the town and destroyed the landing stage – and this was of vital importance.'

Able Seaman Whitmore was equally convinced that a massive British Expeditionary Force was on the way. 'Before embarking on the destroyer we were given a "last supper", which involved two eggs with our chips instead of the usual one. I was a member of the Demolition Party, and remember a few butterflies in my stomach when we were told to keep silence and be prepared for anything. Our job was to transport about a dozen depth-charges to a bridge just outside Namsos and destroy it. The truck we commandeered could get only part of the way, and we had to complete out journey by rolling the depth-charges through deep snow.'

'We were a motley crew,' confirms Marine Reg Bown. 'Most of us were only HOs and our equipment was all 1914–1918 gear. The only training the Royals had been given was on the islands of Scapa.

Anyway, we reached a small village alongside a lake which had a wooden viaduct spanning it. The railway line was the link we had to break, as apparently the Germans were using the railways to infiltrate the country. The stokers and torpedo ratings were there to blow up the bridge.'

Today, the *naïveté* of the Namsos undertaking is almost unbelievable. A handful of sailors and stokers totally untrained in shore operations, supported by marines of whom many had been clerks and factory workers only a few months earlier, and all inadequately equipped and clothed, had been put ashore, in darkness, in a strange, snow-covered location possibly defended by a German battle group, and expected, presumably, to drive off the enemy and hold the area until reinforcements arrived – whereupon, again presumably, the liberation of Norway would follow.

'Everything was a bit of a muddle', Marine Bown confesses, 'as we only had candles for lighting. We had set off on a compass course to bring us to our inland destination, with the stokers bringing the depth-charges along. After an hour of slogging in the cold and snow, in single file, the wits were beginning to mutter about the retreat from Moscow; we were climbing uphill and the men were starting to straggle. The naval ratings were suffering because their footwear was not up to the job, and the depth-charges were difficult to handle in the deep snow.

Worse, the compass had been affected by some magnetic rocks, and we had to retrace our steps, meeting the stragglers and telling them to turn back. Our reputation with the naval ratings was getting low.'

The first grey streaks of dawn were in the sky when *Sheffield*'s men, weary and sodden, reached their destination, only to be met by two Army officers who argued that the railway bridge should not be demolished because it would be needed by the Allies when the invading enemy was driven back. The sailors were now totally disenchanted with the whole business and wishing themselves back in their hammocks. Even a usually abused 'train smash' breakfast – tinned tomatoes with bacon – bread-and-margarine and hot, bitter-sweet tea, would have been wolfed without complaint. With daylight the Luftwaffe would be overhead in force and there were allegedly several thousand German troops beyond Steinkjer, only thirty miles away, who were capable of quickly overwhelming the small British contingent if its landing were reported.

Captain W. F. Edds, RM, commanding, decided to defer the demolition until some sensible information on military intentions was available, to establish a defensive position and get his men under cover before morning. The sailors' opinions are not recorded.

Colin Ross had earlier been ordered to go ahead of the main party to select locations for entrenching, and, not sure that he could make any useful assessment in the deep snow, he hurried on to allow himself ample time to search around before Edds and his marines overtook him.

'It was cold and pitch dark, and I hadn't much idea of what sort of places to choose. Anyway, after falling to my neck into several snow drifts, and handicapped by an enormous pack that grew heavier as the night progressed, I found a few places which looked good.

Subsequently one of these turned out to be a snow drift, into which I floundered. However, the Chief Stoker, with more ingenuity than respect for my rank, proposed a scheme by which I led the way – rather like a human snow-plough – assured by him that I would be rescued by the multitude that followed if I sank too deep! In the event we spent the whole night digging into what seemed solid rock, but we had achieved passable positions before daylight, when the Luftwaffe's dawn reconnaissance was expected. It was bitterly cold each night, although quite pleasant by day. We got water by melting snow over a fire, and we were only allowed out of our cover in driblets, so we must have appeared to be Norwegian civilians to the frequent enemy aircraft.'

Marine Bown and Able Seaman Whitmore had fared slightly better. 'We hid in barns and cattle-sheds,' said Bown, 'which alarmed some of the natives, who did not know who or what we were, but they soon became friendly. Many of us received gifts of food . . .'

After three days – on 17 April – elements of the British 146 Brigade and a demi-brigade of French *Chasseurs Alpines* were landed to relieve the men of *Sheffield* and

Glasgow. Marine Bown records that he was on sentry duty, calf-deep in snow, when he was approached by a youthful Army subaltern who asked to be directed to the Officers' Mess. Bown referred the young man to the small cowshed in which Lieutenants Ross and Hawkes were huddling.

'We were ordered to return to *Sheffield* as quickly as possible,' chuckled Whitmore, 'and I suppose all records were broken as we retraced our steps to the town and the jetty, where our faithful destroyer, *Nubian*, waited to embark us. We were taken out of the fiord to *Sheffield* and transferred to her about eight miles off shore. It was marvellous to have a hot bath and real food after that chilling time ashore. It was great to get home.'

Home was *Sheffield*.

Once clear of the coast, Lucas remembered, Captain Larcom welcomed his men back aboard. 'But I have often wondered what happened to those depth-charges we took ashore!'

One of the ship's errant Walrus aircraft had been hoisted inboard before leaving Scapa Flow, and now, before leaving the Norwegian coast, Sub-Lieutenant Groves was ordered to fly a photographic reconnaissance of Trondheim, southward, and the port's adjacent fiords, in anticipation of the Army's landing. At 1600 a speculative throng, despite the cold, gathered in the waist to watch P5670 catapulted off, with Groves accompanied by Leading Aircraftman Wilson and the observer, Lieutenant-Commander G. Hare. To the spectators' disappointment the stubby little aircraft did not fall off the catapult into the sea. The four-bladed propeller whirled as engine noise tortured the ears. The Walrus shuddered, then lurched forward on the box girder at 80mph and reached into space, dipped momentarily, lifted, climbed, roared upward.

The spectators turned away. It was all very unsatisfying, this efficiency. Nowadays, aircraft were being catapulted successfully four times out of five. It was hardly worth coming up on deck for.

The small amphibian was whirring over Trondheim at 4,000 feet when Groves sighted a number of Heinkel He 115 floatplanes moored in the harbour below, and turned excitedly to Hare. 'Look, sir – Heinkels! Let's go down and machine-gun them!' The prospect of engaging the enemy with a single Vickers gun, and the retaliation such rashness might provoke, was regarded with scant enthusiasm by Hare. 'Be your age, J. Groves,' he responded. 'Be your age. We're here to photograph the enemy, not fight them.'

Even as the Walrus banked over Trondheim fiord they could see fighters climbing from Vaernes airfield to eastward, presumably having been scrambled to intercept the trespassing Walrus, and Groves opened his throttle. 'We fled at high speed, at least 110 knots, low over the hills in the direction of Namsos, carrying away our trailing aerial on the pine trees en route. We landed on the water almost devoid of fuel, hoping the town was still in British hands.'

It was. Hare and Groves were interrogated by a British Intelligence Officer, Major Peter Fleming, and, that done, the crew of the Walrus desired nothing more than to return to their ship by the quickest and easiest route, but it was already late afternoon. The sky between Namsos and the open sea, patrolled by enemy aircraft operating from Vaernes, was 'tiger country', and, in any case, Hare could only guess that *Sheffield* would be off the mouth of Namsosfiord that night. It was cold, and Fleming's offer of hospitality in the officers' mess (the sergeants' mess for Watson) was tempting, but the thought of those warm and noisy below-decks of *Sheffield*, and hot soup, perhaps corned beef surprise, mashed potatoes and hard-boiled peas was irresistible to the crew of P5670.

At dusk two cans of Army benzine were poured into the almost empty fuel tank, and Groves taxied the floatplane along the fiord with all three crewmen straining their eyes as darkness closed down completely. There could be Germans on either shore but, if there were, they would hardly be likely to recognize the passing engine noise as that of a British aircraft, would they? Of course, the enemy might have searchlights, which would be awkward, or the Walrus might run into an enemy patrol vessel.

They never did know what they did run into. 'Our peace was suddenly shattered', says Groves, 'by the hammer of a machine-gun, and then a vessel which looked like a trawler loomed very close upon us in the darkness.' It was impossible to identify the vessel as British, German or Norwegian, and Groves 'blipped' his lights frantically. The gunfire ceased, whereupon all three crewmen bellowed, 'SHEFFIELD!'

Whether or not the shout was intelligible through the roar of the aircraft's engine was debatable, but at least the machine-gun remained silent – probably because the boat's commander was as uncertain of what he had encountered as were the aircrew. The Walrus threshed on into the darkness and, astern, the stranger disappeared from sight.

Another hour of anxious taxiing brought them to the mouth of the fiord, evident by the increasing undulation of a sea-borne swell. Otherwise all was a black void. The crewmen might have only exchanged one predicament for another, but, says Groves, 'Sure enough, there was *Sheffield* at the mouth of the fiord, and we were duly hoisted inboard. Having been out of radio contact for some seven hours we were about to be logged as missing, but I got the impression that relief at seeing us again was slightly tempered with annoyance at having to call out the aircraft handling party at 2300 after a tiring day. We might have had the decency to delay our escape until morning.'

As a result of this operation, Walrus P5670 was named *Terror of Trondheim*.

Scapa Flow was not quite as inadequate as earlier when *Sheffield* anchored at noon on the following day, Friday 19 April. The sunshine of early spring glittered on the waters of the Sound and, ashore, the first wild fuchsias and lupins fluttered. Boat crews had abandoned oilskins, the mud of winter had hardened, and the West Mainland Sheepdog Trials, postponed last September, were being re-advertised in the *Kirkwall Herald*. Since the sinking of *Royal Oak* in the anchorage, more blockships had been placed, the nets doubled. Eighty more guns had been mounted ashore, and the airfield at Wick, forty miles away, had been enlarged to accommodate four RAF squadrons.

With luck there would be at least one run ashore to the vast new beer canteen, where men queued for strings of tickets from cash windows and exchanged them for pints of beer at a long, puddled counter. There was nothing else ashore for ratings, unless one counted Tombola, or the little corrugated-iron cinema screening *The Thirty-Nine Steps*, or the Salvation Army canteen where one could be served baked beans on toast and tea by two 'Sally Ann' lassies already dubbed 'the Flotta Twins'. Men went to the canteen just to look at them; they had plenty of baked beans on board.

The BBC – when there was time to listen – and two-day-old newspapers from the mainland were referring to the second battle of Narvik. The *second*? What had happened in the first? Anyway, apparently the 2nd Destroyer Flotilla had knocked ten bells out of German shipping off occupied Narvik and, later, old *Warspite* had fired her guns in anger for the first time since 1916. Denmark had surrendered after losing thirteen soldiers, and the Russian Foreign Minister, Molotov, had told the German Ambassador, 'We wish Germany complete success in her defensive measures.' The German cruiser *Königsberg* had been sunk by Fleet Air Arm Skuas in Bergen harbour and her sister *Karlsruhe* torpedoed by the submarine *Truant* off the Danish coast. King Haakon had called on all Norwegians to resist the German invaders, and, with British and French troops pouring ashore, it was plain that Germany, having overstepped, was about to experience a humiliating come-uppance.

During the following forenoon orders to secure for sea were received with mixed feelings. *Sheffield* was to proceed to Rosyth, and that could only be an improvement, assuming there would be shore leave. They had not seen streets, shops, pubs or skirts for five weeks. The ship weighed at 1430 and followed *Glasgow* into the Pentland Firth, increasing to 20 knots. The Inchkeith Gate was reached just before midnight and a half hour later both cruisers were anchored off Rosyth. The fo'c'sle party, turning into their hammocks at 0100 on Sunday morning, were turned out of them at 0630 to prepare to weigh. It was diabolical and someone ought to write to their bleedin' MP. *Sheffield* tied alongside the South Wall. The light cruiser *Galatea* was already moored at the North Wall, embarking stores. At 0830 bosuns' pipes shrilled as Rear-Admiral M. L. Clarke stepped onto the quarterdeck; his flag climbed the foremast and the forecastle party secured for a late breakfast. At 0830, having barely got their leathery fried eggs and fossilized fried bread from the messdeck heaters, they were ordered to muster yet again. It could give a bloke soddin' diarrhoea, mate. *Sheffield* moved to the North Wall to tie up ahead of *Galatea*. The forecastle party secured for breakfast.

Embarkation of Army stores began almost immediately – and that could only mean a return to Norway. Well, the BBC was issuing glowing news bulletins of Allied successes, and Gaumont-British, Pathe and Movietone newsreels screened British troops in the snow, warships bombarding alleged enemy concentrations, and old Spanish Civil War clips of German aircraft now claimed to be Russians bombing Helsinki. Virginia Cowley of the *Sunday Times* described 'some of the most spectacular fighting in history', which she had never seen. In Britain, Local Defence Volunteers were being drilled, and Richard Tauber was singing at the Stoll Theatre.

Sheffield continued to load military equipment during the whole of Sunday 21 April and off-loaded her aircraft so that the hangar deck could accommodate stores that totalled 100 tons and included two Bofors AA guns, two 30-cwt trucks, two 3-inch mountings and thirty motor cycles. Men of the 1st Battalion, The Yorks and Lancaster Regiment began filing aboard at 2000, and by dawn on the 22nd the cruiser had embarked 38 Army officers, 650 other ranks and a special Naval Party of seventeen. The soldiers, encumbered with rifles, greatcoats, packs, helmets, respirators, anti-gas capes and massive, noisy boots, negotiated every ladder with extreme care and filled every corner of every messdeck and flat on the main deck. Bungy Williams said they were going to start being sick any minute. At 0600 the ship slipped, and at 0830 formed up with *Glasgow* and *Galatea*, both equally loaded with troops and stores. Six destroyers assumed screening positions. Course 040, speed 22 knots. The liberation of Norway was about to begin.

Of course, these pongoes – the Army – did not have the Norwegian campaign experience of *Sheffield*'s marines and stokers and would not be required to haul depth-charges through the snow all night. The Army had trucks and motor cycles, and footwear that would not be reduced to wet blotting-paper within a few hours; they also devoured the ship's bread as if a famine was scheduled for dawn, not to mention duty-free cigarettes and nutty bars from the dry canteen. In the event, none of them was sick. The 780-mile excursion was, as OA Lucas commented, 'The flattest I have ever known in *Sheffield*, which was most fortunate, as, packed with soldiers, the results of a rough trip is better imagined than described.'

The day's hard steaming passed without incident until evening, when, at 2138, the destroyer *Vansittart* reported an Asdic contact and was detached to attack with depth-charges. Evening darkened into night, calm but heavily clouded, and the cramped soldiers in messdecks and passageways listened in silence to the BBC's news bulletin, which told of British and French troops driving towards Trondheim. Iceland had proclaimed independence, and Holland declared a state of siege, reaffirming the desire to remain neutral. Nobody in the vibrating, red-lit forward

messes knew precisely where *Sheffield* was heading, but it must surely be Norway; the course had been north-easterly since departing Rosyth. Of course, the soldiers speculated, they might get ashore to find it was all over bar the shouting; the 1st Yorks & Lancs had already been passed over for duty in France, and now seemed likely only to pick up the crumbs in Norway. There must be someone in Whitehall with a grudge . . .

The dawn was cold, snatching at the throat, which was hardly surprising; they had almost reached the Arctic Circle. It was impossible to tell where the slow, leaden sea met a sombre sky from which a few snowflakes swirled. Gun crews stamped feet, blew on fingers, and Morning watchkeepers, relieved, trod among the wakened, swollen-eyed soldiers, reluctant to venture too far in search of hot water for fear of getting lost in a labyrinth of ladders and compartments.

Sheffield's destination was disclosed later in the forenoon. It was Molde, a disembarkation point some eighty miles south of Trondheim. The soldiers cleaned their rifles and checked ammunition, gas masks and field dressings. At 1824 an Asdic contact by the destroyer screen set the action alarm hammering, and the soldiers braced themselves as the ship turned to starboard to drop her few depth-charges. Minutes later they heard the distant rumble of underwater explosions, and wondered if it really were a bad thing to be overlooked by someone in Whitehall . . .

A mountainous, snow-stippled coastline spread ahead, and at 1900 the three cruisers were nosing into the confines of Buddybed Fiord with all gun-crews at their stations. The AA cruisers *Carlisle* and *Curacoa* were in the fiord, covering troops already ashore. *Sheffield* tied alongside Molde's little timber pier while *Galatea, Glasgow* and four destroyers pressed on ten miles up-fiord to Andalsnes. Molde, it was learned, had been bombed only once, but the Luftwaffe's return was expected at any time, and at Trondheim, Namsos and Lillesjona the tethered British transports and their escorts had been sitting ducks for the Ju 87s. *Sheffield*'s troops needed no urging to disembark, and all were ashore with their vehicles and stores by 2230. The destroyer *Vansittart* came alongside also to disembark and to oil from the cruiser, followed by *Campbell*. One hour after midnight, with no interference, all three slipped their lines and eased their way thankfully from the fiord to the open sea.

Later that day a similar force of troops was to be put ashore by the cruisers *Birmingham, Manchester* and *York*. The landing was just in time. Namsos was being relentlessly pounded by squadrons of Ju 87s, provoked by the euphoric bulletins broadcast by the BBC. The Allied drive on Trondheim had foundered, and the entire Norwegian campaign was already becoming a logistics nightmare, with British troops, of whom many were inadequately trained Territorials, bereft of air cover and with negligible armour and field artillery, being outclassed by specialist Germans on the ground and progressively bombed into bewildered impotence by the Luftwaffe.

Left: On 23 April 1940, men of the 1st Battalion Yorks & Lancaster Regiment were landed at Molde, about 80 miles south of Trondheim, to be thrown into the débâcle of the Norwegian campaign. They were re-embarked from Aandalsnes seven days later.

The men of *Sheffield* knew nothing of these things. The ship, accompanied by *Vansittart* and *Campbell*, was speeding south-westward for Scapa Flow, mail and Younger's Ale. *Galatea* and *Glasgow* were about forty miles astern, and during the forenoon *Ark Royal, Glorious* and *Berwick* were sighted – surely an omen that all was going well.

But it was not quite. Shortly before midnight, as the Middle watchkeepers were being roused, a signal from Admiralty ordered both *Sheffield* and *Glasgow* to alter course, to locate and escort the light cruiser *Curacoa*, which had been badly damaged by two direct hits off Andalsnes, suffered fifty casualties, and was now limping home.

Contact was made with *Glasgow* and *Curacoa* during the forenoon of 25 April. The little first-war cruiser, despite her damage, still managed 18 knots, but the three ships were dangerously exposed. At 1330 a Heinkel He 111 was sighted, and shadowed at a distance, but eventually turned away. Evening laid down a curtain of mist for which the ships might have been grateful had it not reduced their speed even further. *Sheffield*'s log for Friday 26 April

records: *Seven Asdic contacts between 0001 and 0600.* Four of these were almost certainly U-boats, and the cruisers dropped depth-charges at 0425 and 0530. The scattering of Orkney islands was sighted fine on the starboard bow just after 0600; they were almost safe, but nobody relaxed until they slid past the Hoxa anti-submarine boom into the Flow. The anchor cable thundered in to the water and protesting deadlights were being lifted.

'D'yer hear there? Away first motor-boat. Mail corporal lay aft.'

Scapa, *bloody* Scapa.

Nobody thought about long weekend leave any more, but they did expect a make-and-mend, with shore leave piped for the First part of Starboard Watch. *The Four Feathers* was being screened in the Nissen cinema ashore, while, in the Naafi beer canteen, the 'big house' Tombola prize was expected to be more than £300. A lighter was alongside, off-loading frozen meat, margarine, and a consignment of

Martins' cigarettes – a gift to the ship's company from the Overseas League Tobacco Fund – and both the Walrus aircraft were being lifted aboard.

No shore leave was piped. Instead, *Sheffield* was ordered to raise steam for full speed with despatch. With boilers cold, warships were expected to raise steam for 20 knots in four hours; they were required to raise steam *with despatch* in two. The Forenoon watchkeepers had scarcely cleared away messtraps and emptied refuse buckets.

'Tinkle, tinkle, little spoon,
Knife and fork will follow soon . . .'

In the engine room, a labyrinth of steel ladders and walkways under organ-lofts of white asbestos-clad pipes and channelling, Artificers and Stoker POs watched pressure gauges, and the immaculate Engineer-Commander sucked his teeth. Sweat began to soak.

During the afternoon, with the ship ready for sea and all boats hoisted, orders to proceed were cancelled.

The next forenoon, again, orders were received to raise steam for 24 knots. Junior officers who anticipated that their Saturday flag-hoisting exercise might, as a consequence, be suspended, were disappointed, and Captain Larcom's routine inspection of the ship was carried out as normally. Secured, and with no yearned-for cancellation received, *Sheffield* weighed at 1240 and passed the Hoxa boom thirty minutes later, under orders to substitute for the damaged *Curacoa* as RDF guardship for *Ark Royal*.

Contact was made with the carrier during the forenoon of Sunday 28, about 150 miles west of Namsos. In company was the big cruiser *Berwick* and four destroyers. The BBC was still describing British and French gains in central Norway, while William Joyce on the European Service of the *Reichsrundfunk* – after enquiring about the whereabouts of *Ark Royal* – announced that the 'first and last purpose of German measures in Denmark and Norway is to force Britain to her knees'.

And to prove it, only fifteen minutes after *Sheffield* had assumed station on *Ark Royal*'s port bow, and just as the carrier signalled her intention to fly off aircraft, two Heinkel He III bombers came in high from eastward, and the warships' HA guns engaged immediately. Throughout the war, gunners confident of their ability would always find it incredible that level-flight aircraft were so frequently able to remain unscathed in a barrage that filled the sky with criss-crossing tracer and scattered lethal shrapnel for miles. This enemy, however, was flying too high and fast to be caught, and for that reason its eight 250lb bombs fell wide of any target. *Sheffield*'s gun crews watched the Heinkels escape frustratingly beyond range, but whooped to see three Skuas take off from *Ark Royal*'s flight-deck in pursuit.

The sortie could have been only a morale-boosting gesture, because the British aircrafts' best speed was inferior to that of their quarry, but this time there was an unexpected development. As the fleeing raiders vanished in the direction of the Norwegian coast, the following Skuas

ran head-on into six more Heinkels, apparently intending a further attack on *Ark Royal*. Surprise was mutual, but the British pilots were quicker to react. In the snarling hurly-burly that followed, three of the Heinkels were shot into the sea and the others decided that tomorrow was another day. The three *Skuas* – dual-purpose fighter-bombers that were less than convincing in either role – returned to their carrier unharmed, their crews dazed but very happy.

So far, very good, but the squadron seemed to be contributing very little to the campaign ashore, which, anyway, the BBC claimed, was progressing very much in accordance with plans. The phrase 'according to plan' was becoming overworked, but it was comforting to the men at sea, who remained almost totally ignorant of the war's fortunes.

On the following evening, with the squadron now north-westward of the Shetlands, *Sheffield* was ordered to detach, rendezvous with the 2nd Cruiser Squadron fifty miles off the Norwegian coast, and then proceed to Aandalsnes.

'I recall going into the wardroom at about 1800', said the navigating officer, Charles Hall, 'and asking what the BBC news was. The reply was that there was none, except that the Norwegian campaign was still going on. The British Army had advanced here and there, and fallen back somewhere else. So I joined the others in a gin. At about 1820 the Yeoman of Signals entered with a signal ordering us to Aandalsnes with all despatch to evacuate the British and Norwegian Armies and any civilians who might wish to leave. It came as a great surprise after the calm tone of the BBC news, and no suggestion of a grave situation.'

Almost immediately Captain Larcom sent for me. 'Do you know Aandalsnes?' he asked. I replied that I had never even heard of it. The Captain said, ' "Weil, find your way up there tonight." '

Parting company with *Ark Royal* soon after 2100, the cruiser steamed hard, north-eastward. There was not much that the ship's company could be told; nothing was known to tell. Admirers of Bing Crosby and Ginger Rogers, who had anticipated seeing them in *East Side of Heaven* in the office flat that evening, or having their hair cut for sixpence in the canteen space, or dhobeying in the seamen's bathroom, were closed up at cold gun stations, flag-deck or Asdic cabinets, reading Admiralty's continuous BN broadcast, or sweating in some overheated, steel-walled cavern below decks, questioning why anyone should choose the Navy when they might have lived out the war in the RAF, which provided real beds, a beer canteen *in situ*, Brylcreem and WAAFS.

The familiar shapes of *Galatea*, *Aurora* and *Southampton* were sighted during the afternoon of the 30th in position logged 63°52′N, 03°15′E. The news was almost beyond comprehension. Allied operations in central Norway had foundered in the face of snow and mountainous terrain, unapposed air attacks and the sheer professionalism of the enemy; the chilled and confused soldiers of Stickle Force were to be evacuated from Aandalsnes and Molde under cover of darkness. Other warships and transports would be lifting off troops from disembarkation points elsewhere, and the British Army's first encounter with the Wehrmacht had ended in failure after sixteen days.

In the sequence *Galatea, Sheffield, Southampton* and *Aurora*, the cruisers probed their passage into Isfiord at 2130 with four destroyers screening ahead and one astern. The water of the fiord was black, floating with clotted snow, and dusk was turning to darkness. This was a ragged, jig-saw coastline; nobody, not even the Norwegians, would say for certain where Buddybed Fiord became Romsdal Fiord or if it was really Isfiord here or further, but abeam, to port, there was the yellow flicker of fires and viciously soaring sparks, with an offshore smell of smoke they could detect at more than a mile. It was little Molde, where only a week before they had landed the men of the 1st Yorks & Lancs. Captain Larcom, ordered up-fiord to Aandalsnes, had detached the destroyers *Winchester, Windsor* and *Walker* to reconnoitre inshore, to ascertain the situation and, at the same time, lift off any British troops that might be sighted. The destroyers, darkened, slid into the night. There were other ships – a sloop and a light AA cruiser, but *Sheffield* moved on until Hall said the cluster of fires to the north-east could only be Aandalsnes, and the cruiser came to port anchor with five shackles in 26 fathoms. It was 2300, with snow falling.

Within forty-five minutes the destroyers were returning with troops evacuated from the burning Norwegian town. They were mostly Yorks & Lancs, but included a few stragglers of the Green Howards – all, says Charles Hall, 'In a sorry state, not having eaten or slept for five days, having been almost continuously bombed while trapped on the road around the fiord, with the fiord on one side of them and the blazing forest on the other.' The Yorks & Lancs, in fact, had held up the German advance at Kjorem, a hundred miles inland, and the Green Howards had done the same at Otta. The British small 2-pounder anti-tank guns had dealt reasonably well with the enemy's light armoured vehicles, but there was little answer to the German field artillery. The absence of air cover was fatal. 'Where's the bleedin' RAF, then?' the exhausted infantrymen snarled at the sailors as they climbed aboard and stumbled below. 'Thank Christ, we're safe now.' Recalling the soldiers' golden rule that anything remotely eatable should be consumed immediately, the ratings resigned themselves good-humouredly to mess-lockers being plundered of everything except pepper, salt, vinegar and yellow soap.

The destroyers were returning to report that Aandalsnes and its vicinity appeared to be cleared of troops, but they had taken aboard a number of Norwegian civilians, both men and women, and including small children – one an infant only hours old. All were transferred to *Sheffield* and taken aft. Larcomb, anxious to be quit of the fiord before dawn, ordered the destroyers to make a final sweep inshore before following the cruiser into the open sea.

'I felt extremely relieved', Hall went on, 'to be conning *Sheffield* down the fiord at 26 knots; a bombing attack could be expected at dawn, and there was little room for manoeuvre in those narrow waters. Then, just before we reached the first bend, which would take us beyond sight of Aandalsnes, *Winchester* signalled that *Windsor* was ashore.'

The situation was instantly critical. Even at this moment

Left: Norwegians of both sexes and all ages, including one infant only hours old, took the opportunity to share the British troops' evacuation. In *Sheffield*'s wardroom they discovered that hot Navy cocoa richly reinforced with Nestlés milk was something worth leaving home for.

Ju 87s could be warming up on some airstrip minutes away, waiting for the dawn's first flush to enable them to lift off the trampled snow, and *Sheffield* had hundreds of evacuated troops and civilians aboard, yet the thought of abandoning a grounded ship and its crew to be taken by the enemy was intolerable. In just a few seconds *Sheffield* would be beyond visual contact with both destroyers. Larcom glanced at the Admiral, Clarke shook his head, and on *Sheffield*'s flagdeck an Aldis lamp click-clacked in the direction of *Winchester*. 'Do your best for *Windsor* then follow me.'

Everyone was staring anxiously into the cold void astern, but suddenly the Yeoman shouted: 'From *Winchester*, sir – "*Windsor* off. All's well." '

Clear of the bend, they could see the flames of Molde to starboard and the silhouettes of *Galatea* and *Aurora*, apparently still embarking troops. The little town had been reduced to ashes and rubble; fires were burning at dozens of points across the black face of the mountainside beyond, curtained occasionally by drifting palls of smoke. Astern of *Sheffield* the sky was beginning to pale. In the wardroom ante-room the Norwegians were gratefully sipping hot, thick cocoa heavily laced with Nestlés milk, while the ratings' galley was doing a roaring trade in everything that could be quickly heated for the six hundred troops scattered among the forward messdecks – huge tubs of soup, tins of M&V (meat and vegetables, which the sailors referred to as 'Muzzle Velocity'), sausages, bacon and tinned tomatoes, baked beans, more soup as it reached the boil, tea and cocoa – and bread, which, when the supply of other comestibles flagged, the famished soldiers spread with margarine and sugar.

The ship reached the open sea, working up to full speed, just as dawn broke. Some distance astern *Galatea* was following, enveloped in the smoke of her 4-inch guns as she snarled furiously at the first of the day's Ju 88s, but there was nothing *Sheffield* could do for her. It was going to be a beautiful day of brilliant sunshine, and someone recalled, poetically, that this was the First of May when, in pleasant England, children brought fragrant lilac and hawthorn to school, and danced about a maypole.

At 30 knots the sea was creaming astern as the screws rowelled deep. There was no pursuit; the Luftwaffe had easier targets ashore than a gun-bristling cruiser. The soldiers had told of thousands still retreating on Molde, Aandalsnes and Namsos, and some, known to be cut off, were thought to making for neutral Sweden.

The Norwegian coastline had faded from sight when, at 1100, *Manchester* and *Birmingham* were sighted, bound for Aandalsnes. 'And the best of bleedin' British,' someone offered. Romsdal Fiord was not going to be a pleasant place in which to loiter on 1 May 1940. Below, the troops were sleeping exhaustedly in every awkward space that offered itself, and blankets and cigarettes had been distributed among the civilians, nutty for the children. Already the German radio news programme, read at dictation speed in English, was boasting of the British Army's shattering defeat in Norway. Britain, who had started the war, was now about to feel it on her own body. William Joyce asked, yet again, 'Where is the *Ark Royal*?' and went on to tell the British that their's was a 'retrogressive land of slums, unemployment and social inequality' which could never hope to prevail against Germany, the *Heldenvölk*, the nation of heroes. 'After you with the HP Sauce, mate,' said Bungy Williams.

Hoxa Boom was passed at 0600 on 2 May, with the ship anchoring a half hour later. Passengers began disembarking almost immediately, the soldiers transferring to the troopship *Lancastria*, ex-Cunard. *Sheffield*'s watchkeepers secured, but if, as anticipated, another rescue mission was to be undertaken, the day must be given to refuelling and storing; the concert party on Flotta could wait. The Naafi drifter was alongside and a fresh water lighter was waiting, while several days' back-log of defaulters and requestmen mustered outside the Regulating Office. A travel-stained coterie of newly joining ratings, after four days in the squalor of *Dunluce Castle*, piled kitbags and hammocks below the catapult, and a representative of Bernards, Naval Tailors, was aboard to measure men for new serge suits and lobby for allotments of one pound per month, which would maintain a rating sartorially elegant during his seafaring career, not to mention the provision of gifts by proxy for those wives and sweethearts who must never meet. Mailbags came up the midships ladder, and one of the ship's cats had delivered four kittens in the ERA's workshop. Leading hands of messes were ordered to collect their allocations of Martins' cigarettes donated by the Overseas League Tobacco Fund, and a few hours later the ship's hull was surrounded by floating thousands of Martins' cigarettes, jettisoned as unsmokable. Several old but as yet unseen films had been collected from the library ashore, and, in future, piped the quarterdeck, films would be screened in the starboard hangar when the ship was in harbour.

The BBC was still talking urbanely of 'movements according to plan' in Norway. The Allied Supreme War Council, it was claimed, was in possession of important facts regarding Germany's intentions. It could be said that the German invasion had not come as a surprise to British and French strategists, and Allied plans had been made accordingly.

The day passed, gratefully, with no orders to raise steam, and during the following afternoon it was learned that the evacuation of the Namsos and Aandalsnes area was now complete, although convoys were still supplying troops in northern Norway, where fighting would continue for another six weeks.

But long before the last Allied forces withdrew from Narvik, all attention would move from the Norwegian campaign to the shattering series of events further south – the German invasion of Belgium, Holland, Luxemburg and France, the evacuation of the BEF from the beaches of Dunkirk. Britain would have a new Prime Minister and a coalition government.

5

'Steam will be required at ten minutes' notice'

IT WAS a period of tension, of alarms and exhortations. Holland, Belgium and finally France capitulated, and the evacuation of the BEF, which began on 26 May, achieved the rescue of 340,000 Allied troops who, however, left behind 11,000 machine-guns, 1,200 artillery pieces, 1,250 AA and anti-tank guns, 6,500 anti-tank rifles and 75,000 vehicles. In Britain the newly formed Local Defence Volunteers were equipped with pikes and clubs, Martini-Henrys, shot-guns and petrol bombs. At sea it was a time for the little ships – the Navy's destroyers and sloops, the paddle-steamers, fishing boats and pleasure craft. The larger warships waited at a distance, patrolling or berthed in east coast harbours, ready to move against any German naval threat to the French Channel ports. The Kriegsmarine, however, at this time, could no longer be considered a major surface force. During the Norwegian campaign the Germans had lost three of their eight cruisers and ten of twenty destroyers, and could offer no effective challenge to the withdrawal of Anglo-French forces from the Continent. The giant *Bismarck* was three months from completion, and there were no other surface warships, alone or in concert, able to take the war to the British except as sneak-thief commerce raiders in distant waters. The Channel was safe.

This, however, was not apparent to the Admiralty in May and June of 1940, and certainly not to the men in the forward messdecks. They were still at sea, or if in harbour could expect, at best, only canteen leave, which meant a couple of hours in the Naafi in Scapa Flow, or in Rosyth's beer bar, but no leave beyond the dockyard gate. *Sheffield*'s midshipmen and boys were landed and taken for an exhausting run, and on Sunday the crew mustered for Divisions followed by a church service in the starboard hangar. In the afternoon the midshipmen were invited to a picnic ashore by the Commander, and when the Commander invited, midshipmen did not decline. They were already jaded, and, although it was May, there was a cutting wind across the Flow. The centre-plate of the 1st Motor Cutter refused to fall, but they made the Calf of Flotta. Ashore, it was muddy and cold; they were unable to sit anywhere. The primus stove refused to ignite and the portable wireless remained obstinately silent. Just as they decided to abandon the excursion, they heard the wail of an air raid siren.

Standing orders were explicit; they must remain where they were. They did, until the all-clear at 1700, by which time they were chilled to the bone and thoroughly miserable. Still with no centre-plate, they regained the anchored *Sheffield* at 1900, shivering and ravenously hungry. 'It was', they wrote home, 'a most enjoyable afternoon.'

The ship's company might have been amused had they known that *Sheffield* had been awarded a period of rest. True, Tuesday 7 May was logged 'a normal day', but on Thursday the ship was at sea in the Pentland Firth with sister *Manchester* and the battle-cruiser *Repulse* to carry out full-calibre battle practice firing during the forenoon and AA practice against drogue targets in the afternoon. The concussion from 120 rounds fired from the heavy guns shook out the five years of dust that had accumulated in the ventilation system, smothering mess-tables, wardroom linen and cabin furnishings, shattered a few light bulbs and spilled fifteen hundred fried sausages onto the deck of the ratings' galley.

Returned to Scapa Flow, a weary crew secured, but at midnight *Sheffield* and *Manchester* were ordered to sea to make contact with and escort to safety the destroyer *Kelly* from the mouth of the Skaggerak, where she had been hit and crippled by a torpedo during an encounter with German light craft. Fortunately *Bulldog*, a destroyer of another flotilla, had taken in tow the heavily listing *Kelly*, whose commanding officer, Lord Louis Mountbatten, has told his own story.

'Late the first night a German E-boat hit *Bulldog* a glancing blow, bounced off her and came right inboard onto *Kelly*, firing her 20mm gun. Then she sheared off our davits and guardrails as she passed down our side and vanished into the night. Then came the Luftwaffe. The first attack was driven off, but we knew they would be back – and they were.'

Bulldog and the wallowing *Kelly* were being screened by the destroyers *Fury*, *Khandahar* and *St Laurent*, and the two cruisers sighted the group at 1330 on Friday 10 May. Within minutes *Sheffield*'s 4-inch guns were pounding, driving off a Heinkel He III, which dropped a stick of three bombs wide to port.

'By now', Mountbatten said, 'quite a few ships were clustered around us, and the Admiralty signalled me, saying that with Hitler invading the Low Countries this was a waste of force; it was suggested that we should scuttle *Kelly*.

To this I replied: "I absolutely refuse to scuttle. We do not want any help. We have enough ammunition to defend ourselves. Please send tug to complete the tow." '

Two Dornier seaplanes were now shadowing, and at about 1700 three RAF Hudsons reappeared (having been sighted earlier but, for some unknown reason, having immediately disappeared.) These three circled protectively and, later, were reinforced by three more. At dusk, however, all six turned away westward for base and supper. *Kelly* was being towed at about three knots, with a list of ten to fifteen degrees to starboard, her bows well down; it was going to be a long and cold night's crossing of the North Sea, with the Germans determined to destroy this extrovert great-grandson of Queen Victoria. As the chill darkness approached, a single Hudson, flying low without lights and disdaining to offer a recognition signal, came directly towards *Sheffield*. The sailors below had long become disenchanted with the quality of co-operation conceded by the RAF, and eight 2-pounder pom-poms opened fire.

The aircrew's surprise could only be imagined. The Hudson's engines roared as the pilot hauled it up. Recognition lights flashed frantically and the aircraft clawed for height, distance and the safety of the night. 'And next time, matey', the sailors warned darkly, 'we won't bleedin' aim off.'

Sheffield and *Manchester* steamed ahead of the plodding destroyers, waiting for dawn. At 0340, as the sky paled, RDF reported aircraft approaching from westward, presumably friendly and which, indeed, materialized into three of the paunchy, American-built Hudsons, this time meticulously flashing the day's recognition signals before approaching to within gunnery-range. It was a nasty morning with the sea leaden and sullen, the sky under-quilted with low, heavy cloud that favoured the predatory bomber. The Paymaster and the Chief Cook agreed that, if it was going to be one of those days when the entire ship's company was at action stations, then it was a day for thick pea soup and corned beef. The Canteen Committee had already voiced an objection with regard to the frequency of tinned herrings-in-tomato sauce, baked beans, kidneys-on-toast, and reconstituted egg which, after cooking, reheating, warming-up and finally reheating, reached the mess-table fit only for the bucket. Pea soup ('pea-doo') required only periodical reinforcements of water and an enthusiastic stirring, and corned beef demanded nothing except resignation.

Kelly's plight was so serious that, at one stage, Mountbatten and his crew prepared to abandon ship and transfer to the escort. Four Heinkels attacked *Sheffield* and *Manchester* at 1430 and, helped by heavy cloud, flung down four sticks of bombs. AA fire, however, had kept the Germans above 7,000 feet, and all bombs fell wide, leaving only great puddles of white froth in the sea.

Four days' steaming, although slow, had brought the mangled *Kelly* to within two or three hours of the Northumbrian coast, and tugs from the Tyne were closing. At 1830 *Sheffield* and *Manchester*, ordered to Rosyth, left Mountbatten to bring his brave ship into Hebburn.

The country was in the grip of invasion fever. Leave was cancelled; all warships not already at sea were at two hours' notice for steam, and no ratings were permitted to leave the dockyard. *Sheffield*'s crew began immediately to change her colour from overall medium grey – Admiralty 507B – to Admiralty Disruptible Camouflage, which meant a jig-saw of differing greys and blue-greys, with the deck areas painted brown. An elderly Chief who had served at Jutland recalled that, in his day, it was described as dazzle paint, but to everyone else it was simply a pig's breakfast. It was confirmed that two ratings, natives of the Irish Republic, who had enlisted at the beginning of the war, had deserted and could not be recovered. It was a story that would be told many times during the war years. Men from the Irish south enlisted in the British armed forces, usually in Ulster, where there was no conscription, and were permitted to spent leave periods, in civilian clothes, in their native republic, but when (in the case of the Army and RAF) overseas service threatened, or (in the Navy) they realized that the war at sea was real, and not compensated by a few hours of braggadocio in Murphy's Bar, many deserted at the first favourable opportunity and thumbed their noses from Dublin. There remained a handful of commendable exceptions to that trend, in all three services, who fought and died to help defy the advancing tide of Naziism and bestiality across the face of Europe, always embarrasingly unable to explain their own government's decision to refrain from the conflict, yet maintain amicable relationships with the Axis powers and harbour an army of German espionage agents who could cross and recross the UK border at will.

With warpaint completed, *Sheffield* moved into the Firth for degaussing trials. A report during the Middle watch that *Scharnhorst* had left harbour was cancelled as incorrect only after it had sent *Renown* hammering to sea and *Sheffield*, *Southampton* and *Manchester* raising steam.

General Drill was ordered, covering several days. Fifty of the younger ratings, with junior officers in charge, prepared to tow aft. Others fought an exercise fire on the starboard side of the hangar deck, rigged a machine-gun nest to cover a landing party on an imaginary jetty, rigged sheer-legs and ran out a sounding boom. On 22 May all hands went to quarters to exercise damage control while supposedly engaging an enemy cruiser and simultaneously fighting off aircraft, thus suffering damage by both shells and bombs. On the 24th, with an enemy invasion expected almost hourly, the ship's company was organized in preparation for dealing with paratroops who might land near the ship. Rifles were brought from below and loaded.

The BBC announced to the weary sailors that oranges would now be sold by weight at 6d per pound, and although retailers might still sell the fruit singly, 'the maximum price by weight must not be exceeded, and the buyer may ask for the oranges to be weighed in compliance'. This was war indeed. Motorists were warned that they *must* return any unused petrol coupons when a new ration period began. They must not be deposited with garages against future purchases.

Oh, yes – In France, British and French troops were withdrawing to prepared positions, according to plan, inflicting heavy casualties on the enemy. Allied losses were light.

With the evacuation of Dunkirk in progress, Calais fell to the Germans on 27 May – and Calais was only 22 miles from Dover. 'It is realized', the *Daily Mail* declared desperately, 'that the great battles of Flanders have taken the sting out of the German attack, and that Hitler enters on the second stage of the war considerably weaker on land and in the air.' In Rosyth, *Sheffield* slipped from the North Wall, passed under the Forth Bridge, and joined *Manchester* and *Birmingham*, to pass Spurn Head at 1630. Forty-five minutes later the squadron anchored off Immingham.

Being anchored in the constant swell of an estuary, so near and yet so far from the delights of shore, and with leave restricted to tedious boat journeys for an hour or two in a beer canteen – it could strain the patience of a saint, and there were few saints aboard the three cruisers. It was painful to think of all those nubile 'parties' just over there in Grimsby and Cleethorpes who were just waiting for an

Below: 1940. The same as before but worse. The enemy now holds all of Europe's coastline from North Cape to Spain. On *Sheffield*'s bridge the fatigued watch stare at a grey sea and sky – Captain Larcom (centre); Chief Yeoman Fuller; the Commander. Hour after hour, rain, sleet, a wind that penetrates icily, stings the lungs and blisters lips. Tomorrow will be the same, and the next day, and the next . . .

excuse to lose their virginity, not to mention the booze and the fish-and-chips. There were frequent air raid warnings but no air raids, and all three ships were at short notice for steam. All of the few films held on board had been screened several times; nobody could stomach another showing of *Sanders of the River*. A sailor considered that his ship should be tied alongside or out at sea, not hooked to the bottom, a mile offshore while a sea-born tide pushed and nudged, day after night after day – especially when so much was happening in the Channel, and still off Narvik. On 30 May Captain Larcom found it necessary to address a frustrated ship's company, to explain that *Sheffield* and her two sisters were resources held in reserve, to be launched only if invasion became fact. On the following day it was learned that arrangements had been finalized to blow up the dock entrances of Immingham and Grimsby. That, Bungy Williams pronounced, was the last bleedin' straw.

To keep the ship-confined men occupied and their minds off the deprived maidens of Grimsby, Larcom ordered a programme of quizzes and competitions in which both officers and men were to take part. An obstacle-course included a horizontal greasy spar, scrambling nets, suspended lifebelts, a canvas tunnel with unspeakably revolting hazards, a canvas swimming-pool with submerged trip-wires, and then, at the final stage when competitors were staggering with exhaustion, the 6-inch dummy loader.

Sheffield's guns were basically hand-loaded; shells weighing 100lb were rammed manually into the breech followed by a brass charge. Some of the times achieved by turret crews and individual gun crews in putting ten rounds through the loader were almost incredible. 'The best I can remember', says Lieutenant-Commander Hubert Tresder, 'was something like 55.2 seconds. A lot of money changed hands on the results, and a crack seaman crew taking on the best the Royal Marines could offer was something worth watching. The officers were never in the same class, but it was good for slimming.'

On 8 June the aircraft carrier *Glorious* and the destroyers *Ardent* and *Acastra* were sunk by the battlecruisers *Scharnhorst* and *Gneisnau*. It was unfortunate that *Glorious* had no air patrols flying. Her flight-deck was crowded by ten RAF Gladiators and ten Hurricanes, evacuated from Norway; her own Skuas could not be ranged for take-off. The destroyers, after laying a smoke-screen, made a gallant assault on their massive enemy, and, before being overwhelmed by 11-inch shells, *Acastra* fired her torpedoes, of which one struck *Scharnhorst* aft. The German forces turned back to Trondheim. *Acastra*'s action had saved a lightly escorted convoy with 14,000 troops, a hundred miles northward and in the Germans' path, but 1,200 sailors were left in the sea, of whom only 44 would subsequently be found and rescued. Only the cruiser *Devonshire* heard a garbled wireless report from *Glorious*, and she had to remain silent because she was carrying the King of Norway

to England, and was only four hours' steaming from the German battle group.

And so, at 2100 on Sunday 9 June, the cruiser squadron idling in the Humber received the Admiralty's order to raise steam for sea. Special sea duty men closed up, all ships shortened to three cables. Nobody yet knew why. There was a flurry of last-minute letter writing, although no further mail would go ashore. At 2200 the order to slip and proceed was cancelled, but the ships must be ready to comply at 0430, a diabolical hour that only the old men in Whitehall armchairs could devise. Still, it was June and becoming milder every day. Steam was at ten minutes' notice.

The sky was only just beginning to pale, with the shore in slumbering darkness, as *Sheffield* weighed to join *Manchester* and *Birmingham* in mid-stream. Heavy mist floated on the surface of the Humber as *Manchester*, flying the flag of CS18, Vice-Admiral Sir Geoffrey Layton, led her sisters past Spurn Head and into the North Sea, working up to 22 knots. Rumour – the inexplicable *buzz* – had it that the squadron had been ordered to intercept *Scharnhorst*, *Gneisnau* and *Hipper* off the coast of Norway. If that were true, it could prove to be a somewhat unequal contest. The German battlecruisers, each mounting nine 11-inch and twelve 5.9-inch guns, also had the speed to maintain the three 'Towns' at a distance while pulverizing them at leisure. The British might get off two maximum-range salvoes (the Marines said three) before Nemesis came screaming, to tear through armour and explode with shattering concussion in the confined spaces beyond, wreck gun positions, machinery and circuitry, scythe down men and turn below-deck areas into reeking death-traps.

At 1700 the squadron anchored off Rosyth. It was very anti-climactic. *York* joined them. The following day, although steam was still maintained for 2½ hours, canteen leave to part of watch was granted from 1800 to 2130. Parties of dockyard workers climbed aboard and, as sluggish as only dockyard workers can be, eventually got down to blanking off all lower-deck scuttles, vulnerable to shrapnel and blast from near misses.

Italy declared war 'against the plutocratic and reactionary democracies who have always blocked the march and frequently plotted against the existence of the Italian people . . .'

Mussolini's price for remaining neutral was already known. From Britain he demanded Malta and Cyprus, and from France he wanted Nice, Savoy, Corsica and Tunis. Gibraltar was to be internationalized, and Egypt, Syria and Iraq would become Italian protectorates. Unknown to the British people, there was a chilling period, albeit brief, when these terms hung in the air, neither accepted nor rejected, but since mid-May there had been a new master in Downing Street.

The Italian Army advanced only a few hundred yards into Menton before fighting ended, but Mussolini's war had only just begun.

6

'Get yer knees brown!'

THE Phoney War was over, although the adjective was to be exercised by a Fleet Street that apparently shrugged aside the months of gales and sleet in the North Atlantic; there had been nothing phoney about that, nor about the Battle of the River Plate, or the heroism of ships like *Jervis Bay, Rawalpindi, Glowworm, Ardent* and *Acastra*. For the Royal Navy it was still the mixture as before, only stronger, because the fall of France meant a European coast occupied by the enemy from Norway's North Cape to southern Biscay. In mid-June *Sheffield*, with others, was despatched in abortive pursuit of *Scharnhorst*, and was air-attacked several times without suffering damage, but also enjoyed a four-days boiler clean in Rosyth which allowed each watch an all-night leave. A few lucky Scots dashed for their homes, but most settled for Edinburgh, McEwen's and Younger's. It was during this post-Dunkirk period, too, that the popular Commander G. V. Dolphin, First Lieutenant since *Sheffield*'s commissioning, left the ship, and the log records, with mild surprise: *Spontaneous clearing of the lower deck for cheering Cdr. Dolphin.* He was, L/SA Clay confirms, 'a most popular officer both forward and aft. It's a common thing to cheer a Captain over the side, but this was the only occasion during the whole of my service (and that was 27 years including Boys' time) that I have known of a First Lieutenant receiving the same treatment. And it was not arranged; it was an absolutely spontaneous gesture by the ship's company!'

As Bungy Williams had so succinctly observed, 'There's some that's soddin' pigs, and there's some that's gentlemen . . .'

An enemy invasion attempt was regarded as highly probable; the American Ambassador, Joseph Kennedy, told President Roosevelt that Britain would not survive beyond the end of that month. Britain, however, did, and on 3 July a Royal Naval battle squadron under Vice-Admiral Sir James Somerville shelled a French fleet anchored off Mers-el-Kebir – an action that sent shock waves throughout the service. *Sheffield* patrolled between Rosyth and Sheerness, and then up to Scapa Flow, and was exercising the new 'slick' method of recovering her aircraft while steaming at

12 knots. In company with the battle-cruisers *Repulse* and *Renown*, the cruisers *Devonshire, York, Australia* and ten destroyers, *Sheffield* participated in yet another abortive sweep off the south-west Norwegian coast in pursuit of *Gneisenau*. During the evening of 28 July, returning westward, it was a subdued ship's company that listened to Captain Larcom's voice over the address system. Tomorrow, he told them, *Sheffield* was proceeding to the Clyde for a ten days' service of minor defects. There was something in Larcom's tone that dampened any desire to cheer. Afterwards, he went on, the ship was ordered to a foreign station, the identity of which he was not in a position to yet divulge. There would be nine days' leave from Greenock; with the ship under sailing orders he expected every man to return on time. Make the most of this leave, he advised. It might be a long time before they enjoyed the next. That was all.

They slung their hammocks thoughtfully, with hardly one among them not experiencing that slow convulsion in the pit of the stomach that men have known for a thousand years in anticipation of the unknown or dangerous. When they reached their homes, and their mothers and wives, kids, their sweethearts, they would pose as the laughing, carefree sailor with jingling pockets, stories to tell and an amusing repertoire of seafaring terminology. It was expected of them, but the leaden lump in the gut would always be there. The older men had known it before, but before had been in peacetime when faced with a long and barren foreign commission of years, during which men and wives became distant strangers, photographs of someone once known and loved, but shy aliens when they met again.

Anchoring off Greenock, they could see in the fairway the corpse of the French submarine, *Maillé-Brézé*, which had sunk on 30 April after one of her own torpedoes had exploded in its tube. On the following day *Sheffield* was dry-docked in Fairfield's yard, Govan, and, released, the ship's company raced for their trains for a bitter-sweet nine days. Dockyard men filed aboard.

The welded 'A' bracket, legacy of the ship's 1937 acceptance trials, was found to be sound, but an attempt to repair the leak in Y2 fuel tank would later show to be unsuccessful; the oil from that source would always be contaminated by sea water. Other matters were minor, and all were finished, except for engine-testing and repainting, when the crew rejoined on 9 August to messdecks and flats littered with dockyarders' refuse and reeking acridly of acetylene. The few smiles among them were forced.

By mid-August *Sheffield* was in Scapa Flow with painting cradles hoisted outboard. Now, the three-badgemen declared, the ship's overseas destination would be revealed, and, when white paint came up from the paint store, they nodded knowingly. Hong Kong. When the ship's sides had been painted white, they said, the funnels would be painted buff. Well, there was no war in the Far East, and the China Fleet Club was the finest ratings' hostelry and restaurant east or west of Suez. Chicken soup and *lobster*, mate, and waiters in penguin rig – not to mention those slant-eyed little darlings in Happy Valley with slit-up skirts.

Sheffield's hull was painted 507A Dark Grey, her upperworks MS4 Light Grey, and the messdeck pundits decided it was all a ruse to baffle the enemy.

Final preparations for departure were delayed by southwesterly gales, but during the rain-swept afternoon of 22 August *Sheffield* weighed, and in company with the carrier *Illustrious*, the cruiser *York* and four destroyers, steamed westward at 16 knots. The force, Larcom was now able to divulge, was first to rendezvous with a convoy out of Liverpool and then proceed to Gibraltar for onward routeing. That told the ship's company very little, since Gibraltar could conceivably be the first stage of almost every passage other than to the North Atlantic, and that

was hardly reckoned a foreign station. There was a firm messdeck conviction that *Sheffield* was bound for the tropics, and a few older hands dug deep into lockers for their white caps. One three-badgeman produced a topee which, he said, he had worn in the old *Ladybird* up the Yangtze.

Turning southward, the weather continued bad, but the convoy was sighted on 23 August, 120 miles west of the Hebrides. Transporting troops and military stores, the ships were *Duchess of Bedford*, *Sydney Star*, *Denbighshire*, *Wairotora* and *Royal Scotsman*, while the old carrier *Argus* was loaded with fighter aircraft for the RAF. All were escorted by the old battleship *Valiant*, the cruisers *Ajax*, *Coventry* and *Calcutta*, and several destroyers. With such a massive escort of warships, and *Illustrious* flying off patrols of Swordfish and Fulmars, the six transports must have been regarded as extremely valuable. It *has* to be Somaliland, invaded by the Italians, pronounced the messdeck strategists; there was nothing else happening in this direction to justify such a powerful armada. And there wasn't much of a run ashore in Somaliland except sand, goats and scraggy black parties with rings in their noses, who stank. Shave off!

It had not occurred to anyone that the transports' destination might have nothing to do with *Sheffield*'s. Achieving longitude 20 degrees West on the afternoon of 24 August, three destroyers were detached and ordered back to Scapa Flow, while the main body of the convoy, escorted by *Ajax*, *York* and three destroyers, turned away for the long Cape voyage, leaving only *Royal Scotsman* in company

Right: 'Terror of Trondheim' was being flown every day to perfect the new method of taking up an aircraft at 12 knots. Two of the aircrew, Lieutenant Charles Fenwick (centre) and Lieutenant (E) Hawkes (right) simulate unconcern as their obsolescent little biplane is prepared for launching.

fin

with *Valiant, Illustrious, Sheffield, Coventry, Calcutta* and a destroyer screen on course for Gibraltar. The transports faded into the south-westerly sun haze.

The ship, Captain Larcom told his crew at last, had been assigned to Force H, the other components of which were the battle-cruiser *Renown*, flying the flag of Vice-Admiral Sir James Somerville, the carrier *Ark Royal*, and the 8th Destroyer Flotilla, based on Gibraltar. Italy's entry into the war on the side of Germany had compelled the Mediterranean Fleet under Admiral Cunningham to move its base from Malta to Alexandria in Egypt, and so it was no longer in a position to cut the enemy supply routes to North Africa. In effect, the Italians now controlled the central Mediterranean while the British held both ends, but, between them, Cunningham and Somerville intended to change that arrangement, and *Sheffield*'s company were unaware that their ship was about to begin the most celebrated chapter of her war service.

She had been attached to Force H not because of any earlier outstanding performance – several cruisers had done more – but because of her RDF facility, still a closely guarded secret. Since the Norwegian operation the equipment had been manned by four RNVR ratings – Eves, Piggott, Ravenscroft and MacIver – under the jurisdiction of the Chief Telegraphist, but now RDF was considered sufficiently important to be assigned an officer. The first was a 23-year-old Canadian, Al Hurley.

'On May 1st, 1940,' says Hurley, 'I was still at university in London, Ontario, and I joined *Sheffield* on 9th July,

Above: Suddenly, the scene on the bridge has changed. The sunshine is dazzling, the sea and sky are blue, and white drill is the order of the day. In August 1940 *Sheffield* joined *Renown* and *Ark Royal*, Vice-Admiral Somerville's Force H in the Mediterranean, and the most distinguished period of her life had begun.

announcing myself as the ship's RDF officer. I was not too well informed on RN tradition; my new Gieves uniform with its single stripe didn't mean a thing. I was promptly told, "Yes, we do have an RDF set, but we never use it." '

Al Hurley, however, adapted quickly, with a little tolerant help from his British superiors. 'My action station was at a plotting board in the Plot, just aft of the Captain's sea cabin. Here I recorded the aircraft positions relayed by the operator and advised on course, altitude, speed, etc., of the approaching planes. I had not got my sea legs, and the Captain, who was a chain smoker, always filled the Plot with dense smoke. On one occasion he was watching the progress of the plot over my shoulder. Suddenly feeling very unwell, I pushed my pencil into his hand and ran for the bathroom, a deck below. On returning, I found Captain Larcom calmly continuing with the plot – probably the only RN four-ring Captain ever to sub for a wavy-navy one striper! He was a great guy who commanded everyone's respect.'

The original four RDF operators had also been reinforced before leaving the UK by Ordinary Seamen Allen, Brassington, Wood, Eyre and McDowell, all 'Hostilities Only' ratings. They were the first formally trained RDF operators to ship out on active service.

'But we were not popular,' says Allen. 'We were seamen but did not work part of ship. We messed with the Communications Branch and wore Telegraphists' badges, but we didn't know a dot from a dash. The seamen regarded us as loafers and the Sparkers considered us imposters. We saw ourselves as outcasts.

Secrecy was so rigidly maintained that only a handful of the ship's officers had any real idea of RDF potential. Our unpopularity was relieved only when the sailors tried to pump us for information on those continually rotating aerials. We were able to respond, with an air of superiority, that we were not permitted to divulge such information.'

A dawn rendezvous 250 miles west of Cape St. Vincent, was achieved with Force H – *Renown, Ark Royal*, a screen of destroyers and the old light cruiser *Enterprise*. The latter was almost immediately ordered to escort *Royal Scotsman* to Gibraltar, but the remaining, combined squadrons, now consisting of one old battleship, one battle-cruiser, two modern aircraft carriers, three cruisers and seventeen destroyers, assumed formation for battle practice. Orders by hand from the Admiral, Somerville, in *Renown*, informed Larcom that Force H, and that included *Sheffield*, was shortly to undertake Operation 'Hats' – but more of that to follow. First, the Swordfish of *Ark Royal* and *Illustrious* were to carry out dummy bombing and torpedo attacks against the Fleet while the Fulmars attempted to intercept. Only three days earlier four airmen had been killed when two Fulmars from *Illustrious* had collided in mid-air, with only two bodies being recovered for burial, but today's exercises were thankfully free of accident. The Swordfish biplanes with their open cockpits and slung torpedoes came low over the sea, so slowly – 90 knots – that opposing fighter pilots and gun crews were tempted to miscalculate. It was said in jest that the 'Stringbags' could not be hit by shells aimed ahead, only by those aimed astern. The Swordfish's 1914–18 Lewis gun was irrelevant, and the crew depended totally on the pilot's ability to throw his obsolete aircraft around the sky in avoidance of attacking fighters. Ironically, the Swordfish was to be the only British aircraft which was already flying operationally when the war began and to be still combat flying at the war's end.

Somerville's fleet steamed into Gibraltar harbour during the forenoon of Thursday 29 August 1940, with *Sheffield* mooring alongside the Coaling Wharf, No. 38 Berth. The Gibraltarians had experienced an ineffective air attack by Vichy French bombers, and had little regard for the Italians, but the intentions of the Madrid government, which had already expressed its willingness to join the Axis in exchange for Gibraltar, French Morocco and Oran, were more worrying. The arrival of Somerville's big guns was comforting.

The blue Mediterranean was scattered with thousands of dazzling, golden coins, and the sun was hot. Dress of the day had been suddenly changed from blue serge to tropical white shorts and shirts. With all ships in harbour at two hours' notice for steam, leave was nevertheless given to

1900, and *Sheffield*'s pale-skinned libertymen, fresh from Scapa Flow, ran the gauntlet of good-humoured shouts of 'Get yer knees brown!' from those who had already acquired that hall-mark of Mediterranean service. To the bar-owners and restaurant proprietors of Main Street, currency was good whatever the colour of the knees.

As any officer of the watch will confirm, the achievements possible to a sailor during a few hours of liberty are beyond calculation. He can get drunk, tear his collar, lose his paybook and his cap-ribbon, be involved in a fight, lose all his money in a brothel, get arrested, fall into the dock, and finally reel up the gangplank clutching a monkey or a parrot and loudly claiming he has just enjoyed a bleedin' marvellous run ashore. *Sheffield* had her full quota of irresponsible and hard-drinking ratings, but three hours was just too brief a period of freedom for men to get more than a little tipsy, or to bring aboard anything more exotic than Spanish oranges and Canary bananas.

At 0800, with all ships refuelled, Force H steamed slowly out of Gibraltar harbour, turned eastward into the Mediterranean and increased speed.

In the eastern Mediterranean, Cunningham's Fleet consisted of four battleships (*Warspite, Malaya, Ramillies* and *Royal Sovereign*) three cruisers (*Gloucester, Liverpool* and *Sydney*) the old carrier *Eagle*, the netlayer *Protector*, sixteen destroyers and three sloops. The main object of Operation 'Hats' – the first of many similar undertakings by Force H – was to provide cover for reinforcements for Cunningham consisting of *Illustrious, Valiant, Coventry, Calcutta* and eight destroyers (this group being Force F) which, on passage, would have to pass very close to an Italian-held coastline, either Sicily, Pantelleria or Libya. The old carrier *Argus* was also carrying two flights of Hurricane fighters for Malta – the half-way stage at which Force F would be met by the Mediterranean Fleet, steaming from Alexandria. It was a hazardous venture because, if the Italians had the resolution, their fleet had the weight seriously to disable the British in the Mediterranean. On the other hand, if Force F forced a passage, Cunningham's resources would be richly reinforced, and he would be able to send home the slow and geriatric *Royal Sovereign*, which had been a millstone for months.

As a secondary but important diversion, Somerville's fast squadron (*Renown, Ark Royal, Sheffield* and seven destroyers) was to carry out two air attacks – Operations 'Smash' and 'Grab') on the port of Cagliari, the capital of Sardinia, while detached destroyers, off the Balearics (Operation 'Squawk') transmitted wireless signals calculated to persuade the Italians that the British were five hundred miles from where they really were.

Very little of this complex plan was known aboard *Sheffield*, in either wardroom or messdeck. The weather was superb, the sea an impossible blue scattered with gold and crested with dazzling white. The destroyers danced like excited puppy dogs, plunging, climbing, exploding spray, and within their protecting screen the floating grey citadels of *Renown* and *Ark Royal* rolled majestically, exactly as Gaumont-British News had screened to enthralled, spearmint-chewing audiences in Golders Green. *Sheffield*'s sailors stripped to the waist and were sorely punished; the Mediterranean sun was not, as one Ordinary Seaman insisted, only about the same as the sun at Bognor Regis.

'As the only RDF ship in the squadron,' Al Hurley recalls, 'it was our job to pass data on enemy aircraft to *Ark Royal* – and by flags, incidentally, which might seem a bit primitive in retrospect. On our first operation we picked up enemy echoes and passed the information to the carrier, reporting "more than 9 aircraft at 90 miles", adding that it looked like a large group. There was no response from *Ark Royal*; she had three Skuas up and did not fly off any more. I guess this was her first experience of radar, and there was still a credibility gap.

Well, the Italian bombers were there all right – all twenty-seven of them, and they came for the biggest target, *Ark Royal*. The carrier was unscathed, largely because the Italians flew too high to bomb with any accuracy, but when we warned of the next attack she was much more aggressive, putting up more Skuas and pushing us for continuous reports. RDF had sold itself, and at the end of that operation we were visited by a party of *Ark Royal* officers seeking instruction on our equipment's capabilities with regard to fighter direction.'

After twelve months of war, the performance of *Ark Royal*'s aircraft had been less than distinguished, and her aircrews were anxious to enhance their image before the limelight was stolen by *Illustrious* and others of her class, soon to be operational. It was hardly dawn on Sunday 1 September, chill, with accompanying ships distant, black shapes that ploughed through a sea still streaked with emerald phosphorescence when the Swordfish lifted off from *Ark Royal*. Armed with six 250lb bombs and full long-range petrol tanks, they clawed for height at maximum throttle and with exhausts flaming. An Aldis lamp blinked. In succession the gawky biplanes climbed to 10,000 feet, assumed formation, and then vanished into the darkness of the north-east and Cagliari, port and capital of Sardinia. *Ark Royal*, having steamed twelve miles into the wind, resumed station with her attendant destroyer.

Sheffield, equipped with both Asdic and RDF, was inevitably positioned with the screen, but her normal speed in that role was too slow for her easily to manoeuvre in the event of an enemy torpedo attack. 'I think we needed more than 20 knots to swing quickly,' says Hurley. 'Larcom kept one eye on the RDF plot, dropping astern of station if enemy aircraft were reported, so that if an attack developed he could push *Sheffield* back into position but now at a speed that would enable her to move about more easily.'

Ark Royal's strike force returned at 0700 and were counted aboard; there were no losses. At debriefing the aircrew were to report that Operation 'Smash' had been only a qualified success. All bombs had been dropped on the target area but visibility had been too poor for results to be observed. Somerville turned the Fleet westward for three hours in anticipation of retaliatory action by the Italians. Action AA armament remained closed up and the Skuas were ranged on deck for immediate take-off, but the blue sky remained empty, the RDF screens blank. Mussolini's vaunted Regia Aeronautica was not accepting the challenge, so Somerville wheeled his force north-eastward, and at 2200 ordered *Illustrious*, *Valiant*, *Coventry*, *Calcutta*, *Argus* and their destroyers to proceed towards Malta and a rendezvous with the Mediterranean Fleet. Force H set course westward, for Gibraltar.

There was still, however, Operation 'Grab'. At 0400, in semi-darkness on 2 September, the Swordfish strike force flew off *Ark Royal* to hit Cagliari for the second time and hopefully tempt the Italian Air Force to come within range of the twenty-four Skuas remaining with Force H. Three hours later all Swordfish returned and touched down safely, their crews disappointed that, again, heavy cloud had prevented any accurate assessment of the operation and, as before, the Italians could not be tempted into giving chase. In the event, Somerville had good reason to be satisfied. The Mediterranean Fleet had been usefully reinforced without interference, his carrier-based aircraft had twice attacked an Italian port, and Mussolini's bombast had suddenly become comic opera. 'Oh, *what* a surprise for the Duce,' carolled the 4-inch gun crews who sheltered on the after galley flat, 'He's had no spaghetti for weeks!' It wasn't John Wayne stuff, but it wasn't bad, either.

Sheffield secured alongside Gibraltar's Coaling Wharf at 1000 on Tuesday 3 September. Leave was piped from 1330 to 2245, dress for libertymen Number Six white drills, twenty cigarettes or one ounce of tobacco, the Rock and Bristol Hotels being out of bounds to ratings. Condoms were available from the Sick Bay, one per rating. Caps must be worn at all times. The squadron was at two hours' notice for steam. Libertymen must not return aboard with animals. Snakes were animals . . .

Rome Radio was stridently claiming that the British Mediterranean Fleet, foolishly challenging the Italian Navy, had lost an aircraft carrier, a battleship and a cruiser, and had run for Gibraltar with tail between legs. 'Of course,' Bungy Williams declared in the Casablanca Bar as a middle-aged señorita breathed in his ear, 'yer don't know 'arf of what goes on.'

The old battleship *Barham* steamed slowly into harbour that day with mail from the UK. *Barham* had fought at Jutland in 1916, suffering 26 killed and 37 wounded, and had been torpedoed in 1939, so even *Renown* had respectfully to concede seniority. The great grey lady lay at her moorings in complacent dignity. 'Start something, Franco,' the Gibraltarians taunted. 'Come on, start something!' They painted their doors and window-frames red, white and blue.

7

'Blackshirt, Blackshirt, have you lost your balls?'

IN BRITAIN it was learned for certain that the Germans were massing an invasion fleet; the ground was being prepared by relentless Luftwaffe attacks intended to smash all RAF opposition over the southern half of England. The London skies were reddened by the fires of the Blitzkrieg, and the city was rocked by explosions as its people crouched in shelters. From hill and headland armed men waited, peering into the night. The enemy, which had with such contemptuous ease outfought the armies of Europe, could come at any time.

In Gibraltar, most of *Sheffield*'s company were asleep in bunk or hammock when, shortly after midnight on 5 September, the ship was ordered to raise steam and secure for sea. At 0300 *Sheffield* was under way, ordered to the Clyde at her best possible speed.

It was unbelievable. When the Forenoon watch, swollen-eyed, climbed on deck the cruiser was hammering north-westward at 28 knots, a speed that would be maintained for the next three days, blistering the paint on the funnels and tearing the ensign to rags. Captain Larcom warned his crew. They must not assume that their orders held any promise of leave in the UK. They might not put foot ashore. It was cruel planning that brought a ship home from the Mediterranean for its crew to gaze only at the shore before being ordered away again – but the country was under imminent threat of invasion. The warships of the Home Fleet were strategically positioned and ready, and it would be wrong to disrupt that deployment, weakening the battle plan, in order that a slow-plodding convoy could be escorted several thousand miles from the crucial theatre.

The men knew the Captain was right, but it didn't make the choke in the throat any easier. *Sheffield*, Larcomb told them, was to be sheepdog to a convoy from the Clyde to Freetown in the first instance, possibly further. After that, the ship would rejoin Force H.

Sheffield anchored off Greenock during the early morning of Sunday 8 September, then, on the following day, moved downstream to lie off Gourock, just inside the Dunoon boom. The river was crowded with ships and the late summer weather was superb. Just over there, a stoker pointed, there were milling thousands of Glasgow lassies on holiday, all looking for a chance to be ravished before they returned to their shop counters and factory benches for another year. In Lamlash, where there were only long walks and a bracing wind, a sailor had to fight off predatory females. 'I've known matelots that's been stripped,' he claimed, but perhaps that was going a bit far.

The merchant ships lay at the entrance of Lough Foyle – *Dunbar Castle, Athlone Castle, Britannic, Brisbane Star, Imperial Star, Dominion Monarch, Clan McArthur, Clan Campbell* and *Glaucus* – a trickle of smoke rising from every funnel. Aboard *Sheffield* spirits rose slightly. No plodding eight-knot convoy, this. Someone intelligent in the Admiralty had assembled nine ships all capable of twenty knots, and the eight *V&W* escort destroyers were good for twenty-five. With luck, and in the absence of any bloody-mindedness among the mercantile skippers, the convoy could be jockeyed into three columns within two or three hours and be pushing westward before noon.

It was better. With Malin Head to port, *Sheffield* hoisted 'K12' to order a convoy speed of 12 knots, and fifty miles further on, as Bloody Foreland faded astern, increased to 15. W/T silence had been imposed, with the warships reading only the Admiralty's continuous broadcast HD, Fleet Wave, and the merchant ship frequency, 500 kc/s. It was a fine morning, fresh enough for duffle coats, but with the sea easy under a bright sun. At 1030 one of the destroyers reported a possible submarine contact right ahead, and two depth-charges were dropped. The convoy ploughed on, and the day passed.

The following morning dawned equally fair, but these were U-boat waters and there could be no relaxation. For certain, there would be no screening of *Snow White and the Seven Dwarfs* in the office flat that evening.

It was just after midnight that an Operational Priority wireless signal, addressed to all cruisers in Home Waters, was passed up to the Officer of the Watch. *Sheffield* was to hand over the convoy to the armed merchant cruiser *Wolfe* and return to Greenock at high speed. The deciphered signal said nothing more, but the meaning was loud and clear to everyone on the bridge. Invasion.

Wolfe, sometime *Montcalm* of the Canadian Pacific Steamship Company, impressively twice *Sheffield*'s tonnage, was sighted just before dawn. There was a brief exchange of flashed signals and a throaty roar from the the AMC's siren. 'Have a good leave,' said *Wolfe*, and *Sheffield*'s men groaned. The cruiser heeled when she pulled around to eastward, her telegraphs chang-changed as she began working up to 28 knots. Larcom lowered his binoculars and took a mug of coffee from the wardroom steward. The navigating officer was at the chart-table, pencilling, and the ratings' galley below was boiling haddock for breakfast. Galley cooking smells always permeated the Marines' messdeck and, they claimed, turned their brasses green. The seamen said that all Bootnecks were naturally green anyway, by definition.

'We are ordered to return to Greenock', Captain Larcomb explained, 'and our mail has been directed to Freetown, Sierra Leone. I do not think there will be any leave from Greenock.'

The BBC's placatory news-reader conceded that the Luftwaffe's raids on London had been 'heavy', which meant that they were devastating. Buckingham Palace and St. Paul's Cathedral had been damaged, and the city's firefighters, reinforced from the surrounding counties, were stretched almost to breaking-point.

Many of *Sheffield*'s company were Londoners, familiar with the short weekend dash from Chatham Barracks to London Bridge, twelve shillings return, with dirty dhobeying in a bundle handkerchief, and they tried not to think of the smoking streets of Rotherhithe and Woolwich. At two in the morning *Sheffield* elbowed her way through a tangle of anchored shipping to secure to the Flagship buoy off Greenock. Dunoon's signal station challenged, but nobody else seem to care.

Six days later the cruiser was still infuriatingly swinging on her buoy while distant London burned, and the BBC's assurance that 'blazing AA guns and daring young RAF fighter pilots worked in perfect co-ordination, taking turns to break up enemy formations' was dismissed as bullshit. Larcom granted afternoon shore leave for organized sport – football, hockey and rugby – and tension was briefly relieved when the ship's second Walrus amphibian chose to land at Campbeltown airfield with its wheels up, promptly to be christened *Clot of Campbeltown*.

During mid-forenoon on Wednesday 2 October a lighter tied alongside to transfer several hundred bags of mail for Force H and the Mediterranean Fleet, but none for *Sheffield*, which the GPO insisted was halfway to Freetown. Captain Larcom spoke to his crew, telling them they were now to escort a convoy southward to about 30 degrees North, possibly as far as Sierra Leone, after which the ship would rejoin Force H at Gibraltar. 'This', decided Bungy Williams, 'is where we soddin' came in.'

The forecastle party mustered at 0600, shivering in a cold wind, and, weighing at 0630, *Sheffield* moved into the Firth with the destroyer *Versatile* astern. It was a grey morning, the choppy sea white-flecked, and there were few men other than watchkeepers above deck to see Arran slide past

to starboard. Most were at breakfast – reconstituted egg, fried bread and tea – as the BBC's 7 o'clock news bulletin described continuing bombing raids on London and several seaports, the torpedoing in mid-Atlantic of *City of Benares* with the loss of 77 of her several hundred child passengers being evacuated to the USA, while Germany, Italy and Japan had signed a ten-year mutual assistance pact.

The convoy, overhauled by 2000, consisted of *Oropesa*, carrying the Commodore, *Dorset, Port Chalmers, Clan Campbell* and *Clan McArthur*, with seven destroyers escorting, beginning to roll and plunge in conditions that were ominously deteriorating. There was a sixth merchant ship somewhere, the Commodore reported – *Highland Brigade* – which had apparently wasted no time in getting herself detached and was assumed to be following. It was enough to make anyone want to shit, but the main body would press on. The glass was falling as officers on every bridge searched for Bloody Foreland's light; at the briefing in Greenock nobody had said it was extinguished. Buckets of thick cocoa and Camp coffee on *Sheffield*'s bridge and flagdeck were shared by officer and rating alike, sandwiches of pink salmon and corned beef, and slabs of the Chief Cook's Aggie Weston's Special Bread Pudding with currants, very solid and guaranteed to immobilize the human gastric function for two days. At midnight *Highland Brigade* was still unsighted.

The weather had worsened, with a full gale blowing and the sea handling the destroyers viciously. By noon on 4 October *Sheffield* had been compelled to reduce to 8 knots, and there were only occasional glimpses of other ships of the convoy. Green seas were exploding over the cruiser's quarterdeck and both Carley floats were stove in; the calcium flare of one was ignited and burned blindingly for hours. God help those poor sods in the Boats – the little destroyers that climbed and plunged like crazy fairground amusements, where cramped below-decks reeked of men's bodies, wet clothing and vomit, and the bulkheads streamed with condensation. All food was coldly prised from tins, and happiness was a single hour of uninterrupted sleep, clinging to a mess-stool.

Another day passed, of winds and heaving sea, before the convoy, less *Highland Brigade*, had reformed, and on the next, Sunday 6 October, two destroyers were detached to search for the missing freighter. All other destroyers were recalled by CinC Western Approaches before evening, and it was assumed that *Highland Brigade* had either overtaken the convoy during the night, unseen, or had been torpedoed.

The weather was improving, and during the forenoon of 8 October *Sheffield*'s No. 1 aircraft, the veteran *Terror of Trondheim*, was launched, piloted by Lieutenant Johnny Groves accompanied by Lieutenant C. E. Fenwick and Telegraphist/Air Gunner Pike.

By noon the Walrus had returned, her Aldis lamp reporting that her search had achieved nothing. Then Groves put the aircraft down perfectly into a long swell, taxiing to come alongside the crane for hoisting. Pike, hampered by his harness, reached for the hook but missed. At the second attempt he managed to couple hook and lifting eye, but, as the aircraft was falling astern of the crane, Groves revved slightly. Simultaneously a wave broke over the nose, and the sudden strain on the hook tore out its safety-pin. The crane wire tautened and the Walrus nose-tipped, its cockpit flooding in seconds.

Fenwick and Pike were thrown clear, and Groves, after switching off the ignition, decided to scramble to the highest point of the swamped and sinking aircraft until taken off by the crash whaler, already lowered. An appreciative audience watched from *Sheffield*'s deck. 'Swim for it, Johnny,' shouted Fenwick, 'before you get sucked down with the aircraft.' Groves declined. 'Come up here, you fool,' he shouted back. 'You'll be eaten by sharks.' All

three crewmen were hauled into the cutter, and *Terror of Trondheim*, beyond salvage, was finished off with a burst of pom-pom fire, to sink in 1,300 fathoms.

Cumberland – one of the dignified 8-inch 'County'-class that always seemed so superior to all lesser-breed cruisers – relieved *Sheffield* as convoy chaperon during the afternoon of 9 October. There followed a frustrating patrol of the neutral Azores area to intercept, if possible, two German freighters reported about to break out of quarantine. They did not, and *Sheffield* halted only a dirty little Spanish tramp, *Mar Rojo*, which was allowed to proceed, and this time Larcom ordered 25 knots for Gibraltar; there were times when the staunchest of ships' companies became

Below: On board HMS *Sheffield*, shown here making smoke.

stale and moody, a condition generated by a lack of contact with shore, no mail from home, a diet reduced to basics, adequate but repetitive and defeating. The most reasonable of men will eventually rebel against an interminable cycle of corned beef, baked beans, mystery soup, reconstituted egg, hard-boiled peas, corned beef in batter, baked beans, hard-boiled-pea-soup, corned beef surprise, reconstituted egg omelette, corned-beef-shepherd's pie . . .

Gibraltar was just beginning to stir as *Sheffield* entered harbour. Except for a few destroyers the base was empty of warships, which boded well for the cruiser's Watch ashore – until massive *Renown* arrived at 1100, meaning a few more blue collars in Main Street than had been anticipated, and the price of a brief, panting exchange on a crumpled bed in Line Wall raised by fifty per cent; it was the old law of supply and demand. Worse, old *Barham*, the cruiser *Australia* and three more destroyers arrived during the following forenoon, following their involvement in the abortive attack on Dakar, of which *Sheffield*'s men knew nothing. Nor did they know that when, that day, the Admiral Commanding Force H, Vice-Admiral James Somerville, was piped aboard *Sheffield*, he was anticipating his own dismissal by the Admiralty for failing to intercept a Vichy French battle squadron on passage from Toulon to Casablanca. In the event it would be Admiral Sir Dudley North, Flag Officer North Atlantic, whom the Admiralty was to pillory, and Somerville would survive to fight again, but he could not anticipate this when he stood on *Sheffield*'s quarterdeck on Tuesday 15 October. He welcomed the cruiser back to his command, especially with that priceless 'cuckoo' device revolving above her bridge – but, he added, ships, weapons and equipment were only as good as the crews that manned them. At sea, it was the efficiency of men that mattered more than anything.

'D'yer hear there? There will be watchkeepers' leave from 1330. Leave to the second part of Port from 1600. All leave terminates at 2300. The Rock and Bristol Hotels are out of bounds to lower deck ratings. Condoms are available from the Sick Bay at 1200, one per rating. The film showing on board tonight at 2000 will be *Each Dawn I Die* . . .'

'So do I, mate,' said Bungy Williams, 'every time I get shook for the soddin' Morning watch.'

The ship's company were beginning to develop a certain fondness for the 'cuckoo'. While others patrolled the Straits and the vicinity of the Azores seeking U-boats and blockade-runners, *Sheffield*, the only warship with RDF, remained AA Guard in Gibraltar harbour, tied alongside the Coaling Wharf, for the next twelve days. There were Yellow alerts almost daily, but only once was a distant Heinkel sighted, to be driven off by the AA fire of warships and shore batteries. To counter the possibility of underwater attack from Algeciras, across the bay, *Sheffield*'s No. 1 Motor Boat was armed as an anti-submarine patrol launch, with three depth-charges and two Lewis guns, while the remaining Walrus made a number of flights to exercise AA director crews. Finally, despite unsettled weather, the ship

was painted, but this was a small price to pay for a daily run ashore. The sun shone, there was Worthington and Bass in the bars and the canteen of *Rooke*, girls in Alameda Gardens, while the more erudite sought out the Moorish Castle, the Trafalgar Cemetery, the Museum. Some stalwarts even climbed to the Upper Rock to see Gibraltar's apes, although why anyone should want to walk miles, during drinking time, to see a few monkeys was beyond the comprehension of most. It took all kinds.

This Utopian interlude was terminated on 27 October when, in the early evening, the cruiser slid past the breakwater into the Atlantic, ordered to the Azores area. It was a repeat story. Two enemy merchantmen, interned in the port of Horta, on the island of Fayal, were reported to be preparing to leave. It was thin fare for a cruiser, but North Atlantic resources were stretched to breaking point, and if the only uncommitted warship was *Sheffield*, tied to a Gibraltar jetty, well, so be it – and *Sheffield*'s men could hardly complain. Course 260, 20 knots.

The validity of RDF, soon to be known as radar, was being accepted only cautiously by some watchkeeping officers. Ordinary Seaman Allen, RDF operator, aged 19, recalls that five minutes of silence from the RDF office aft could prompt some worried officers of the watch to enquire: 'Anything on the screen, RDF?' If there were not, the operator was unfailingly instructed, 'Well, keep a good look-out, RDF.'

'On the other hand,' says Allen, 'during an otherwise uneventful watch, the bridge could be infuriatingly sceptical when a contact was reported. There would be a pause, then – "Can't see anything, RDF." We might have reported "an aircraft at forty miles, height ten thousand", or, on a black night, "a small surface vessel, ten miles dead astern", and the answer would come back: "Are you sure, RDF? Can't see a thing up here." On one such exasperating occasion I was moved to retort, "I know you can't see anything, sir. That's why they've sat me in front of this bloody machine." '

Nine days of prowling the waters around the Azores were not rewarded by the interception of any enemy ships. During the first evening the Vichy French trawler *Marcella*, from Newfoundland bound Casablanca, was questioned but allowed to proceed. Two days later three British armed trawlers, bound Freetown, were sighted and during the early hours of 2 November the Portuguese fishing boat *San Miguel* and the Norwegian steamer *Tyr* were both challenged. After these the seas remained empty until Tuesday 5 November, when the cruiser turned back to Gibraltar. At 1300 a large, three-funnelled merchant ship was sighted on the horizon, and *Sheffield* altered course to intercept, sending her crew to quarters. In these waters large vessels steaming alone were treated with caution. German surface raiders like *Atlantis* and *Orion* were equipped with 5.9-inch guns and torpedo tubes, capable of severely mauling an unwary challenger. Today, as *Sheffield* closed, the hull of the strange vessel could be seen to be painted with a Vichy French tricolour and, in large letters, the name *Messilia*.

Everyone relaxed. *Sheffield* had earlier received a signal regarding *Messilia*. A passenger ship of 15,000 tons, of the French Sud Atlantique Company, she was to be allowed free passage as she was bound for Liverpool to embark French servicemen who, having been evacuated from Dunkirk, or had brought their warships to British ports, had now elected to be repatriated, and were to be conveyed to French West Africa.

Sheffield allowed the Frenchman to proceed northward, then resumed her own course of 090, for Gibraltar, speed 20 knots. And I'm soddin' watch ashore tomorrow, said Bungy Williams, so let's stop pissin' around.

To everyone's chagrin, Gibraltar was crowded with warships – the old grey lady, *Barham*, the carrier *Ark Royal*, the cruisers *Berwick* and *Glasgow*, the 30,000-ton French transport *Pasteur* (of the same company as *Messilia*) with 2,000 troops embarked for Malta and beyond, and, far from least, two flotillas of destroyers.

It was not that the presence of other warships was resented, but the availability of English beer in Gibraltar was a matter for concern, while Spanish beer was like boiled liquorice. Besides, the price of twenty minutes upstairs in Rosia Road with that party who said she had a brother in Swansea would be twenty-five bob and two stokers and a marine waiting on the stairs.

The film on board tonight in the starboard hangar, piped the quartermaster, would be *Union Pacific* with Joel McCrea. Tombola in the office flat.

The Italians were being hammered by the Greeks, and British troops and RAF units had already been landed in Greece. The Government of the neutral Republic of Eire had firmly rejected a British suggestion that ports on the south-western coast of Ireland might be used by Allied ships. A Dublin spokesman said, 'When the agreement (to hand over the ports to Eire in 1938) was signed it was made clear what the position would be in the event of Britain being involved in war.' Subsequently President Roosevelt, campaigning for re-election, declared to an Irish-American audience in Boston: 'I have said this before, but I shall say it again and again and again. Your boys are not going to be sent into any foreign wars.' However, just in case, 16,400,000 American men had already been registered for compulsory military service. In the Atlantic the U-boat offensive was mounting in intensity; it seemed impossible that the devastating losses of September and October could be suffered much longer – and in sunny Gibraltar equally unlikely that the Mediterranean could be allowed to retain cruisers and destroyers that might more profitably be fighting in defence of Atlantic convoys. And without cruisers and destroyers, Cunningham's carriers and battleships must withdraw or die. That would mean the loss of Malta, possibly Gibraltar, with the Mediterranean

becoming, *ipso facto*, exclusively Italian. The passage to the Middle East, India and the Orient could only be via the Cape. Alexandria would wither on the vine, Egypt, the Sudan and Cyprus would be isolated, and nothing could prevent Greece being crushed.

Such matters were beyond the comprehension of those ordinary men who lived, slept and blasphemed among the forward messdecks of *Sheffield*. More relevant were the clogged drains of the seamen's bathroom, the Naafi canteen's acquisition of Sweet Caporal cigarettes and Canadian Neilson's chocolate to the exclusion of any other, and the fact that the Chaplain, having lunched a little unwisely in *Rooke*'s wardroom, had returned aboard with the film *Sanders of the River* yet again.

At 1800 on Thursday 7 November Vice-Admiral Somerville, temporarily flying his flag in *Ark Royal*, led *Barham, Berwick, Glasgow, Sheffield* and the 8th and 13th Destroyer Flotillas out of Gibraltar harbour, ordered 18 knots on a course due east.

This was to be the first of the many 'club runs' executed by Force H, the insolence of which would be a constant and annoying distraction for the Italians. On this occasion *Pasteur*'s 2,000 troops had been transferred to *Barham* and *Berwick*, and Operation 'White' was to ensure their safe passage as far as Malta, at which point they would become the responsibility of the Mediterranean Fleet.

To the men of *Sheffield*, more usually an operational 'loner', the company of *Ark Royal*'s aircraft and *Barham*'s big guns was comforting. These were enemy-dominated waters, and it was too much to expect that they could cover eleven hundred miles without detection. Even so, the remainder of that day and the following night, with a good moon, passed with incident. So far, so good. At dawn the sea was calm, the sky an unflawed blue, the sun growing steadily warmer. In the afternoon a school of dolphins raced the ships, leaping. The men on flag-deck and gun platform unbuttoned their shirts, deadlights were lifted, and the demand for hot soup and cocoa had fallen sharply. It was not until 1800, as night clothing was piped, that RDF reported an unidentified aircraft approaching from north-easterly, and with all ships alerted, the contact flew into sight a few minutes later. *Sheffield*'s log recorded a Caproni aircraft, but it was almost certainly a Fiat BR20, ocean patrolling from a Sardinian airfield, whose five crewmen were far more startled to encounter the British squadron than the British were to receive them. In the event, identification was largely academic. *Ark Royal*'s AA guns opened fire. The Italian aircraft turned tail and fled but, beyond sight of the ships, was shot into the sea by the carrier's fighters.

And that, claimed the messdeck pundits, was all good stuff for an Errol Flynn film, but the Italians had almost certainly wirelessed an enemy report, and, any moment now, the Regia Aeronautica would be arriving, screaming

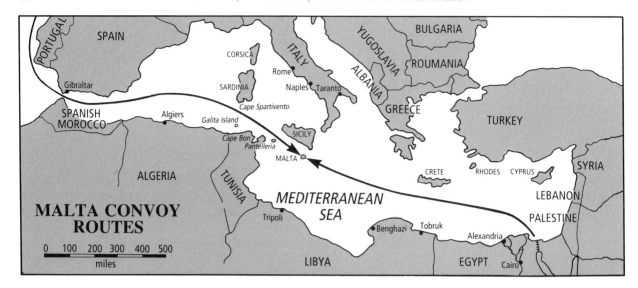

MALTA CONVOY
ROUTES

0   100 200 300 400 500
miles

blue murder. Tonight the moon would be almost full and the weather perfect for a torpedo attack; Somerville ordered all ships to expect bombers at any time this night.

An hour later, however, *Sheffield* and *Ark Royal* detached to ENE and increased to a lively 26 knots so that, by first light tomorrow, they would be only a hundred miles from Cagliari and deep into Mussolini's *Mare Nostrum*. Saturday 9 November dawned fine, and the carrier pushed her bows into a light wind. Her latticed wireless masts fell slowly down, outwards, and fifteen minutes before take-off all nine Swordfish of the sortie were manned and waiting. At ten minutes the order was given to 'man the chocks, stand clear of propellers, stand by to start-up,' and at exactly 0430 the strike leader was launched over the bows, its load of six 250lb bombs dragging it down almost to the wave-tops before maximum throttle pulled it upward and clear. The second aircraft was already airborne, and the third, on the flight deck, was in motion, roaring. Height six thousand, course zero six zero. The sun was exploding, golden, in the eastern sky. When the operator in *Ark Royal*'s bridge wireless office had confirmed that all nine Swordfish telegraphists had 'told off' – six, seven, eight, nine – carrier and cruiser swung back to easterly to rejoin Somerville's main force, heading for Malta. This time, with Cagliari bombed from the sea yet again, the Italians must surely hit back, but, it was hoped, not before the carrier had recovered and struck down her Swordfish. No warship was more hopelessly vulnerable than a carrier during the period of landing-on.

Sheer good fortune arranged that, at 1015, the returning Swordfish, all unscathed, were reported visual just as the carrier's flag-deck was sighting *Barham* and her fellows ahead. There was no time to de-brief aircrews. The deck-landed aircraft were taxied forward, wings folded and struck down into the hangar in twenty minutes, and then Al Hurley, in the Plot, was shouting a warning of twenty plus aircraft closing fast and no bullshit. Moments later the same

warning was being relayed to *Ark Royal* and the squadron – by wireless on Fleet Wave, by lamp, and by flag 'A' at the yardarm. Emergency Enemy Aircraft. And Hurley was just in time; twenty-four Savoia-Marchetti bombers were spilling out of the sun.

Hanson Baldwin, correspondent for the *New York Times*, and taking passage with the squadron, would later telegraph his despatch from Malta, written in that staccato prose of which only an American was capable.

'The lookouts behind the weather screens on the destroyers stare unceasingly, faces creased from long vigil, at sea and sky. The crew is at battle stations; splinter mats are up. Astern, with the solemn majesty befitting a Queen of the Seas, steams a battleship, her great guns loaded and lifted. She is the destroyers' charge. They circle and weave about her, the white wash of their passing mixed with the scud of the wind-whipped sea.

A black dot to northward – one, two, three, a horde of them – and now is heard the faint hum of their engines above the wind and the voice of the ships moaning in the lifting sea. The destroyers' guns rise towards the targets; on the battleship the anti-aircraft batteries – eight 4-inchers – elevate to the heavens, train to starboard. The planes grow bigger, too high for the pom-poms and the machine-guns, but the great guns speak, and soon the shells are bursting around sea power's new and bitter enemy, in cotton balls of white. But this is only the beginning, and the men at the guns know it.

They have not long to wait. The hum of the engines quickens to a terrible roar. All about now the guns of the fleet are firing, first the short, sharp bark of the four-inchers, and then, as the planes come closer, the quicker, deafening rattle of the pom-poms and machine-guns.

You can see the bombs, now, in the racks. You feel very naked and lonely and insignificant and afraid, but you keep your glasses trained upward, at sudden death.

Suddenly, as the nearest gun barks again, the awful roar

changes and you known that the bombs have dropped. In one second of immortal time you will know if you've been hit. The bombs drop and the ocean opens up in a rush of water; you feel the wind of death on your face and the sound of it in your ears – but you are not hit. The ship shivers, but steams on.

You look about you, at the wreckage of several planes upon the water, at the bomb geysers subsiding into the sea. Your muscles are tense and your jaws are set and aching, but the guns are still firing and the fleet steams on . . .'

'Shave off,' Bungy Williams marvelled. 'Was that *us*?'

It was, but the exploits of Force H on this occasion were to be completely overshadowed by another. Having executed Operation 'White' without loss, Somerville turned his own ships back to Gibraltar at 26 knots, and signalled Admiral Cunningham: 'I trust goods to your esteemed order arrived safely. Further consignments will follow shortly in very plain van.'

The Commander-in-Chief replied 'I nearly caught a chill waiting one and three-quarters of an hour at rendezvous for a coat. I still have no trousers but propose to take off Mussolini's in due course.'

And even as Force H was thankfully berthing in Gibraltar's sun-drenched harbour during the forenoon of 11 November, *Illustrious* was positioning herself for Operation 'Judgement', a twenty-Swordfish night raid on the harbour of Taranto. The obsolete 'Stringbags' carried out a text-book attack. The Italian battleships *Conte Di Cavour*, *Littorio* and *Caio Duilio* were all sufficiently crippled to keep them out of action for most of the war and three cruisers were badly damaged – nearly half the Italian battle fleet. Only two British aircraft were lost.

Almost unheeded, the BBC announced the death of Neville Chamberlain.

Illustrious had stolen the limelight from *Ark Royal*, but Somerville immediately signalled Cunningham: 'Our best congratulations on so successful a debagging accompanied by such a lovely crack on the navel. Another one like that and our friend will join Uncle George singing alto in the choir.' Cunningham responded: 'Thank you for your 0850/13 November. Uncle George now learning to pipe tune "Blackshirt, Blackshirt, have you lost your balls?" '

Renown had rejoined Force H, *Sheffield*'s lost aircraft had been replaced, all ships had provisioned and reported ready in all respects for sea. The old carrier *Argus* was oiling. Escorted by *Despatch*, she had arrived from the UK, ferrying eighteen Hurricane fighters for Hal Far, Malta. The aircraft, desperately needed by the island, represented a top priority consignment; Somerville's orders required Force H to ensure that *Argus* was safely escorted as far as Galita Island, off the Tunisian coast, at which point the Hurricanes would be flown off and the ships would return to Gibraltar. There would not, as before, be any distracting air attacks on Cagliari. Rumour had it that the Germans, impatient with the performance of their Italian allies, were transferring six squadrons – a hundred bombers – from France to Sicily in order to disrupt the sea traffic between Gibraltar, Malta and Alexandria. The Italian Regia Aeronautica was one thing, the German Luftwaffe something different. There was nothing to be gained by kicking providence in the teeth. *Sheffield*'s armed cutter, which had been patrolling the mole, was hoisted inboard, and at 0400 on 15 November, as Gibraltar slept, Force H slipped quietly into the Mediterranean, joined by *Argus* and *Despatch*.

The old engines of *Argus* were capable of only 16 knots, which was uncomfortably slow for Force H, but the first day eastward passed without incident, although the wind, right astern, was rising. The following day, too, was uneventful. It was almost too good to be true, but perhaps the steadily worsening weather was a blessing in disguise. That night all hands were at action stations as the ships were passing close to the coast of Algeria, nominally Vichy French and so presumably enemy-sympathetic. Dawn was unexpectedly cold, the sea grey and wind-whipped. All ships were plunging their bows into lakes of white froth, climbing again, their ragged ensigns streaming from jacks and tangling. At 0545 *Argus* and *Despatch* turned away into the wind to fly-off the Hurricanes. At this stage of the operation an RAF Sunderland was expected to rendezvous with the squadron and subsequently escort the Hurricanes towards Malta, but no plane was sighted. Well, the sailors shrugged, the weather was a bit wet for the RAF. Old *Argus* got her aircraft into the air, and by 0800 the squadron was reformed and steering 280 degrees for Gibraltar, warm beer and cheap Marsala, vaccinations and kit inspections for junior ratings, midshipmen's examinations and Fat Mary's belly-dancers from Tangier's Casbah via every working man's club east of Cardiff's Queen Street.

By mid-afternoon of 17 November the wind had risen to gale force and the sea was sufficiently violent for the squadron's speed to be reduced to 15 knots. In *Sheffield* bad weather routine was piped; hatch-covers, equipment, furnishings and messtraps were secured, lines rigged and many ladders blanked off. The galley cancelled soup.

At 1545, with the squadron labouring westward, *Sheffield* was ordered to push on to Gibraltar independently in response to a report of an enemy surface raider, possibly *Admiral Scheer*, in the vicinity of the Cape Verde Islands. The cruiser increased to 18 knots.

'Shortly after 1800,' says Warrant Shipwright Pack, 'with the ship's company at night action stations, there was a very loud crash from forward. The ship shuddered, and the Forward Damage Control Party believed that we had been torpedoed. However, an examination of the forward upper messdeck revealed that an unusually heavy sea had broken over the forecastle, damaging the deck and wrenching up the breakwater. Below, two steel stanchions were buckled, with the deck-head forced nine inches downward. Water was pouring into the forecastle messdeck.

Wooden shores were immediately placed under the deck-head, and some lengths of old railway line welded in as supports, but, with the ship under urgent orders and the Captain unwilling to reduce speed, repairs could only be temporary.

Under the drenching brine, ratings were attempting to rescue gear from their kit lockers while shipwrights were passing up and cutting timber. There was considerable congestion, but the men recalled a film they had recently seen in which the Crazy Gang had tried to saw a length of wood between two trestles which were too far apart. The comedians had sung: "It's a little bit too short, turn it around the other way." Now, as *Sheffield*'s soaked shipwrights sawed and hammered, the equally drenched sailors chanted the ditty, and humour rescued a situation which might have been miserable and exasperating.'

The sea dropped during the night, and with the ship enjoying a degree of shelter from the Spanish shore, Larcom increased to 27½ knots. Gibraltar was reached at 1800 on 18 November, and the ship secured, at a half-hour's notice for steam and no shore leave granted. Alongside, the damage to *Sheffield*'s forecastle was inspected and it was decided that the cruiser was still seaworthy, her fighting efficiency unimpaired; she would not be docked for repair. 'Shave off,' sniffed Bungy Williams, whose best serge suit looked like a wet deck rag and his nutty ration was uneatable. 'If it was the soddin' wardroom, mate, we'd be in dock for bleedin' six weeks.'

Renown and *Ark Royal* secured during the Morning watch, *Despatch* and *Argus* shortly after daybreak, but at 1700 *Sheffield*'s orders for sea were received, and the cruiser passed the breakwater at 1830. She was to patrol westward of Gibraltar for twenty-four hours, then rendezvous with an outbound convoy escorted by *Southampton* and *Manchester*. The BBC's news of the recent bombing of Coventry and then Birmingham had aroused anxiety among the ship's Midlanders; there was little consolation in hearing that the Greeks had pushed the Italians back into Albania, or even that President Roosevelt had been elected to a third term of office. *Sheffield*, passing through the Straits into a sullen, November Atlantic, reduced to a cruising 18 knots on a course of 300 degrees.

Two ships sighted during the forenoon of 20 November proved to be a Portuguese trawler, *Fafe*, which was allowed to proceed, and a Brazilian freighter, *Sequeira Campos*. This vessel was on the suspected list, and Larcom ordered her to heave to for investigation. The starboard whaler was called away as, a half-cable distant, the rust-streaked Brazilian sat sulkily in a long, greasy swell, her single funnel spiralling lazy smoke.

As *Sheffield*'s whaler was being lowered, however, the after slipping grear failed to disengage, leaving the boat swinging and suspended by its stern. Four of the crew were flung into the sea, but all got safely clear. The port whaler was immediately sent away, and *Sequeira Campos* also lowered a lifeboat – which had hardly wet its keel before all men in the water were recovered unhurt and the miscreant whaler re-hoisted. Even so, the whole business was an embarrassment that was only compensated by the boarding party's discovery; *Sequeira Campos* was indeed carrying German war exports to Brazil. The ship's master shrugged indifferently when told that a prize crew would take his vessel into Gibraltar. It wasn't his war and, anyway, his owners would still get a handsome price for their cargo.

Another vessel was already reported, hull down on the horizon and subsequently identified as the *Duero*, a Spanish tramp freighter bound for Tenerife from the Canaries in ballast. Not on the suspected list, she was not detained, and *Sheffield* altered course to achieve her rendezvous by noon the next day.

The convoy, intercepted in position 38°50'N, 18°27'W at 1115 on 21 November, consisted of the Ministry of War Transport charters *New Zealand Star*, *Clan Fraser* and *Clan Forbes* accompanied by the cruisers *Southampton* and *Manchester*, all on passage to the eastern Mediterranean by the shorter but more dangerous route. For tactical reasons it was necessary to delay the merchant ships' passage through the Straits, so *Sheffield* turned them away westward while *Southampton* and *Manchester* continued to Gibraltar for oiling. Three days later, having steamed almost a thousand idling miles with nothing achieved except a massive fuel consumption, *Sheffield* sighted and investigated a three-funnelled liner which proved to be the Sud Atlantique *Messilia* again, this time laden with French servicemen from the UK, bound for Casablanca and repatriation. The Frenchmen lined their ship's rails in sullen silence as the British cruiser flashed the order to proceed and added a charitable *bon voyage*. Then, relieved by several destroyers from Gibraltar, *Sheffield* parted company with the small convoy and increased to 28 knots. After four days of time-wasting in the cold Atlantic the increased beat of engines and the vibration underfoot suggested that Larcomb was thinking of at least one run ashore. He took his ship past the breakwater at 2200, in half light, ordered to secure alongside an oiler off South Mole.

The harbour was unusually crowded – *Renown*, *Royal Sovereign*, *Ark Royal*, *Argus*, *Manchester*, *Southampton*, *Despatch* – not to mention the destroyers. Main Street, lamented Bungy Williams, was going to be like bleedin' Putney High Street on Boat Race day.

But he need not have concerned himself.

'D'yer hear there? There will be no shore leave tonight. The ship is under sailing orders. Wires will be singled up at 0530 and special sea dutymen will close up at 0630. The Chaplain's confirmation class and the next issue of condoms by the Sick Bay are both postponed until return to harbour. As there has been no opportunity to exchange films, the next showing in the starboard hangar will be *Sanders of the River* . . .'

8

'Our tail feathers were very bedraggled'

SOMERVILLE'S Force H – *Renown* (Flag), *Ark Royal* and *Sheffield*, screened by nine destroyers supplemented by *Despatch* – left harbour at daybreak on Monday 25 November. At sea, the squadron was joined by *Manchester* and *Southampton*, between them carrying 1,370 RAF personnel assigned to Alexandria, the two 16-knot Clan Line ships *Clan Forbes* and *Clan Fraser*, the *New Zealand Star*, one destroyer and four corvettes. On this same day a much more powerful British fleet under Cunningham, in three parts and also including five merchant ships, was departing Alexandria and would steam westward to rendezvous with Somerville, to exchange mercantile convoys. A number of other movements were anticipated (including a bombing raid on Tripoli by *Eagle*'s aircraft) before Force H, joined by *Ramillies, Berwick, Newcastle* and of course the five west-bound merchant ships from Alexandria, turned back to Gibraltar. Interference from the Italian Navy was not expected but, as Larcom told *Sheffield*'s company, the unexpected could happen at any time. The weather was bright, crisply fresh, visibility excellent. If it were not for the men's worries about the Luftwaffe attacks on London and the Midlands, it would be great to be alive, young and ready for anything.

The next day (27 November) just before noon, in position 37°54'N, 08°16'E, Somerville's force was joined from westward by the old battleship *Ramillies*, the 'County'-class cruiser *Berwick*, and *Newcastle*, sister to *Sheffield* and built in the same yard. This, now, was a sizeable force, probably more powerful than the Italian CinC, Campioni, thought he was intercepting when the battleships *Vittorio Veneto* and *Guilio Cesare*, supported by seven 8-inch cruisers and sixteen destroyers were launched from their harbours to intercept. The Italians were still markedly superior, but unfortunately, during the forenoon, a Sunderland flying-boat from Malta had reported an enemy force of five cruisers and five destroyers, sixty miles distant and another force of two battleships and seven destroyers at a distance of 75 miles, but all closing at 15 knots.

Forewarned, Somerville had time to send away to south-easterly the three merchant ships with *Despatch* (an obsolescent and lightweight veteran who could fill no useful role in a surface action against battleships) and add *Manchester* and *Southampton* to his force, which now mustered one slow battleship, one fast battle-cruiser, one 8-inch cruiser, four 6-inch cruisers and ten destroyers. It was not to be expected that the battleship, *Ramillies*,

Right: Off Cape Spartivento on 27 November 1940, the Sheffield ladies' huge battle ensign is hoisted for the first time. Somerville's squadron has sighted the enemy.

would keep up with a fast-moving action, and, indeed, a defect in *Renown*'s notoriously troublesome engine-room had reduced her speed by two knots. Nevertheless, by 1040, Somerville's ships were hammering towards the enemy at 28 knots, all closed up at action stations and spoiling for a fight.

'At 1205', writes Lieutenant-Commander Hubert Treseder, 'masts and smoke were sighted on the horizon, and soon the funnels and superstructures of a group of cruisers and destroyers could be distinguished. By 1216, it could be seen that there were about seven cruisers and ten destroyers steering a south-easterly course, and for a time it was hoped that the Italians would abandon their usual policy of retreat. They had apparently just sighted us, and it could be seen that they were taking up a different formation. The range was now 28,000 yards, and the enemy was bearing 350 degrees. Two minutes later a second enemy group was sighted bearing 020 degrees, soon identified as two battleships and several destroyers steering a north-easterly course at high speed.

At 1222 the enemy cruisers opened fire, but after two broadsides the entire enemy force turned away to the north-east, the cruisers splitting into two groups, one of three and the other of four ships.

At 1230 our first aircraft was catapulted off to spot for *Renown*.'

Fenwick, the observer in *Sheffield*'s Walrus, remembers those uncomfortable few minutes. 'Groves and I were briefed to report the composition of the Italian Fleet. We manned the aircraft in plenty of time and the catapult was extended for launching. The Italians with their 8-inch guns opened fire accurately before *Sheffield* got within range, but eventually we did get into maximum range and opened up. Unfortunately our aircraft was on the end of the catapult

on the engaged side – rather a hair-raising position during broadsides, and for some reason the launch was delayed for what seemed a very long time. When we were shot off at last, it was straight through the wall of water put up by an Italian salvo. Our own [*Sheffield*'s] 6-inch guns were also fired at the moment of launching. After we had been in the air for about a half hour – during part of which we had been the target for some very accurate AA fire – I noticed that our tail feathers were very bedraggled, although Groves was apparently having no difficulty. It was not until we were back in *Sheffield* again that we discovered that it had been the blast of our own guns that had removed the air gunner's hatch and caused the tail damage.'

The second Walrus carried by *Sheffield* had been briefed to spot for *Ramillies*, but the old battleship never managed to get within range of the enemy during the duration of the action.

By 1130 the five British cruisers, led by Rear-Admiral Lancelot Holland in *Manchester*, were steaming for the enemy at 30 knots and had drawn five miles ahead of *Renown* and eight from *Ramillies*. Flag 5 was hoisted at 1223, and they opened fire, *Sheffield* directing her guns against the second enemy in the line. Within a few minutes this cruiser was seen to be hit, and a large fire broke out amidships.

Renown, coming up from astern, also began firing at extreme range, concentrating on the retreating enemy cruisers but occasionally trying a salvo at the Italian battleships which, however, were never really within reach.

But the British cruisers were hitting. 'We shifted our fire to a destroyer that was laying a smoke-screen', says Treseder in *Sheffield*, 'and it is thought that we hit her, as she was seen to be on fire, and later retired behind the other enemy ships.' Campioni was running as fast as his

Left: In the high-speed chase of Italian cruisers and destroyers, *Manchester*, seen from *Sheffield*'s deck, narrowly survives a salvo of 15in shells from the Italian battleship *Vittorio Veneto*. Beyond *Manchester* is *Newcastle*.

battleships could take him. 'We then shifted our fire again to another cruiser, and continued firing at this ship until she was out of range.'

The exchange was not completely one-sided. The Italian ships were firing from their after turrets, and most of them seemed to be ranging on *Manchester*, although several large splashes were seen to fall around *Berwick*. These were probably from the 15-inch guns of *Vittorio Veneto*. The cruiser was also twice hit by 8-inch projectiles and her 'Y' turret training was jammed as a result. *Berwick* was the only British warship to be hit, and suffer casualties, during the action off Spartivento.

'Earlier, when Captain Larcom had addressed the ship's company', said Petty Officer Clay, 'he told us, "If we meet the Italian Fleet during one of our runs, it will be 'A' and 'B' turrets that will be overworked, as 'X' and 'Y' will not be able to bear on the enemy." He was proved right when we met the Italians off Spartivento . . . My action station was Petty Officer in charge of 'A' cordite gallery, and I never had to move so fast in all my life to keep up with the gunhouse crew . . .'

Broadsides were fired whenever possible, but 'X' and 'Y' turrets were firing on extreme forward bearings for most of the time, and frequently could not bear. 'A' turret fired 79 rounds per gun: 'B' turret fired 79; 'X' fired 42 and 'Y' fired 49. The other British cruisers in company fired approximately the same as *Sheffield*, while *Renown* fired a total of 86 rounds (from three twin turrets) and *Ramillies* only managed to get away two salvoes.

It was clear that the Italians, outstripping the British, were heading northward for the Sardinian coast and sanctuary. By 1246 the enemy battleships were beyond sight over the horizon, and Somerville was becoming uncomfortably aware that his battle force was being drawn progressively away from his merchant ships; Article 625 of Fighting Instructions insisted that the safety of the convoy was his first priority, and he could continue in pursuit of Campioni only a little longer.

Just after 1300 the speeding British cruisers sighted two large, three-funnelled passenger liners bearing 320 degrees. They both flew Vichy French tricolours. The reason for their presence in this location was never ascertained; they were left unchallenged and the cruisers smashed on. By now, however, Somerville was less than 30 miles from the Sardinian coast and the only remaining evidence of the Italian warships was a thinning pall of black smoke on the horizon. Further pursuit was pointless; Somerville ordered the cruisers to break off the action and Holland hoisted Flag 6. The fleet reformed, reduced to 27 knots, and set a south-easterly course to rejoin the convoy by nightfall.

Throughout the action Lieutenant Colin Ross had sat in 'A' turret. The steel cavern was hot, reeking of cordite smoke, the noise was deafening – of shell-hoists and cordite hoists, the stinging hiss of hydraulic rams that fed the three 6-inch breeches sunk low in their wells so that their barrels could lift to 45 degrees. Beyond his feet the

turret crew were intent, tensely sweating, at their stations – sight-setter, trainer, loader, layer. They addressed each other as Spud, Smithie, Taff and Scouse, and they were solid gold. Ross had shared their greasy cocoa cups and their doorstep corned-beef sandwiches tainted with gun-oil, the same thick pea-doo. They winked at each other, amused, when, his own cigarettes exhausted, he had tried to roll a 'tickler' from their tobacco. They confided their problems, openly discussed their sex lives, invoked curses on the Master-at-Arms, and had infinite trust in Lieutenant Colin Ross, RN. He loved them.

Two days after the action Ross would write home to his parents.

'It really was a great experience. Towards the end of the afternoon we got the first reports from our aircraft, and it seemed too good to be true. I'm afraid I could hardly believe we were going to have a scrap, even when everything pointed to it. Even when we had actually sighted their battleships, cruisers and destroyers, it seemed more like a practice than a battle. I found that I had so much to do that I forgot all about the enemy.

We opened fire at extreme range, and for the next forty-five minutes I had very little time to think of anything except the turret. We were hard at it, and I never looked out of my periscope at all, which I very much regret now, as I saw none of the enemy . . . I certainly heard the Ity's shots falling but did not see any. The sailors, naturally, loved every minute of it, and it has done as much good as a fortnight's leave. I only wish I could describe every detail of what went on in the turret, but I know that would be censored, and I know you would only find it boring and technical. I enjoyed every minute, and it was only terribly disappointing that such a strong force should run away. In any case we were damned hungry by then, and were ready for a huge lunch of sandwiches.

There's not much more I can tell you about except that our Chief Yeoman found two of the most enormous ensigns for our battle-flags, so we must have looked like one of Drake's ships – all flag.'

Those ensigns, hoisted for an action in which more ships had been engaged than in any battle since Jutland, were those provided by the Ladies of Sheffield and paid for by the hard-earned sixpences of the factory women, typists and shop girls of Tyneside, where now every slipway, every dock, was occupied by a warship building, equipping or refitting; acetylene flared and riveters hammered for twenty-two hours of every day. The action off Spartivento would not figure as one of the war's great moments. The BBC's account of it was only modest, and *Sheffield* was not mentioned. The same bulletin announced that farm workers in the Army were to be granted agricultural leave, that Roumania and Slovakia had formally joined the Axis, and a Kitchen Front was to be launched by Lord Woolton, the Minister of Food.

From *Sheffield*, just having reached Gibraltar, a weary Captain Larcom also wrote home.

'As usual, a hell of a rush, this is the 29th. I am sure you were thrilled at Jamie's (Somerville) success. So was I, until I heard we were NOT on the BBC. Secrecy in official quarters is quite beyond ordinary understanding. I enjoyed the two hours more than anything I remember, and I will, one day, tell you about it. I find the only difference to the last war is that advancing age brings gun deafness. I was as deaf as a post after two hours . . .

Just had my first bath for ten days. Everyone is well and really bucked up; it does no end of good after months of waiting. I was a luck prophet when we sailed. I told the sailors: "I fear a dull trip, but remember, it is the unexpected that always happens in war." What a lucky shot.

Everyone was remarkably cool under their first dose of fire, except one poor soul, and him I shall land . . .'

Larcom, however, could not at this time anticipate the unpleasant sequelae to the Spartivento action which were about to develop. Italian radio, predictably, claimed that the exchange had been terminated by a British withdrawal. Somerville was not Winston Churchill's favourite Admiral because of his outspoken criticism of the controversial attack on Mers-el-Kebir, and the Prime Minister had also admonished Admiral Cunningham (CinC, Mediterranean) for commenting on the gallantry of Italian destroyer commanders. Now the failure of Somerville to achieve more than he had was interpreted in certain departments of the Admiralty as a weakness in leadership, and Churchill seized on this contention to justify a demand for his replacement by Harwood, the hero of the River Plate. 'It is quite sufficient', ruled Churchill, 'to tell (Somerville) to haul down his flag and relieve him by Harwood without giving any other reason than we think a change necessary on general grounds.'

Unfortunately an official Inquiry at Gibraltar had already been ordered, and to cancel it now would have raised embarrassing questions. Churchill reluctantly acquiesed, adding that, 'should the Court of Inquiry consider the Admiral blameworthy . . . I hope the relief will take place this week'.

The Board of Inquiry sat on 3 December for four days. To the delight of the Mediterranean Fleet in general and Force H specifically the resultant decree was that within the context of orders that were clear and precise the action fought by Admiral Somerville was correct, spirited and achieved the purpose of protecting the convoy in face of a superior force. Somerville survived Churchill's disapproval; others would be less fortunate.

The Navy, from flag officers down to able seamen, were frequently to experience annoyance as a result of Winston Churchill's interference in matters of naval strategy, of which he had only a politician's grasp, and the often extravagant demands made from Whitehall were regarded as eccentric or simply beyond capability.

Force H had entered Gibraltar harbour with battle flags flying and all ships already in the anchorage having cleared lower decks to cheer. An Army band played on the jetty. *Sheffield* secured to bow and stern buoys close to the Detached Mole, while *Berwick* was ordered into No. 1 dock for minor repairs. Normal leave was piped; the ship's company had received a month's pay earlier that day, and an unusual number were anxious to get ashore to refight the Spartivento action over pints of black-and-tan or bottled Bass. Ammunitioning would be commencing early during the following forenoon, and the barrels of all 6-inch guns, blistered by a half-hour of continuous firing, were to be red-leaded and repainted.

It was now December, 1940, with the weather in the western Mediterranean squally, wet and chill. Libertymen wore raincoats and boats' crews returned aboard soaked and cold. The motor-boat was blown into the stern wires and damaged, and the second Walrus almost lost when it was dropped some eight feet by the crane when being hoisted. The ensign hung dankly at half mast in honour of *Berwick*'s dead, and the ship refuelled, preparing for sea again. There seemed no end to it.

Sheffield slipped her mooring at 1500 on 5 December to pass westward through the Straits into the Atlantic, subsequently to steer a course of 270 at 25 knots. The ship, Larcom told his company, was to carry out another nine-day patrol of the Azores area – and they groaned. Thankfully, the chaplain had left Paul Robeson and his *Sanders of the River* in Gibraltar, substituted by *The Man in the Iron Mask*, to be screened as and when circumstances permitted, and which, Bungy Williams said, was all about a Maltese canteen manager smuggling thousands of Naafi nutty bars to his relatives in Floriana. Abeam of Cape Spartel, *Sheffield* reduced to 25, then 20 knots at 1915, and the sailors resigned themselves to the steady hum of the ship and the whisper of punkaloolas, supper of corned beef shepherd's pie laced with onions, bread-and-marge and tea.

It was the same story, and it could have been told by the men of dozens of cruisers and auxiliaries, armed merchant cruisers and elderly destroyers that searched ocean wastes hour by hour, day after fatiguing day. Someone had once written that the Navy's role consisted of 'periods of intense monotony alleviated by moments of intense excitement', which was true only if the monotony were known to mean weeks of green and white-shot seas, penetrating cold and vicious rain, indifferent food and consuming tiredness. Any unscheduled event was a welcome distraction, a cause of speculation – such as the sighting of a darkened ship at 0744 on 7 December, identified within minutes as the British freighter *Observer*. Three hours later a floating object was reported dead ahead; it proved to be an abandoned lifeboat with, on its transom, the legend *Klaus Schoke: Hamburg* – a German merchantman which had slipped out of Horta in the Azores a few days earlier, only to be intercepted by a British AMC and promptly scuttled herself. *Sheffield*'s sailors watched the boat as it rose and fell in the long, greasy swell until the cold Canaries Current tugged it away southward and beyond sight. The cruiser continued westward.

Right: Launched to report on the movements of the Italian fleet, *Sheffield*'s Walrus amphibian had her rear cockpit cover torn away and a segment bitten out of her tail by the blast of her own ship's broadside, but continued to shadow the enemy. Later, the aircraft was named 'Spotter of Spartivento'.

Smoke on the horizon during the First Dog watch was found to be that of a dirt-streaked Spanish tanker, *Gobco*, bound for a home port, and she was not delayed.

It was Saturday night, when the sailors recalled, wistfully, the warm and smoke-wreathed Hammersmith Palais or the dark intimacy of the back row of the Odeon; the younger officers might think of that wonderful last evening – *Galetes de Montmartre* at the Prince of Wales or topless girls at the Windmill. Older men, both forward and aft, remembered wives no longer young and with sad faces, armchairs by a fire, children, Radio Luxemburg and the Ovaltinies, home-work, an old dog sleeping on the rug . . .

The midshipmen of the watch made their deck log entries.
Sunday 8 December 1940.
0140: Terceira Light sighted.
0658: Horta and Ribeirino lights sighted.
Noon position: 37°38′N, 26°57′W. Distance steamed: 441.4 miles.

It was an ordinary night – nothing much that Colin Ross could write home about. Marshal Badoglio, said the BBC, had resigned as chief of staff of the Italian Army because of the military disaster in Greece. In *Sheffield*, supper for the forward messes was kidneys on toast, familiarly referred to as 'turds on a raft'.

'There will be no moon tonight,' the Officer of the Watch warned over the ship's address system.

'Then there'd better be two soddin' moons termorrow night,' responded Bungy Williams.

The next day was the same as yesterday, which had been no different from the day before. The United States Lines ship *Artigas* was logged early on the 10th, bound New York from Vigo. On the 11th, Wednesday, nothing

was sighted except the distant, slate-blue islands of São Jorge and Terceira. Before daylight on Thursday *Sheffield* altered course to investigate a darkened vessel which subsequently claimed to be the Greek *Icarion*, bound for Canada. Larcom was not entirely satisfied, however, and the cruiser remained with the merchant ship until 0800, when a whaler was sent away with a boarding party to confirm the other's bona fides.

By the 13th, *Sheffield* was a hundred miles to southward, warned that a German freighter, *Madrid*, of 9,000 tons, had departed Las Palmas two days earlier. At 1000 the cruiser's first Walrus was launched, to return at 1245 after a fruitless air search. The second Walrus was airborne at 1340, recovered at 1550. Nothing had been seen of the German *Madrid* – if she were at sea or, indeed, if she even existed.

In Britain the ration book had become a passport to survival for every man, woman and child of ordinary means, and rations had been steadily reduced in both quantity and quality. Meat was now rationed by price – to 2/2d-worth per ration book, and the cheese allowance fluctuated unpredictably. Eggs, at one per fortnight, had become luxuries, and most other comestibles were tightly controlled. The worst blow was about to fall; tea was to be rationed to two ounces per person per week.

In warships at sea men complained less about the amount of their food (they could in any case supplement their rations with low-priced tinned goods, biscuits, chocolate, etc., from the dry canteen) but of monotonous repetition, indifferent cooking and uninspired presentation. Even the humblest of dishes can be made to *look* attractive, given a little imagination.

RDF Operator Allen remembers.

'A most unpopular meal was Herrings-in – Maconochie's herrings in tomato sauce, served warmed for breakfast. I had known, in my younger days, acute poverty and hunger, but despite this, like most of my companions, I found these no-doubt highly nutritious fish quite unacceptable as breakfast. We therefore had mess competitions to see who could throw most tins through the scuttle without ricochet. One messdeck entrepreneur devised a scheme for taking tins back to Jack Dusty and trading them for jam or margarine, but the Pay Bob soon stepped on that one.

Other unpopular meals in *Sheffield* were 'Oosh' and 'Fuel Oil Duff'. The first was a nauseating, thick and greasy gravy which concealed occasional fragments of doubtful meat together with onion pieces and other floating debris. The more erudite referred to it as 'Potmess'. The other offering, 'Fuel Oil Duff', was basically 'Oosh' but with a thin, rubbery covering of what was presumably a suet pastry, and this deathly white, semi-glazed laminate of throat-clogging stodge tasted exactly like the smell of fuel oil. Some of us named it 'Oosh in a Greatcoat'.

There came the day when a Royal Marine rebelled and took himself to the bridge with a plate of Oosh, cold and congealed by the time he got it up there. He offered it to the Captain, inviting him to "sample a fighting man's dinner" with the spoon he also carried (Oosh was never a knife and fork meal). A few minutes later we heard the familiar click of the broadcast amplifier, and then the Captain's voice. He told us of the Marine's overture, then added that he had given instructions that Oosh would not be served again to the ship's company while he was in command. It wasn't. Mind you, I don't recall seeing the Marine again, after we'd next docked.'

Only one vessel, the Portuguese fishing smack *Alvarea*, was sighted on 14 December, and that day was the last of *Sheffield*'s period of patrol. At 2000 Larcom turned the ship towards Gibraltar and ordered 24 knots.

'D'yer hear there? The ship is expected to secure at 0800 and will begin oiling immediately. There will be no Divisions, but a Church of England service will be held in the chapel at 1000. Roman Catholic and Free Church parties will proceed ashore at 1000. Cruising watch will be maintained throughout the stay in harbour, but normal leave will be granted from 1330 to 2245.'

Gibraltar's peak was wreathed by mist, and Tangier, across the Strait, was lost to sight. A thin rain fell and the Coaling Wharf was deserted. The RFA nudged alongside at 0910, and two weeks' mail, flung aboard by four Marines from *Rooke*, included the first battered Christmas cakes and mince pies from home, handkerchiefs, knitted gloves, Bala-clavas, sweaters and scarves, greetings cards, photographs of the kids at school, and parcels of Devonshire clotted

cream and Manx kippers that were consigned hastily to the waste chute. In the starboard hangar the men hooted the *Man in the Iron Mask* and suggested that even *Sanders of the River* should return; all was forgiven. The Padre protested that *Sheffield* had been promised two Charlie Chans and an Errol Flynn as soon as *Barham* returned them from Alexandria. Failing that, the film library offered *The Arsenal Stadium Mystery* or *Radio Parade of 1935*, which, he said, were both jolly good fun.

AA Guard as previously, the cruiser was again required to provide an armed patrol motor boat and man a watch-post on the Detached Mole as a defensive measure against the midget submarine and two-man chariots which the Italians were known to be developing and which were suspected to be operating from Spanish harbours, including Algeciras. The watch-post, at the northern end of the mole, isolated and exposed to the Atlantic, was armed with a single Lewis gun, while the boat carried one Lewis and one depth-charge. The latter was a full-size pattern embodying an explosive charge of 750lb TNT. Intended to be rolled off the stern of the 30-foot wooden cutter, there was no doubt that, whatever it might do to a submerged enemy, it would certainly destroy those who had dropped it.

Midshipman David Cobb pencilled the next entries of relevance in *Sheffield*'s deck log on Friday 20 December.

0700: Oiler alongside; refuelling completed.

0945: Four destroyers left harbour.

1200: 'No Leave' piped.

1300: Orders received to raise steam; ship secured for sea.

1700: Singled up wires.

1805: Slipped from Coaling Wharf and proceeded out of harbour.

1830: Algeciras Bay. Fleet sequence Renown, Ark Royal, Sheffield, screen of six destroyers.

It was a pig's bastard to be sent to sea only four days before Christmas, and Larcom explained to his ship's company:

'Force H has been ordered to the eastward to rendezvous with *Malaya, Clan Forbes, Clan Fraser* and four destroyers of the Mediterranean Fleet off Galita Island on Sunday – the day after tomorrow. I hope, if all goes well, we shall be back in Gibraltar by Christmas Eve.'

At 2000 Somerville signalled 23 knots, course 080. There would be W/T silence, with all ships at first state of readiness. Clocks would be advanced one hour at 2200.

It was, this time, an uneventful sortie. The rendezvous with big old *Malaya* and the two merchantmen was achieved at 0900 on the 22nd, screened by only three destroyers. The fourth, *Hyperion*, which had destroyed an enemy subma-

---

Right: Vice-Admiral Sir James Somerville – 'Our Jamie' – was a commander who could not tolerate incompetence and never minced words, but he recognized effort and ability; his congratulations were delivered personally, even to junior ratings.

rine earlier in the year, had herself been torpedoed and sunk off Pantelleria during the early hours of that morning. Somerville formed his mixed armada into two columns and, turning them eastward, reduced to a vulnerable 15 knots out of kindness for *Malaya*'s engines, which had not enjoyed a refit since 1934. His intended course ran close to the doubtfully neutral coast of Vichy French Algeria, and when an unidentified floatplane was sighted at 1310, all AA crews closed up. The plane disappeared to southward, and there was no further interference with the ships' progress before Gibraltar was reached.

Normal leave was piped on arrival. There was a dance at the Assembly Rooms, with women overwhelmingly outnumbered by bluejackets. More mail had arrived from the UK, a huge Union Jack flew from the highest point of the Rock. All libertymen were reminded that they should not discuss their ship's activities when ashore, because of eavesdropping enemy agents, but very few men knew very much about what had happened, and nothing whatsoever of anything yet to come, except, according to Bungy Williams, an absolute racing certainty a continued issue of 'Herrings-in or Train Smash fer breakfast, Corned Dog or Dead Baby fer soddin' dinner. If Mussolini's got plenty of spaghetti, we've got all the bleedin' tomato slosh. How's about a meeting off Galita fer a trade-orf?'

On Christmas Day, Wednesday 25th, however, *Sheffield*'s hands were turned out at 0700 for a breakfast of bacon, real fried egg and sausage, bread, real butter and marmalade. Midshipman David Cobb wrote in his diary:

'The ship was cleaned, and lower decks were cleared for Vice-Admiral Somerville, who came aboard to address the ship's company. Having wished us all a Happy Christmas, he told us how pleased he was with the work of Force H. He went on to say that while the war was being fought, we could not expect much rest. We had always to be prepared for unexpected alarms. He reminded us that the sooner the war was finished, the sooner we should get home, and that he thought and hoped we would all be home for next Christmas. Church was held when the Admiral left us, followed by the Boys' Rounds.'

[It has always been customary, on Christmas Day, for the Boys' Division to borrow caps and uniforms from the officers and the Master-at-Arms. The youngest boy in the ship, wearing the Captain's cap and coat and with the musical assistance of the Royal Marine Band, carries out Captain's Rounds.]

'It had been intended that, subsequently, the real Captain Larcom would make his Christmas Rounds at 1100, with all uncommitted officers accompanying him, but just as we were preparing for them, Rounds were cancelled,

Left: Somerville's captains (Larcom, left) were aware that no ship of Force H would ever be misused or left unsupported, which knowledge generated extreme confidence.

and the Captain spoke to the ship's company over the broadcasting system. An important convoy in the Atlantic appeared to have been attacked by a German 8-inch cruiser and *Berwick* had engaged the raider. As the convoy was in our area, Force H had been ordered to raise steam for full speed, and it seemed probable that we would be at sea by the afternoon.'

The alarm had been raised by an attack by *Admiral Hipper* on Convoy WS 5A, of some thirty ships carrying troops and matériel to the Near East. She had been challenged by *Berwick*, still with 'Y' turret inoperative following damage sustained off Spartivento. Now the British cruiser received a direct hit on 'X' turret that killed four Marines and wounded two, but in return she hit *Hipper* abaft the funnel. The arrival of *Bonaventure* to add her fire-power to the exchange persuaded the German to break off the action and run for Brest. The gunnery of the recently commissioned *Bonaventure*, which fired 438 rounds of 5.25-inch shell, was somewhat haphazard, provoking *Berwick* to signal her: 'If you are shooting at me, you have not yet hit.'

By the time Force H, breathing fire, and having steamed 930 miles at high speed in bad weather, reached the scene, there was little to do but assist *Berwick* and *Bonaventure* in rounding up the scattered convoy. *Ark Royal* flew off a search force of nine Swordfish – briefed also to ensure that *Hipper* had not swung around to southward for another tilt at the merchantmen. Frustrated, and robbed of their traditional Christmas Day buffoonery for another year, the ships of Force H turned back for Gibraltar, joined – for the protection of the warships' guns and aircraft – by *Clan MacDonald, Empire Song, Northern Prince, City of Canterbury* and *Essex*.

The earlier heavy pounding had resulted in hull damage to *Renown*; some thirty feet of her internal bulge had been torn or distorted, necessitating a precautionary reduction of speed. After *Ark Royal*'s aircraft had flown low along the length of the battle-cruiser, Somerville called for his Chief Yeoman.

'Ark Royal from Flag Officer Force H: Your boys appear to exhibit a morbid curiosity about the hole in Father's pants. I hope there is nothing sticking out = 1130/25.'

The reply was immediate.

'Flag Officer Force H from Ark Royal: Your 1130. I hope they would be too polite to say so.'

Gibraltar was regained during the early hours of Monday 30 December; all ships of convoy WS 5A had been accounted for, and *Renown*, arriving at 0900, proceeded directly into No. 1 Dry Dock for repair. Normal leave was piped for the non-duty part of watch for that day and the next – the last of 1940.

It was a grey day, gusty and chill, the great Rock darkly sullen above them. There was wetness in the air, and the barometer threatened worsening conditions. Bazaars and bars were still festooned with coloured lights and incongruous cotton-wool snow, but for the comfort-starved men of Force H there was little to do but gaze at shop windows,

huddle into one of the two small cinemas, or drink stupidly. Apart from a handful of Wrens who disdainfully rejected the mildest advance from a rating, there were almost no women other than the pseudo-señoritas from Tangier who demanded payment in advance and watched the clock, or several faded but sincere ladies at the Catholic Community Centre (8.30 p.m. to 10 p.m.) who offered stewed tea and have you been told the wonderful story of the Annunciation?

'So ended an eventful year', wrote Hubert Treseder, 'with no show of confidence, a lot of sea time, not much leave, and 54,000 miles steamed, but Force H is ready to enter 1941 with its tail up. A pattern of life has been established. In harbour, as much sport as possible is organized, and one favourite occupation is to see how quickly one can climb to the top of the Rock. Those with hobbies are producing lovely models – rugs, dolls, felt animals, paintings. The ship has a good concert party, and guest nights in the officers' messes are happy and hilarious occasions. After dinner, one lets off steam with enthusiasm. Finally someone gets down to the piano, and all the old sea songs, mostly bawdy, are sung – as far as a tolerant Commander will allow . . .'

The year that had passed had revealed many myths, such as, in the Navy, the exaggerated effectiveness of Asdic and warship AA gunfire, and, ashore, the belief that ill-equipped British troops with upraised thumbs and comic songs were a match for ruthlessly handled massed tanks and dive-bombers. There were still too many in high places with Great War mentalities, too old or too arrogant to learn new tricks, and there had been a great deal of misdirected activity. The country had been saved from bankruptcy only by the promise of American Lease-Lend.

Still, Britain was fighting, new leaders and new philosophies were emerging; there had been much brilliant improvisation. The British people had closed ranks more firmly than they ever had before. They could not see how they could possibly win this war, but, by God, they were not going to lose it.

In Gibraltar the tethered ships were beginning to strain at their moorings as the wind freshened. The Old Year was not going to depart without a final snarl. *Sheffield*, the Shiny Sheff – or sometimes simply Old Shiny, rose and fell uneasily alongside the Coaling Wharf, nudging the catamarans as an increasing swell pressed in from the Atlantic. The cruiser came to one hour's notice for steam, and during the night the full force of the gale struck. Several of the ships in harbour parted their wires; *Northern Star* broke completely adrift and let go an anchor, but not before she had grounded by the stern. In *Sheffield* four wires parted, and the duty part of the watch was called out in heavy rain to secure new moorings, including hurricane hawsers.

A rating descended to the Seaman PO's bathroom and asked the cleaner, 'Have you any warm water, Townie?' The cleaner replied, 'Sorry, mate – only hot or cold.' The other shrugged. 'Never mind. I'll try the Chief's bathroom.'

9

'Enemy aircraft, fifteen thousand feet and closing'

AMONG the ships of Force H there was an almost incredible faith in the leadership ability of their Admiral – our beloved Jamie. Events would show that faith to be not misplaced, but there were a number of near-run occasions when success and failure were finely balanced. Somerville called a spade a spade, aloud, a propensity that endeared him to his own squadron but frequently caused annoyance in higher circles. He recognized effort and ability, as when, aboard *Sheffield* in Gibraltar, he asked for the eight ratings of the RDF Division to be mustered on the quarterdeck in company with the RDF Officer (Hurley) and their Divisional Officer (the Navigator), the Commander and the Captain. He ignored convention, told the ratings to 'gather around' and, hands in pockets, congratulated them on a

'damn fine performance' in persuading old salt horse sailors like himself that radar had an important role in sea warfare. *Sheffield*'s RDF personnel had probably already saved Force H from destruction, he said, and paused to glare at Commander Searle, who was notoriously unappreciative of RDF. It was almost certainly Somerville's recognition that prompted *Ark Royal*'s Captain to invite the same eight ratings aboard his ship because 'since the carrier owed her continued existence to them, it was only right that they should get to know her better'.

'We were always amused', said Ordinary Seaman Allen, presumably referring to Admiral Somerville and himself, 'by the Italians' practice of attacking out of the sun, for all the usual reasons, not knowing that we had watched them place themselves in just that position. They must have ques-

tioned, in those early days, why they could never achieve the advantage of surprise.'

Operation 'Excess', Somerville had told Larcom, was to be the most important of the 'club runs' so far attempted by Force H in running vital cargoes through the western Mediterranean to rendezvous with Cunningham's ships operating from Alexandria. On the evening of 6 January *Bonaventure* departed Gibraltar with *Clan Cummings*, *Clan MacDonald*, *Empire Song*, *Essex* and a destroyer escort. During the following forenoon *Sheffield* slipped, to join *Renown*, *Malaya*, *Ark Royal* and a destroyer screen in Algeciras Bay. All were aware that German binoculars followed them from both Spanish and Moroccan vantage points, and information on the convoy's departure had already been wired.

Bonaventure and the convoy, however, had first turned westward into the Atlantic on leaving Gibraltar, and the merchant ships' Captains were under the impression that they were bound for the Near East via the Cape. Indeed, they had submitted a concerted complaint that their ships' provisions were inadequate for such a long journey, and replenishment would be necessary somewhere on the route. Doubtless the enemy's agents reported this, too.

During the night *Bonaventure* turned the convoy about, to eastward, and shepherded it through the Straits in darkness and at maximum speed, to join forces with Force H

during the evening of that day. Subsequently, *Ark Royal* intended flying off a squadron of Swordfish to Malta.

Nobody could predict whether or not the subterfuge would succeed, or, if it did, for how long. Neither the Germans nor Italians were fools, and the men from Force H were aware of the reports of several squadrons of German Junkers Ju 87 'Stuka' dive-bombers having been brought down to Sicilian airfields. 'Those of us who had been in the Norwegian campaign', says Treseder, 'were keeping our fingers crossed. The Italians were brave men, their high-level bombing attacks were good, but the German dive-bombers were lethal, their pilots superbly trained. Nobody who has heard the attacking scream of a Stuka will ever forget it.'

During the late afternoon of the 8th *Ark Royal*'s patrol aircraft reported that they had located the convoy from an unusual distance because one of the merchantmen was discharging a monstrous column of black smoke. The offender was *Clan Cummings*. 'She looks as if she's leading the Exodus out of Egypt,' Somerville suggested to his Flag Captain.

Thankfully, evening and night passed without incident as the ships steamed eastward, mid-distant between the Spanish Balearics and the coast of Algeria. Before dawn the squadron altered course into the wind and by 0500 *Ark Royal* was lifting off her aircraft for Malta. Aboard *Sheffield*, following astern of the carrier, the coughing of Bristol Pegasus engines, warming up, was clearly audible; the Swordfish, slow and almost defenceless, had nearly 500 miles to fly over a stretch of sea well within range of the Italian shore-based air force. The British pilots had been briefed to sight Cape Bon light during darkness, pass Pantelleria at dawn, and, by the grace of God and petrol remaining, touch down at Hal Far about one hour later, but it would be a tense period of waiting until Malta's broadcast confirmed that all eight Stringbags had arrived safely.

Somerville's squadron turned back on course to rejoin the merchant ships; *Clan Cumming*'s smoke was sighted at 0820, the ships at 0900. Somerville swore, but at 0940 was relieved to be told that the outriders of the Mediterranean Fleet, the cruisers *Gloucester* (CS2), *Southampton*, and a brood of destroyers had been sighted bearing 084 – on the starboard beam – and forty minutes later *Sheffield*'s two sisters were in company and under Somerville's command.

'Chief Yeoman,' the Admiral ordered. 'Course and speed to all ships, please. Oh-eight-four degrees, fifteen knots. And to *Ark Royal*: Maximum fighter cover is to be provided during the hours of daylight or until otherwise ordered.' He was passing his ships only fifty miles from Italian airfields, and there was no possibility of surviving the day unscathed. It was going to happen.

Left: The battle-cruiser *Renown* and the fleet carrier *Ark Royal* – seen from the starboard quarter of *Sheffield*. These were the three senior components of the fast, hit-and-run squadron, Force H.

'Everyone was scared,'says Allen. 'The only difference was the ability to conceal it. We were at pains to demonstrate lack of concern by facetious comments or jokes about the Eyeties, or yarns about that run ashore in Gib, or that smashing party in Greenock – anything to avoid speculation on what was coming. Everyone talked too much and laughed too readily.'

During the late forenoon *Sheffield*'s RDF fastened on a single aircraft to northwards, as yet unidentifiable. It surely had to be an enemy, probably reconnaissance, and the squadron was alerted. The rum issue, in process of being drawn from the spirit room, was hastily returned, and all hands went to actions stations. Captain Larcom was strolling between compass platform and Hurley's plot, chain-smoking and eyeing the clouds thoughtfully. Flag 'A' streamed from the yardarm and the HA guns were lifting their barrels. Ahead was the white feather of *Ark Royal*'s wake. Her flight-deck teemed with handlers, fuel parties, mechanics and other flight personnel, and aircrew had been piped to man the ranged Fulmars in readiness for take-off. Astern, ponderous *Malaya* ploughed, to beam was *Renown*, and beyond, distant, was *Southampton*, leading the merchantmen. Almost beyond sight, *Gloucester* and *Bonaventure* guarded the squadron's flanks. All flew flag 'A', acknowledging *Sheffield*'s; all were ready.

Hurley reported the approaching enemy at 1320.

'Aircraft bearing two-eight-five, sir. Fifteen thousand feet and closing, estimated speed two-twenty knots. A tight formation – ten, maybe –.'

They were within visual range minutes later – eight Savoia-Machetti bombers flying high, straight, diagonally across the course of the ships below. It needed binoculars to see that they were bigger than Blenheims – the biggest British aircraft in the Mediterranean theatre – and three-engined. *Sheffield* was able to open the action with a 6-inch barrage immediately, but within less than a minute the surprised enemy formation turned into the clouds. It seemed certain that the Italians would work around for an approach from the sun, and *Ark Royal* was launching her Skuas.

The warships' AA guns sniffed at the sky, tracking speculatively as Hurley's operators, double-manned, followed the enemy's movements, while look-outs, flag-deck and bridge, director and fire control teams, gun-crews and magazine personnel waited for the Italians to emerge from cloud cover. They did so at 1352, and *Sheffield*'s HA armament erupted deafeningly. Almost instantly the high-flying enemy planes were surrounded by a rash of black smoke-blotches; it seemed quite impossible that the formation, flying level and straight, could survive the massive barrage thrown up by the two capital ships, a carrier and four cruisers, mounting in total sixty long-range AA guns in addition to scores of lighter weapons. However, at this stage of the war the Navy's system of gun elevation, training and fuze-setting was based on visual estimations and then manually-operated mechanical computers (High Angle Fire Control System) which conceded an error of ± 2 degrees and was resigned to a more usual error of 3 to 4 degrees. Add to this the idiosyncracies of any mechanical or servo apparatus, hand-set shell fuzes transmitted verbally, smoke and weather conditions – and it is now apparent that despite the exceptional ability of gun-crews, who could get away 22 rounds of 4-inch shell per minute, it was incredible that any aircraft were ever hit by warship AA gunfire.

But these Italian Savoia bombers were intent on only one target – the battleship *Malaya*. There was – and would be subsequently – a great deal of British contempt (mostly generated in the tobacco-wreathed haven of Fleet Street's King Lud) for Italian timidity. It was a contempt not shared by Somerville's squadron. Above them eight bombers were in close-knit formation – two had apparently become detached since the earlier sighting – and they were clearly going to concentrate on *Malaya*. The pilots were not going to be distracted by a heavy and accurate AA barrage, and the battleship was completely surrounded and hidden by white bomb eruptions. The other ships watched for a sudden vomit of spume and smoke which would mean a bomb hitting, but *Malaya* emerged from a seascape of white froth and spindrift, majestically steady, to report later that all bombs had fallen just *ahead* of her, and she had steamed through the splashes.

The Italians had turned away, but one of *Ark Royal*'s Fulmars, piloted by Lieutenant-Commander Tillard, had shot two of them into the sea before they had begun their bombing run; Tillard's observer/gunner was Mark Somerville, a nephew of the Admiral. A third Savoia was brought down in flames by the screen's AA fire, ahead of the Fleet, and from this aircraft one surviving crewman was recovered.

The raid had been expensive for the Italians; of ten aircraft, two had never dropped their bombs, three had been destroyed, and no hits had been achieved – but no sailor of Somerville's Force H would ever endorse Fleet Street's shrill jeers at Italian courage, and newspaper correspondents were becoming progressively less welcome in the Navy's wardrooms.

'Up Spirits,' piped the quartermaster.

'And stand fast the "Oly Ghost," ' said Bungy Williams.

That afternoon, at 1500, gun crews were again sent to stations and *Ark Royal*'s Skuas were scrambled to meet a second group of aircraft reported to be 40 miles' distant and closing. The carrier's planes intercepted the high-flying enemy within a few minutes – surprisingly, twelve single-seater biplanes which a senior British pilot later said reminded him of the old Gloster Gauntlet of the early thirties.

But these were Italian Fiat CR42 fighters, similar to those that had recently flown from Belgium towards London, only to be shot to ribbons by the RAF over the Thames estuary. The CR42's wing load was limited to two 220lb bombs, but they were appreciably faster (267mph) than the Skuas (225mph) and could fly 15,000 feet higher.

Unlike the RAF's Spitfires the Navy's honest but plodding fighter-bombers, the Skuas, were unable to come within shooting distance. The nimble Italians danced away, wisely unwilling to force an attack when, obviously, their operation had been compromised. They were only beginning to understand why every approach by aircraft, no matter how devious, irrespective of cloud, time, speed or altitude, was always met by British fighters and then by a blistering AA barrage that had been ready and waiting. The Luftwaffe had already suffered desperately because of a British detection device which must be years ahead of its enemy counterpart.

Gloucester, Southampton, Bonaventure and the convoy parted company at 2200 on that evening of 9 January; Force H turned westward for Gibraltar with all crews at action stations until the following dawn. The base was reached two days later, and *Sheffield* immediately took the oiler *San Claudio* alongside. Ammunitioning began during the afternoon of the following day.

On the 13th the bad news from eastward began to trickle in.

Three days before, the Operation 'Excess' convoy, recently escorted by Force H, had joined forces with Admiral Cunningham's squadron of *Warspite, Valiant, Illustrious* and five destroyers. *Bonaventure* had celebrated her inclusion in the Fleet by engaging two attacking Italian torpedo-boats, sinking one and driving off the other, but that afternoon, still sixty miles west of Malta, the force was attacked by some forty Ju 88 and Ju 87 dive-bombers of Fliegerkorps X. Fulmar fighters from *Illustrious* shot down several of the enemy but could not prevent their carrier being struck by six 1,000lb bombs and *Warspite* by a seventh. The crippled carrier had been assisted as far as Malta by *Gloucester, Southampton* and two destroyers, and then the two cruisers continued their passage eastward.

Neither was equipped with RDF, but considered themselves now beyond the range of the German Ju 87s. They were not. During the afternoon of 11 January, without warning, twelve dive-bombers exploded out of the sun. One 1,102lb bomb sheared into *Gloucester*'s bridge structure, killing nine and wounding fourteen. Two bombs hit *Southampton*, one penetrating to the wardroom, the other exploding in the Petty Officers' mess. Both locations were unusually congested with men who had come below for tea, and the death-roll was horrifying. Moreover, resultant fires could not be controlled. Soon after 1900 *Southampton*'s crew were ordered to abandon ship, and at 2050 the blazing, blackened cruiser was sunk by *Orion*'s torpedoes.

Among *Sheffield*'s company the news was chilling. There, but for the grace of God, they mused, goes Old Shiny. *Southampton* was the first of the 'Town'-class cruisers to be sunk, and that was an event which, in her sisters, exploded the subconscious persuasion that the 'Towns' were, by some peculiar magic, immune from enemy spite. The damage to

Illustrious would keep her out of the war during the whole of 1941, and *Ark Royal*, anticipating a return to the UK for a refit, was ordered to remain with Force H; defects and damage would have to be remedied in Gibraltar's dockyard.

The escort sloop *Folkestone* arrived with *Sheffield*'s first mail since Christmas, and old *Malaya* was eased into No. 1 dock. *Sheffield* was fully ammunitioned and fuelled; it was decided to paint ship, repeating the existing colour scheme of pale grey upperworks and medium grey hull. In *That Certain Age*, Deanna Durbin's trilling filled the darkened starboard hangar for several nights, and the *Gibraltar Chronicle* reported that the Catania air base from which the Luftwaffe had flown to bomb *Illustrious* had twice been attacked by the RAF.

On 15 January a Royal Naval Boxing Tournament was staged in the Alameda Theatre, featuring twelve bouts from Bantam to Light Heavy. For the occasion, leave for Boys was extended to 2300; one of the exchanges involved Boy Morgan versus Boy Duffy at 8 stone 4 pounds. At the evening's end, Vice-Admiral Somerville's speech progressed from his expected congratulation to competitors into an hour of anecdotes and reminiscences delivered in such robust terminology that ratings and officers roared appreciation, while Gibraltarian dignitaries and their ladies eyed the ceiling and sucked their teeth. The *Gibraltar Chronicle* pleaded censorship intervention to justify the failure to print a verbatim report.

Both Walrus aircraft were being hoisted out and then inboard repeatedly for the benefit of the handling parties, and *Ark Royal* had programmed three Swordfish to a period of brief 'experience flights' for midshipmen and junior officers – until one of them force-landed in Algeciras Bay, sinking in seconds but fortunately with no loss of life.

Rumour – the eternal 'buzz' – flared through the messdecks like a dry-grass fire when an ammunition lighter tied alongside, to transfer 500 rounds of 6-inch High Explosive and take off the same quantity of Ordinary. 'The situation's bleedin' grave,' Bungy Williams told two Ordinary Seamen newly arrived from the UK. 'Bleedin' grave.' They nodded.

Force H was, indeed, soon to undertake one of the most audacious operations of the war, but there was first a modest chore. On 27 January, with the light cruiser *Neptune* in company, *Sheffield* was to escort a homeward-bound 7-knot convoy for two days. Among the merchantmen were several Vichy French vessels taken as prizes, and it was feared that an attempt to recover them might be made by French warships out of Casablanca. In the event the convoy's passage was uneventful, and *Sheffield* was back in Gibraltar by noon on the 30th, only to learn that Force H, supplemented by *Malaya*, was under orders to leave harbour on the following day.

Wires were slipped at 1300 on the 31st, and the squadron set course 082 degrees at 16 knots, screened by a mixed bag of destroyers – *Jersey, Jupiter, Duncan, Encounter* and

Isis. With Algeciras Bay fading astern, Larcom spoke to his crew.

The nature of the operation, he said, could not yet be disclosed because bad weather, or some other uncontrollable factor, could mean its postponement to a later date. If this happened, *all personnel* must maintain the strictest silence on return to Gibraltar. The slightest leak of information, the merest hint of action, would not only totally invalidate the operation but make it a death-trap for Force H.

Early on 1 February course was altered to 035 degrees, and at 1450 the Balearics were sighted. Force H turned to 084 degrees, towards Sardinia, but the glass was falling. By first light on the 2nd a half gale was blowing; a heavy sea was making conditions unpleasant for the destroyers and lifting spray over *Ark Royal*'s flight deck, but nine Swordfish, torpedo-armed, lifted off at 0530 and disappeared eastward. Force H reduced to 15 knots, heading north-west. *Sheffield*'s men went down to breakfast haddock and bread-and-marge, but the Forenoon watchkeepers had not closed up when all ships turned into the wind to land-on the returning Swordfish. It was then revealed that a large dam at Tirso, on the Sardinian west coast, had been attacked. Heavy AA fire had been encountered and one Swordfish had been lost. The raid's results could not be observed because of poor visibility.

It was all a little spurious. Somerville, for sure, had not taken a battleship, a battlecruiser, an aircraft carrier, a cruiser and five destroyers into enemy waters just to fuse a few Sardinian lights. Tirso had been the secondary target; the big one – whatever it might be – had been left on ice. Force H turned back towards Gibraltar, all crews exercising action stations with *Jersey* and *Jupiter*, only recently joined from the UK, carrying out a mock night attack. A practice shoot by all ships was carried out on 4 February, but it was all small beer. Gibraltar was regained by evening, and *Sheffield* took an oiler alongside.

During the forenoon of the 6th, it was observed that five destroyers had unobtrusively let go their moorings and, at intervals, slipped past the breakwater. When, at 1430, *Sheffield* was ordered to prepare for departure, men complained that they'd hardly had time to dry their dhobeying. The showing of Charles Laughton in *Jamaica Inn* was postponed, mail was closed, wires were slipped at 1615, and *Sheffield* joined *Renown*, *Malaya* and *Ark Royal* steering westward into the Atlantic at 16 knots.

There had been no intimation, yet, of the squadron's employment, but at 1945, as the dull orange orb of the sun kissed the horizon ahead, *Renown*'s lamp flashed to *Malaya*: 'Proceed in execution of previous orders.' The old battleship turned out of station, wheeled completely about, and settled on an easterly course back into the Mediterranean.

The three remaining warships increased speed to 24 knots, still steering westward, but an hour later *Ark Royal* also parted company, circling around to a reciprocal eastward, which left Somerville's flagship and *Sheffield* still

ploughing westward into the Atlantic. But they had known this trick before. Sooner or later it wasn't going to flannel anyone, and someone was going to get bleedin' shamfered.

At 2100 *Renown* ordered a reversal of course, to eastward, and *Sheffield* took station 3,000 yards ahead of the battlecruiser. 'We are proceeding into the Mediterranean,' Larcom told his ship's company at last, 'to intercept certain Italian merchant ships believed to be at sea. It is quite possible we'll make more than one trip before catching up with them. If, on this occasion, we do not, then you must maintain the utmost silence on the subject when we return to Gibraltar.'

Nobody believed Larcom; nor did Larcom think that anyone did. A few nebulous enemy merchant ships did not justify the repeated deployment of a battleship, a battlecruiser, an aircraft carrier, a cruiser and five destroyers. There was something bigger afoot – something that had already been aborted, a week earlier. *Renown* and *Sheffield* raced through the Straits during darkness; nobody was surprised when, just after midnight, *Ark Royal* joined company and, at 0200 on the 7th, *Malaya* and her brood of destroyers were overtaken and taken under command. To accommodate the old lady, speed was reduced to 18 knots, course 080 degrees. Alboran Island was logged as passed at 0500, and at first light the sea's gentle whisper was shredded by the roar of *Ark Royal*'s first air patrol dragging off her deck.

At 1000 course was altered to 064 degrees, which had the force heading towards the Balearics, and again at 1930 in order to pass between Spanish Ibiza and Majorca. All ships were maintaining strict W/T silence, their operators reading the area broadcast and Fleet Wave, but wireless traffic was routine, and Larcom had made no further statement on the situation. The night passed without incident except for several minor adjustments of course, and by dawn on the 8th the chart showed the force to be north of the Balearics and still heading 050 degrees at 17 knots. Something, surely, must happen soon.

Something did, but it was an anticlimax. The five destroyers that had slipped stealthily from Gibraltar during the forenoon of two days before were sighted at 0830 and joined company. Speed was reduced to 17 knots on 050 degrees. *Renown*, *Malaya* and *Sheffield* streamed paravanes, all crews assumed first state of readiness, and Larcom said nothing.

When, at 1900, the force increased speed to 21 knots, still steaming 050 degrees, and then – just before midnight – a fix was obtained from Porquerolle light on the French Coast, speculation ran riot in both wardroom and gunroom. Force H was in tiger country. Nice and Monte Carlo were just over there, and Somerville was steaming them directly towards the Gulf of Genoa!

Johnny Groves, one of the Walrus pilots, was aware that, for several weeks, spotting aircrew sworn to secrecy had rehearsed observations on a model of Genoa in Somerville's flagship, but during the night of the 8th he (Groves) could not believe that a bombardment was imminent because he was required to keep the First watch on *Sheffield*'s compass platform. 'It was only later', he said, 'that I vaguely recalled that officer aircrew were not excused ship's duties prior to a bombardment; only four hours' rest was considered necessary between watchkeeping and flying. We came off watch at midnight and were not expected to fly-off until 0500. I didn't even get four hours; the Chaplain hammered on my cabin door during the Middle watch to ask if there were any messages he could send to my mother if I did not return!'

Below decks the air was stale and warm; all deadlights were clamped shut and messdeck refuse-buckets reeked, but, above, the night had been clear, with visibility daylight-clear under a bright moon. These were superb conditions for the enemy's destroyers or MTBs, but the Italian Navy seemed to be slumbering. At 0400 *Ark Royal* parted company, taking with her three destroyers, and Force H went to action stations. *Renown*'s masked lamps ordered, 'Course 024. Execute.'

A swollen-eyed Johnny Groves pulled on his overalls. 'We had an excellent "last breakfast" of Lancashire Hotpot from the ship's company galley, and flew off before first light. The Bristol Pegasus VI engine – the "flying gas-ring" – was the only light in a darkened *Sheffield*.'

By now the mountains eastward of Genoa were becoming visible through a light dawn haze. Hammocks were hastily lashed; it was difficult to remain indifferently cocooned when, in enemy waters, bombardment aircraft were being catapulted.

At 0645 a fix was obtained from Portofino Point, only twenty miles eastward of Genoa.

It was Sunday morning. Colin Ross, in 'A' turret, recalls that during the night a messenger had brought him a sealed envelope marked *Not to be opened until ordered*. 'At about 0530 we were told to open our envelopes, and I read, "Prepare to bombard." A few minutes later the Captain spoke to us.'

'In a few minutes' time', Larcom told *Sheffield*'s company, 'we – with *Renown* and *Malaya* – will open fire on Genoa. The Admiral hopes that, between us, we shall put five hundred high-explosive shells into the port, concentrating on the important Ansaldo ship-yards and electrical works, and also on the docks area . . .'

Somerville turned his ships to 290 degrees and reduced speed to 18 knots, with *Sheffield*, having flown off her second aircraft, steaming 15 cables ahead of *Renown* and with *Malaya* following last in line. Dawn was just beginning to break. A grey mist hid the immediate coastline, but, above and beyond, the Appenines were clearly visible against a sky turning to pearl. There was a crackle of light

Below: *Sheffield*, ahead of *Renown* and *Malaya*, turns her guns on unsuspecting Genoa. For thirty minutes hundreds of 15in and 6in projectiles would smash into the docks, moored ships, marshalling yards and factories of the Italian port.

AA fire as the spotting aircraft circled over the city, but the approaching ships, now only ten miles distant, had still not been observed. 'One doesn't feel one's bravest at 5.30 in the morning,' Ross wrote, 'but I poked my head out of my lid to clean my periscope, just as it was getting light – a rather cold, damp morning – had a final look around the turret, and then we all settled down to wait for the show to start.'

At 0715 *Renown* hoisted flag '5' and opened fire with a salvo of 15-inch shells, followed seconds later by *Sheffield* and *Malaya*. It had been planned that if any Italian battleships had been spotted in the port, these would first be engaged by all three bombarding vessels. No major enemy warships, however, could be seen, so *Malaya* concentrated her fire on the docks area to the east of the city, where there was a large basin with wharves, jetties and two naval dry docks. *Renown* and *Sheffield* turned their guns on the industrial area to the eastward, in which was the vast Ansaldo ship-building and armament complex, electrical and boiler works, a huge marshalling yard, a rail junction and a number of other important factories. Johnny Groves was flying at 10,000 feet, just off shore.

'It was at least twenty minutes before the Italian shore defences realized what was happening. At first they thought they were being bombed, and a heavy AA barrage was thrown up, immediately overhead, leaving the spotting aircraft unmolested. The shore batteries' long-delayed reply to the bombarding ships was pathetic, and must have caused far more alarm and despondency aboard two Italian coastal freighters which were steering peacefully down the coast, midway between the shore and the bombarding squadron. One moment they were plodding serenely on their way – and you could almost imagine their Sunday morning breakfast of spaghetti simmering gently in their respective galleys – and the next moment they were zigzagging frantically in all directions.'

And two days later Captain Larcom would write to his family:

'It was grand. Incidentally, greatly bucked up James's shares . . . It was a perfect party, in which everything went right down to the last detail. We made the Italian coast in mist at 6.50 a.m. on the Sunday morning, picking up Rapallo, and then through the mist we stood along the coast for 10 miles or so, and there was Genoa wrapped up in mist. Surprise was complete. Not a destroyer, trawler, E-boat or aircraft was about, and the first that the town knew was the crump of our first salvoes . . . Sunday morning, just as the devout were on their way to Mass; I could not help thinking of it that way . . . *Sheffield* gave them 782 high-explosive shell in area about the size of, say, Gosport . . .'

Perhaps the integrity of both British and Italian versions of the bombardment's effectiveness can be regarded with caution. The neutral New York Daily News, however, subsequently printed the communiqué of its own correspondent, Hal Lehrman, writing from Italy, which, in

the newspaper's words, 'dodging the Fascist censorship, reached the News with the *true* story of what the battleship *Malaya*, the battle-cruiser *Renown*, the cruiser *Sheffield*, a flotilla of light warships and planes from the aircraft carrier *Ark Royal* did to Genoa in 30 minutes on February 9'.

'When the giant guns of a British naval squadron opened up on Genoa they ravaged miles of that vital Italian port's waterfront, sank or crippled at least 28 commercial vessels, burned down scores of harbour installations, and fomented a near-insurrection among the Genoese against Mussolini and the war.

At first everyone thought this was an extra heavy air raid, but no alarm was sounded. It didn't matter, because Genoa's bomb shelters are too few and skimpy to be of any protection. Then, as huge flames began shooting into the growing light and clouds of smoke poured over from the docks, the Genoese made out the sinister boom of the enemy guns offshore.

Their immediate reaction was amazement followed by humiliation and rage. How could our navy allow this? they wanted to know, when the British had retired without a hit scored by the coastal defences. By 8 a.m. the throngs jammed the narrow streets leading to the port – roped off by Fascist guards to keep them from seeing the devastation. The newspapers were hours late, but with not a line about the bombardment. Only next morning was there a communiqué, which insisted that nothing of military value had been hit. All the destruction was civilian, it was officially asserted; 72 non-combatants had been killed and 226 wounded.

[These figures were substantially correct. A few stray shells had smashed half a business building in the fashionable Via Venti Settembre and demolished a half-dozen houses in the populous Lower Town.]

For two days the populace was kept completely uninformed of the real destruction. On the third a Commerce Ministry commission arrived, the Maritime Prefect was discharged, and the naval commander of the Portofino district, allegedly having been caught by surprise, was arrested. The city magistrates issued an appeal for calm, the Cardinal Archbishop called for Genoese charity for the homeless and orphaned, and in due course a commemorative tablet for the victims was ordered to be installed in the principal square, the Piazza Deferrari.

Italy's two major insurance companies, the Assicurazione Generale and the Riunione Adriatica, announced that the bombardment was not covered by ordinary fire policies. They refused to meet the huge damage claims until ordered to do so by the Government. The damage, in fact, was enormous. Four ships were sunk in the port's cargo area. Their masts are still sticking up. We could count sixteen others smashed or listing. The big liners in the passenger port, among them the *Rex*, were intact, but all the warehouses between the industrial suburb of San Pietro d'Arena and the principal Ponte dei Mille had burned like matchwood. Many hundreds of yards of buildings along

Above: 'It was grand,' wrote Larcom later. 'It was a perfect party. *Sheffield* alone gave them 782 high-explosive shells . . .'

Right: With Genoa devastated, and La Spezia, Livorno and Pisa bombed, it was time to run. Somerville signals, 'You know where home is. Get going.' *Sheffield* pounds after *Ark Royal* and *Renown*.

the water front are completely burned down – the grain silos of Fratelli Pozzani, the warehouses of Gondrand, of the State Railways, of the Lloyds Sabaudo, the dry dock, the launching slipways of the Odero Company, the nine grey buildings of the Capitaneria del Porto, each 100 yards long, are no more. The Coal Port is entirely smashed.'

Several weeks would elapse, however, before Lehrman's story reached New York, and he knew nothing of events aboard the British ships. *Sheffield* was firing rapid broadsides, but, records Midshipman David Cobb, 'The HE shells we were using had very sensitive fuses, and the projectiles from the centre guns of our turrets were frequently being exploded, at the muzzle, by the blast of the two outer guns. These premature bursts were not only wasteful but could also be very dangerous to our destroyers on the engaged side. After fourteen broadsides, during which there were nine premature bursts, *Sheffield* shifted to salvo-firing, and we continued firing salvoes for the remainder of the bombardment.'

The low-lying mist that had earlier been so valuable was now obscuring the target, although, as Larcom would comment, 'You can't miss a haystack; we plugged shell after shell into the town and docks.' At 0740 *Sheffield*, as an amusing aside, poured her fire into an Italian oil tanker, helplessly tethered and becoming rapidly obscured by the smoke-screen now being vomited by the Force H destroy-

ers. *Renown* was flying flag '6' – Cease Fire – and two small Italian fishing craft that chuttered frantically to starboard were left untouched.

Somerville broke off the action at 0745 and the British ships turned away in succession to 270 degrees at 22 knots. 'It sounds incredible,' Colin Ross marvelled, 'but (the Italians) had nothing there – no destroyers on patrol, not even a drifter, not even a motor-boat! If their shore batteries opened fire, well, certainly nobody noticed it.'

An hour later *Ark Royal* was sighted approaching from eastward. While Somerville had been bombarding Genoa, the carrier's Swordfish had attacked targets at La Spezia, Livorno and Pisa, concentrating on the railway yards, factories, an oil refinery at Livorno, the airfield at Pisa, and had laid magnetic mines at the entrance to La Spezia harbour. In total, some five tons of bombs had been dropped. Now it was time for Force H to show a clean pair of heels, and Somerville signalled: 'You know where home is. Get going.'

The British force was by no means out of the wood; there were still a thousand miles to steam before the questionable safety of Gibraltar was reached; the Italians had sufficient air and sea forces available to destroy Force H. At 1030 RDF reported a group of aircraft to northward, apparently heading – too late – towards Genoa, and a second group at 1100. Two Cant Alcione bombers approached

Left: Never a dull moment for Observer Charles Fenwick. Force H's withdrawal is too rapid for a lift-on recovery. This spotting Walrus must make a first time landing on *Ark Royal* and subsequently take off for Gibraltar. 'I've never done a deck landing before,' Pilot Johnnie Groves confesses to Fenwick, who responds, 'Now he tells me.'

Left: The blistered barrels of 'X' turret after the action. *Sheffield* had fired 782 6in shells in thirty minutes.

Right: Regaining Gibraltar after the bombardment of Genoa, Force H is greeted by cheering base staff, ships' crews and garrison troops, even a pipe band – but not inspired entirely by admiration. Gibraltar's bars had halted the sale of beer, in short supply, until the squadron's return.

belligerently, but a blistering barrage persuaded them to drop their bombs almost a mile from *Ark Royal* and then run for shore. (Radio Rome subsequently described this incident as a 'well pressed home attack in which HMS *Sheffield* was hit and later sunk'.)

In fact, Force H was blissfully ignorant that, at 1430, in deteriorating visibility, an Italian force of three battleships, three heavy cruisers and seven destroyers, under Admiral Angelo Iachino, had passed only thirty miles northward, breathing vengeful fire. Fortunately the Italians were misdirected into intercepting a convoy of seven French merchant ships that Force H has also sighted, and ignored, three hours earlier. An Italian reconnaissance seaplane was shot down by one of *Ark Royal*'s Fulmars, and, at dusk, course was altered to 232 degrees, speed reduced to 17 knots for the benefit of *Malaya*, who was breathing hard.

Meanwhile, *Sheffield*'s spotting Walrus aircraft was still in the air. 'We had been instructed', says Johnny Groves, 'that the ship would be unable to slow sufficiently to recover aircraft after the operation; we were thus to make either for Corsica and internment or, if possible, locate *Ark Royal* (whose aircraft were carrying out a diversionary raid on Livorno) and land on her.

The prospects of internment were not appealing, and Fenwick, observer and commander, decided that sitting beside Groves on his first ever deck landing (I had gone

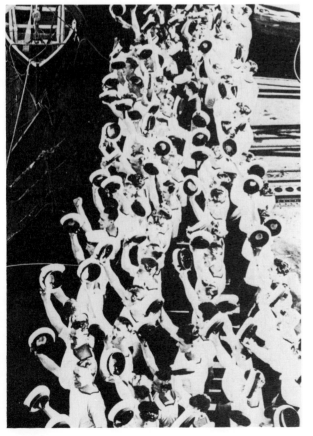

on to seaplanes without ever doing a deck landing) was the lesser of two evils. So we duly located *Ark Royal* – as also did Ewing and House in the other Walrus – and I had the satisfaction of performing my first deck landing in the old girl, finding it, in fact, considerably more relaxing than landing on a slick sea in bad weather. While on passage back to Gibraltar, Fenwick and I enjoyed listening to William Joyce – Lord Haw-Haw – telling us repeatedly that *Ark Royal* had been sunk.'

Following the bombardment, *Sheffield*'s guns were blistered and too hot to touch. Chief Stoker Tom Bolton recalls being on the quarterdeck when the Captain of Marines drew his attention to a seagull *actually marking time* on a gun barrel. 'And that', Bolton swears, 'is no sailor's yarn!;

The cruiser, with her silk battle flags still flying, secured at her usual berth at 1430 on 11 February. All ships in Gibraltar had cleared lower decks, troops cheered from both sides of the harbour, and the Black Watch had launched two boats filled with pipers. 'No wonder they were glad to see us back,' said Ordinary Seaman Allen. 'All the cafés ashore had withdrawn beer from sale [in short supply and 2/6d a bottle] until Force H returned for its share.'

Winston Churchill had already told the nation, 'Our Western Mediterranean Fleet entered the Gulf of Genoa and bombarded in a shattering manner the naval base from which a German Nazi expedition might sail to attack General Weygand in Algeria or Tunisia . . .' It was heady stuff, and the first time the ships of Force H had been named – although the sailors were slightly puzzled by the reference to General Weygand, commander of the Vichy French colonies in Africa. The Prime Minister also signalled Somerville: 'I congratulate you on the success of the enterprise against Genoa –,' but added churlishly, '– which I was glad to see you proposed yourself.'

But the war in the Mediterranean was about to increase momentum, the battle for Malta become more savage. The Luftwaffe was already flying from Italian airfields, and on 12 February, as *Sheffield* replenished her magazine, refuelled and provisioned alongside a Gibraltar jetty, and her off-duty watch anticipated leave from 1630, the Afrika Korps was being landed in Libya and General Erwin Rommel had arrived in Tripoli to assume command. During the early afternoon *Sheffield* was ordered to raise steam; all magazines were replenished by 1630. Just as libertymen were preparing to fall in, leave was cancelled. Mail would close in twenty minutes. Tombola was cancelled. Once again, the Chaplain's confirmation class was postponed, as also was the vaccination party for *Rooke*. It was bleedin' diabolical, stormed Bungy Williams, who regarded both confirmation and vaccination sessions as legitimate opportunities for being somewhere else when there was paint-scraping.

And worse. The double film showing in the starboard hangar – Charles Laughton in *Jamaica Inn* and Ginger Rogers in *Primrose Path* was postponed.

10

'Shove off and take your nasty friends with you!'

THE raiding enemy heavy cruiser *Hipper* had intercepted an unescorted convoy, SLS 54, north-east of the Azores, sunk seven ships and scattered the remainder, but, by the time Force H reached the area, the marauder had fled for Brest to refuel. *Sheffield* was back in Gibraltar on the 17th, leaving *Renown* and *Ark Royal* at sea in a north-easterly gale. If there was any messdeck gloating, however, it was quickly frozen. The ship was to slip again at 0900 on the morrow.

In a letter, Colin Ross wrote: 'This really is a grand force to belong to. We call ourselves "The Club", and there is the most wonderful team spirit, which one seldom gets in a squadron – although frequently in a ship. I doubt if you can realize what a difference it makes when people don't curse the Flagship, and are even tolerant of the next ahead. It's odd how one's next ahead is always worse at station keeping than anyone else in the Navy. It's a recognized fact, but there's no ill feeling about it with us; we just blame the design of the ships. *Malaya*, for instance, is quite, quite round, and the *Ark* looks more like a haystack every day . . .'

A passage of 840 miles brought *Sheffield* to 31°24′N, 22°25′W, within the triangle formed by the Azores, Madeira and the Canaries, and smoke was sighted at 1100 on 20 February. In this position it should be the convoy, and, thank God, it was – but a slow-plodding, unwieldy collection of sixty vessels, from Freetown, many of which had been reprieved from the scrapyard only by the war's demands. All were between 4,000 and 7,000 tons, British, Norwegian, Danish, French and Greek – battered, smoking, rusting, and wallowing northward at 7½ knots. These were the dead-beats, the geriatrics of the sea, but eleven of them were tankers and the others were loaded to capacity with food and war materials. They carried a total of more than 360,000 tons that the UK desperately needed. Two convoy Commodores, in the freighters *Deido* and *John Holt*, were supported by the modern cruiser *Kenya* and a seasoned AMC, *Bulolo*, but no anti-submarine escort. Incredibly, the ships were not yet regarded as being vulnerable to submarine attack, and so were not zigzagging, partly because most mercantile skippers considered the procedure to be unnecessarily laborious, but also because zigzagging sixty old merchant ships, in unison, was an undertaking

hardly less hazardous than taking on the U-boats.

Relieved, *Kenya* turned away north-eastward, for Gibraltar; *Sheffield* took station ahead of the convoy and commenced zigzagging 50 degrees either side of the mean course at 14 knots. At dusk the cruiser dropped astern of the convoy, reducing to 10 knots. On the 23rd the long lines of ships were herded between the Azores islands of São Miguel and Fayal, and two more merchantmen joined from Ponta Delgada. The glass was falling steadily and visibility was deteriorating, which, it was hoped, would make matters difficult for U-boats, but also meant that the rag-bag convoy was becoming progressively less manageable. Every alteration of course was a nightmarish procedure, signalled by flags to which attention had to be drawn by siren blasts. Neither warships nor merchant ships had yet been equipped with TBS VHF voice radio which, later, would make convoy control so much simpler. In February 1941 a shepherding warship had to rely on bunting, signal lamps, shaken fists and shouted oaths.

The sky was blackening. By the morning of the 27th, after a lashing thunderstorm, a full gale was blowing, and *Sheffield* was unable to overtake the convoy before 0900. The Norwegian tanker *Morgenen* had already been defeated by the sea and had turned eastward to run before the weather. *Sheffield* passed her at 0820; she plunged helplessly, her low-slung waist hidden by heaving water. Another ship had lost her rudder, three others had become detached, but fifty-three old hulls, smoking and leaking from every seam, still clung together, pitching and rolling, making 6 knots against a Force 10 gale on a course of 290 degrees.

The spray was so whipped up, said *Sheffield*'s Officer of the Watch, that it was like smoke, reducing visibility to about two cables. 'It was an extraordinary sight, everything white; you could hardly see any colour in the sea at all – just spindrift and foam.' The barometer rose 20 millibars in a few minutes, the sharpest change ever seen at the lowest point. Several men felt the change of pressure in their ears.

By 0800 on 1 March the convoy, still butting into an easing north-westerly at 6 knots, had reached 50 degrees North, some 800 miles west of Land's End. *Sheffield*'s responsibilities were now ended, and she turned away as the merchantmen continued northward. In three or four days they would be docking in Liverpool and the Clyde, their crews hurrying for their homes or seeking dockside pubs and brothels. Substantially better paid, particularly in wartime, than their Naval counterparts, many freighter sailors took to sea only the barest minimum of necessaries – a single change of underclothes and a razor. If torpedoed, they lost little. *Sheffield*'s men watched SLS 65 wallow determinedly towards England; the cruiser assumed course 145 degrees, speed 18 knots, for Gibraltar. Larcom stood down one watch to cope with messdeck shambles, and pumping began. Old Shiny, the shipwrights reported, was making water.

Cape St. Vincent, distant, was sighted during the Morning watch of 4 March, and at 0900 Captain Larcom ordered a full-power trial. Progressively, *Sheffield* worked up to 31 knots, but could do no more. To many of the crew (in this eighteenth month of the war, three of ten were now Hostilities-only ratings) who had never known full speed, the experience was exhilarating, but Larcom and his engine-room personnel were less than enthusiastic. *Sheffield*'s hull was thickly encrusted with barnacles and leaking; her Asdic dome was already waterlogged and useless. Her engines, long overdue for dockyard attention, had to be nursed, and the rudder collar was badly strained.

'D'yer hear there? The ship is expected to arrive Gibraltar at 1800 on Tuesday and be warped immediately into No. 1 dock for bottom scraping and repair. Leave will be granted to one watch from 1830 to 2215. The ship will be docked for four days but will remain at eight hours' notice for steam.'

The cruiser was still endocked on 8 March when, at 1830, the recall was hoisted for the libertymen of *Renown*, *Ark Royal* and *Arethusa*, patrols scoured the bars and warnings were flashed from cinema screens. The three ships left harbour at 2100, heading at speed for the Cape Verde Islands, in the vicinity of which *Malaya*, escorting an east-bound convoy, had reported contact with *Scharnhorst* and *Gneisenau*. The German commander, Admiral Günther Lütjens, might have lured the old slow battleship away with one of his ships while attacking the convoy with the other, but his orders forbade any risks; *Malaya*'s guns were formidable and, in any case, the alarm had been raised. Lütjens made for the safety of the French coast, and Somerville's search force, again frustrated, regained Gibraltar on the 10th.

On the following day, her bottom scraped and painted, the Asdic dome replaced, several seams re-riveted, the rudder repaired and hawsers, wires and cables overhauled, *Sheffield* was eased out of the dry dock, and Larcom reported her ready in all respects for sea. *Renown*'s sister *Repulse* had that morning entered harbour, accompanied by the trooping P&O liner *Strathmore* and the carrier *Furious*, which landed an infantry battalion for the Rock and a number of drafts for Force H. The new men for *Sheffield* had barely piled their bags and hammocks amidships and presented their draft note to the Regulating Office when Gibraltar's guns opened fire at an aircraft over Algeciras

Bay and the ship's AA guns were manned. The alarm passed, but there was to be more disconcertment for the newcomers from the UK. *Sheffield* secured for sea at 1830 and all boats were hoisted inboard. Wires were singled up at 1920. The cruiser slipped four minutes later and passed the breakwater at 1932 followed by *Arethusa*, *Strathmore* and three destroyers. The draft from RNB Chatham, who had spent the past two weeks confined to the draughty hangar of *Furious* on passage to Gibraltar, listened, bewildered, as Captain Larcom addressed his crew.

'We have orders to escort *Strathmore* to the Clyde, but also to return to Gibraltar almost immediately with the depot ship *Maidstone* – so you will understand that, at best, there can be only local shore leave in Greenock to each watch, perhaps not even that. Today is the 11th; we must be back in Gibraltar and ready to resume operations before the end of the month.'

'Of course', Bungy Williams told the pallid Ordinary Seaman with the barracks haircut, 'yer can get a Greenock-ter-Gibraltar season ticket.' He sniffed. 'Have yer drawn yer tickler issue yet, Townie? I'm gettin' a bit short.'

The three destroyers were ordered back to Gibraltar late on the 12th, and *Sheffield* took station five miles ahead of *Strathmore*, speed 18½ knots. A Vichy French merchant vessel, *Thisbé*, escorted by a destroyer, was sighted but allowed to proceed, and apart from a stiff wind which provoked an uncomfortable swell, the passage was unusually free of incident until 0334 on the 15th, when *Arethusa* was detached to investigate a darkened ship. The light cruiser subsequently signalled that the intercept was a straggling member of a UK-bound convoy, known to be in the vicinity. There was, however, an interesting item of news. On the previous day the convoy's escort sloop had sighted two armed trawlers incongruously flying Norwegian colours, and which, on being approached, quickly scuttled. The crews of both, taken aboard, had been found to be German.

It was reasonable to assume that the convoy's position and course had been reported by the trawlers. Larcom decided to leave *Arethusa* as additional protection for the convoy while *Sheffield* and *Strathmore* pushed on to rendezvous with four destroyers already deployed from Falmouth as anti-submarine escorts.

In deteriorating visibility and a rising sea the first was sighted at 1700. She was *Legion*, a single-funnelled, modern destroyer of almost 2,000 tons, with eight 4-inch guns in four fully-enclosed turrets and eight torpedo tubes – a superb product of Hawthorn Leslie's yard, plunging and climbing, shrugging off green water from her forecastle as she closed on *Sheffield* like a spirited hound and ready for anything. Two more of the A/S escort were met within the hour – but these were four-stacker veterans already retired by the United States Navy – HMSS *Burwell* (ex-USS *Laub*) and *Broadwater* (ex-USS *Mason*). They were the first of Roosevelt's lease-lend ships that *Sheffield*'s men had seen, and they sucked their teeth, not wanting to be unkind towards these old-timers that were plugging the Royal

Above: *Sheffield*'s Warrant Officers' mess during 1941, with members, pin-ups and midday gins. Shipwright A. E. Pack, later to be critically responsible for limiting action damage, is seated sixth from left.

Navy's critical shortage of escort vessels. Beggars weren't choosey.

Assuming their stations, the liner with her escort of one cruiser and three destroyers turned to 068 degrees and increased to 20 knots. England in springtime was only two days away. The trees would be greening and daffodils and narcissi were stippling the lawns and parklands from Plymouth to Aberdeen; children would be two inches taller.

One destroyer, *Ripley* (ex-USS *Shubrick*) had not achieved the rendezvous – but that was war.

On approaching the Irish coast Larcom had ordered paravanes to be streamed but, despite the poor visibility, 20 knots were being maintained with *Strathmore* keeping pace; the ships' estimated time of arrival of 1300, coupled with a request for berth off Greenock, had already been passed to CinC, Western Approaches.

Just before 0500 on the morning of Monday 17 the Marine bugler tongued his lips and watched the clock's minute-hand climb to vertical; Telegraphists reading broadcast BN wrote *Quiet. Gear Correct*, on their logs. On the flag-deck Signalmen shrugged themselves into their duffle coats – it was a soddin' cold morning; the duty Petty Officer Cook switched on the oil heaters that were about to shrivel nine hundred paper-thin rashers of bacon and transform sixty pounds of dampened powdered egg into sixty pounds of *warm* dampened powdered egg; the Chaplain dragged

himself from his bunk, questioning if yet another 6.30 a.m. Watchkeepers' Service performed for nobody was really worth his gastric turmoil and thinning hair. Perhaps he should have remained with St. Barnabas in Godalming. Several cats in widely separated locations climbed out and stretched, thinking of their watered Nestlés, bacon scraps and a licking of egg. The Officer of the Watch turned to the midshipman. 'Snot – slope down to the galley for a bucket of coffee, will you? And I mean coffee, not bloody kye . . .'

It was 0552. From under the starboard side there was a sudden, momentary flare of dull red followed by a sharp explosion which shuddered every forward messdeck and flickered the lights on the main deck. Ominously, *Sheffield* hesitated, as if she had been kicked. 'Stop both,' Larcom ordered immediately. He had reached the compass platform only seconds before. 'Sound the Still.'

Slowing as her engines died, the cruiser rolled gently. *Legion*, who had earlier pulled out of the screen to investigate an Asdic contact, was now closing fast. Nobody seemed to know what had happened; Damage Control HQ could give the bridge no information except that the forward lower damage control party was investigating. Captain Larcom ordered all hands to quarters.

'The forward party began to investigate', recorded Shipwright Lieutenant A. E. Pack, 'and when we reached the lower store, just above the port bilges, a second explosion occurred. I have never seen two men move up ladders more quickly. All relevant watertight hatches were secured – but the mystery remained.'

It was now 0620. *Sheffield* was stopped, wallowing. There was a strong smell of explosives throughout the forward flats and passageways, and a number of lights were extinguished. Consensus of opinion had it that the cruiser had struck two mines, an opinion reinforced by the discovery of several metal fragments on the hangar deck, but the absence of any obvious damage was puzzling. Larcom decided to restart engines and, cautiously, resume passage.

'Orl these explosions', said Bungy Williams, 'is getting bleedin' monotonous.'

Paravanes were taken in before arrival at Greenock. The cutters of each were found to have snared plaited copper wire, identified as antennae of British anti-submarine mines.

'On berthing,' reported Pack, 'a more detailed inspection of compartments was carried out. The large oil fuel tanks A1 and A2 were opened up and it was found that oil was being contaminated by sea water. The explosion initiated by the port paravane had caused an inward bulge of the ship's side and framing over the whole of the twenty-foot length of the A1 tank. Water was seeping in through shaken rivets.'

It was estimated that the damage had reduced *Sheffield*'s steaming endurances by two days, and her hull was undoubtedly weakened. Under normal circumstances docking would have been considered imperative, but these were the days when British fortunes hung on a hair. Every man, gun and ship was vitally of value; if a warship could float, she could fight.

'Repairs', sighs Pack, 'were not considered urgent as the damage did not impair the seagoing and fighting ability of the ship, but the damage did affect the supply of fuel from the tanks, with water leaking in. The problem was to some extent overcome by the ship's engine-room staff removing the lower end of the suction pump, allowing water to remain in the bottom of the tank, while the pumps picked up only oil fuel.' This was only improvisation, but, continues Pack, 'Subsequent dockyards would not undertake full repairs of this damage because it entailed removing the forward armoured plating. Gibraltar's dockyard carried out temporary repairs by cutting out distorted frames and rivets and fitting new pieces of framing shaped to the large bulge in *Sheffield*'s plating – but I have often wondered if that damage was ever properly repaired with a new plate!'

Dunoon boom was passed at 1315 on 17 March and the ship berthed with eight shackles on the port anchor. The Clyde was crowded with vessels; the battleship *Revenge*, the cruisers *Suffolk*, *Hermione*, *Dido* and *Cardiff*, the old

carrier *Argus*, depot ships *Maidstone* and *Hekla*, destroyers, AMCs and auxiliaries of all types. Shore leave to the off-duty watch was granted to 2230 with the warning that there was yet no information on the length of *Sheffield*'s stay, so the ship must be assumed to be under sailing orders. Mail, presumably, was still being routed to Gibraltar, but a Naafi lighter nudged alongside and another from Saccone & Speed, to transfer duty-free spirits and cigarettes, Lifebuoy and Wright's Coal Tar toilet soap, war quality chocolate and Horlicks, Brylcreem and OK Sauce. The BBC was talking cautiously of British successes against the Italians in Somaliland and Ethiopia – cautiously because earlier euphoria over the campaigns in Norway and France had proved embarrassingly premature. Returning libertymen who had not made a crazed dash for homes in the Glasgow area or sat drinking determinedly in the first pub outside the dockyard gate had rejected Shirley Temple's *The Blue Bird*, preferring *Dr. 'X'*, featuring Humphrey Bogart. It would now be fashionable to threaten (from the side of the mouth) a graveyard in the East River (twitching an upper lip) if the bread, or sugar-and-tea issue had been forgotten, or nobody had peeled the mess's potatoes.

If *Sheffield*'s brief passage to the Clyde had been regarded as a few days of respite, then it was mistakenly so. On a foreign station, with no expectation of home leave during the foreseeable future, a sailor became progressively more resigned and his nostalgia blunted, but to be anchored in a UK port, to tread UK streets, yet be forbidden to travel beyond the city's precincts, was to open old wounds of home-sickness. Better by far, most would have agreed, if the ship had not come. The announcement that *Sheffield* would sail at 1800 on 19 March was greeted almost with relief, but then the orders were cancelled; heavy fog had reduced visibility to less than a quarter mile. A frustrating two days would pass before the anchor was lifted from the dirty river, and a further eight before the ship came alongside her old berth, the Coaling Wharf in Gibraltar harbour. A wind was rising, and the palm trees that fringed the air strip were swaying on their slender stems. *Sheffield* secured at 1600 on Saturday 29 March.

'D'yer hear here? All shore leave is cancelled. The ship is under sailing orders and is expected to slip and proceed to sea before nightfall.'

The lines were thrown off their bollards at 2200 and *Sheffield*, nosing past the breakwater, joined the destroyers *Fury*, *Fearless*, *Fortune* and *Forester* steaming eastward at 27 knots, which was faster than was wise in the conditions prevailing.

The ship's company, having resignedly resumed their watchkeeping stations, waited for an explanation. *Sheffield*, Larcom told them, had been ordered to overhaul and intercept a convoy of four French freighters escorted by the Vichy destroyer *Simoun* which had passed eastward through the Straits, from Casablanca, bound for Oran. It was believed that the ships, originally from Indo-China, were carrying war materials. One, the *Bangkok*, was reported to be heavily loaded with rubber. The Germans were increasingly obtaining vital war supplies through France, and the British felt justified in halting them, but the reaction of the French to a British interception could not be guessed at. Since July of the previous year the Royal Navy had been very unpopular with the Marine Nationale.

The four destroyers had been joined by the remainder of the 8th Destroyer Flotilla led by *Faulknor*. The weather was filthy, and nobody could understand why the Frenchmen had not been stopped and searched as they came through the Straits; they would now hug first the Spanish and then the French territorial waters of the North African coast, and Larcom's brief had been made unnecessarily complicated. He ordered a course of 100 degrees and increased speed. The force smashed its way through the dark hours until reasonable light at 0620, when the battered destroyers were deployed on a line of search, three miles apart, concentrated on Captain D8 in *Faulknor*. This was a wretched business for which few could generate much enthusiasm; both cruiser and destroyer men were exhausted. Bungy Williams asked his associates whether, faced with a choice of all night under a blanket with Betty Grable and no holds barred, or an extra daily tot of rum for six months, which would one choose? It was agreed that the mere thought was torture except for teetotallers or eunuchs, and there were none of either in *Sheffield*.

The convoy was sighted at 0830, its ships steaming hard on a course parallel to the Algerian coastline, which was a slate-coloured thread on the southerly horizon. As the British closed, one of the freighters could be seen to have the name *Bangkok* painted conspicuously on her side, and a French *torpilleur d'escadre* followed to seaward. It was almost too late. At 0900 *Faulknor*, leading the destroyers already deploying to intercept, signalled *Simoun*:

'Please order your ships to heave to for inspection.'

The French freighters, however, had already altered course and were racing for the Algerian three-mile coastal limit beyond which British interference would be illegal. *Simoun* was plainly delaying her answer to *Faulknor* for as long as possible, and the British destroyer, moving even closer, flashed: 'Order your ships to stop.'

In a few more minutes the freighters, laden with war contraband, would be beyond interception unless Larcom was prepared to defy international law. And *Simoun*'s commander knew it. It was only necessary to play for a little more time.

'My ships', he returned at last, 'are carrying only food supplies for the French population of Algeria, and I implore you in the name of humanity that you waive your rights under international law and allow these ships to proceed . . .'

The French signal lamp flickered on and on, slowly, as the smoke-vomiting freighters piled on speed for the sanctuary of the Algerian shore . . .

The shore-line was nearer now – a flat, dun-coloured strand stippled with green, white buildings, a lighthouse,

the momentary flash of sun-glare from a glass window or vehicle windscreen, and, through binoculars, a train crawling from right to left, lifting white steam into an azure sky. There was an offshore, desert-warmed wind. The French freighters had almost achieved the out-reaching extremities of a wide bay, steering for the white chalk-line of a breakwater that must have been all of a mile long. Mers-el-Kebir Bay, someone said, unnecessarily. The British had been here nine months before to hurl two hundred tons of high-explosive shells into a tethered French battle-squadron, to provoke the alienation of a French Navy that had hitherto been totally pro-British. The bombardment force had been led by James Somerville, who had no hesitation in describing Churchill's orders as 'a filthy job' which was 'too bloody for words and I curse the day I was landed with this appointment', while dubbing himself, bitterly, as 'the unskilled butcher of Oran'.

Simoun was now less than a mile from *Sheffield*, while the freighters were still racing for the shore with the British destroyers fast closing astern. Then, from among a scattering of white buildings, just visible off the starboard bow, a sudden mushroom of black smoke erupted. Glasses turned immediately, 'That's Arzew, about twenty-five miles east of Oran,' the Navigator said, then, 'Good God, are they opening fire?'

The answer came within seconds. A column of splintering white lifted from the sea, intimidatingly close to *Faulknor*, then another, and a third. 'Port ten,' Larcom ordered, then, 'Prepare to engage, and tell the destroyers to withdraw.'

Sheffield leaned softly to starboard as she turned, two points to port, opening her firing arcs to bring all guns to bear on a Vichy French fortification. At 0945 the cruiser opened fire. Larcom knew that he was navigating on thin ice; his destroyers had almost certainly ventured within French territorial waters, and the Vichy batteries' response was predictable, but since he was already hanged for the lamb, he might as well go for the sheep. Yet another salvo from the distant shore batteries tore up the sea, obviously clawing for *Sheffield*. The cruiser's turrets snarled back.

The French had ceased firing, and for several minutes it seemed that *Sheffield*'s warning salvoes had made their point. There might still remain an opportunity to put a few shells into the *Bangkok*; Larcom's orders were that the rubber-laden freighter was to be brought into Gibraltar or, in the last resort, sunk, but any attempt to do so now, in Vichy territorial waters, would be not only of doubtful legality but would also bring the British into direct conflict with the French. As with the Mers-el-Kebir affair, Vichy would be incensed, the already sensitive relationship further eroded, and the British action would be frowned on by neutral governments, exploited by Germany and Italy.

One cargo of rubber was not worth the possible consequences, and Larcom reluctantly prepared to retire, return to Gibraltar and report failure.

Ashore, however, the French military had been stung into further action. Their honour, country and valour had all been insulted – again by the British Navy. In the coastal forts of Lamoune, St. Gregorio, Santa Druz and St. Thérèse the loaded 6-inch guns were turning their barrels; bearings and elevation were shouted. As the recall signal climbed to *Sheffield*'s yardarm, the batteries opened fire. It was 0950, and Bungy Williams had been debating whether the off-duty watch might get ashore to the Casbah, where there were sloe-eyed dancing girls with veils, bangles and oscillating navels. 'Did I ever tell yer about that party in the Gyppo Queen, in Malta? Shave off. . . .'

Speculation could venture no farther as the surrounding sea was shredded to white ruin by a drenching barrage that had ranged on the British destroyers with vicious accuracy. *Simoun*, out-gunned, wheeled uncertainly in a wide uncompromising circle. *Faulknor* sheared through shell-burst spindrift and the bridge personnel of both *Fearless* and *Fortune* would later claim, in *Rooke*'s mess, that they were soaked by French shell-spray. They knew it was French, they said, because it was perfumed. Chanel No. 5.

Larcom lowered his head to the Director Control Tower voicepipe: 'Resume firing.' From the DCT the Gunnery Officer ordered, 'Shoot!' His guns were already ranged, held on target by the Transmitting Stations below. The turrets roared, barrels recoiled, and black smoke billowed along the ship's side, flattening over the sea, thinning slowly as *Sheffield* left it astern. Fresh projectiles and charges were already being rammed into breeches, the range fractionally corrected and gun-ready lamps glowing red. 'Shoot!' The Navigating Officer leaned over Admiralty Chart No. 812, covering Mers-el-Kebir, Oran and Arzew. The French, he mused, weren't going to like this a bit. The midshipman of the watch made a pencilled note in the deck log. *0952: Opened fire on shore battery . . .*

At the western extremity of the Gulf of Arzew, from the crumpled thread of white that fringed the sepia coastline, there was a flash of flame that, momentarily, filled the lenses of searching binoculars. It was followed, seconds later, by a duller, red flare that could only be that of a massive fire. A dense vomit of smoke climbed into the blue sky, slowly, and the French batteries had ceased firing. The target was obscured, and *Sheffield* turned westward. The midshipman's blunt pencil wrote again.

0952: Observed cordite fire near battery.

0954: Ceased firing. No damage or casualties.

Two hours later, at noon, *Sheffield* and her destroyers, steaming fast, had achieved position 35°36'N, 02°45'W, almost half-way to Gibraltar and just north of the Spanish Moroccan coast. Afternoon watchkeepers had been piped to dinner – tinned silverside, potatoes, hard-boiled peas. To follow, Chinese wedding-cake (the sailors' boiled rice laced with currants) and, if the mess caterer had provided, a lick of Lyle's Golden Syrup. At twelve minutes past noon the Vichy French aircraft came out of the eastward sky, 'going like smoke', recorded Colin Ross, and determined to answer the insult suffered earlier.

During the next five hours *Sheffield* was subjected to five bombing attacks by Vichy aircraft flying from Algerian fields. The first, at 1212, involved two Martin Marylands flying high and fast to drop several bombs wide to seaward. At 1220 two more aircraft that carried out shallow dive attacks with 500kg bombs were also logged as Glen Martins, but were in fact Bloch 174s. The art of aircraft recognition never did achieve a high standard in *Sheffield*; it was apparently considered sufficient to merely identify approaching planes as either hostile or friendly and never mind irrelevant details.

A single, high-altitude Maryland attacked at 1223 and three Blochs dive-bombed at 1252. In this fourth attack the French pilots survived a drenching AA barrage to place several bombs very close to *Sheffield*. 'One exploded deep beneath us,' said Shipwright Lieutenant Pack. 'The shock of this threw many of us, who were in the messdeck forward, off our feet. Mess-tables came off their hooks and mess lockers jettisoned their contents.' From one of the destroyers, *Sheffield*'s fore end was seen to lift from the sea.

The final and heaviest French attack was mounted at 1748, just as the force was closing Gibraltar. Eight Maryland bombers were reported by RDF to be overhauling fast from astern, and it was very possible that, if Larcom entered harbour, the French would persist, which might mean damage and casualties ashore. Somerville, monitoring the situation from Gibraltar, ordered Larcom by wireless to 'shove off and take your nasty friends with you'.

Being only early evening, the off-duty watches in both cruiser and destroyers were anticipating a long-awaited shore run and were already borrowing funds and clean collars, frantically polishing shoes and searching for station cards. Larcom's flag signal to reverse course was greeted with howls of disbelief until the Vichy dive-bombers howled over the mast-tops. Off Europa Point the ships fought off the vengeful French, weaving and counter-weaving. 'We turned away eastward to draw off the attack,' wrote Ordnance Artificer Lucas, 'and I understand we gave the people ashore in Gibraltar a magnificent show. From five miles they saw the planes diving, our guns firing and the bombs exploding; those who missed it were quite annoyed.'

And so were the off-duty watch. *Sheffield* and her destroyers docked at midnight.

'I always had the feeling', Al Hurley remembers, 'that Larcom was censored for that North African action. There was the possibility of Vichy France declaring war on Britain as a result, and Larcom certainly had trouble in composing the signal reporting the incident.'

Pack agrees. 'Larcom was never promoted to flag rank, and when he was relieved by Captain Clarke many of us wondered if he had incurred the displeasure of Winston Churchill and My Lords . . .'

If he had, he was in good company.

11

'Hood blown up. Sink the Bismarck!'

MORE sensational events, however, had captured public attention. Off Cape Matapan the Italian cruisers *Pola, Zara* and *Fiume* and two destroyers had been sunk by warships of the Mediterranean Fleet, while in the Atlantic, within a space of days, three ace U-boat commanders, Kretschmer, Prien and Schepke, had been eliminated. Both Britain and the USA had warned Stalin that the Germans would shortly attack Russia. Addis Ababa, capital of Abyssinia, had been recaptured, but six British generals, including Sir Richard O'Connor and Sir Philip Neame, had been taken by the Germans after being lost in a sandstorm. The RAF had dropped their first 4,000lb bombs on Emden.

Eight hundred miles away, in the Baltic, the battleship *Bismarck* had finally completed her long programme of trials, training and weapon calibration; she was ready for sea, fuelled and her magazines filled to capacity. In Gdynia

she had been joined by the new heavy cruiser *Prinz Eugen*, and operational orders were received on 2 April. At the end of that month the two ships were to rendezvous with *Gneisenau*, now in Brest, and with her in company embark on a wide-ranging voyage of destruction against Allied trans-Atlantic shipping.

The Germans had assessed, correctly, that this sea-going force (which, originally, had also incorporated *Scharnhorst* – docked for boiler repairs) could outspeed any British warships of comparable armament or, conversely, out-gun any ship capable of overhauling, including that geriatric darling of the British public, the battle-cruiser *Hood*.

In Gibraltar, *Sheffield* had spent five days in dry dock to repair hull damage inflicted by French bombs. The ship's company were well satisfied; any damage that had caused

Left: *Sheffield* nudges alongside a Gibraltar jetty following an escort run to the UK with all leave denied. Exacerbated homesickness is not soothed by the lack of interest in Gibraltar; no bands or singing crowds this time – only dockyard personnel anxious to finish work and go home. It was 1600, and *Sheffield* would be at sea again within six hours.

no casualties but merely docked a ship for a week was – like the 'Blighty' wound of 1914–18 – a very desirable thing. Gibraltar's weather was at its best. There was an ENSA concert at the Alameda Theatre and a new consignment of beer had arrived from England. The resident wives of servicemen in both Malta and Gibraltar had been advised to return to the UK, but most insisted on remaining; the admission of women ready and willing from Spain and Tangier had not been curtailed. The bicycle of Gibraltar's pompous RN Assistant Provost Marshal had been consigned, one night, into the dark depths of the harbour, but only the Assistant Provost Marshal displayed any concern.

There was, of course, always a price to pay. On 5 May, Force H, including *Sheffield*, and joined by the veteran battleship *Queen Elizabeth* and the cruisers *Gloucester*, *Fiji* and *Naiad*, steamed eastward on escort Operation 'Tiger', covering the merchant ships *Clan Campbell*, *Clan Lamont*, *Clan Chattan*, *Empire Song* and *New Zealand Star*. This was another of Somerville's 'club runs' carrying important armoured reinforcements for the Eighth Army in the Western Desert now retreating before Rommel.

The first two days of 'Tiger's' passage were uneventful except, according to a laconic entry in *Sheffield*'s log on 7 May – *1540: Avoided torpedo attack.* – indicating that an incident which, eighteen months before, would have inspired shouting headlines was now hardly worth mentioning. It was fortunate that the German Fliegerkorps X was suffering heavily over Malta and North Africa at this time, and the task of disputing 'Tiger's' passage through the Mediterranean fell on the Italian Air Force.

The first wave of attackers – eight torpedo-carrying Cant bombers escorted by fighters – attacked at 1345 on Thursday 8 May in position 37°41′N, 07°59′E. They came in bravely and low, despite being intercepted by *Ark Royal*'s patrolling fighters and a blistering AA fire from the powerful British escort. All released their torpedoes in a copybook operation of which the Fleet Air Arm would not have been ashamed. 'It was quite the best we've had yet,' Colin Ross wrote in his next letter. 'There were aircraft and shells everywhere . . . I was able to stick my head out through my manhole for part of the time and had a grand view, including one of their aircraft drifting down our side with only its tail above water . . .'

There was only one understandably hurried entry in *Sheffield*'s deck log during that first attack – *1349: Altered course to avoid torpedoes. Passed 20 yards to starboard.* The Italians' spirited attack deserved better than negative hits and three bombers shot down in exchange for one Fulmar. Tragically, the observer of that British Fulmar, of which both crew members were lost, was Mark Somerville, the Admiral's nephew.

The ships of 'Tiger' pressed on eastward. Sardinian airfields were only twenty-five minutes' flying time away for the Cant Alcione bombers; they would surely come again, at least once before dusk.

The second attack came out of the northerly sky at 1620, concentrating on *Ark Royal*, with the aircraft too high for accuracy and beyond the reach of anything except the heavier AA ordnance. A third attack by five aircraft was held off at 1730. The eastern horizon was beginning to shadow and all crews were exhausted, having been at their stations since dawn with no sustenance other than corned beef sandwiches staled by the heat and tea scooped from a bucket. Spent brass cartridge cases littered the decks, and pom-poms and 0.5-inch guns manned by sweat-soaked ratings with red-rimmed eyes had hardly begun to cool when, at 2037, three Cants were reported coming in low and fast from north-westerly.

'Target enemy aircraft red two-six-oh, angle of sight oh-one-five. Commence tracking . . .'

The Cants launched their torpedoes at a range too distant to have any real hope of success, and the weary British glimpsed the bombers' pale blue under-bellies as they banked, low over the sea, turning away and apparently hardly concerned with the fate of their missiles; they could plead bad light. The British gun-crews blasphemed and tongued salt, peeling lips. *Renown*'s lamp was blinking. In accordance with previous orders six destroyers of Force H would remain with *Queen Elizabeth*, *Gloucester*, *Naiad*, *Fiji* and 'Tiger's' merchantmen as far as Malta, where they would refuel and then rejoin Force H, which would have turned back towards Gibraltar. Bunting climbed to yardarms, fell, and Force H wheeled. The convoy continued, and *Sheffield*'s men watched their sister cruiser *Gloucester* until, hull down, she faded into the easterly dusk. They could not guess that only fourteen days later both *Gloucester* and *Fiji* would be sunk and *Naiad* damaged in the battle for Crete. The war in the Mediterranean was about to enter its most desperate phase.

Two days later Force H was far to westward, only thirty miles off the Algerian coast in position 37°20′N, 03°58′E, almost beyond the reach of aircraft from the Sardinian airfields of Costelvetrano, Sciacca, Gela and Comiso, but still waiting to be overtaken by the four destroyers of the 8th Flotilla detached on 8 May. During the early afternoon, however, it was reported that one of the four, *Fortune*, had been badly damaged by bombing and was in difficulty. There was no obligation on the part of Somerville to hazard his squadron by turning back, but he did, risking censure. It was important, he considered, that the smaller vessels of his command should know that 'Uncle Jamie' never abandoned even the most junior member of his club. *Fortune* was sighted at 1758, deep in enemy-dominated waters and struggling to make ten knots. The destroyer was nursed back to Gibraltar by *Sheffield*, securing at 2100 on the 12th.

Under other circumstances *Sheffield* would have been a candidate for dry dock and extensive repairs. Her hull had been distorted in several places, both forward fuel tanks were leaking and the meat room's bulkheads were buckled. The forecastle deck had fallen six inches and was held in place by the welding of old rail lines. Bungy Williams, who was attending the Sick Bay twice daily for the treatment of *pubic phthirius inguinalis* (more usually referred to on the messdeck as 'crabs') and as a consequence was fully cognizant of the Surgeon-Commander's exchanges with the Captain, informed his fellows that *Sheffield* was shortly going home to the Tyne for a full refit and three weeks leave for each watch. After that, said Williams, they were all going to have *night vision treatment*.

Night vision – or the ability to see more clearly in darkness than the enemy – was a fashionable subject. To draw attention away from the role of RDF, the RAF's night fighter pilots were claimed to be taking carrot juice to improve their ability to see Luftwaffe bombers in the dark. Two earnest Canadian doctors had spent three weeks aboard *Sheffield* investigating the relationship between diet and night vision, and now reported that, to improve the sailors' night eyes, they should be fed more tomatoes and/or milk.

Larcom, less than convinced, nevertheless authorized additional milk for lookouts. These, in turn, were even less convinced, and were only persuaded to drink more milk if it were issued in the form of Ovaltine. Unfortunately the nightly Ovaltine queue at the galley was joined by everyone, including stokers who saw no reason why they should be victims of night starvation. Then several lookouts blamed Ovaltine for sending them to sleep on watch.

The experiment was terminated; a subsequent Admiralty Fleet Order stated that a normal ship's diet was adequate and special issues for lookouts were unnecessary.

Early on 19 May Force H had left harbour for an Atlantic rendezvous with the carrier *Furious*, following which the combined force turned back through the Straits. At dawn on the 21st *Ark Royal* and *Furious* flew off 47 Hurricanes and 4 Fulmars for Malta, all of which, it was learned later, landed safely. *Sheffield* was back at her usual berth by 0100 on the 23rd.

It had been an uneventful club run, satisfactorily concluded, and as the sea dutymen, secured, swung into their hammocks to sleep the remaining five hours to Reveille and, on the flag-deck, less fortunate signalmen of the Middle watch gazed wearily at the speckle of distant lights of Algeciras and La Linea, nobody knew that four days earlier and seventeen hundred miles away the German battleship *Bismarck* and the cruiser *Prinz Eugen* had steamed out of the Bay of Danzig, intending to slip unreported through the Kattegat. Aboard *Bismarck* was Admiral Günther Lütjens with orders to proceed first to the Arctic, oil from one of five tankers already on passage to position themselves, and then turn southward at high speed through the Iceland-Faroes gap into the Atlantic.

The story of *Bismarck*'s breakout has been told and re-told many times – first a despatch from the British Naval Attaché in Stockholm, then an illicit radio transmission from Norway. The dramatic series of events that followed, the interception of *Bismarck* and *Prinz Eugen* by *Norfolk*

and *Suffolk* on 23 May in the Denmark Strait and the despatch of *Hood* and *Prince of Wales* from Scapa Flow – all these things were yet unknown to the darkened ships of Force H in Gibraltar. Later that day Somerville and Captain A. G. Talbot of *Furious* climbed the Rock, to sit in the sun among sun-bleached wild flowers. Anything happening in the Arctic or North Atlantic was of interest, of course, but only academic interest, to ships anchored in the sunshine of Gibraltar. Below the two officers the eastern face of the Rock fell to Catalan Bay, and beyond the expanse of water catchment they could see the blue Mediterranean, sparkling golden in the evening light. A dozen Spanish fishing boats rose and fell in the swell, and the screams of gulls carried faintly on the warm breeze. Talbot shared in common with Somerville the disapproval of Winston Churchill. Until recently Director of the Anti-Submarine Warfare Division in the Admiralty, he had dared to dispute the then First Lord's highly colourful claims with regard to U-boat sinkings and, as a result, had been ordered to sea – but perhaps not entirely to Talbot's regret.

Far to the north, in that bitterly cold, white-shot corridor of water between Greenland and Iceland, the Denmark Strait, *Bismarck* and *Prinz Eugen* were speeding southward, but the British cruiser *Norfolk*, on White Patrol, had just made her preliminary enemy report on H/F.

GBR v AD – 0 – 1822z/23 = 1BS 1CR – 020 7 25 = +

Hood and *Prince of Wales*, ordered to intercept and now pounding northward through swirls of snow at 27 knots, were eleven hours away from the enemy. Aboard *Hood* was Vice-Admiral Lancelot Holland, who had led the cruisers, including *Sheffield*, in the action against the Italians off Spartivento, and he had not hesitated to engage battleships. If he met *Bismarck*, he would fight.

And in Scapa Flow, Admiral Sir John Tovey, CinC Home Fleet, ordered his remaining ships to raise steam

– his own flagship *King George V*, the carrier *Victorious*, the cruisers *Kenya*, *Hermione*, *Galatea* and *Aurora*, and the destroyers *Punjabi*, *Inglefield*, *Intrepid*, *Active*, *Lance* and *Windsor*. The carrier was already loaded with crated aircraft for transport to the Mediterranean (by courtesy of Force H) and had accommodation only for nine Swordfish and six Fulmars flown on two days before by pilots most of whom had landed on a carrier for the first time and were completely lacking operational experience. Finally, in the Clyde estuary the old battlecruiser *Repulse*, sister to *Renown*, was only hours away from departure, with convoy WS8B, to southern climes, palm trees and tropical beaches when the change in orders was piped and the messdecks howled with disbelief. *Repulse* was to leave the convoy and rendezvous with *King George V* north of the Hebrides during the next morning.

Somerville glanced at his watch. 'It's nineteen-thirty. We'd better begin walking back.' It would take them an hour; he was anxious to see the latest situation analysis and the weather forecast.

In London, just after midnight GMT, in the Admiralty's below-ground wireless centre, the Routeing P.O. Telegraphist placed a ciphered Operational Priority signal on the Service 5 bay, from which the operator was in uninterrupted communication with Gibraltar. The signal was addressed to Flag Officer Force H, repeated to CinC Home Fleet, CinC Med., FO Gibraltar, D.8 . . .

In Gibraltar, an hour ahead of London, naval police from the base establishment *Rooke* were deployed to seek out the privileged few personnel of Force H granted leave to sleep ashore. All ships of the force were ordered to raise steam for 20 knots with despatch, which meant two hours.

'We were singing "Drink to me only with thine eyes" in the wardroom', Colin Ross would write only a week later, 'when I first saw our sailing signal, and very regretfully got a little sleep before we left, in the middle of the night – regretfully because we were singing jolly well.' Returning libertymen had brought aboard string bags of oranges, bananas, smudged reprints of Lady Chatterley's Lover, equally smudged pornographic postcards and a few smuggled bottles of explosive Spanish near-brandy.

Sheffield's lines were thrown off at 0305, and she passed the breakwater in moonlight, her bow wave spilling silver and the Gibraltar dock, astern, in darkness except for a few masked jetty lights. Clear of Algeciras Bay, Somerville ordered 25 knots. Four hours later, when the hands turned out for breakfast – chopped kidneys on fried bread – everyone waited for the familiar click-click of the Captain's microphone.

Bismarck and *Prinz Eugen*, Larcom told them, were loose in the North Atlantic, steaming southward with *Norfolk* and *Suffolk* shadowing. Heavy units of the Home Fleet had already left Scapa Flow to intercept, but meanwhile Force H was to place itself between the German ships and Brest, their usual bolt-hole, to meet the unlikely event of the enemy evading the British ships closing, including *Hood* and the new battleship *Prince of Wales*. However, the two German warships were still far to the north, in the vicinity of Iceland, so the likelihood of Force H becoming involved was remote.

There were groans – not all of disappointment. 'I think most of us feared that they would slip through,' confessed Ross. *Renown* and *Sheffield* were totally outclassed by

---

Below: The German 'Schlachtschiff' *Bismarck* was of 45,951 tons displacement, with eight 15in guns. Even her secondary armament outclassed *Sheffield*'s best. With her companion *Prinz Eugen*, the battleship *Bismarck* was overwhelmingly superior to the ships of Somerville's Force H, but *Sheffield* found herself alone in the ring with *Bismarck*. The German's first two salvoes erupted alarmingly close.

Bismarck and *Prince Eugen*, while meteorological reports suggested that *Ark Royal* would be unlikely to fly off her aircraft.

During the whole of that day, and the night following, the weather was deteriorating. By noon on the 25th, with Force H in position 41°47'N, 17°07'W, a north-westerly wind – from dead ahead – had increased to Force 7, and still threatened to worsen. The '*F*'-class destroyers in company were being savagely handled and running low on fuel, so Somerville ordered them back to Gibraltar. The three larger ships smashed on, northward, into a sea so vicious that at midnight on the 26th even Somerville was compelled to order his squadron's speed to be reduced to 19 knots. Below decks in *Sheffield* the situation was impossibly chaotic; it was almost preferable to be on watch, above. The shipwrights were becoming concerned over the creaks and groans in a forecastle supported by old railway lines. Christ help us, they mused, when Old Shiny's two forward turrets next fire a salvo.

At 0112 on the 26th Somerville reduced to 17 knots. In *Renown* rivets had sprung, deadlights had collapsed and both forecastle deck and quarterdeck were untenable. The oil-tanks forward of 88 bulkhead were showing signs of leakage.

Rear-Admiral Frederick Wake-Walker, in *Norfolk*, had transmitted the dramatic signal: '*Hood* blown up.' to generate a nation-wide shock-wave as traumatic as any during the war. *Hood* had been not just a warship but a legend that symbolized all the proud strength of the Royal Navy. Now the legend was dead and that navy was stunned. The crews of many ships refused to believe the news for hours; it was just a variation on the German taunt, 'Where is the *Ark Royal*?' In Force H, smashing its way through massive seas, scraps of information gleaned from intercepted wireless signals told a story that was beyond credibility. It must be a mistake – and yet the BBC's news bulletins, when they could be heard through storm static, were confirming that *Hood* had been sunk with heavy loss of life, that next of kin were being informed. Nobody, yet, could imagine that, of the battlecruiser's complement of 1,419, only three survivors would be recovered. Somerville's distress at the loss of his nephew only sixteen days earlier was now compounded by the sinking of *Hood*, a much-loved ship in which he had flown his flag until the previous August.

In *Sheffield* young Colin Ross wrote home: 'I don't think even the loss of *King George V* herself would have been such a heavy blow to us. As you know, *Hood* was almost a legend in the service. She was always thought of as the ideal ship, and anyone who served in her took a pride in telling of it. There will never be another like her . . .'

So despite, or perhaps because of, the catastrophe, there was a cold, fatalistic determination among the warships in baying chase of *Bismarck*. Whatever the cost, the German battleship must be sunk. The news that shadowing *Suffolk*

had lost contact with the enemy, that *Bismarck* and *Prinz Eugen* were again running wild, turned even the meekest into implacable avengers. *Bismarck must be sunk.*

Somerville had not only *Bismarck* to consider but also *Scharnhorst* and *Gneisenau*, last reported to be in Brest, but which were perhaps even now at sea to support *Bismarck*. He needed to know; no firm information had come from the Admiralty, and the distance between Force H and the probable area of interception was shrinking hourly. With daylight on Monday 26 he ordered *Ark Royal* to fly a reconnaissance in the direction of Brest.

The carrier, however, was taking the weather badly, incredibly shipping green seas, her weather decks swamped. She had steamed a hundred thousand miles since her last engine refit, and twice in recent weeks the centre of her three shafts had ruptured its stern gland. Like her two Force H companions, she had rivets sprung and bulkheads warping, but Loben Maund, her Captain, turned her into a wind that scythed over the flight-deck at 50 knots. The wireless masts sank and flag 'F' streamed from a halyard – 'Am landing-on or flying-off aircraft.' Oilskinned handlers jostled around the coughing Swordfish, leaning into the wind as the deck heeled thirty degrees, then scattered as the leading biplane trundled into the drenching spray.

Somehow all ten aircraft lifted off the see-sawing deck, plunged almost to the level of the vicious sea ahead, then clawed upward for the sky, roaring desperately as the gale snatched at them. Minutes later, altitude gained, they had disappeared from sight northward, followed only by *Sheffield*'s RDF until out of range and beyond wireless contact. Of course, getting airborne was one thing. Landing-on – particularly if the weather worsened by only a little – was something quite different.

It was, however, a Catalina flying-boat of Coastal Command, flying from Lough Erne, that sighted *Bismarck*, now alone, and reported her position as 49°33'N, 21°47'W at 1030, steering 150 degrees. This placed the German about 700 miles due west of Land's End and a similar distance from Brest, for which presumably she was now making.

Since sinking *Hood*, two days before, *Bismarck* had enjoyed some incredible luck, which, in retrospect, can hardly be considered undeserved. Several British units, including the battleship *Rodney*, had missed her by only a few miles, and now the pursuing forces were far astern.

Except one. Force H was only 120 miles to the eastward of *Bismarck*'s position and, more relevant, between the German battleship and Brest.

The Catalina's sighting report was hammered out on area broadcasts HD, BN and CN within minutes by Whitehall W/T, read by *Renown*, *Ark Royal* and *Sheffield*. At this time the carrier's search aircraft were still airborne, but minutes later one of them, Swordfish 2H, reported to *Ark Royal* on H/F the sighting of a heavy cruiser which could only be *Prinz Eugen*.

Sheffield's Walrus was not employed, and her observer Charles Fenwick, was on the ship's bridge. 'For some reason', he remembers, 'Charles Larcom had a personal feud with the German cruiser *Prinz Eugen*, and he was often saying that he wanted to meet her in single combat. I believe . . . he would rather have found her than the *Bismarck* herself . . .'

But it was decreed otherwise. Within seven minutes Swordfish 2F reported the same enemy – but this time a battleship.

'I was PCO of the Forenoon watch', Ross's next letter told, 'when the voicepipe from the W/T Office buzzed at us, and the Sub hauled up a pink signal on the end of the usual piece of string, then read aloud that the *Ark*'s aircraft had found [*Bismarck*] steering towards Brest – which was just the sort of shot we were meant to field . . . It was a thrilling moment . . .'

Somerville, however, was not totally convinced; it was vitally necessary to know if both Swordfish were referring to the same ship and, if they were, whether it was indeed a battleship or a cruiser, so that the depth settings of torpedoes could be adjusted accordingly. He ordered off two more search Swordfish and all others to be landed and armed. The Admiralty had already ruled that Somerville's *Renown* was not to engage *Bismarck* unless *King George V* and/or *Rodney* were in company, but the Admiral was intending to get to the north-west of the enemy and engage from astern, compelling *Bismarck*, if she wished to respond, to turn away from Brest, into a Force 6 wind and towards other British heavy units closing at speed. If *Renown*, older even than *Hood*, outgunned and creaking in every joint, was going to fight, then Somerville needed to steal every advantage possible.

And he would make quite certain that the enemy battleship would not twist away this time. At 1300 he ordered Larcom to increase speed, make contact with *Bismarck*, shadow and report.

Sheffield, released, lifted her bows as she smashed into the swell, and, on both flanks and astern, the sea creamed. In the boiler rooms below, the fans were roaring, burners and turbines screamed, artificers among the labyrinth of ladders, catwalks and asbestos-covered pipes watched their brass-rimmed gauges. Within minutes the paint on both funnels was beginning to blister and peel. By 1500 the cruiser was steaming at 31½ knots and increasing, the wind WSW, Force 6. Above the funnels the heat shimmered, smokeless.

At 1630 it was piped: 'The ship is now steaming at 38 knots' – which was six knots more than her engines had been designed for. 'It thus seemed rather unfair', recalls AB Allen, 'that when a small puff of smoke escaped from the forward funnel, we heard the double click of the Captain's microphone, and then his voice. "Stop making smoke." A few minutes later there appeared another smoke-ball – and again the ominous click-click. Larcom's voice was coldly angry. "Engines – come up here!" The sympathy of the

entire ship's company followed Engineer Commander Baily as he climbed ladder after ladder to the compass platform. After all, we were doing thirty-eight knots!'

Meanwhile *Renown* had raised Portishead W/T on ship/shore H/F to inform the Admiralty, in cipher, of the detachment of *Sheffield*. At this time *Ark Royal* was several miles away, landing-on aircraft and beyond visual range, so *Renown*'s signal – which would be immediately re-broadcast by the Admiralty to all ships in the area – was repeated in its address to CinC (Tovey) and *Ark Royal*. This procedure might seem to be cumbersome, but it was the surest means of acquainting *Ark Royal* with the intentions of her own squadron.

When the signal regarding *Sheffield*'s deployment was received in *Ark Royal*, however, the carrier's communications personnel were already occupied with a back-log of incoming signals traffic. Fresh shadowing reports were still being read. One Swordfish of the returning reconnaissance sortie had crashed on landing, while newly armed aircraft were being lifted from the hangar in the bell-clanging after lift. Somerville's signal, seen to be merely 'repeated for information', was not immediately deciphered. Thus when, at 1450, fourteen attack Swordfish lifted off *Ark Royal*'s deck, their crews knew nothing of the presence of *Sheffield* on their flight path; the first warship to be sighted, they had been briefed, would be *Bismarck*.

Within Force H, only *Sheffield* was equipped with air surveillance RDF (Radio Direction Finding), soon to be renamed Radar (Radio Detection and Ranging) but several of *Ark Royal*'s Swordfish had been burdened with ASV (Anti-Surface Vessel) radar assemblies, the use of which nobody had confidently mastered. Within only forty minutes of lifting off, the cockpit radar warned of a vessel just ahead, and it had to be *Bismarck*. The strike CO, Lieut-Commander Stewart-Moore, waited for a gap in the cloud – and there she was below, pounding into the grey sea with a tumbling, silver wake stretching astern.

Ark Royal's airmen were thoroughly acquainted with *Sheffield*; she had steamed thousands of miles in company, shared the same anchorage on numerous occasions. *Sheffield* had two funnels to *Bismarck*'s one, while the German was 330 feet longer and almost five times the cruiser's tonnage. It might seem impossible that *Ark Royal*'s aircrew could fail to identify *Sheffield*, but they saw only what they expected and wanted to see, and Stewart-Moore led his aircraft above the cloud to deploy for attack.

'We had closed down our RDF for fear of enemy detection,' says Al Hurley. 'I will always remember the words coming down the voicepipe that the *Ark*'s bombers were sighted, and then the excited retort, "My God – they're attacking us!"'

Larcom called for emergency full ahead and ordered all guns to refrain from firing. Hurley had hurriedly climbed to the after end of the bridge where, he recalls, 'the scene was one of dismay, but certainly no panic . . .

Larcom was a cool customer. As each group of three (aircraft) lined up to make a run at us he would bring *Sheffield* beam on to their approach, hoping they would recognize our profile. When they failed to do so, and dropped their torpedoes, he had to bring the ship around smartly to meet the fish head on. We had just avoided one such attack on the port bow when I saw, from my vantage point, another three forming up to starboard. I could not resist shouting: "There are three more attacking on the starboard bow, sir!" – which was a bit presumptuous for a Sub-Lieutenant, RCNVR, Special Branch, from a position in which I should never have been in the first place!'

Only three pilots realized their mistake in time; nine released their torpedoes. 'I reckon that *Sheffield* showed great restraint,' wrote Charles Fenwick, the cruiser's own pilot. 'It was certainly a very frightening affair. The last straw came when one of our Swordfish, having dropped its torpedo, flew across our bow and sprayed us with its rear gun.'

Larcom had handled his ship with remarkable skill. Even so, *Sheffield*'s survival was hardly less than a miracle. As the incredulous sailors stared up at the Swordfish climbing away, torpedoes gone, an Aldis lamp was blinking apologetically from the tail-ender: 'Sorry for the kipper!'

In *Sheffield* there was little time for anything more than a few obscenities, because at 1740 *Bismarck* was sighted off the starboard bow – according to the deck log at 068 degrees 10 miles. Hurley says, 'The first man to sight her masthead was Sub-Lieutenant Paul McLaughlan of Toronto, the only other Canadian aboard.' From that moment until a destroyer flotilla joined the action four hours later *Sheffield* never took her eyes off *Bismarck*.

The Germans had sighted and correctly identified *Sheffield* almost simultaneously. They had also seen the reconnaissance Swordfish earlier that day, which meant an aircraft carrier in the vicinity. The carrier must almost certainly be *Ark Royal*, who, they knew, was accompanied by the old battle-cruiser *Renown*. The combination presented little threat; only the carrier's aircraft were capable of slowing *Bismarck* with torpedoes, but the weather was unfavourable, with a Force 6 wind from WSW, an ugly sea, visibility reduced by frequent rain squalls and a cloud base at 600 feet. *Bismarck* was running low on fuel, but so were her pursuers. It would soon be dark, and by dawn the battleship would have almost reached the French coast, with the Luftwaffe overhead. The possibility of *Bismarck* being prevented from reaching the sanctuary of Brest was diminishing hourly.

In *Sheffield*, Colin Ross was closed up at his station in 'A' turret. 'We were all ready to loose off,' he wrote later, 'but we didn't fire as we could have no effect at that range and, anyway, we were only required to shadow. I said to my Captain of Turret, "Every ship in the Navy must be plotting us on their charts now. If we lose him we'll never be able to lift our heads again." '

The cruiser was transmitting her position, course and speed every fifteen minutes. At 2030 the second strike of fifteen aircraft from *Ark Royal* was sighted, this time briefed to first home on *Sheffield* and obtain a positional report before proceeding. *Sheffield* flashed, 'Enemy is twelve miles dead ahead of me.' Larcom then increased speed to bring his ship to within eight miles of his massive opponent.

'The second run of torpedo bombers,' recalls Hurley, 'which was the first attack on *Bismarck*, was a gratifying sight, especially the spout of water that accounted for the hit on her stern. I suppose we were about nine miles away as she laid down white smoke and vanished . . .'

Ross agreed. 'At about 8.30 . . . the *Ark*'s strike force went in and got one definite hit, which was most encouraging. We saw them from the turret passing overhead with their fish and returning without them.' All, it seems, was forgiven. 'The good old Swordfish – which look as though they came out of the original Ark – always come up to scratch.'

Meanwhile, *Bismarck* was defending herself with every AA gun she could bring to bear on the biplanes that emerged from the leaden cloud only 700 feet above and came on, almost at sea level. Eight miles away, in *Sheffield*, everyone with a pair of binoculars had them to his eyes, levelled at the indistinct, grey shape far ahead. The deck log noted: *2107: Sighted gun-flashes bearing 130 degrees and 3 Swordfish returning from T/B attack.*

Of the fifteen Swordfish that made the final attack on *Bismarck*, the torpedoes of eleven missed. Two were not launched. The fourteenth struck fairly amidships but did not embarrass *Bismarck*'s 12½-inch 'Wotan' armour. The fifteenth, approaching from starboard as the ship was turning evasively to port, exploded under her starboard quarter to wreck the steering mechanism. *Bismarck* had three screws and might normally be expected to steer on her engines, but the rudders had been jammed hard over to port; nothing could move them. She began to turn in a wide circle and, no matter how her three screws were used to counter the discrepancy, she insisted on returning her bows into the wind and steering an erratic north-westerly course, which was only slightly to be preferred to steering a continuous circle.

'Larcom's tactics of shadowing,' said Fenwick, on *Sheffield*'s bridge, 'of coming astern of *Bismarck* until we sighted her, then immediately turning 360 degrees and coming in again, worked well until . . . we sighted her bows-on instead of stern-on, and the fat was in the fire. She opened up and straddled us from the very first salvo.'

Bismarck, however, had not turned in order to savage the only British warship in sight. *Sheffield* was a nuisance but not a threat; the German battleship had circled because she had no choice, and, since the British cruiser was within range, she was engaged. The first two salvoes cleared the German guns of HE projectiles (which had been used against the Swordfish) and it was these that were just short, bursting on impact and causing all of *Sheffield*'s casualties and damage.

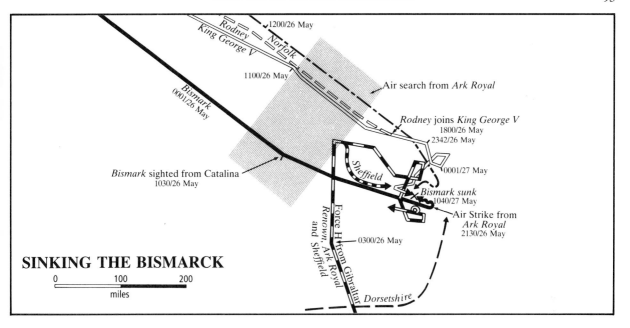

SINKING THE BISMARCK

0   100   200
miles

Rodney
King George V
1200/26 May
Norfolk
1100/26 May
Bismark
0001/26 May
Air search from *Ark Royal*
Rodney joins *King George V*
1800/26 May
2342/26 May
0001/27 May
Bismark sighted from Catalina
1030/26 May
Sheffield
Bismark sunk
1040/27 May
Air Strike from
Ark Royal
2130/26 May
Force H from Gibraltar
Renown, Ark Royal
and Sheffield
0300/26 May
Dorsetshire

Paymaster-Commander R. Q. Pine had joined *Sheffield* in Gibraltar only two weeks before, and had just discovered that two months' supply of flour in a forward store had been ruined by sea water, the result of the mine explosions in March. He was passing the starboard pom-pom and apprehensively watching *Bismarck* when the dark shape twinkled prettily and was immediately lost to view behind a pall of black smoke. Pine decided that this was probably not the right time to tell the Captain about the flour.

2137: Bismarck *coming towards out of smoke. Range 9 miles.*

2140: Bismarck *opened fire at* Sheffield.

2142 Made black and white smoke. 6 salvoes 15-inch HE and AP fired. All straddles. Suffered minor damage from splinters and 14 casualties, some serious.

'We were lying on our stomachs on the decks,' recalled Shipwright Lieutenant Pack, in charge of the forward damage control party. 'The first salvo burst near the ship, which gave a vicious whipping movement. The Gunner (T) said he could not get the smoke floats overboard fast enough on receiving the order. The wounded were brought below, and I can remember the odd whimpering of one young lad . . .'

The sea was erupting raggedly around *Sheffield* as Larcom ordered maximum helm. 'It was the most awful experience of my life,' confessed Able Seaman Allen. 'I was standing at the door of the RDF office on the flag deck, looking aft, when an enormous black curtain rose in front of me, and never before or after have I heard a sound of more terrifying quality.' Lethal splinters of steel scythed down AA gun crews, clawed at *Sheffield*'s bridge structure. Ross flinched as the Krupps shrapnel flayed 'A' turret without penetrating. 'I must say it was not much fun; they were too close to be comfortable. [*Bismarck*] sent over

six salvoes, and we were not answering back, so there was nothing to do except wonder where the next was coming.' *Bismarck*, after all, had destroyed *Hood* in six minutes.

The enemy's change of course to 340 degrees was assumed to be only temporary; its real meaning had not yet dawned on anyone, and daylight was fading fast. Larcom was toying with the possibility of carrying out a torpedo attack, which might be the last and only way of stopping *Bismarck* – but then, at 2152, *Sheffield* was no longer alone. In company, steaming hard, were the Tribal-class destroyers *Cossack, Maori, Zulu*, and *Sikh*, and the Polish-manned *Piorun*. Ross could see them through the turret periscope, 'being at the time indisposed towards opening up my lid!' The destroyers, rearing and plunging, overhauled and swept on, to assume responsibility for the night's pursuit of *Bismarck*. D4, in *Cossack*, was Captain Philip Vian, VC. 'Where is the enemy?' his lamp blinked across a darkening, torn sea. 'Bearing 155 ten miles course 340,' Larcom returned. 'Good luck.' Darkness came down like a curtain.

There was still a tense, sleepless night ahead for *Sheffield*. Inspection showed that the Germans' shell-fire had not damaged the hull, but the after superstructure was holed and lacerated and the RDF aerial smashed. The port searchlight had been taken away, and a plunging shell or very large splinter had passed through the forward leg of the tripod mainmast, almost severing it. Another large splinter had disintegrated in the wardroom, damaging the portrait of Princess Marina.

Early in the Middle watch, logged as 0100 Tuesday 27 May, Ordinary Seaman D. T. George died of his wounds in the Sick Bay. RDF was inoperative, and most men had not enjoyed anything better than 'action feeding' during the previous two days; the cooks were closed up in the after magazine. At 0105 lookout positions reported gunfire flashes, distant, bearing 155 degrees. It was probable that Vian's destroyers, clinging to *Bismarck*'s flanks, were tormenting her with long-range torpedo attacks, and the battleship was snarling back. God be with those little ships, the men on *Sheffield*'s bridge muttered.

The sun rose reluctantly at 0715. A Force 8 gale from NNW whined through stays and halyards, streaming the ensign and drenching the weather decks with cold rain. But there was boiling water available from the galleys and pails of cocoa were coming up. The watchkeepers stood, shrugged into their collars, with hot cups clasped in dirty hands, sipping meditatively as they rocked on their feet to placate cramped muscles. Intercepted signals were reaching the compass platform from the W/T office every few minutes – position, course and speed reports from *Maori*, *Sikh*, then *Maori* again. *Bismarck* was trapped and doomed, but nobody was looking for a blaze of glory, only to get the thing finished with as quickly and inexpensively as possible. By 0830 Larcom had again brought *Sheffield* up to within fifteen miles of *Bismarck*'s position. *King George V* and *Rodney* were also closing, *Norfolk* was in visual contact. At 0851 all ships were ordered to move in for the kill.

Ordnance Artificer Lucas recalls feeling annoyed that *Sheffield* had not been allowed to finish *Bismarck* with torpedoes, and Pack protested, 'It had been Force H aircraft that had successfully stopped *Bismarck* for the big ships of the Home Fleet, but we were not allowed the honour of giving the *coup de grâce*. There were some bitter remarks on the messdecks.'

But this was bravado. *Bismarck*'s fire power was unimpaired; she was far too strong for *Sheffield*, and Admiral Lütjens had already signalled Berlin to assure Adolf Hitler that the battleship would fight to the last shell. She did, being totally crippled by the close-range fire of *Rodney*, *King George V* and *Norfolk* before being despatched by *Dorsetshire*'s torpedoes. In any case, *Hood* had been a unit of the Home Fleet, and it was her Home Fleet sisters who were entitled to the reckoning.

By mid-forenoon on 27 May the three principals of Force H had rejoined company. With the fire-eating Somerville ordered to remain away from the scene of action, twelve of *Ark Royal*'s Swordfish had got airborne in the teeth of a Force 7 north-westerly, intending a final torpedo attack. Arriving over the battle area, however, they could see that their involvement would complicate rather than help the situation, and turned back to their carrier.

'*Bismarck* sank at 1040 this morning with her flag still flying,' Larcom told his ship's company. 'I take off my hat to her.'

Right: After the action and glad to be alive, the nervously jubilant crew of the After Director Tower point to the splinter holes caused by *Bismarck*'s very near misses.

Below left: And the foremast has suffered a severe gash.

Below: Shrapnel has damaged the picture of HRH the Duchess of Kent, which she had presented to the wardroom. For the next twenty-five years the portrait will hang with its honourable scars left untouched.

Opposite page, bottom: Splinters from German shells have punched through *Sheffield*'s 4½in side armour into the wardroom, where . . .

. . . Paymaster Lieutenant G.B.R.S. Harris assesses damage to a bulkhead. Portraits of the King and Queen are dislodged, but undamaged.

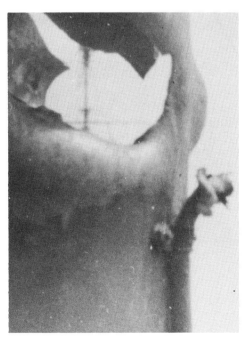

Left: On 28 May 1941 off-duty men muster on the quarterdeck for the burial of Ordinary Seaman George and Able Seaman Ling. Hours later Able Seaman A. C. Taylor will die of his wounds in the sick bay, to be buried on the following day. *Sheffield*'s casualty list, however, is astonishingly modest, and successive crews will always regard her as lucky.

Everyone was exhausted, completely and utterly drained, wanting nothing more desperately than to stretch out anywhere, on mess-stool or table, locker, deck or hatch-cover, to sleep. Food could wait, the foul sweatiness of bodies and the tobacco-sour mouths, the fetidness of messdecks long deprived of clean air, the piled messtraps and over-spilling refuse buckets – all could wait in exchange for the bliss of sleep. The Admiralty, however, was warning that U-boats were closing fast on these few square miles of Atlantic in which British battleships, carriers, cruisers and destroyers had gathered. There could be no sleep yet. As soon as *Ark Royal* signalled that her final sortie had jetti-soned torpedoes and landed-on, Somerville ordered course and speed for Gibraltar.

It was considered inevitable that enemy aircraft would attempt to intercept from French coastal fields but, in the event, the Luftwaffe's performance on 27 March was fee-ble. *Sheffield*'s log records, somewhat wearily, *during the forenoon firing intermittently at enemy aircraft shadowing*. Ordnance Artificer Lucas is a little more specific. 'A Focke and a Condor came to have a look at us and made a half-hearted attack. We made a lot of noise, but weather conditions were so bad that our shooting could not have bothered either of them. A number of returning Swordfish fouled the range on one occasion as we spotted the Condor through a gap in the clouds; the [Swordfish] manoeuvres to keep out of the way were most amusing. They probably thought we were seeking revenge for their attack on us during the previous day.' Even enemy air attacks aroused little concern in men almost comatose from lack of sleep, and AB Allen remembers the only meal he had during that entire twenty-four hours – one sausage, one hard-boiled egg and a slice of bread.

At 2130 that evening Able Seaman A. Ling died of wounds received during the encounter with *Bismarck*.

By dawn on the 28th the wind had eased to Force 5, north-west by westerly, and the ship's routine was resuming a normal pattern. At 1045 lower deck was cleared of off-duty personnel and in position 41°09′N, 15°08′W Ordinary Seaman George and Able Seaman Ling were buried from the quarterdeck with full honours. Only three hours later the ship's company learned that Able Seaman A. C. Taylor had also succumbed to his wounds. He was buried at 1050 on the 29th in position 36°11′N, 08°16′W, the waters in which so many British sailors lay, of Cadiz, St. Vincent, Trafalgar.

Somerville had signalled from *Renown*: 'Much regret to hear of your casualties whilst shadowing *Bismarck*. I wish to express my sympathy in the loss of your shipmates. I trust the wounded are progressing favourably. I consider your tenacity and your shadowing was to a large degree responsible for the striking force and destroyers making contact which fixed the *Bismarck* and led to her eventual destruction.'

In truth, *Sheffield*'s losses had been very modest. A total of 1,416 men had gone down in *Hood*, 1,977 in *Bismarck*, while during the few days covered by the action, some 2,000 more had perished in the cruisers *Gloucester* and *Fiji*, and the destroyers *Greyhound*, *Juno*, *Hereward*, *Imperial*, *Kashmir* and *Kelly*, all sunk off Crete. Even so, a few empty places at the mess-tables, a missing voice at tot-time, the emptying of the deceaseds' lockers, the unclaimed oilskin – all sobered the horseplay and waggery which was so much an ingredient of shipboard life.

Right: With Force H safely returned to Gibraltar, Vice-Admiral Somerville boards *Sheffield* to congratulate her company. The cruiser's tenacious shadowing, he tells them, had been largely responsible for the final interception and sinking of *Bismarck*. The operation had cost *Sheffield* a total of seven lives.

Sheffield's death-list, however, was not yet complete.

At 1334 on 29 May both Walrus aircraft were catapulted off. The first, piloted by Johnny Groves, was to carry out an anti-submarine sweep around the squadron. The second was crewed by newcomers to the ship – Lieutenant (P) B. A. H. Brooks, Lieutenant (A) A. Nedwill and Leading Aircraftsman J. A. Saville. The pilot was required to first drop a message on the flagship, *Renown*, and then proceed to Gibraltar to pick up mail, and for this reason was carrying one passenger, Regulating Petty Officer J. W. B. Marjoram, who would wait on the jetty for *Sheffield* to berth.

On reaching *Renown* four minutes later, Brooks flew over the forecastle, and then, for reasons only to be guessed at, decided to make a low pass over the stern. In doing so he steered through the hot gases rising from *Renown*'s funnels. The Walrus was flung over by the hot up-blast, out of control, and fell, to strike the stern awning tripod and then crash into the sea. Only RPO Marjoram was picked up by the destroyer *Wishart*, unfortunately to die of his injuries. His body was taken on to Gibraltar, reached by Force H at 1900.

Force H was welcomed by cheering crowds, bands and scores of small boats. The *Gibraltar Chronicle* erupted with patriotic fervour not endorsed by many in *Sheffield*. That evening, in the quiet of his cabin, Captain Larcom wrote his own story to his wife.

'Just back from sinking the *Bismarck*. Our share was small, but she was a tiger trapped, and gave me hell for four or five minutes. We escaped, but lost three men dead and five seriously injured. And then today, after two funerals at sea, another tragedy. A young Lieutenant, not fourteen days on board, took my aircraft to drop messages on *Renown*, and cutting a dash, as I guessed he would, killed himself, another young officer and two men. It is too much at once.

However, in spite of my fifty years I have survived, and Synge (the chaplain) and I are booking Gibraltar Cathedral tomorrow evening for a memorial. I have said I will have no strangers and no 'marching men' to the Church. Synge will do it all, and anyone who cares to be present can be. I expect a full house of *Sheffield*'s, but no strangers ordered to attend. I shall tell James, if he likes to come, no-one else.

It is not only a memorial service, but also a thanksgiving to Almighty God for a miraculous escape.

You should see the wardroom, shot to ribbons; and Marina, Duchess of Kent, is just a mass of shot holes, and all the time I never knew it. But I knew that God had been very kind.

James's reception in Gibraltar was marvellous, so was ours, but I am sad for the eight dead. Tomorrow I will give you names and addresses to write to, and I will write as well.'

And two days later, on Friday 30 May:

'We had a wonderful memorial service in the Cathedral. The only stranger was James, and he is not a stranger. About four hundred troops (ratings) turned up, and no-one was sent. I expressly said I would not have a man marched up, but if they cared to come, they could. There was a full house. Synge was excellent; the only thing that harried me was the Last Post. I had heard it at our last funeral, I had hoped for the last time, earlier in the day.

James came and spoke to the troops this morning, and afterwards privately . . .'

12

'Inside, Jack!
All your ship's company here!'

PRINZ EUGEN had reached Brest. The German airborne invasion of Crete and the subsequent evacuation of Allied troops had reawakened fears of a similar assault on Britain. Conscript the Home Guard, demanded the Daily Mail, while to foil the landed enemy, recommended the Bishop of Chelmsford, 'barrels of soft soap judiciously applied to the roads at hairpin bends might have results both striking and surprising.' In Gibraltar it was hot. Dress for libertymen was compulsorily No. 6 white drills and, ashore, the pavements burned through the soles of pipe-clayed shoes. There was a water shortage; the trees in Alameda Gardens drooped in the sun, and an unwary hand placed on one of the big old muzzle-loaders would be burned. 'Inside, Jack!' the cafe-owners wheedled. 'All your ship's company here!' There were rumours that the Mediterranean Fleet had been badly mauled in the battle for Crete, that the damaged *Formidable*, Cunningham's only operational carrier, had been withdrawn for repair, but there were no details. *Furious*, loaded with aircraft for Malta, was moored in Gibraltar harbour awaiting orders to proceed.

When they came, the orders took the ferrying carrier to sea on 5 June with Force H in company, and during the following forenoon *Furious* and *Ark Royal* flew-off 43 Hurricanes and 3 Fulmars for Malta, escorted by a long-range Blenheim. Twenty-four hours later all ships had regained Gibraltar.

Sheffield's respite, however, was brief. That same evening she singled up wires and slipped at 2246, assigned to a fourteen-days Atlantic patrol. It was, Bungy Williams protested, another diabolical liberty; every time he resolved to visit Gibraltar's museum instead of Murphy's Bar in Rosia Road, the ship went to bleedin' sea.

But, Captain Larcom broadcast as soon as the ship had settled on course westward, when the patrol had been finished, *Sheffield* would proceed direct to Rosyth for a six weeks' refit. Promises, promises.

The first few days of the patrol were pleasantly uneventful, and Thursday 12 June promised to be no different; the sea was like glass, visibility superb, and during the First Dog watch, in position 44°48′N, 24°00′W, the off-duty hands were dhobeying, playing cribbage, queueing at the dry canteen for cigarettes or 'nutty', or merely yarning over mess-tables. At 1722 they were called to action stations.

A ship had been sighted bearing 340 degrees, 18 miles distant, and *Sheffield* altered course slightly to port to intercept, increasing speed. Within twenty minutes the stranger could be identified as a tanker, and *Sheffield* hoisted the international flags 'WBA' – '*What ship?*'

The tanker did not respond, and at 1810 *Sheffield*'s signal lamp hammered: 'Show signal letters.'

This time the tanker flashed back, slowly. 'Panamanian *Leda* bound Land's End.'

It was slightly odd. A ship's destination might be expressed as a port, an anchorage, an estuary, even – vaguely – a country, but hardly as a coastal feature of no relevance to mariners other than as a navigational reference. Larcom brought *Sheffield* closer, cautiously. German raiders, disguised as Allied or neutral merchantmen, were capable of embarrassing even a cruiser if approached carelessly. At 1916 *Sheffield* signalled: 'I intend to board. If you scuttle I shall fire.' All 6-inch guns were tracking, the turret crews hoping. This could be better than Tombola.

There still remained some three hours to sunset, but the tanker was showing no willingness to heave to. At 1926 *Sheffield* flashed: 'Stop.'

'Suddenly she altered course towards us', says Lucas, 'and disclosed a number of boats being lowered on what had been her blind side; she appeared to be settling lower in the water.' At 1943, having allowed the boats to pull clear, *Sheffield*'s 6-inch guns opened fire at point-blank range. Almost every salvo hit. The seventeenth smashed into the tanker's waist, and yellow flames vomited dense smoke skyward. She turned over to sink at precisely 2000, and *Sheffield* closed to pick up the survivors.

Eighty-eight, including twelve injured, were taken from four boats and a raft, and the ship was quickly identified as the German supply auxiliary *Friedrich Breme*, recently built, of 15,400 tons gross and fourteen days out of Brest. Deployed as a source of fuel and provisions for U-boats and surface raiders, only twenty-five of her seamen taken were tanker crew members; most were Kriegsmarine replacement personnel. All were well fed and healthy, many wearing their best uniforms and carrying suitcases crammed with personal effects. The tanker's Captain, during interrogation, claimed that he had he been an officer in the 1914–18 raider *Moewe* and later a POW in British hands. A few of the prisoners were arrogant and argumentative, and two or three, on being searched, were found to be carrying knives. Most, however, were compliant, and all were accommodated in the Boys' messdeck, evacuated for that purpose, under guard. Commander Pine recalls that one German flushed, embarrassed, when he whispered that he lived in Adolph Hitler Street.

Larcom turned *Sheffield* away eastward at 24 knots. He would later be criticized for stopping his ship for 37 minutes in waters known to be frequented by U-boats and particularly in the vicinity of an enemy auxiliary on which

German submarines were probably homing. If RN warships were forbidden to halt for British survivors in dangerous waters, why had an exception been made for those of the enemy? In the event, *Sheffield* ran clear.

During the early hours of 14 June a change of orders was received by W/T. The ship was to join forces with *Cumberland*, already escorting a UK-bound convoy of 50 ships. Two of the crew of *Friedrich Breme* had died of their wounds and were ceremonially buried in the presence of their erstwhile comrades. The Germans were exercising on deck when the convoy was joined soon after noon; they were clearly nonplussed at the sight of fifty merchant ships

Right: The 15,400-ton German tanker *Friedrich Breme*, posing as a Panamanian ship, is intercepted in mid-Atlantic and quickly destroyed; here 88 enemy personnel are taken aboard *Sheffield*.

steaming unconcernedly through seas which, they had been convinced, had been swept clean of all Allied shipping by U-boats. One young prisoner insisted that the freighters that stretched to the horizon were all German. If that was so, an amused Marine sentry enquired, why wasn't *Sheffield* attacking them? The German sneered. Because, he said, the English navy was frightened. The young man was less assured when *Sheffield* and *Cumberland* flashed nautical witticisms at each other, and totally crushed by the time he and his fellows were disembarked at Rosyth during the afternoon of 20 June.

Old Shiny was nudged into dry dock during the following day, but already the first leave party had been put ashore at South Queensferry, to race for Edinburgh's Waverley Station. At the end of the refit Captain Larcom would no longer be in command, and many others would be making the long journey back to Chatham for redrafting to new ships commissioning; their experience in *Sheffield* would be worth more than rubies. They would be replaced by Hostilities Only conscripts from training establishments that had once been Butlin's or Cunningham's holiday camps but now, stripped of all frivolities, were as bleak as only the Navy could make anything. Apprehensive, mildly bewildered, the newcomers with their ill-fitting, issued uniforms and barracks haircuts would find messdeck candour and camaraderie initially intimidating, but they would become progessively less sensitive and would quickly learn new expletives, respond more confidently, and for the rest of their lives remember the bonds of comradeship forged across the white-scrubbed mess-tables.

The Canadian, Al Hurley, was one of those who departed *Sheffield* for oceans new at that time. 'I never saw her again until she visited British Columbia around 1950, when I remember that Princess Marina's photograph was still damaged. As for my memories of serving in Old Shiny, I was always amused at the way almost the entire ship's company came on deck every time we flew off a Walrus, to debate whether the droopy creature would really fly off this time. I remember the way Larcom would fill those Capstan tins with cigarette butts as he chain-smoked his way through the day, and the flying of the tremendous silk battle ensign to start an action. I remember the Army Bofors gun crew on the dockside in Gibraltar that just about shot off our bridge when they fired at a lone enemy plane, and I remember when Lieutenant Scroggy Phillips fought in the boxing tournament at Gib, and blasted the much-vaunted Army champion, and so on . . .'

The ship was dry in the dock at 0930 on Saturday 2 August 1941 when Captain Arthur Clarke assumed command. Larcom left an hour later. The refit was taking longer than had been planned, and attention to a number of less urgent defects had to be postponed. Captain Clarke, however, wrote of another problem that would repeatedly be met by commanding officers throughout the war – the periodical drain-off of experienced seamen in exchange for novices.

'Of the officers, only five remained of the original forty-eight manning the ship in September 1939, and, more significantly, the replacements were to a considerable extent from the RNVR; the regular, long-service officers had to be thinly spead throughout the Fleet and Staff appointments. The policy for first-line units was still to provide regular officers for the posts of Executive Officers, Heads of Departments (Engineering, Accountant, Medical), and to the various specialist appointments (Gunnery, Torpedo, Navigation), but to replace other regular officers by war service volunteer officers to the maximum to which such officers with the necessary qualifications were available. Such replacements were not possible in the Warrant Officer class, with their long experience, but elsewhere it was being taken with a ruthlessness never experienced during the First World War.

On the lower deck the changes were just as drastic, if not more so. A seaman is not made in a day, and the modern seaman . . . requires not only very considerable training but also a great deal of experience before he can be relied upon "by day or night, in fair weather or foul, whether fresh or tired to the point of exhaustion". Again the burden fell upon the long-service officers and men . . . the newcomers were largely taught as quickly as possible to do one job properly . . . Supervision was intensified, and no opportune moment was lost for drill, and more drill . . .' The efficiency of the old Royal Navy, the envy of the world, was being alarmingly reduced by the need to get bank clerks, builders' labourers and bus conductors to sea as quickly as possible, hopefully transformed into fighting seamen by a few weeks of bullying by Gunners' Mates.

'At times the continued dilution of ships' companies', says Clarke, 'seemed more than harassed commanding officers could bear. Our consolation was that the enemy's plight must be as bad, and we resolutely purged our minds of too many thoughts with regard to desirable standards of appearance, smartness and discipline – to which we ourselves had been born and bred. The essential thing was that the machinery should work, the guns fire, and the ship be always be ready for the demands made on her.'

Clarke's comments indicate a concern for his ship's efficiency and the decline in quality of personnel, even for 'harassed commanding officers', but he makes no reference to the conditions imposed on the thousands of young men who had no desire to be seamen or stokers, to serve in his ship, or to be his subordinates. It is doubtful if he possessed the slightest knowledge of life in the messdecks' quarantined squalor; he was of a different caste, as distinct as the Brahmin to the common Vaisya or a feudal overlord to his peasantry. Clarke, like others of his generation, was a graduate of the inter-war period during which the Washington Treaty and governmental cheeseparing had drastically slashed the Royal Navy's strength, seen the Atlantic Fleet mutiny of 1931 and the shrinkage of the sailors' tolerant loyalty to, and total confidence in, their officers.

But Clarke was right, of course, in that the enemy's plight was worse. The Kriegsmarine was confined to the safe waters of the Baltic for trials and training, which might seem a desirable arrangement, but it meant that, now, few left that sanctuary until their first operational assignment, which – as in the case of *Bismarck* – frequently proved to be their last. The psychological differences of the Royal Navy and the Kriegsmarine were indisputable and interesting. There was never an engagement during which the British considered defeat, while the tendency to scuttle when the going got rough was a German penchant, almost a death-wish.

During *Sheffield*'s period in dry dock the entire anatomy of the war had changed dramatically. Germany had invaded the Soviet Union along an 1,800-mile front from the Arctic to the Black Sea, while Roumania, Hungary, Finland, Slovakia, Croatia and Albania had also declared war on Russia. Sweden was permitting the passage of German troops from Norway to Finland. 'Any man or state who fights against Nazidom', Churchill had promised, 'will have our aid. Any man or state who marches with Hitler is our foe.'

The House of Commons had been told, in secret session, of the staggering shipping losses in the North Atlantic; now convoys carrying war materials were to be steamed to Russia's Arctic ports.

Undocked on 7 August, decks hosed clean of refit grime, *Sheffield* took on ammunition, fuel and stores for several days before being hustled into an intensive training routine calculated to knock some degree of efficiency into the green hands recently joined from Depot. There was no time for anything else, Lucas remembers. 'The morning after our arrival in Scapa (12 August) we started working-up exercises, doing little shoots, big shoots, day shoots and night shoots in addition to launching and recovering our aircraft, firing torpedoes, damage control exercises and fire drill.' Clarke had hoped for a month in which to work up the cruiser. He was given fifteen days, and many recently joined men had neither locker nor slinging-billet, and were still getting lost on their way from stokers' messdeck to the forward paint store when *Sheffield* stood off Greenock on Saturday 30 August 1941. She weighed anchor in darkness, at 0055 on Sunday morning, and the duty part of watch blasphemed.

'Cable Party and Special Sea Duty men muster at the double. Close all scuttles and watertight doors. Stand by for leaving harbour.'

Nobody told soddin' nobody about nothing, Bungy Williams gritted as he struck his head against the bulkhead. Somebody in seaboots trod on his bare foot. On the compass platform Captain Clarke's feeling were not widely different. *Sheffield* was to join *Furious, Repulse, Cairo*, the AMC *Derbyshire* and nine destroyers in escorting a convoy bound for the Cape – but for Clarke this was all too

soon. Apart from the high percentage of less-than-efficient ratings among his crew and his own lack of experience in handling *Sheffield* in confined circumstances . . .

'. . . the wind had been steadily increasing during the day [writes Clarke] and by nightfall was blowing heavily down river. It was also pitch dark and raining. There was nothing extraordinary in this, but my own lack of experience of my new command made the general departure more difficult than might otherwise have been the case. It so happened that both *Repulse* and *Furious* were anchored up-harbour above *Sheffield* and it had been arranged for good reason that *Repulse*, the senior ship, would lead the force through the boom to sea. In my anxiety not to be too late in the sequence, I weighed a bit too early, and then found myself blowing down river, beam on to the wind, with *Repulse* above me trying to find room to pass and take the lead. It would have taken a long time to turn again, head to wind, and this would in any case have put the two large units in a very difficult situation. To turn down wind would have accelerated my inevitable progress towards the narrowing approaches to the exit. So there the ship was – occupying a great deal more of the channel than she should. *Repulse* just squeezed past, and her Captain [Captain 'Bill' Tennant] was extremely nice about my apologetic signal, but he cannot have been very pleased at the problem I set him, with 32,000 tons of ship to handle through that narrow opening, and with a strong wind behind him.'

That night *Furious* was compelled to put back to Greenock with engine trouble, and two days later, 400 miles due west of the Irish coast, *Sheffield* was ordered to return immediately to Scapa Flow. *Repulse*, with convoy WS 11, steamed on for the Cape, then Trincomalee and Singapore, to die with *Prince of Wales* off the coast of Malaya.

Sheffield's drifter put her libertymen ashore on Flotta's landing pontoons, and they followed the uneven, cindered road to the beer canteen and cinema. They had expected to be in Gibraltar by now; Scapa Flow was an anti-climax. The vast anchorage was scattered with silent, anchored ships, most in the twilight camouflage of Arctic seas, weather-beaten, with bows red-scarred by ice-rubble and ensigns grey and ragged from months of funnel smoke. The little tin cinema was showing *Pimpernel Smith*, and the Salvation Army canteen offered the same tea, beans on toast, rock cakes and bread-and-jam. At least it was not raining. Over Hoy and Mainland thousands of lapwings wheeled and shrilled, gathering for the autumn migration, and the gulls still lamented over *Royal Oak*'s buoy below the cliffs of Gaitnip.

There was no explanation for *Sheffield*'s return to Scapa Flow, but the men had long ceased to reason. They only knew that Old Shiny did not belong here among the grim, white-grey ships from the Arctic Circle, for theirs was a different war from *Sheffield*'s in the Mediterranean, and the cruiser's men were grateful for the order that took them again to Greenock, to embark Rear-Admiral Harold

Burrough, commanding the 10th Cruiser Squadron. A hundred other passengers were taken aboard, assigned to several ships at Gibraltar and now to be accommodated in several unlikely and equally uncomfortable locations for the passage. The last mail was ashore, gate requested, and *Sheffield* slipped at 2205 on 12 September. The new arrivals from Chatham told themselves that, at last, they were on their way to foreign parts.

In Gibraltar, when they arrived on the 17th, *Ark Royal* and *Furious* were in harbour, and Somerville's flag flew from the battleship *Nelson*. Burrough transferred to his own flagship *Kenya*, and all passengers were deposited ashore.

Nothing had changed in Gibraltar. Lights still blazed at night from late-opening hotels, bar and cafés; there was no blackout, and the bazaars were stocked with foreign goods, imported through Morocco and Spain, that had not been seen in Britain for two years. Men of the King's Regiment and the Devonshires, in starched khaki drill, paraded in Casements Square. There were perm-haired prostitutes of uncertain nationality and equally uncertain age, English beers with every convoy, a plentiful supply of oranges, bananas and melons, fried fish and chips.

It was suspected that, across the bay at Algeciras, the several Italian freighters were not as shabbily innocent as they pretended, and there was no doubt that the enemy maintained a constant watch, from Spanish vantage points, on British warship movements in and out of Gibraltar. Three attempts by Lieutenant-Commander Prince Valerio Borghese to launch underwater craft from the submarine *Scire* had failed, but the fourth, during the morning of 20 September, succeeded in severely damaging two freighters. If the sun did shine on Gibraltar, life was not all beer, skittles and señoritas. Clarke confessed to an uneasy couple of hours 'wondering whether some similar noisome and lethal agency was ticking away under our keel', but there was not, and at 1051 that forenoon *Sheffield* slipped, steaming westward into the Atlantic for the first phase of Operation 'Halberd'.

At the end of July, Operation 'Substance', covered by *Ark Royal*'s Fulmars, had got six freighters through to Malta. Now Somerville, with 'Halberd', was to attempt to fight through nine, laden with troops and vital stores, aware that the Regia Aeronautica had 200 strike aircraft on Sardinian and Sicilian airfields ready and waiting for him. Of these, fifty were torpedo-bombers, thirty were dive-bombers; only Fleet Street made music-hall jokes about Italian pilots. And there was the Italian Fleet yet, incensed over criticism from the Germans and totally unpredictable.

'Two days later [22 September] we took over the convoy', writes Captain Clarke, from the battleship *Rodney*, who went ahead to refuel at Gibraltar. The convoy at that time contained not only the nine large merchant ships bound for Malta but also another nine intended in the first instance for Gibraltar only. On the 24th, still to the westward of Gibraltar, the convoy was joined by the cruisers *Kenya*, *Edinburgh* and *Euryalus* [the first two with Rear-Admirals Burrough and Syfret aboard], the new battleship *Prince of Wales*, and nineteen destroyers. The Atlantic escorting destroyers then detached to hurry on to Gibraltar for refuelling.'

The escort was massive, but it would need to be if the Italian Fleet put to sea in earnest. Somerville, recalling the criticisms levelled at him after the Spartivento action, added a pointed rider to his signal to the Admiralty, outlining his intentions. 'I do not intend to fall into the trap of being led away from [the] convoy by an enemy who has the means and desire to avoid action and whose object may well be the reduction of [the] convoy escort in order to facilitate air and submarine attacks.'

During the early hours of the 25th the ships bound for Gibraltar were detached, the main body passing through the Straits eastward, in darkness to avoid speculative eyes on the Spanish shore. As breakfast was piped, Somerville and the remainder of the covering force hove in sight, and pre-arranged dispositions were assumed during the forenoon. *Nelson* (Somerville), the cruiser *Hermione* and six destroyers constituted one group that steamed on ahead, beyond sight of the convoy, while *Prince of Wales*, *Rodney*, *Kenya*, *Edinburgh*, *Sheffield*, *Euryalus* and twelve destroyers formed the second as close protection to the nine merchantmen. The weather was superb.

The men of Force H were less than grateful for the company of *Prince of Wales*; although in commission only since early 1941 she had already acquired a reputation for being a 'Jonah'. Within minutes of leaving her Liverpool fitting-out berth she had been run aground on a sandbank. Pulled off, she had steamed for Rosyth with two of her four screws lashed to her upper deck; there had been no time to fit them. In Rosyth a pom-pom crew had accidentally fired two rounds, injuring a dockyard worker. Three small fires had erupted in the shell-room of 'B' turret, and two ratings had been badly injured by falls. In May, when, in company with *Hood*, she had steamed from Scapa Flow to intercept *Bismarck*, civilian armourers of Vickers-Armstrong were still working on her defective 14-inch turrets which, in the subsequent action, were to fail and *Hood* would be destroyed. 'The best place for 'er', opined Bungy Williams, 'is the bleedin' Far East, mate, where she can't bleedin' hurt anyone.'

They steamed eastward in conditions as flawless as only the Mediterranean can provide, unaware, says Captain Clarke, that every hour brought them nearer to trouble. *Sheffield* was assigned to the centre and apex of the covering anti-submarine screen ahead, but apart from a possible submarine contact during the evening of Thursday 25th, which the destroyers handled, there was no excitement. Most of the next day, too, passed quietly. Fine weather continued, everything was going to plan, but that evening Intelligence was received that the convoy's passage had been reported by enemy reconnaissance aircraft; within hours the ships would be in easy flying range of the Italian Air Force.

There was no hope, now, of getting past Cape Bon without punishment, and nothing to be gained by continuing in two groups. Somerville, with *Nelson* and *Hermione*, rejoined the main body by dawn on the 27th and ordered a new deployment in anticipation of air attacks. Every ship went to first state of readiness.

Colin Ross began his day with the Morning watch in the Director Control Tower.

'I got the call at 0330 to give me time to collect all the things I'd need during the day, including a stop-watch and some abstruse calculations I'd been making for shooting down Italians. And I always take *The Compleat Angler* to action stations; it's the most soothing and peaceful book imaginable. I also took a sketch-book, but hardly had a chance to use either. I stupidly forgot to get any chocolate the day before, and of course couldn't get any at four in the morning. However, we had a jolly good breakfast in the DCT – bangers and bread and marmalade, and some grand coffee which warmed us up beautifully. I love these

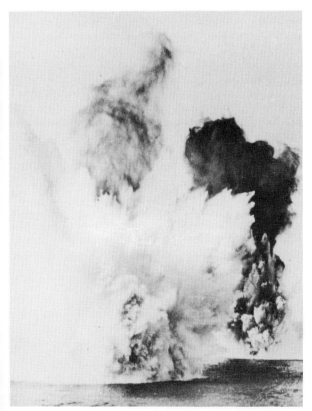

The Italian airmen, far from being the spiritless cravens that Fleet Street named them, attack determinedly through a storm of gunfire, and some of their bombs (above) fall alarmingly close to the convoy. The freighter *Imperial Star* is hit, and is finally finished off by the destroyer *Oribi*.

action stations meals; they are a real picnic, and darned funny because one is too cramped to do it in style.

The lunch might have been good, too, but after some soup we had an alarm and the fun started . . .'

The merchantmen were steaming in two columns; one of four ships, the other of five. The port column was led by *Kenya*, the starboard by *Edinburgh*, while *Sheffield* brought up the rear, as 'Boots', by being stationed between both columns to provide a defence against aircraft coming in from astern. The three battleships placed themselves abeam of the merchantmen – two to port, one to starboard – a deployment that gave their considerable AA armament maximum freedom. The eighteen destroyers were disposed farther afield in a great arc in order to unsettle enemy formations in the final stages of closing. *Ark Royal*, with *Hermione* and *Euryalus* in attendance, was to manoeuvre independently inside the destroyer screen.

It was a beautiful day, with the skies golden blue and flawless. Dolphins, drunk with ecstasy, leapt ahead of the speeding ships, bright silver as they raced through a sea that sparkled with gilded confetti and tumbled astern like snow. The air was like wine. This was the first time that Captain Clarke had commanded *Sheffield* in action; for many aboard it was simply the first time.

'It was not until 1300', Clarke recorded, 'that the first attack by a dozen Italian torpedo-carrying planes, escorted by fighters, appeared ahead of the Fleet. *Ark Royal*'s Fulmars got at them. One of the enemy was shot down and the formation broke up. Six Italians only managed to get into firing positions, and the convoy turned towards them to present a minimum target; their torpedoes failed to find any billets. Of the six that did come in, three failed to survive the concentrated fire from the ships, and a fourth was caught by one of our Fulmars during retreat. This was encouraging. As the attacks, so far, were from ahead, *Sheffield* was not playing a conspicuous part in the action, but we had sufficient long-range firing to relieve the tension on board and warm up guns and crews.'

The BBC news bulletin that morning had announced that the new USA Ambassador, Mr John Winant, had arrived in Britain and German armies were thrusting towards Leningrad. During the forenoon, however, Jack Payne, Alfred Van Dam and Victor Silvester were all making music to deserted messdecks. Sandy Macpherson was switched off, and nobody ever knew about Joan Baker on a piano – whoever she was.

'The next attack came a half hour later from the starboard side; some coming in on the bow and some on the quarter, where our particular interest lay. There were a half dozen or more low-flying torpedo planes, fairly well timed together, but much spread out. Fulmars from *Ark Royal* broke up the quarter attack and shot down one enemy. We and the other ships poured out a good deal of fire, but with no particular result except that of forcing the Italian machines to drop their torpedoes too far off to be effective.'

Ross had taken his gramophone into the DCT. 'The speaker is packed with socks to muffle it, so that we can hear if any of the voice-pipes suddenly gives tongue. When the loud passages of music come on, I just shout, "Put a sock in it," and the duty musician stuffs another sock in the long-suffering gramophone. So, on the whole, we get quite a lot of fun when things are going well.'

It would be known later that the Italian attack was carried out by Lo Stormo del Sacrificio – the Sacrifice Wing – and during this sun-drenched afternoon the Italians would lose thirty-four men including the commanding officer and three squadron leaders. On *Sheffield*'s bridge, Clarke was watching one of those enemy sacrifices.

'Meantime, though, *Nelson*, in turning towards the bow attack with the object of combing tracks, was torpedoed well forward on the port side by one Italian who very gallantly closed almost to point-blank range through heavy fire. In so doing, he ran the gauntlet not only of the merchant ships' fire but also that of *Prince of Wales* and ourselves. The Italians passed so close that I could see the crew plainly, bent over their instruments as if urging their machine to greater speed. They must have sensed that they had only seconds to live. *Prince of Wales*'s pom-poms were roaring away, and close-range armament, which should have done better, appeared to chip bits off the aircraft's rear as she went past. To make certain, one of our Fulmars flashed down on her tail; a moment later an ominous splash astern wrote *finis* to a brave effort.

In the general uproar I did not at first realize that *Nelson* had been hit, but it soon became evident. Although still maintaining the convoy's fourteen knots, she took a noticeable dip by the bows. Admiral Somerville, however, made no move to transfer his flag, and we all assumed that the damage was something that could be kept under control for the time being. At the same time it meant that *Nelson* could not be considered one hundred per cent available offensively if a surface engagement developed.

The attack that had caught *Nelson* was followed by another, involving a dozen enemy aircraft, which again split up and fired their torpedoes from outside the destroyer screen.

Some of the destroyers themselves had narrow escapes, but the barrage and the excellent Fulmar pilots disposed of at least three of the enemy. Further attacks threatened as the afternoon wore on, but these were generally drive off by our fighters, and the convoy had little more than a ringside seat. So far, matters had been most satisfactory; a third of the attacking aircraft had been destroyed in exchange for only, I think, three of our fighters and an unpleasant but manageable hole in *Nelson*'s forecastle.'

And Ross had been enjoying his day – 'the lovely exciting smell of cordite smoke and that strange punch on the nose which you feel when one of your own guns goes off near you. There seemed to be T/Bs everywhere . . . it's exactly like a grouse shoot, but more noise . . .'

At 1530, as the third attack was being beaten off, *Prince of Wales*, *Rodney*, *Sheffield* and *Edinburgh* were ordered to detach and proceed at maximum speed to the north-eastward. An enemy surface force comprising two battleships, four cruisers and sixteen destroyers had been reported in position 38°15'N, 10°30'E, some sixty miles away, and Somerville intended that the enemy warships should be intercepted as far from the convoy as possible. He also ordered *Ark Royal* to fly-off her entire torpedo-carrying strike force of eighteen Swordfish.

Sheffield and *Edinburgh*, overwhelmingly outgunned by the force they were to intercept, were working up to 30 knots, while the two battleships were doing their utmost astern. Clarke was not optimistic of making contact with the enemy, but . . .

'Some minutes after we had set off we sighted the Swordfish force passing overhead in beautiful formation; we wished them luck in their intention to pin down the enemy for us. But I had been right, the enemy vanished as the summer mist. At 1700 we were recalled, and by 1830 we were back with the main body, while the Swordfish

Below: Repeated attacks are made by Italian torpedo-bombers against the ships of Operation 'Halberd', fighting through to besieged Malta, and the battleship *Nelson*, temporarily flying Somerville's flag, is struck. Although down by the bows, she pushes on.

searched to the limit without a smell of the enemy and landed on again with a bare minimum of fuel.'

The Italians were not quite as craven as British propagandists subsequently suggested. The sighting report's position was certainly in error, and the Italian force, determined to oppose the passage of the 'Halberd' convoy, was hamstrung by both poor air co-operation and its orders to remain under shore-based fighter cover at all times.

Yet by 1900 (27 September) the convoy, still intact, was only north of Bizerta and facing a perilous night run through the narrows of the Malta Channel. The destroyers closed around the merchantmen in anticipation of E-boat attacks. *Kenya* and *Edinburgh* still led the two columns while *Euryalus, Sheffield* and *Hermione* followed close astern. Enemy aircraft were already prowling above a purple horizon, primrose in the west, their distant engines inaudible above the whisper of the sea and throbbing of the ships' engines. The friendly dolphins had fled and the waves were laced with green fluorescence as they tumbled. The men of every ship, merchant or fighting, were fatigued and hungry, the sweat dried on their bodies and smelling, their mouths dry.

Unfortunately for the British, the night was superbly clear, cloudless with a bright moon on the starboard quarter, i.e., to southward. The enemy very sensibly came in towards the convoy's northern flank, out of the darkness.

'The difficulty in such circumstances was, first, of seeing the aircraft in time to do anything, secondly of knowing whether they had dropped torpedoes and, if so, in what direction, and finally of observing, in time, what avoiding tactics one's own ships were carrying out. The heavier the gunfire, the less it was possible to distinguish what was going on.'

Following astern of the starboard, and therefore up-moon, column, *Sheffield*'s only warning of attacking aircraft was the streams of tracer from other ships, firing out to seaward, while the repeated, dazzling flare of gunfire from the cruisers and destroyers tended to confuse vision. The ships were beautifully silhouetted against the moonlight, and everyone watched for the distant splash in the darkness that meant a torpedo dropping into the sea, and Clarke would alter course evasively, towards or away.

'We were to meet these problems again later, but that night in the Skerki Channel was our first introduction. Soon after 2030 we clearly saw the splash of a dropped torpedo on the other side of the port column, almost certainly aimed at one of the merchant ships. It still required a full wheel to starboard on our part, which was just as well because our neighbour to port was swinging towards us in avoiding the same threat, or, more possibly, to avoid the next ahead, *Imperial Star*, which had just been hit aft.'

With this success, however, the enemy had shot his bolt, and turned away for home. There was still a hazardous distance ahead of 'Halberd', and Somerville pushed his ships on. *Imperial Star*, now unmanageable, had to be left. The destroyer *Oribi* struggled for several hours to get her in

tow, but the task was beyond her capabilities; it would have required a couple of ocean-going tugs and far more time than the situation allowed. At 0340, crew and passengers taken off, *Imperial Star* was finished off by *Oribi* to prevent her cargo falling into enemy hands.

Meanwhile, the remaining ships of 'Halberd' were pressing on towards Malta. There could be no question of relaxing to even second state of readiness; there were still the possibilities of attacks by E-boats and submarines, for either of which conditions were excellent. About midnight the fatigued British watched the coastal lights of Sicily slide past to northward, and, at 0100 (28th), to distract enemy attention *Hermione* was ordered away to bombard the harbour and base of Pantelleria and to make smoke as if covering a convoy. Her gunfire flashes were clearly visible to the ships of 'Halberd' as they steamed eastward at *Nelson*'s best speed of 15 knots.

At dawn on Sunday an RDF alarm sent gun-crews stumbling numbly to their stations, but the approaching whine of aircraft proved to be friendly. 'I'll never forget the relief of that moment', claimed the Torpedo Officer, Hobson, 'when we saw first Beaufighters and then Spitfires, flying out from Malta to meet us.' And Ross, writing in his next letter, was very tired. 'Having been closed up since 4 o'clock the previous morning – 29 hours either in the DCT or the After Tower – we were very glad to see the sun rise next morning, and warm up in it. We fell in for entering Malta. I was very weary and not much looking forward to securing to a buoy aft, but it was so good to feel that we were through.'

Sheffield, like the other ships of 'Halberd', entered Grand Harbour with seamen on the forecastle cleanly mustered and the Royal Marine band playing – a simple tribute to the hard-pressed people of the island. On this occasion, however, 'Halberd' found the population assembled in full to cheer home the convoy.

'On this day, every vantage point, high and low, on each side of the harbour, was packed with Maltese people. Our band played as we steamed into Grand Harbour, past the Barracca, the Castile and Customs House. It was Sunday, and the people's gay clothes added just that relief to the all-pervading dun of the sandstone walls and buildings. As we entered we heard, faintly at first – then as we drew closer, in ever increasing volume, the sound of thousands of clapping hands – and all along the waterfront, and from the housetops and balconies, the fishing boats and dghaisas. They cheered and cheered and waved their hats until the next ship following came in sight, when they began cheering again. I confess it brought a lump to my throat, and I am sure to many others.'

'They continued cheering', agreed Lieutenant Colin Ross, crawling into his bunk, 'until we were all accounted for, so I turned in knowing we had done a worthwhile job.'

Bungy Williams was already deeply asleep on the deck under the table in 30 Mess, covered by an oilskin. He should not, he ordered, be roused until tot time.

13

'Ice drifting past ship. Deep fog. Deep fog.'

T HE jaded ship's company had been consoled by the anticipation of a run ashore to Valletta's notorious 'Gut', that quarter-mile of bars and sleazy cabarets, custom-designed for sailors with jingling pockets, of sampling Blue Label bottled beer in the Egyptian Queen, the Wheel of Fortune and the Mae West with their tarts and bawdy floor shows. They were to be disappointed. At 1852, just six hours after securing, *Sheffield* slipped for sea and steamed westward to rejoin 'Halberd's' covering force, on course for Gibraltar. With only one merchantman lost, the operation had been a success, although *Prince of Wales*, during the torpedo attacks, had lived up to her 'Jonah' reputation by shooting down one of *Ark Royal*'s Fulmars. Somerville jokingly admonished *Sheffield*, his RDF 'guardian angel', for allowing the flagship to get a kick up the arse; it did not contribute towards his recommendation for Clarke's promotion to Archangel. Cunningham signalled both congratulation and sympathy:

'Flag Officer Force H from CinC Med: – Please accept a slap on the back from me to compensate for a slap on the belly with a wet fish.'

Winston Churchill was compelled to convey to Somerville his approval of 'the latest of a long series of complicated and highly successful operations for which you and Force H have been responsible'.

And several weeks later, after *Sheffield* had parted company with Force H, Sir James Somerville was appointed a Knight Commander of the British Empire, and Cunningham could not resist another quip.

'Flag Officer Force H from CinC Med: – Fancy, twice a knight at your age.'

The return to Gibraltar was uneventful and, securing to buoys at 2030 on Tuesday 30 September, *Sheffield* took an oiler and a water boat alongside immediately. Three teenage stokers had been gulled into officially requesting a licence to smoke a pipe – one of the oldest of gags on the lower deck – and they got it at the Captain's table from a solemn Captain Clarke. And tonight, everyone said, there would be an uninterrupted all night in the sack, a make-and-mend tomorrow, then a stroll ashore for cold beer and an hour of leisurely carnalism behind dingy lace curtains in Flat Bastion Road.

The luxury of sleep, however, was rudely interrupted at midnight by the noise of steel-shod boots descending the midships ladder and moving along the main deck. Eighty-seven Army and RAF personnel had boarded with their kitbags, packs and suit-cases and were being lodged for the remainder of the night in the canteen flat and the seamen's locker space. An hour passed before all were found a sleeping billet and the messdecks again sank into silence.

But it was not to last. At 0300 everyone groaned into their pillows as a bosun's pipe shrieked.

'D'yer hear there? Duty watch to muster aft. Away first cutter. Special Sea Dutymen will close up at oh-four-thirty . . .'

As OA Lucas observed, 'They didn't intend to let us get into a rut, did they?'

Sheffield slipped at 0507, eased past the breakwater and turned westward, working up to 27 knots and followed by *Kenya*.

The capture of the German U-boat *U-110* by the destroyer *Bulldog* during May of that year, and with her a complete Enigma cipher machine with its vital rotor wheels and settings, was to prove one of the most important Intelligence break-throughs of the entire war. As an immediate result the six tankers (including *Friedrich Breme*) deployed for the replenishment of *Bismarck*, plus two other supply ships, were quickly rounded up or sunk by hunting British cruisers. The German programme of deployment for blockade-runners and supply ships never recovered from that crippling blow of 1941, but the Admiralty was still faced with a problem. The continued success of the Admiralty Tracking Room would surely suggest to the Germans that their ciphers had been compromised, and they would take measures accordingly; it could be only a matter of time. The British penetration of the enemy's communication system, therefore, must be exploited for all it was worth before that system was changed, and *Sheffield* and *Kenya*, Captain Clarke told his company, were after a suspected German supply ship north of the Azores.

'The first day was rough', OA Lucas recalls with relish, 'and seasickness was rife among our guests.' The soldiers and airmen huddled with glazed eyes fixed on a bulkhead in the vicinity of the heads or a bathroom and did not present themselves for their breakfast 'train smash' (bacon and tinned tomatoes) or their dinner 'dead baby' (meat suet pudding). 'But within a couple of days they were fit again, and we were able to give them a show for their money – we depth-charged a submarine, halted and boarded a Portuguese merchant ship, flew off both aircraft and then mauled one of them in recovering it, and all this time we were chasing a German supply ship.'

During the evening of 3 October, sweeping the area of anticipated interception, the two cruisers were thirty miles apart, and at 1800, in mist and failing light, *Kenya* sighted a distant vessel at the same time as her airborne Walrus was reporting that she, also, had sighted a ship with a submarine alongside. *Kenya* closed at 29 knots and opened fire from 14,000 yards. Asdic was detecting a second submarine in the vicinity, so, wheeling, *Kenya* loosed a salvo of torpedoes, and the target, to be later identified as the German supply and reconnaissance ship *Kota Penang*, erupted in flame, smoke and flying debris that narrowly missed the Walrus, circling at 1,000 feet.

Five boat-loads of the crew had been lowered from the sheltered side of the enemy ship, but many were trapped aboard. Knowing that U-boats were in the area, *Kenya* did not stop to pick up survivors.

Sheffield anchored off Greenock at 1014 on 6 October to disembark her passengers and take aboard mail covering several weeks. The Clyde, as before, was crowded with vessels of all kinds, under a dark-clouded sky, loading or discharging over their sides into lighters to reduce berthing time, the estuary floating with oil and debris that fouled ships' boats with a greasy scum. Ashore, the passing of two years of war was beginning to show in the general shabbiness of streets, buildings, vehicles and people. There were surface shelters, water tanks and First Aid posts, sandbagged doors and windows, British Restaurants offering shepherd's pie, macaroni cheese or fish cakes. Still, there was beer in the pubs and Vera Lynn singing 'We'll Meet Again', while Scottish lassies' morals were gratifyingly relaxed after blackout time. The Lord Mayor of Sheffield wrote to announce that the cruiser was to be 'adopted' as a part of the city's forthcoming Warship Week effort; the accompanying parcel of table games from the Sheffield Newspapers War Fund was the first fraternal gesture made to the ship since 1937. Press and BBC spoke of the crisis battles for Leningrad and Moscow, but no amount of semantic sophistry could disguise the fact that the Russians were suffering enormous casualties. The first British convoy had just reached Russian waters without interference, and more and more resources were being directed towards the northern seas.

'We spent four days off Greenock', Lucas noted, 'which enabled us all to get two nights ashore. Although we did not know it at the time, this was to be our last run ashore in a civilized place for 25 weeks exactly.'

The ship departed Greenock during the afternoon of Friday 10 October and, twenty-four hours later, anchored in Scapa Flow. On Sunday, Rear-Admiral E. N. Syfret, CS18, was piped aboard to meet the officers and inspect Divisions. *Sheffield* was now a component of the 18th Cruiser Squadron, Home Fleet.

OA Lucas recalls the period as involving 'shoots, more shoots, torpedo firings, oiling destroyers at sea, AA guards, and salvaging our motor boat from the rocks'. The Germans still had a substantial surface force in addition to the widely flung U-boat fleet. *Scharnhorst*, *Gneisenau* and *Prinz Eugen* were in Brest, while *Admiral Scheer*, *Hipper* and the massive *Tirpitz* were poised on the sidelines of the North Atlantic and Arctic convoy routes.

In Scapa Flow newly joined midshipmen grappled with sextants, the seamen weighed anchor manually, lowered and raised boats, and scoured paintwork, signalmen hoisted make-believe flag signals and telegraphists manned the Fleet's exercise frequency. Lieutenant J. M. Larder tells the story of the junior ratings who had been sent away in the cutter for instruction in boat-pulling.

'As was not unusual in Scapa Flow, a gale blew up. The boat could be seen about two cables astern of the ship with the crew pulling hard but making no headway. Commander Searle gave orders for a 2½-inch grass hawser, with a float attached, to be floated out to them. The boat's crew saw the float bobbing on the waves and proceeded to pull towards it, thinking that, when they picked it up, the men on board would haul them in. Instead, they found themselves alongside, having pulled their boat to the ship. The Commander had given orders for the rope to be hauled in slowly while the boat's crew were still rowing hard to reach the float.'

Several officers had unintentionally left bills unpaid at the Tontine Hotel in Greenock, expecting to return shortly, but on 3 November *Sheffield* nosed into Hvalfiord, south-west Iceland. British forces had landed in the Faroes and Iceland in May 1940, to be largely relieved by American troops in July 1941, and when *Sheffield*'s anchor plunged in to the fiord's dark water, the American flag was flying from the old battleships *Idaho* and *Mississippi*, the cruisers *Wichita* and *Tuscaloosa* and a number of smaller warships, including *Kearsay*. All were immaculately painted, with brightwork gleaming, decks whitened, and crewmen impeccably laundered, so that those on war-stained *Sheffield* were half expecting, at any moment, to see Fred Astaire and Ginger Rogers tap-dancing on the *Idaho*'s quarterdeck supported by a chorus of Hollywood sailors.

From the shore the hills climbed skyward. There was absolutely nothing on landing other than a narrow road that followed the water's edge in each direction until out of sight, no buildings, no trees, and only the green-covered,

steeply rising walls of the fiord. Libertymen could climb laboriously to the empty sky, to look down at the tiny, toy-like ships below, or they could tramp three miles up-fiord to an Anglo-American complexity of Nissen huts, among which was included a canteen, the Falcon Club. The beer was Canadian, markedly more potent than British, of which the gravity had been progressively reduced since the beginning of the war, and there would subsequently be some concern felt by ships' officers with regard to ratings returning from shore unfit for duty when all ships were at short notice for steam. Several Army personnel stationed in Hvalfiord, with access to Reykjavik, the capital, had laid in stocks of imported luxury items, rationed or difficult to obtain in the UK, and they now resold them profitably to the shore-going sailors. These included ladies' underwear, costume jewellery, shoes, cosmetics and *nylon stockings* – of which the men had received wistfully glowing reports from their womenfolk at home. For a pair of nylons, it was said, a woman would go to bed with a pig.

'Du Pont fifteen denier, mate, gun-metal grey – and that's the latest fashion. Only three quid a pair, and I'm makin' nothing. Ground bait, did yer say? Even the Bishop's missis will drop her pants behind the lilac if yer flash a pair of fifteen denier . . .'

Joe Honywill, then a junior midshipman, had been in the ship for only five weeks. 'The libertymen had been sampling the Black Horse beer in the shore canteen, and a Royal Marine corporal, who shall be nameless, made a highly improper suggestion to me in the Gunroom bathroom after the Morning watch. Needless to say the offer was refused – but it did my ego good.'

On 5 November 1941 the ships in Hvalfiord were joined by the battleship *King George V*, flying the flag of the CinC, Sir John Tovey, accompanied by the heavy cruisers *Suffolk, Kent, Berwick* and the carrier *Victorious*. The following week *Rodney* and *Cumberland* arrived, and the bleak Icelandic fiord was beginning to resemble Scapa Flow but with even fewer facilities. The flagship had ordered a low-power exercise frequency for junior telegraphists, flag-hoisting sessions for signalmen and midshipmen, sunrise and sunset colours routines, Sunday Divisions in blue suits and church services for all denominations. *Sheffield*'s men were not sorry to be ordered to sea on the 13th for Black Patrol duty, covering the area between Iceland and the Faroes (White Patrol lay in the Denmark Strait between Iceland and Greenland).

A northern cruiser patrol lasted for seven to nine days and almost inevitably, at some stage of it, bad weather was experienced. On this occasion *Sheffield* lost her starboard whaler and a great deal of chinaware from messdecks lockers, and on the 21st, reaching Scapa Flow, the ship heard the news of *Ark Royal*'s sinking in the Mediterranean, miraculously with the loss of only one rating, but dampening spirits among *Sheffield*'s crewmen. If only Old Shiny had still been with her, they vowed, it would never have happened. William Joyce, on German radio, pounced gleefully on the event. *Ark Royal* was sunk, he jeered, repeatedly and venomously – but he had made the claim too frequently before, and now nobody believed him.

Back in Scapa Flow by the afternoon of 21 November, *Sheffield* refuelled to capacity, replenished all stores and disembarked aircraft. These were sure signs of a coming operation. The days were grey, overcast and rain-swept now, the nights black and the ship darkened. There was speculation. Where would it be this time? Iceland again? The fatiguing monotony of Black Patrol? Or Russia? They dug into their lockers for football stockings, long forgotten Balaclavas and the recently distributed knitted 'comforts' from the Ladies of Sheffield. The ship was under orders to leave Scapa Flow at 0400 on the morning of 25 November.

The hands dragged themselves from their hammocks at 0245. The night was wild, with a full gale screaming across the dark Flow, and the forecastle party could hardly stand upright. Further orders were subsequently received, postponing departure, but by that time the lee anchor had been weighed and the weather anchor was almost home. The ship, taken by the wind, dragged through the Fleet, causing considerable anxiety before Clarke brought her under control, undamaged, and again anchored. There was scrambled egg and fried bread for breakfast, and the BBC's 7 o'clock new bulletin reported that the rapidly advancing British Army in Libya had closed around Rommel's armoured forces, whose situation was hourly becoming more desperate, but did not mention the sinking of the battleship *Barham* in the Mediterranean, with heavy loss of life. The news was followed by gramophone records, *Exercises*, and the *Thought for Today*. Both watches mustered at 0815, and *Sheffield* weighed at 1030.

Twenty-four hours later the cruiser was 500 miles to the north-west, passing through the Iceland-Faroes gap, and *Sheffield*'s destination, Clarke revealed, was first Seidisfiord on Iceland's east coast, and then Russia's Kola inlet. It would be the farthest north ever travelled by Old Shiny, her first visit to Russia – a country towards which there were mixed feelings. Nobody had forgotten the Nazi-Soviet pact of 1939, as a result of which Russia had provided Germany with war materials and assisted the passage of German vessels to and from the Far East by the northern route, but, as Winston Churchill had said, any enemy of Hitler was an ally of Britain; necessity introduced strange bedfellows.

For the moment, however, the atrocious weather was all that anyone could think about, and for Captain Clarke in particular there were moments of serious concern.

'The gale continued to blow, and by the 26th it rose to hurricane force. By the middle of the forenoon our progress had come to a full stop. At 7½ knots the ship was pounding head-on into a gigantic sea, lifting her fore-foot clear and smashing down into the trough with sickening momentum, shuddering her length and then reluctantly rising again, only to repeat the process again and again. The seaboats turned to matchwood, deck fittings were twisted and torn, the depth-charges vanished over the side, and lashings thrashed and parted. The huge, steep seas made the handling of the ship a real problem. It was out of the question to turn in such a sea without major damage. Consequently we strove to remain hove to, juggling with the engines and waiting for the barometer to rise out of the pit of Gehenna into which it had dropped so rapidly.'

'It was on this occasion', recalls Operator Allen, 'that Captain Clarke showed his faith in radar, as RDF was now known. During the night, in that terrible weather, I reported a small surface vessel not only precisely ahead but, as successive reports confirmed, on a reciprocal course. We were keeping head to sea, and my understanding of such matters was that under those sort of conditions a vessel presenting her blunt end to the sea would undoubtedly be pooped. The Captain thought so, too, because he indicated that he didn't think there could be a small vessel, in that area, on a reciprocal course. Still, he conceded, if I was absolutely convinced of what I had seen, he would alter a maximum of five degrees, which was as much as would allow the quartermaster to hold the ship on course. I insisted, and the Captain altered course slightly.'

Allen, aware that, if he was mistaken, he could expect an uncomfortable reprimand from the bridge, not to mention the plot and the wheelhouse, turned over his screen to his watch-mate and dashed for the nearest lookout point, the flag-deck. 'And there it was –' he says, 'a drifter or MFV type of vessel, almost within arm's reach! I had to look *upwards* to see it.'

Hours later the Radar Officer, Sub-Lieutenant Rivington (Hurley's successor) conveyed to Allen the Captain's thanks – a never failing courtesy, records Allen, of which the lower deck would always be appreciative.

'Our purgatory lasted seventeen hours,' Clarke writes, 'before welcome signs of improvement. The barometer climbed as rapidly as it had descended, visibility improved, the wind dropped from a howl to a whistle, and gradually we were able to increase speed and move on our way. We were very glad to drop anchor in Seidisfiord, take stock of the damage and begin to clear up the mess. Every sailor, with little encouragement, will tell you of his worst gale. This was certainly mine.'

Old Shiny, however, under another commander, would later experience a storm of even greater violence, with devastating results – but we are ahead of ourselves.

Seidisfiord had its charms if, as Bungy Williams said, you liked that sort of thing. Long, narrow, with a small fishing village at its inner extremity, the fiord was certainly peaceful after days of Arctic gales. For the sailor, however, the holding ground was not too good, and the wind could pounce without warning out of the mountains, demanding constant alertness and many hours of maintaining steam while at anchor. On *Sheffield*'s arrival it was learned that the recent gale at sea had been experienced as a blizzard ashore; a number of British soldiers, caught in the open, had died of exposure. All *Sheffield*'s company were issued with an extra blanket – 'making two all told,' says OA Lucas, 'an ominous sign. Those of the crew who worked on the upper deck each got a pair of leather, fleece-lined gloves and a sheepskin coat.' It was still considered unnecessary to provide anything extra for the majority, who were apparently

Left: For the ships in the Arctic the winter of 1941–2 is atrocious. In late November *Sheffield* runs into a gale of hurricane force, repeatedly pushing her bows into massive walls of water, shuddering . . .

Left: . . . as thousands of tons of brine thunder over her fo'c'sle. Then she gathers her strength and heaves upward, straining every rivet, but winning clear. But another giant roller is ahead, approaching, and the cold and sodden lookouts tense.

expected to remain below decks for eight or nine weeks.

An oiler was waiting, and liberty was granted. There was a ramshackle wooden jetty and a number of equally dilapidated houses, but a mile tramp brought the men to a small white church, more houses and several well-stocked shops, but prices were high. Three hundred troops lived in corrugated iron huts, and *Sheffield*'s Top Division played football against the Marines on a make-shift pitch that was frozen iron hard.

The days had become shorter, the air colder, but it was a dry, crisp cold, and scuttles could be opened to clear messdecks and flats of staleness. On Sunday 30 November,

however, the deadlights were clamped shut again, and the ship disengaged the oiler. The following day, in position 70°34′N, 03°33′W, well north of the Arctic Circle, the convoy was met – five British merchant ships accompanied by the minesweeping sloops *Sharpshooter*, *Hazard* and *Hebe*. Darkness, now, was almost total, and *Sheffield* would not see the sun again for the next three weeks.

For several days, however, the weather remained tranquil, although becoming progressively colder with frequent flurries of snow. It was warm below decks, smelling faintly of warm oil, and men were still slinging their hammocks at night; several earlier convoys had reached Russia and

Right: In Greenock, weeks before, the men of *Sheffield*'s RDF Division had gone ashore immaculately shaved, in 'tiddley' suits, pressed collars and polished shoes . . .

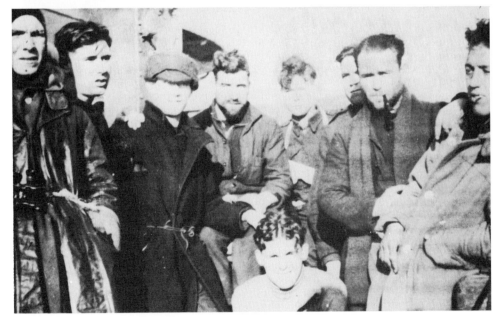

Right: Now, in the bitter temperatures of the Arctic, those same men would be almost unreconizable in a miscellany of oilskins, Balaclavas, football shirts and old coats tied with string. The Royal Navy provided very little protective clothing for the men who served in polar seas.

returned without enemy interference. Condensation was beginning to form on bulkheads, but BBC programmes were being relayed from messdeck loudspeakers until too indistinct to be worth receiving – *In Town Tonight, Sandy's Half-Hour* and the music of Geraldo, Joe Loss, Victor Silvester and Rawicz and Landauer. The Russians, said the news bulletins, had recaptured Rostov; it could be the turning-point of the war. The Admiralty had announced the formation of a new and expanded Eastern Fleet; the battleship *Prince of Wales* and the battle-cruiser *Repulse* had arrived in Singapore. In the UK, egg production was rising, and a magistrate in Manchester, sentencing two

men who had behaved offensively in a public lavatory, announced, 'You two men have to take yourselves in hand and pull yourselves together.' No news agency reported that a Japanese task force was only hours away from a massive air attack on Pearl Harbor. 'The film in the office flat tonight', said *Sheffield*'s SRS, 'will be *The Seahawk*, featuring Errol Flynn. Smoking will be permitted.'

With only five merchantmen, and the weather moderate, there were few station-keeping difficulties, but on the 3rd, in semi-darkness and whirling snow, *Sheffield*'s north-bound group steamed head-on into another convoy returning from Russia.

'This should not have happened', Captain Clarke confesses, 'and maybe somewhere error had crept in. Consequently there followed those tense moments during which both bodies of ships were endeavouring to determine, in the darkness, whether the other was a friend or enemy, followed by some drastic lateral movements to extricate the two masses of ships from head-on entanglement. Thanks to the merchant ships' alertness the episode passed without mishap, and we proceeded on our way, relieved.

The good weather did not last long. The next day [4 December] a sharp gale set in, and progress became slower and slower until, with the wind and the darkness, the convoy became dangerously scattered. *Sheffield* and the escorting fleet sweepers circled the ships, ever pressing them to close up and keep together, so that the anti-submarine screen might be effective. One merchant ship was particularly unfortunate. During a heavy roll, two of her deck cargo of Churchill tanks broke adrift from their moorings, and she had to heave to into the wind for a couple of miserable hours while her crew struggled to re-chain the monsters before serious damage was done.

On 7 December – one is not likely to forget this date of Japan's treacherous act of war against the USA – we reached the approaches to the swept channel into the White Sea, and I turned over my responsibility to Captain J. H. F. Crombie, commanding the British minesweeping flotilla maintained in those waters. *Sheffield* turned about for the Kola Inlet.'

The Kola Inlet was ice-free throughout the entire year. At its head was Murmansk, through which most of the British and subsequently American war supplies, carried by the northern convoy route, passed southward to the Russian armies desperately defending Leningrad and Moscow. The vital railway line from Murmansk ran unpleasantly close to the Finnish frontier, but although frequently attacked by the Luftwaffe, the line was never reached on the ground, and when damaged from the air was inoperative for only hours. The life-blood supplies continued to flow southward.

The inlet, between Murmansk and the sea, provided occasional anchorage for visiting ships close under the hills,

and the black water was just shallow enough for an anchor to reach and hold. The shore was snow-covered, cold and bleak, with spiky sedge reaching to the frozen mud at the water's edge. At the entrance to the inlet lay Polyarno, the Russian naval base and headquarters of the Soviet Naval CinC in the North, which boasted a wooden jetty, its piles clogged with filth and frozen excreta from the latrine shacks built over the river, several rusting Soviet trawlers and a scattering of wooden buildings spreading haphazardly towards distant pine trees. It was difficult to imagine a location more desolate or, indeed, an anchorage more ill-equipped. A sullen party of Russian men and women, almost indistinguishable in heavy swathes of ragged clothing, dog-skin coats and felt boots, shovelled snow from an alleged road, and an occasional ramshackle motor truck churned through the grey slush. After Polyarno, Scapa Flow was going to be paradise.

Sheffield remained anchored in this miserable waterway for a week. The temperature had already been falling on the day of arrival, and by nightfall a black, icy fog enveloped the entire inlet, halting all boat traffic and severing the ship from all outside contact. On the third day the fog was still dense, and the temperature had dropped to an appalling 52 degrees below freezing. The cruiser lay alone in claustrophobic darkness. One hour on the upper deck was as much as any man could tolerate, and teams were organized to work the movable fittings frequently to prevent permanent seizure, but even the torpedoes froze in their tubes, rigging and halyards were as rigid as iron. Rails and wires would burn the skin from unwary hands on contact. Below, every radiator and steam coil was worked to its limit, yet, although the temperature on the centre-line of accommodation areas kept to 60 or 70 degrees, the bulkheads became sheathed in ice that dripped incessantly onto the decks, so that it was impossible to walk anywhere except in filthy water. Throughout the ship – in wardroom and gunroom, cabins, the POs' messes and the stokers' messdeck, the forward broadside messes, workshops and offices, everyone huddled around heaters as the hours dragged slowly on. Ordnance Artificer Lucas remembers

Left: A weather-battered *Sheffield* in Admiralty Disruptive camouflage punctuated by sea rust. After April/May 1940 all ships of the 18th Cruiser Squadron except *Edinburgh* were painted up in camouflage, usually a mix of greys and blue-greys with occasional splashes of brown or green. Camouflage was not to disguise a ship, but to impose a vital few seconds of doubt as to identification in the mind of an enemy observer.

Right: It gets worse. 'Hell ain't bleedin' hot,' says the frozen Oerlikon gunner behind a frozen gun, 'and it ain't Down There, mate. It's up here in the Barents Sea behind this soddin' shooter.'

Right: Members of a 4in gun crew test each other's skill in aircraft recognition. The Navy's opinion of RAF co-operation was not high, and many gun crews would be tempted to fire first and identify afterwards.

well his first week in Russian waters . . .

'Fifty-two below zero was a new experience for most of us, especially as only two months before we had been sweltering in the Mediterranean. Here the sea was smoking with intense cold and the anchorage was blotted out by impenetrable fog. Every exposed mechanism had to be moved at least every half-hour, night and day. Even oil froze. Our messdecks and bathrooms had a quarter-inch of ice on the outer bulkheads. Men were suffering frost-bite, and life was just miserable. Then we received the shocking news that *Prince of Wales* and *Repulse* had been lost. We had been in company with them only a few months earlier.'

Even the cruiser's deck log was confounded:

Wednesday 10 December: Ice drifting past ship. Deep fog.
Thursday 11 December: Deep fog.

Friday 12 December: Deep fog.
Saturday 13 December: Deep fog.

And at this point the pages remain blank for the next three days.

On the 12th, however, the thermometer had risen by ten degrees, and a day later climbed to a mere 22 below zero.

'The fog dispersed', says Lucas, 'and the ship's below-decks began to thaw. There was water, water everywhere – dripping, pooling, puddling, soaking everything that could soak. On the 16th we were able to get away, and none of us was sorry.'

Sheffield slipped and proceeded at 1335 on 16 December, hopeful that the UK would be reached by Christmas Day. Britain had been at war with Japan since the 12th.

Left: Anyone passing beyond the Arctic Circle for his first time will receive a Bluenose Certificate, signed by the Captain.

'Be it known that on this day – in Latitude 79°0' North and Longitude 23°03' East, the Worthy and Esteemed Hubert Treseder, Lt.Cdr., HMS *Sheffield*, defied the elements, regardless of the dangers roaming my Arctic Kingdom, and became an Honourable Blue-nose. I exort you, whales, icebergs and other terrors, leave him in peace – else you incur the iciness of my Royal Displeasure.'

Left: There is a freezing, heaving sea; this is a world that the folks in Bethnal Green could never imagine. The guns must be frequently traversed and elevated to forestall iced-up immobility.

Below left: In the comparative warmth of *Sheffield*'s charthouse, Captain Clarke (right) and the Navigator, Lieutenant-Commander Eric Back, share a dawn discussion on the ship's course.

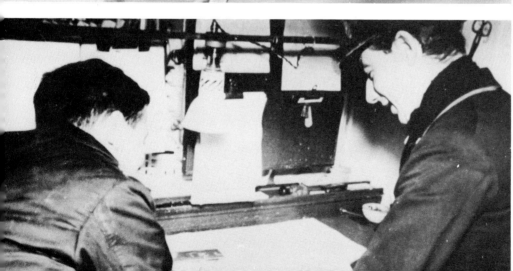

Right: But beyond clamped doors the cold is insufferable; nobody ventures above decks unless on watch and swathed in every towel, scarf and garment from his locker, football stockings and even wrapped newspaper.

Below: *Sheffield* reaches the Kola Inlet, anchorage for Vaenga and Polyarnoe, where British convoys off-loaded war cargoes. The waterway is shrouded in freezing fog which halts all boat traffic. The temperature is 52° below freezing, and the cruiser remains in blind isolation for a week.

Below right: Torpedoes freeze in their tubes, every bulkhead is sheathed in ice, and men are unable to tolerate more than one hour above decks. Can anything be more miserable? It can – when the thaw floods every messdeck and cabin with filthy water.

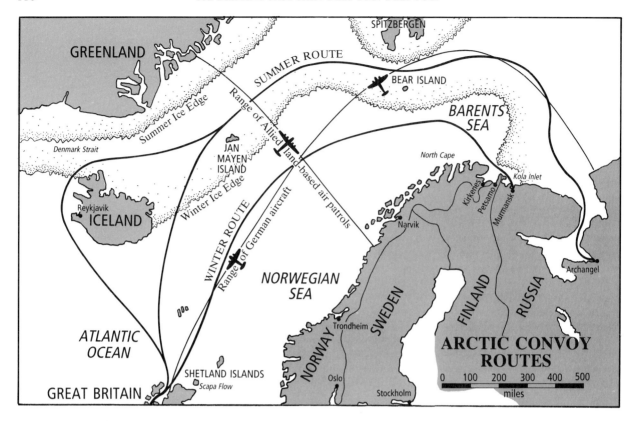

Scapa Flow, indeed – dear old Scapa Flow – was reached by 20 December. An oiler was alongside within twenty minutes, followed by a stores RFA and the Naafi drifter. The ship's own duty cutter made several journeys to Flotta to bring back aboard 168 mail bags of letters and parcels; the mess-tables were strewn with brown paper and string and the First Dog watchmen's pipe was ignored. Watchkeepers were sidling below, and Chiefs and POs were unusually uncaring; most of them were doing the same. The BBC, now loud and clear, told *Sheffield*'s men that Hong Kong's garrison was still fighting and, although Penang had been evacuated by its British garrison, the defence lines on the Malayan mainland were holding firm, and 'the marked enemy inactivity during the last twenty-four hours is probably due to their very heavy casualties and the exhaustion of their troops after their 100-miles advance in eleven days'.

Sheffield's next four weeks were to be spent in Scapa Flow, on several occasions her cable tautening uncomfortably as gales tore at the Orkneys, and on Christmas Day morning the entire Fleet was ordered to one hour's notice for steam. There were howls from forward. Since the previous day the hands had been preparing their messes; bunting was draped, Christmas cards adorned bulkheads, and the torpedo party had rigged coloured lights. The contents of parcels from home were spread on tables –cakes, sausage rolls, pies and confectionary, black puddings, even cigarettes, with many items spoiled in transit. Most men would have preferred that mothers, wives and sweethearts did not

draw on domestic food rations in order to send Christmas fare, while the Navy's duty-free cigarettes and tobacco were both cheaper and of better quality than those available to civilians, but how could anyone churlishly deny the sacrifice that a loved one wanted to make?

On conclusion of Church the ship's company was piped down and the Captain led his rounds of all messes, to be offered sips of rum or taste of a haggis from home, while the officers who followed him ran the gauntlet of a storm of badinage – bearded officers, for instance, were usually greeted with goat-like bleats – before retreating to the wardroom to open a few precious bottles of champagne and receive a visit from Santa Claus. Both ratings' and officers' galleys had cooked turkeys, a gift from the WVS of Canada, followed by pudding, fruit and nuts. The BBC was broadcasting carols, but news bulletins, at intervals, were grave. The Japanese, already driving southward in Malaya, had also taken Wake Island, while General MacArthur, in the Philippines, had withdrawn his surviving forces to Bataan. In the United States many influential voices were urging the President to forget about Hitler and to concentrate all effort in the war against Japan, and in Britain radio and newspapers provided recipes for Spam fritters and dried egg omelettes. *Sheffield*'s men could have contributed corned beef surprise and Webster's first edition liver (leather-bound) but the messdecks were silent during that make-and-mend afternoon until 1530, when Dog-watchmen were piped to the galley to collect mince pies. That evening the BBC announced that Hong Kong had surrendered to the Japanese, and British fortunes, it was clear, had sunk to rock bottom.

That evening's film showing, in the office flat, would comprise a special Christmas double feature – *Pimpernel Smith*, starring Leslie Howard, and *Listen to Britain*, sponsored by the Ministry of Information.

On Wednesday 14 January 1942 *Sheffield* hoisted the flag of Rear-Admiral Sir Stuart Bonham-Carter, CB, CVO, DSO, sometime Commodore, RNB Chatham and Naval Secretary to the First Lord, now commanding the 18th Cruiser Squadron. Bonham-Carter, a shortish, portly man with several chins, did not meet the Boys' Own Paper concept of a lean and intrepid naval commander, and, indeed, his own men would later refer to their inflatable life-belts as 'Bonhams' – although this was also partly the result of his penchant for having ships sunk under him. Still, he was a highly professional seaman and a perceptive and sympathetic officer with an effervescent sense of humour. His most severe trials were yet to come, but he was well equipped to meet them.

Bonham-Carter took *Sheffield* to sea at 1600 on 16 January 1942, leading *Kenya* and *Suffolk*, while an hour astern followed the CinC, Tovey, in *King George V* accompanied by *Rodney*, *Nelson*, *Nigeria* and a destroyer screen. Enemy units were at sea, Clarke said, and were believed to be attempting a break-out. Neither Clarke nor his men knew that an alarm had been raised by reports that *Tirpitz*, the monstrous sister of *Bismarck*, had left the Baltic. If this meant another German berserk sortie into the Atlantic, all British resources must be deployed accordingly, but with Japan rearing her snarling head in the Far East and America's contribution at this time negligible, British resources were being spread cobweb-thin.

Tirpitz, however, was to anchor in Foettenfiord, near Trondheim, her very existence a menace. Tovey turned

Above: Scapa – dear old Scapa. A mixed group of *Sheffield*'s hands enjoy fresh, unfrozen air on the upper deck. They will never again revile the bleak Orkneys, because they have experienced much worse.

Below: On 14 January 1942 *Sheffield* hoists the flag of Sir Stuart Bonham-Carter, CS18 (left) seen here with Admiral Sir John Tovey, CinC, Home Fleet. A highly professional seaman, Bonham-Carter had a reputation for having ships sunk under him and, when he came aboard, men tested their life-belts.

his ships away to Hvalfiord, where *Renown* and *Berwick* were already berthed with the American cruisers *Wichita* and *Tuscaloosa*. The Americans were carrying films from the USA that had not yet been screened in the UK, and *Sheffield*'s men were hoping to see *Dumbo* and *Blood and Sand* in the starboard hangar, but on 27 January the cruiser was ordered to relieve *Kenya* on Black Patrol.

At sea, at least, there were no Sunday Divisions in blue suits and lanyards, no kit inspections or bedding musters for junior ratings. The weather was moderate, but carefully-phrased BBC bulletins could not hide the gravity of the Far Eastern situation. British forces were withdrawing from the Malayan mainland to Singapore and were retreating 'to prepared positions' in Burma. North Borneo had been surrendered, and the American defence of the Philippines was crumbling. In Libya the Eighth Army was retiring in the face of an Afrika Korps offensive, while it was debatable whether the news of US troops arriving in Britain was good or bad.

For the next five weeks *Sheffield* would be sharing the Iceland-Faroes gap with *Kenya* and *Trinidad*, refuelling and provisioning in Hvalfiord, where very few men now considered local shore leave worth while. A destroyer had taken a party down-fiord to Reykjavik, but the returning libertymen complained that the capital's prices were exorbitant, there were no pubs that could be called pubs, and the citizens were coldly unsociable, although less so towards the wealthier Americans. Morale was beginning to sag; the ship's company had not trodden pavements since those four days in Greenock in early October, almost

five months before, and everyone was sick to his back teeth with confinement, over-crowded messdecks, over-crowded bathrooms, the daily, monotonous diet of slushy tinned tomatoes and fried bread or warm tinned herrings-in-tomato-sauce, reconstituted powdered egg that tasted like chopped and warm, sodden blotting-paper, and, not least, corned beef with potatoes boiled in string bags. Most important, few experienced a meal that was hot. By the time it had been hauled from a cooker, consigned to a queuing mess-cook, negotiated through a hundred yards of flats, messdecks and ladders, then shared over two dozen cold plates, the resultant meal had lost any small charm it might once have had.

Yet conditions aboard the smaller vessels frequently in company – the destroyers, minesweepers and trawlers – must, it was recognized, be inconceivably worse; it was a matter of amazement for the cruiser men that the little ships, in the atrocious weather of the Arctic, were able to keep station or achieve a rendezvous, but somehow they always did, despite decks awash, waterlogged electrics and galleys cold for days. In Hvalfiord they came alongside for bread, and their crews might come aboard for hot baths, canteen purchases, or to watch a film, and *Sheffield*'s could look down at the worn deck and rust-streaked hull, their grievances silenced. Perhaps Old Shiny wasn't so bad.

Below: Black Patrol was just that – blackly monotonous, with snow-storms, fog and grinding boredom relieved only by the occasional clear day when the Walrus would be launched on a reconnaissance and anti-submarine flight.

On 3 March 1942, having relieved *Trinidad* on Black Patrol, *Sheffield* had been ordered to leave her patrol line, return to Seidisfiord for refuelling, and then await orders. Clarke complied. The weather was foul, with frequent snow storms and visibility reduced to a mile, but *Sheffield* anchored, took an RFA alongside, and by 1800 was at sea again. The cruiser was to effect a rendezvous with the CinC in *King George V*, in company with whom she would undertake a covering operation for a Russia-bound convoy.

Sheffield, however, was never to reach the rendezvous position.

'Three hours out from Seidisfiord, at 2116, to be precise,' says Captain Clarke, 'there was a sudden, dull and distant roar. The ship lifted, shuddered convulsively, and then lurched forward as if pushed by a giant hand.

I had always determined that if the ship suffered an underwater explosion, the engines should be stopped immediately to prevent a possible collapse of bulkheads abaft the damage from the inrush of water under pressure from the ship's continued forward motion. I had reasoned that even if the explosion had been caused by a torpedo – the most likely calamity – the enemy would probably have fired a full salvo at such an attractive target as a cruiser, and the U-boat would not be in a position to renew the attack until her tubes had been reloaded. That could mean twenty minutes' grace at least. Meanwhile the danger of self-inflicted destruction is a real one until the extent and nature of the original damage has been determined and, to my mind, a greater hazard than the possibility of a further enemy attack.

I stopped engines and ordered night action stations. On the bridge there was nothing more that could be done at that moment. If the drill worked properly, reports could be expected from the damage control headquarters and the engine-room as soon as the facts had been determined. The night was very dark, with a strong south-easterly wind that had been rising steadily since sailing – so much so that our speed of advance had been reduced to fourteen knots, shortly before, to alleviate the bumping we were suffering from the increasingly short sea. The barometer was dropping fast and there was every symptom of a coming full gale. The nearest anchorage was Seidisfiord, about seventy miles away; the nearest base with reasonable repair facilities was more than 700 miles distant. We had no escort.'

At the moment of the explosion, Commander Searle and Shipwright Lieutenant Pack had been standing outside the wardroom abreast the mainmast, and it was impossible to say whether the explosion shock came from forward or aft of them. The Commander went aft and the Shipwright forward, and thus it was Searle who reached the bridge with the first news. As far as could be determined from a cursory examination, *Sheffield* had been holed on the port side aft, midway between the bulkhead before the steering compart-

---

Below: More usually the weather was foul. The smaller vessels came alongside the larger to take on fuel and fresh bread. Below the decks of those little ships existence was crude, cold and always wet and foul-breathing. A day's calm was a day sent from Heaven.

ment and the next watertight cross bulkhead forward. The damage ran the whole length of this watertight section; the main deck and everything below it had vanished from the port side to the centre-line, with the hole itself reaching down and inward to the keel. There was also a hole in the upper deck amidships, apparently from the upward blast of the explosion. Nothing was left of Captain Clarke's day cabin, and very little of the adjoining sleeping cabin, which meant the loss of almost all his personal effects. It had been either a torpedo or a mine, with the point of impact a foot or so below sea surface. As *Sheffield* had been turning to starboard at the crucial time, it did seem more likely that a floating mine had been the culprit. Meanwhile, the engine-room was confirming that all four propeller shafts appeared to be in working order, which was incredible. The damage was immediately abaft the port outer propeller, which was ominous enough, but the port inner shaft ran directly through the area now open to the sea, with its final securing bracket apparently unsupported. In all reason this shaft should have been fractured, or at least bent and usless. So far, so good, but Old Shiny could be only minutes away from an icy grave, and the assessment of the senior shipwright was desperately needed. Pack went aft, to find that nobody knew what had happened beyond the final watertight door. The clips of a manhole escape hatch were kicked off, and, as *Sheffield* rolled in a beam sea, wounded, he lowered himself into a black unknown. The faces of the after damage control party, apprehensive, filled the circle of light above him.

Pack's own account is worth reading.

'Water was beginning to slop around, the hatch to the steering compartment was open, and the watertight door to the main cabin was open. Just inside this door my torch shone on a large fountain of water falling from the broken fire-main overhead. The cabin flat was also in darkness and the water swirled over my rubber boots as the ship rolled. I began to make my way forward by the starboard cabin doors when I trod on something soft that gave out a groan. It so startled me that I dropped my torch, and while I was groping for it the ship rolled to starboard; I could see the moonlight coming through the huge hole in the port side.'

Recovering his torch, Pack realized that he had trodden on the badly injured keyboard sentry, Marine F. W. Wint. He yelled up for a first aid party, which soon tumbled down accompanied by the CPO Shipwright, and both turned their attention to the damaged area.

'In the limited light of my torch we could see the after capstan engine standing up on a part of the torn-up steel deck. From the huge hole in the ship's side a large part of the deck had been torn away, and the sea was washing into the flat and swilling in and out of the cabins on the starboard side. Commander (E) joined us going forward and closed the isolating valve to the fire-main. No further casualties could be seen, so we abandoned that compartment, clamping the after watertight door tight behind us. By this time the hand steering party of Marines had arrived to man the manual steering gear below the Captain's flat.'

However, the crucial bulkhead that now stood exposed

Left: During the evening of 4 March 1942, three hours off Iceland, a contact mine explodes under *Sheffield*'s port quarter, blowing a hole 35 feet by 2 feet in the outer bottom and causing severe structural damage between the keel and the upper deck. All compartments in the vicinity are flooded up to the waterline, all electrical circuitry in the area destroyed. Steering gear and 'X' and 'Y' turret pumps are out of action, with speed reduced to six knots.

to the pounding sea had been fractured. The steering compartment was threatened; its loss would be disastrous. Pack ordered his damage control party to begin shoring for their lives, then climbed to the bridge to report to the Captain as *Sheffield* wallowed, stopped in the cold darkness.

Clarke wasted no time in speculating on the consequences of steering collapse. He ordered a wireless signal to be made immediately, and then decided to ascertain if the ship could steam without exacerbating the damage already sustained.

The emergency report hammered out on Ship/Shore H/F was received a thousand miles away and within minutes had been relayed to the Admiralty's Operations Room, CinC Home Fleet and Flag Officer Iceland. Tovey at once broke W/T silence to indicate that he had detached two destroyers to provide assistance, while FO Iceland alerted the Norwegian-manned aircraft under his command and FO Clyde was ordered to despatch two deep-sea salvage tugs even although the crippled cruiser was a thousand miles away. Intercepting the interplay of signals, the men on *Sheffield*'s bridge were comforted; things were beginning to happen. The vital bulkhead was leaking like a sieve but still holding, and Pack's men were working like madmen to erect a coffer-dam around the steering compartment, with all timber and portable pumps being dragged over the quarterdeck in darkness as the weather worsened and the ship rolled sickeningly.

'But a confession must be made,' says Captain Clarke. 'The violent wallowing while the ship was stopped had created quite a welter of odd books, dirty cups and papers on the plot and, as it happened – although we know it should not – part of the edge of the chart had become obscured. The plotting officer, in reading off the position, glanced down the side of the chart and, alas, read the latitude one whole degree wrongly, which meant that the signal transmitted placed the ship exactly sixty miles southward and, worse, in the middle of the minefield.'

Many years later the Captain, in retirement, could chuckle over an incident that almost certainly blighted his further advancement in the Service. In the Admiralty the First Sea Lord, Sir Dudley Pound, had gazed disbelievingly at the pin pressed into position by the Duty Operations Officer, then enquired accusingly, 'Who's her Captain?' There was, as always, the bright officer with the correct answer, and Pound nodded. 'Just what I would have expected,' he grunted, and had returned to his bed when, twenty minutes later, *Sheffield* discovered her error and signalled a correction.

Meanwhile, Clarke was fighting to save his ship, and had decided to make for Seidisfiord, the nearest sanctuary. Anywhere further was very risky, and indeed even Seidisfiord was unlikely with the ship's crippling damage and the threatening weather.

'I went ahead tentatively at four knots on the port outer shaft and the two starboard shafts,' Clarke recalls, 'exactly seventeen minutes after the initial explosion. Our ship-wrights were still trying to establish the extent of damage to the bulkheads involved. Further flooding through leaks was a danger that, if not arrested, could lead to instability, while if the bulkhead abaft the damage was carried away, the steering gear would become useless, and we could never control the ship, in that weather, without a rudder. Anyway, the general weakness aft would have become so great that the stern of the ship might have dropped off . . .'

Reports from below, however, were encouraging. Only a trickle of water was entering the steering compartment from the damaged area, and the steering party of Marines was following orders from the bridge through emergency communication circuits. Shipwrights were preparing a concrete coffer-dam to secure the most sensitive bulkhead and had already raised a wooden breakwater and shored up adjacent bulkheads with timber. It could not be ascertained how far the rupture of the hull extended inboard below sea level, and it was clear that the ship could only progress at minimum speed; the submarine risk had to be accepted. All hands, wearing life-belts, were at their stations, most of them anticipating the shock of further explosions or the sudden collapse of *Sheffield*'s stern. It was icily cold, the sea vicious, with much of the ship reduced to emergency lighting. 'It was a miserable night in the after steering compartment', says the Torpedo Officer, Hobson, 'with men hauling water out with buckets, getting the portable pumps down, and running emergency cables over the quarterdeck to supply the steering motors and the after gyro repeater.'

Had the explosion occurred only twenty minutes later the loss of life might have been considerable, with the ship's company at Action Rest stations and 'Y' shell room crews and Pack's damage control party mustered in the damage area. In the event, miraculously, only the unfortunate keyboard sentry had been killed – 'Poor old Tubby Wint,' remembers Marine Thorndyke. 'He loved his books; I found one of them in his tattered uniform pocket.'

Having got the ship moving, Clarke now had to turn her towards Iceland, and anything could happen.

'Slowly the ship was brought around, trailing the port inner shaft for fear of overstraining the hull abaft the hole, and we began to crawl homeward. Unavoidably the new course brought the weather to the damaged side, and both wind and sea were continuing to rise. The ship laboured heavily, each roll to port driving the sea into the hole, to smash against our life-saving bulkhead and finally erupt spectacularly through the ruptured quarterdeck. Everyone watched anxiously, the damage control personnel, sodden and cold, labouring in the darkness aft. The roar of wind and sea, the surrounding blackness and continuing uncertainty, demanded strong nerves.

But then, just after 2300, we were cheered by the arrival of Captain Alan Scott-Moncrieff with the destroyers *Faulknor* and *Eskimo*, detached by the CinC from a force operating to northward. They had been driven relentlessly, with some damage, into a head sea to our succour, and their company was a positive tonic.'

'I could have cried to see those destroyers,' admitted Marine Thorndyke, one of the S2 gun crew. 'They appeared like two white angels astern. Now we felt safe.'

Sheffield, however, was very far from safe. Ahead were twelve hours of painfully slow steaming, with every heavier-than-usual roll bringing hearts to mouths and life-belts clutched. The journey seemed endless, with the destroyers tirelessly circling the crippled cruiser as she limped towards sanctuary. In every circuit of twenty minutes each escort was exposed to every vicious characteristic of the weather – first pitching heavily into a head sea, then turning to take the weather on the beam, turning again to surge down as the pursuing sea crashed up over the stern, and concluding with another leg of sickening rolling. Then the circuit had to be repeated, again and again; the below-decks squalor in those little ships must have defied description. In *Sheffield*, on several occasions, the timber shoring that had been hastily raised in support of the steering-room bulkhead began to disintetrate under the sea's pounding, and the crouched shipwrights, keeping watch, fought, blaspheming, to mend the damage. During the Middle watch, very gingerly, *Sheffield* increased to 6 knots, and the Commander reported from aft that, so far, all was good.

'At last,' Clarke records, 'at 1000 on 5 March, we closed Seidisfiord and entered at 1100. With the protection of the land the wind died and the distressing rolling ceased. The ship reached the head of the fiord and we dropped anchor. Phase one was over.'

But only phase one. Seidisfiord offered only a temporary respite from the sea and time to assess damage. There were no repair facilities, still nearly a thousand miles to Rosyth or Belfast, more to Newcastle or the Clyde. Meanwhile, *Sheffield* at anchor was still visible from the fiord's entrance and was not beyond the reach of an enterprising U-boat.

Shipwright Lieutenant Pack, however, could now descend to undertake a full inspection of *Sheffield*'s damage.

A massive, diamond-shaped hole in the port side, 35 feet long, extended from just below the upper deck – the quarterdeck – reaching almost to the keel. There was a huge crater in the main deck, and some ten compartments and store-rooms were flooded; the Spirit Room had been completely demolished and this, with the flooded and inaccessible wardroom wine store, 'caused some dismay throughout the ship'. Cabins and offices on the starboard side had been washed clean of furnishings and artefacts; lookouts had earlier reported seeing what appeared to be mines bobbing astern, and it was now realized that these must have been rum barrels and the Captain's furniture.

(The quarters here referred to were normally occupied by the Commander, but they had been temporarily appropriated by the Captain, who, in turn, had conceded his own accommodation to Rear-Admiral Bonham-Carter. It had therefore been a fortunate exchange for Commander Searle, while Bonham-Carter was maintaining his reputa-

tion for being a Jonah to any cruiser in which he flew his flag.)

The first move was to clear away as much debris as possible, and as the main deck was above sea level, this was quickly done. The ship's safe and the confidential books boxes were intact, but some difficulty was experienced in extracting the code-books as many of them were swollen by water. One heavy volume had to be drilled out by the shipwrights.

The ship's stern was then lightened by lifting all 6-inch ammunition from 'Y' shell room, the hatch of which was four feet under water, and transferring it forward. This operation entailed constructing a timber coffer-dam around the hatch and pumping out the enclosure, with the shipwrights working in icy water and without pause.

There could be no attempt to rebuild the hull. Most of the 500 square feet of the hole was submerged and, in any case, no steel plating or essential equipment was available in Seidisfiord – or, for that matter, in Iceland. A salvage specialist, Lieutenant-Commander McLaughlin, RCNVR, had arrived by tug from Reykjavik and, meanwhile, the body of Marine Wint was buried ashore, with full honours, in the little cemetery outside the village.

Somehow, Clarke had to repair *Sheffield* sufficiently to permit a safe passage to a UK dockyard while, at the same time, ensure the safety of the disabled cruiser during the weeks of repair.

'The obvious things to do were, first, improve the longitudinal strength of the ship in the vicinity of the damage with girders, to further bolster up the contiguous bulkheads, and to provide some means of breaking the force of the sea entering the ship under way. McLaughlin proposed the construction of a wooden shield, in no sense watertight, but so made as to be flexible, rather like a Venetian blind. This was to be bound over the hole with wire cables rove around the ship abreast the damage, and braced on to further cables similarly rove – rather like darning a sock. First the hole would be crossed vertically by six wire hawsers passed right around the ship and hauled taut. Then heavy wooden planks would be placed edge to edge, in the fore-and aft line horizontally on the vertical wire background. This done, further vertical wires were to be wound around the ship, over the timbers. Everything must be built up on the quarterdeck, secured plank by plank to its outer binding wires, and then eased section by section over and down the side, hauled by the securing cables in the blue-frozen, numbed seamen's hands until the shield built itself around the hull, from the top strake of the damage to the keel line.'

This task promised to consume every foot of wire hawser in the ship, while timber was another problem; Iceland is almost bereft of trees. Fortuitously the Army ashore had recently taken delivery of a shipload of 4-inch and 2-inch planks, intended for the construction of a jetty, and McLaughlin persuaded the soldiers to surrender it. Clarke, tongue in cheek, claimed that he 'had no detailed recollection of the transaction which was brought to a sat-

Right: Miraculously, only one man – Marine F. W. Wint – is seriously injured, to die within hours. *Sheffield* is nursed slowly into Seydisfiord, and during the next two weeks her crew labours under difficult and icily cold conditions to fashion a huge patch over the hole with timber, cables, concrete and coke, just sufficient to get the ship back to a repair dock in the UK.

isfactory conclusion through the forceful character of the naval officer'.

The timber lengths were too short to cover the length of the hole, so the shipwrights and carpenters applied themselves to making adequate lengths by scarfing and bolting pieces together, end to end. They worked in the waist, surrounded by canvas screens, to make up fifty jointed units, while the blacksmith heated and hammered steel rod into 200 U-shaped bolts. Artificers sweated at benches below, drilling metal and cutting threads, and while some seamen worked at the wires, others strained and hauled at the timber baulks. The pumps panted endlessly. It was bitter and fatiguing work, and Clarke knew it.

'From dawn each day the work went on, and slowly the shield took shape. There was a great deal of snow, which did not make the exercise a picnic. An occasional visit to the scene with, I fondly imagined, a sage remark or two, was the limit of my personal interference. This was the Commander's province.'

The Captain, of course, was right. His men did not want to hear platitudes from an officer with clean hands and polished shoes, even if he was the Captain. They would far rather have their midday tot; the loss of that palliative without which the sailors' day had become misery was a serious blow to the ship's morale. It was sufficiently serious for Clarke to send the Paymaster Commander ashore to request another favour from the Army; he returned with the motor cutter loaded to capacity with jars of Army rum. It was of the same high quality as that issued to the Navy – from whom, Bungy Williams snorted, the soddin' Army had probably bleedin' pinched it in the first place.

It was only reasonable that an attempt should be made to reach the Wardroom's wine store. The Commander agreed, providing only officers handled any bottles recovered. Again the flat was pumped clear and, with difficulty, a small coffer-dam was built around the wine-store hatch. Then the hatch was opened and the store also was pumped free of water. This time the operation was repeatedly interrupted; the pump's suction pipe was clogged by bottle labels. However, to the Wardroom's delight the stored bottles had suffered very little damage. True, vintage selection thereafter was very much a lottery, but that was a small price to pay. After all, a subsequent and similarly laborious operation that penetrated to the Admiral's store on the port side yielded only a single bottle of sherry.

Clarke applied himself to the question of his ship's security. Immobilized within the confines of Seidisfiord, *Sheffield* was vulnerable to U-boat attack and shelling from seaward, and the Commander-in-Chief could afford little in the way of protection, but he did detach two destroyers for the duration of the temporary repairs. One patrolled the mouth of the fiord while the other, within, remained at short notice for steam. A flight of Norwegian-manned Northrop aircraft provided routine reconnaissance coverage, and *Sheffield*'s own two planes were worked hard. Finally, two anti-submarine trawlers, based on Hvalfiord, steamed inshore patrols, and it was one of these, *Stella Capella* of 440 tons, that disappeared without trace on 11 March. Clarke's concern was not unfounded.

It was more than likely that, by now, the enemy knew of the cruiser's predicament. The possibility of bombardment by a heavy warship was unlikely but not to be entirely dismissed; *Sheffield* must be able to hit back. An officer with two telegraphists, portable wireless equipment and fourteen days' provisions were landed to establish an observation post in an old building that stood on high ground at the fiord's entrance. It was Clarke's intention that *Sheffield*'s guns, firing blind at a seaward enemy, could be controlled from this point, but fortunately it never became necessary to test the plan. Portable wireless equipments were invariably of Army origin and never seemed to be operationally compatible with ship-borne installations. Clarke conceded that a few practice salvoes would have been a good thing, but *Sheffield* usually lay with her stern to the sea, and any suggestion that 6-inch guns might be fired over the shredded after-end of the ship, just for practice, would have been met with obscene howls of disbelief from shipwrights, carpenters, artificers and raw-fingered seamen. It was better, Clarke sighed, to let sleeping dogs lie.

On 12 March, Rear-Admiral Bonham-Carter, politely expressing his regrets, departed aboard the destroyer *Maori* for Scapa Flow with his staff. The 10th Cruiser Squadron needed him. *Sheffield*'s men, equally polite, did not feel bereaved; flag officers and their patronising staff were more highly appreciated when in some other ship.

On this occasion Bonham-Carter transferred his flag to the cruiser *Edinburgh*, at Scapa Flow, and that ship, during her next assignment – escorting convoy QP11 from Murmansk to Iceland – was torpedoed and sunk. Bonham-Carter, his entire possessions contained in a suit-case, having lost most of his gear in *Sheffield* – took his flag to *Trinidad*, in the Kola inlet. This cruiser, already damaged by torpedo and crudely repaired by the Russians, began her homeward run but was the victim of savage air attacks, caught fire, and finally sank. Bonham-Carter had yet again lost his flagship.

Above: The body of Marine Wint is buried with full honours in the little village cemetery, in company with other British servicemen killed on active service in the northern theatre.

In the fiord, radio reception of BBC programmes was very poor, but news in English was broadcast by Reykjavik, and most of it was bad. The surrender of Singapore had been confirmed, and apparently a coalition of British, American, Australian and Dutch warships had suffered a reverse in the Java Sea. Java had been lost to the Japanese, and British resistance in Burma seemed to be collapsing. There was a confused report of the German warships *Scharnhorst*, *Gneisenau*, *Prinz Eugen* and six destroyers departing Brest and forcing a passage eastward through the Channel to reach Germany.

By the eighth day the massively knitted mat of timber and wire hawser was in place and attention was transferred to reinforcing it by internal bracing. Short lengths of wire were rove through the timbers and bolted to cross-beams under the quarterdeck. 'The whole thing', Captain Clarke sighed, 'looked like a cat's cradle, but the additional bracing did help to shape the shield to the lines of the ship. It now only remained to give our masterpiece a trial.'

The Fleet Constructor Commander had arrived to give his opinion on the temporary repair, and a weary Shipwright Pack's labour was rejected as unsound. 'Our spirits touched bottom when he condemned our patch out of hand as useless, then said that, before he could approve, steel girders must be made and fitted across the damage, reinforcing the internal bracing.' Such steel reinforcing was simply not to be found in an Icelandic fiord, but the Canadian, McLauchlin, 'was completely unperturbed by the Constructor Commander's rebuff; like all salvage men he was entirely practical. He dismantled the girder rails that transported torpedoes in the waist and welded them together to make a single length. This was secured fore and aft across the damage.' The patrolling destroyers,

Faulknor and *Eskimo*, were ordered to contribute all wire hawsers not in immediate employment.

The additional work demanded six more days, and then Clarke ordered steam for a trial. *Sheffield* moved cautiously down-fiord towards the open sea and the long grey rollers that waited, but even as the ship's bows met the first sea-borne swell, McLaughlin was reporting that the patch was showing movement. Clarke turned back into Seidisfiord.

What was required, McLaughlin decided, was firm over-all pressure against the huge timber patch from within. He repaired ashore, purposefully, although what he hoped to find in this frozen wilderness nobody could imagine. When he returned, however, he announced that he had 'negoti-ated the acquisition' of several hundred tons of coke.

Coke –?

And, yes, McLaughlin wanted it bagged, transported aboard, and packed tightly into the compartments inward of the damage. The timber-and-wire shield would be sup-ported and, if any water intruded, the coke would absorb it like blotting-paper.

The embarkation and stowage of coke took two days – 1,200 bags on the first and 1,500 on the second – with the men urged to their utmost effort by the Commander. On 23 March McLaughlin declared himself satisfied and, again, Clarke took *Sheffield* slowly down the fiord. Despite a stinging wind, off-duty men thronged the upper deck watching the sullen sea ahead. The swell was markedly heavier than before, and McLaughlin, they breathed, had better bleedin' know what he was doing, or one of H.M. cruisers was going to be lost, any minute now, and next of kin would be informed. *Sheffield* rolled ominously.

Gingerly, Clarke increased speed to ten knots, then twelve. A modest bow wave was lifting, the wake creamed astern and all was well. Twelve knots; the patch was holding – so far. 'Fourteen knots, please,' Clarke ordered Back, the Navigator, and on the quarterdeck McLaughlin, one knee on a bollard, peered over the port side. Fifteen minutes later the Shipwright Lieutenant, Pack, joined him from below. 'It's holding,' he confirmed. 'Tight as a drum. Given good weather, I'd say we're ready.'

Clarke, however, did not intend to gamble. The first leg of *Sheffield*'s passage to a home dockyard was 700 miles to Scapa Flow with the Faroes as a possible half-way refuge, and he needed not less than three days of good weather, par-ticularly free of sizeable swell. He was prepared to wait, and the Admiralty's meterological broadcasts began to include unusual emphases on the Iceland-Faroes area. The causes of a sea-swell, however, may originate hundreds of miles away, and Clarke was aware that, under war circumstances, he could not expect more than, at best, a 48-hours specu-lation.

In anticipation, however, of dockyard repair and home leave, libertymen were returning from shore with nylon stockings and cheeses, the only items available locally which, it was considered, would keep unspoiled. After sev-eral days a certain aroma escaping from kit lockers provided a degree of doubt. The early morning meteorological report of Friday 27 March was optimistic; there were no signs of approaching bad weather, and such swell as existed would progressively decrease. It had to be today, if only for the sake of those cheeses.

McLaughlin and his salvage tug departed for Reykjavik, *Faulknor* and *Eskimo* were ordered to sea for a final Asdic sweep of the approaches, the harbour defence party was withdrawn, and at 1000 *Sheffield* weighed, moved out of the fiord and began to work up to 13 knots.

For the first few hours the swell caused worry, but it steadily subsided. The wind was only light and the sun shone, while with each hour the BBC's signal was stronger. A church service was being broadcast during Stand-easy, and the one o'clock news bulletin announced that General MacArthur had landed in Australia – with the implication that the war against Japan was all over bar the shouting – the destroyer *Vortigern* had been lost in the North Sea, and, in the UK, coal rationing was soon to be introduced.

During the afternoon a segment of the timber shield broke away and a stream of coke emptied into the sea for the rest of the day.

It was during the afternoon of the second day, however, that *Sheffield*'s crew became uncomfortably aware that they were still far from home and safety. The ship had passed beyond the Faroes and a vicious southerly wind was whip-ping up the sea. Clarke reduced speed, but within minutes another portion of the timber shield had been torn away. Damage control parties were piped aft and pump hoses connected. If the disintegration continued and the weather deteriorated further, the cruiser could again be in serious trouble.

'Just before sunset', Clarke recorded, 'I considered turn-ing back to shelter in the Faroes, but as this would have brought the damage to the weather side, I decided against it. It was at this time that our Chaplain [Revd. M. H. R. Synge] overheard me say, "Only God can fix this weather. There's nothing we can do about it, so let's press on." Synge went immediately to his cabin and offered up a prayer for fine weather; within the hour the weather began to abate, and by daylight we were again bowling along in a light breeze, a smooth sea and not a vestige of swell.

Six hours later, at 1000 on Sunday 29 March we passed triumphantly through Scapa Flow's boom defences and dropped anchor.'

Several tiresome days were given to repairing the dam-aged shield; everyone was anxious to get away to the Tyne, the designated venue for dockyard attention. On Wednesday 1 April 1942, promised a further spell of rea-sonable weather, *Sheffield* slipped southward through the Hoxa gate and into the Pentland Firth. Twenty-four hours later she secured alongside at North Shields to disembark ammunition and to cut away and jettison the big timber patch from the port side. Then, with leave parties mustered and ready to depart, Old Shiny was received into the hands of Palmer's Yard at Hebburn.

14

'We are setting out on a great enterprise'

I N HEBBURN, Captain Clarke went ashore for the first time in nine months. Some two-thirds of the ship's company, on completion of leave, were to be returned to Chatham for re-allocation, and all midshipmen were drafted away for three months' hard-lying experience in destroyers. The yard's performance, however, fell very short of expectation. 'The refit', simmered Hobson, the Torpedo Officer, 'so cheerfully started with the firm promise of everything we asked for, was followed by the gradual realization that the dockyard was completely crooked.'

Hobson was perhaps a little unjust; neither he nor any-one else aboard *Sheffield* could understand why, as soon as repairs began, the yard's platers went on strike for higher pay, although they were already earning several times more than any of the cruiser's sailors and sleeping in warm beds every night. The trades unions were a law unto themselves; the war was a convenient element of the old law of supply and demand. Meanwhile those workers engaged on board stole everything they could smuggle over the gangplank in their tool-boxes – rations from the mess-lockers, shoes and clothing, watches, money and cigarettes left momentarily unguarded. Finally, the dockyard's management failed to disclose that all dockyard employees would be proceeding on their annual holidays before the termination date of the refit, leaving all final work in the hands of the Admiralty overseers and the ship's own technical personnel.

When the midshipmen rejoined on 10 July, however, they were to find many modifications. The gaping hole, of course, had been repaired and, throughout the ship, watertightness had been improved; one watertight door in every bulkhead was blanked off. Oerlikons had been installed on 'X' gundeck in place of the 0.5-inch machine-guns. The planking had been stripped from the quarterdeck and replaced by a non-slip, non-inflammable composite material. There was a new after tower. The chain system for paravanes had replaced the old bar system, and there were now two new motor cutters and a 25-foot motor boat.

The most important installation was that of a compre-hensive range of radar equipments covering air search, surface search, main armament control, secondary arma-ment control and close range AA direction. There was no longer a single 'cuckoo' but, as Bungy Williams observed, a bleedin' aviary.

Sheffield undocked on 11 July, to reberth at North Shields. On the previous day a large lower-deck draft had joined, representing two-thirds of the ship's company – and that meant an uncomfortably large percentage of crew who were strangers to the ship. The process of ammunitioning, storing and provisioning was chaotic, with green ratings stumbling aimlessly among a labyrinth of flats and passageways as the Commander, Searle, and the First Lieutenant, Hobson, snarled blasphemies at an absent, sun-bathing work-force and an equally chairbound drafting authority that could send three hundred wide-eyed youths to a cruiser that was desperately needed in that white-shot hell of Arctic convoying. True, in England it was July and midsummer, but in only three or four weeks Old Shiny would be nudging through ice rubble and frozen fog in the Arctic, with messdecks streaming with condensation, the bulkheads iced and the below-decks puddled underfoot. A contingent of Boys, aged 16½ years, climbed the brow on the 15th. Repainting in Admiralty Disruptive Camouflage, 507A, 507C and B5 – convoluting dark and light grey, and pale blue – was finished, just in time to be spoiled by the tanker *Shearwater*, which, passing up-river, scraped the port side, tore off the refuse chute and imposed a small dent in the side armour. Nothing seemed to be going well for *Sheffield*.

One of the newly joined officers during this period was Lieutenant-Commander Hubert Treseder, to assume the duties of Air Defence Officer, Snotties' Nurse and Boys' Divisional Officer in addition to organizing all seaman training. On arrival Treseder was immediately sent off to the old seaplane carrier *Pegasus* with Lieutenant (E) Jane to learn something about Walrus catapulting. He wrote to tell his wife that 'Jane and I are going to Arran for a fort-night,' only to receive in return an angry demand: 'Who is Jane?' He was, he says, still trying to answer that question twenty years later.

With a number of equipments still working only fitfully or not working at all, *Sheffield* departed the Tyne at 0759 on Monday 20 July 1942 and secured to a buoy off Rosyth that same evening. On the 24th she proceeded to Scapa Flow, to be boarded and her company inspected by Vice-Admiral Bonham-Carter, still commanding the 18th Cruiser Squadron. *Sheffield*'s men eyed their mainmast apprehensively but, to their relief, no red-crossed flag was hoisted, and Bonham-Carter returned to *Cumberland* – who, said Bungy Williams, could bleedin' keep 'im.

Asked later about the proportion of Hostilities Only to Long Service personnel in *Sheffield* at the end of 1942, the Commander, M. W. St. L. Searle (later Rear-Admiral Searle, CB, CBE) said that he had carried out an analysis about twelve months before [end of 1941], 'and I think the proportion then was about 30 per cent. We lost quite a number of the regulars at Newcastle [end of 1942] and accepted a much higher dilution. However, I don't think the overall dilution exceeded 60 per cent, as very few Leading Seamen and above [about 40 per cent of the complement] were H.O.s. Of the men who surrounded one on the bridge or upper deck, fully 75 per cent were H.O.s, but there were a lot of hard-core regulars out of sight.'

If Searle was right, then Old Shiny was exceptionally fortunate to have retained so large a number of long-serving professionals after three years of war. Undoubtedly *Sheffield*, at this time, was far from being an efficient fighting machine, and Clarke desperately needed both time and opportunity to drill his ship.

'Our first requirement was an intensive programme of exercises, so the ship was in and out of Scapa Flow, engaging in main and secondary armament firing practices, night encounter exercises, aircraft handling, general drills and damage control exercises. All this carried us through August. Occasional fog disrupted activities but, when the ship was called upon for operational involvement, I felt satisfied that she was ready and that all of the refit troubles had been overcome.'

There was no further doubt, now, that the days of Mediterranean sunshine, Gibraltar, blue water and dolphins were long passed, and the old men among the messdecks could stop reminiscing. There were to be no more runs ashore under hot, golden skies, Main Street and Alameda Gardens, sloe-eyed Moroccan parties flaunting their nipples to entice innocent Stokers 2nd Class into Line Wall and a damp, urine-reeking room that five others were waiting for. *Sheffield*'s officers, who always occupied the first two rows of seats, were entertaining the simpering ENSA actresses and high kickers, none of whom ever ventured further forward than the midships ladder. On 4 September Clarke informed the Admiral, optimistically, that *Sheffield* was 'ready in all respects for sea', and two days later he was ordered to leave Scapa Flow in company with *Cumberland* and the destroyer *Eclipse* for Greenock, the reason unspecified.

On arrival in the Clyde early on the 7th both cruisers took lighters alongside and began embarking a range of commodities that included, in the case of *Sheffield*, three Bofors guns and associated ammunition, drums of diesel oil, petrol and paraffin, boxes of canned provisions, tents, sledges, skis, stoves, and a 35-foot motor launch. All were accommodated in the hangar deck and available space

below, even the Admiral's dining cabin, while *Cumberland*, loading similar stores, also took aboard a number of dogs. There was to be no shore leave for the ship's company; nobody was to leave the ship for any reason. Nobody seemed to know anything, or, if they did, they swore ignorance.

Soon after midday there was another development to set rumours aflame. Up the quarterdeck ladder climbed two Norwegian Army officers, two sergeants and six corporals followed by a Petty Officer and three seamen of the Royal Norwegian Navy. They were quickly ushered below. Someone suggested that the other half of the Norwegian armed forces had probably boarded *Cumberland*. The BBC was still referring to the massive raid on Dieppe, three weeks earlier, as an outstanding success. In response to a question in the House, the Prime Minister had answered: 'It is not the practice to give exact figures of casualties sustained in individual operations, and I see no reason to depart from this practice in the present instance.'

At 0900 on 8 September the three warships slipped, turning northward into black skies and a nasty sea that warned of unpleasant things to come, and by the following noon the group was 500 miles to north-westward and butting into a Force 9 gale. There would be no film tonight, but *Island of Lost Men* would be screened on arrival in Hvalfiord tomorrow, ETA 1630. *Sheffield* smashed her bows into a tumultuous sea, shuddering her entire length as green brine exploded over her forecastle and avalanched over 'A' turret. Little *Eclipse* disappeared again and again, each time clawing upward for breath, for buoyancy and life. Thinking of *Cumberland*, the stokers' messes debated whether dogs were susceptible to seasickness and, if they were, if they were the responsibility of the Sick Bay or the duty part of watch. Speed was reduced to eight knots, and the little force anchored gratefully in the quiet, dark waters of Hvalfiord at 1640 on 10 September. Already in residence were the three big cruisers, *Norfolk*, *Suffolk* and *London*, with a string of destroyers extending up-fiord. *Cumberland* and *Sheffield* were ordered to anchor short, well away from other ships, and communication was forbidden.

To provoke speculation further, orders were now given for the construction of cargo trays and slings for the offloading of guns and stores, with, in addition, a raft to accommodate the Bofors guns. All this suggested that, wherever *Sheffield* was going, she was not to enjoy the benefit of a jetty. That meant wild stuff.

Meanwhile, in Hvalfiord, the weather being sunny and clear, 'Hands to bathe' was piped. 'A dozen hardy souls', says Treseder, 'went over the side and pretended that they were enjoying it – then climbed from the icy fiord, painfully laughing and blue-lipped, to run for a hot shower.'

On 14 September all ships weighed and proceeded to sea, with CS18 – Bonham-Carter – flying his flag in *Norfolk*. This was no mean force; something was about to happen somewhere. *Sheffield* was the lightest of the cruiser strength, most of her company not yet blooded, and Clarke spoke

Left: The Spitzbergen archipelago, only 700 miles from the North Pole – the farthest north that man had permanently settled and, equally, the farthest north that *Sheffield* would ever venture – is distantly sighted on 16 September 1942 . . .

Below: *Sheffield*'s damage means dry-docking, and she goes to Palmer's yard at Hebburn, on the Tyne. When she returns to sea she has installed a completely new range of updated radar equipments – air surveillance, surface, gunnery and direction-finding, in addition to improved VHF radio. In July 1942 *Sheffield* was the most sophisticated cruiser in any navy, but now half of her crew were conscripts.

Right: . . . and the cruiser anchors off Barentsburg, the population of which – 3,000 Norwegians and Russians – had been evacuated by the British during the previous year. The Germans, however, were showing new interest in Spitzbergen, and a modest Anglo-Norwegian force is re-established.

to them as soon as the ship had settled down to a sea routine.

At this time, he said, the largest convoy to Russia, PQ18, was attempting a passage to northern Russia to stave off the collapse of the Soviet Army, and the enemy was going to make every effort to deny that convoy's progress. Clarke could not know at this time that PQ18, steaming from Loch Ewe on the west coast of Scotland, comprised forty merchant ships laden with aircraft, tanks and petroleum, escorted by the cruiser *Scylla* (Rear-Admiral T. L. Burnett) 29 destroyers and the escort carrier *Avenger*. This was the maiden operation for *Avenger*, the first of three converted merchantmen supplied to the Royal Navy from the USA, and it would prove to be the fiercest convoy battle of the entire war.

While the enemy was preoccupied with the convoy, *Cumberland* and *Sheffield* were to make for Spitzbergen, to land their parties and stores. During August 1941 the Navy had evacuated the several mining stations on the Arctic archipelago, transporting 900 Spitzbergen miners and their families to the UK and 2,000 Russians to Archangel. Canadian and Norwegian commandos had destroyed the mine installations and fired 450,000 tons of coal.

The weather remained poor, and on the afternoon of 16 September *Cumberland* and *Eclipse* were detached to close Spitzbergen before *Sheffield*. It was understood that a German air reconnaissance was flown over Spitzbergen every morning, and Bonham-Carter wanted the unloading operation completed and his ships out of the fiord as quickly as possible. *Sheffield* detached on the following evening, proceeding northward as far as the impenetrable ice barrier, 78°02′N, only 700 miles from the Pole and the farthest north the ship would ever venture. It was icily cold but visibility was superb, and at 1420 on Friday 18th, after meeting *Cumberland* returning, *Sheffield* anchored off Barentsberg. Ashore, all was silent, with spirals of smoke climbing from the huge, white-mantled piles of coal. There was one tiny jetty and, beyond, the wreckage of a small mining town, the ribs of collapsed roofs and sagging walls softened by a deep covering of snow. There were no roads, but the weather sparkled, with temperatures rising to 26° Farenheit, and in the far distance a massive ice glacier glinted greenly in the sunshine.

The Commander's plans for off-loading had allowed six hours. All boats were lowered and, although fully half of the ship's seaman strength was closed up in anticipation of an air attack, disembarkation proceeded rapidly. The first problem involved the Bofors guns, and Pack had constructed a raft of planks fixed to empty oil drums. He had decided by some obscure arithmetical formula that his raft would safely support the travelling weight of a Bofors gun (5,418lb). Commander Searle, less than convinced, ordered that Pack should be standing on the raft when the first gun was lowered on to it, but to the disappointment of a speculative audience the raft proved adequate and the

shipwright did not even get his feet wet. The guns were successfully landed, watched by a large herd of reindeer on the opposite side of the fiord.

Meanwhile the fourteen Norwegians had been put ashore and a solitary souvenir brought back – a portrait of Joseph Stalin which was hung in *Sheffield*'s OA's mess. At this period of the war, of course, 'Uncle Joe' was held in high esteem for his leadership of Russian resistance to German aggression; it was only later that the Russians' ingratitude, their lack of co-operation amounting almost to hostility and their deplorable treatment of British survivors would progressively erode and finally erase all desire for rapport.

Sheffield was under way by 2141, grateful to be free of the fiord in which, in the event of air attack, she would be a helpless target. There were still many men aboard who remembered the narrow fiords of Norway. Now, above Barentsberg, the sky was empty and infinitely blue, although the northern horizon was walled by rolling, dense cumulus cloud, three thousand feet high and so blindingly white that unwary eyes were dazzled. That cloud, all knew, must be shrouding the North Pole itself. The Canteen Committee had earlier, in anticipation, purchased a stock of Bluenose Certificates, each of which, signed by the Captain, confirmed its owner's service north of the Arctic Circle – and Clarke must now resign himself to scrawling his signature nine hundred times before his ship's next home-coming. *Sheffield* nosed southward through a sea almost black, floating with ice rubble and clotted snow. Bonham-Carter and the other ships of the force were joined at 0800 on 19 March.

It had been a minor and apparently simple operation, but it had also required careful planning and timing. No BBC bulletin or newspaper would mention it because no battle had been fought, no ships lost, and thus it was of no interest to Fleet Street, and it appeared that the small force landed in Barentsberg remained undetected by the enemy. By the same token, however, Bonham-Carter's men knew very little of the massive convoy battle to their southward. Enemy attacks on PQ18 had begun as early as 13 September and continued remorselessly until the 21st. When the entire operation was completed (including attacks on a returning convoy, QP14) the British/American losses were thirteen from forty outbound merchant ships, three of fifteen home-bound empty ships, plus a tanker, a destroyer and a minesweeper of the escort group and four aircraft. In return, the Germans had paid with four submarines and forty-one aircraft.

Having regained Hvalfiord on 22 September inconvenienced only by an easterly gale, Bonham-Carter transferred his flag to *Sheffield*, who early the next day led *London*, *Cumberland*, *Bulldog* and *Amazon* out of the fiord and south-eastward as far as the Butt of Lewis, at which point *Sheffield* turned away for the Orkneys and the remainder went on to Greenock and long-awaited home leave. In Scapa Flow, Bonham-Carter (CS18) lowered his flag (subsequently to be promoted and appointed VA Malta)

Right: Regaining Scapa Flow, the ship's company is ordered to clear lower deck, with a total lack of enthusiasm, to listen to a 'rousing speech' from Sir Stafford Cripps, Lord Privy Seal, raised between Captain Clarke (left) and Commander St. L. Searle, who appear no more emotionally inspired than their shivering men.

and on the following day, 5 October, Rear-Admiral Cecil Harcourt was appointed CS10 and in command of all Home Fleet 6-inch cruisers. He elected *Sheffield* his flagship. The ship's company, never enamoured with the superior types imposed upon wardroom and messdeck by an admiral's flag, watched *Lady Hamilton* in the starboard hangar, which was becoming very chilly, purchased 'goffers' – aerated soft drinks – in the forward recreation space, and played Tombola. Naafi confectionery was predominantly Canadian – assorted Neilson's chocolate bars and canned fruits – and a representative of Bernard's, Naval Tailors of Harwich, held court in the office flat, measuring ratings for new serge suits and recruiting new allotment-paying clients. It was only now that it was learned that the ship's two Walrus aircraft, offloaded in Scapa Flow before the Spitzbergen operation because their hangars were needed for cargo storage, had been exercising together on a clear, fine day and had collided in mid-air, with the crews of both killed. Indirectly, then, the Spitzbergen operation had demanded a price after all.

Winter was beginning in earnest with drizzling rain and thin fog, weather-deck fittings always wet and bunting hanging sodden and listless on their halyards. Drifters puttered among the warships, loaded with stores or mail, libertymen or new drafts from the mainland. From messdeck loudspeakers Vera Lynn shrilled, 'Yours till the stars lose their gloree . . .', Germany had threatened to chain all POWs taken at Dieppe, and Britain promised that, if the threat were fulfilled, all German prisoners would be similarly shackled. On Friday 9 October the destroyer *Faulknor* anchored in the Flow carrying the Prime Minister and Sir Stafford Cripps, Lord Privy Seal, both of whom transferred to the CinC's flagship *King George V*. On the following day Cripps, accompanied by Vice-Admiral Sir Bruce Fraser, boarded *Sheffield* to tour the messdecks and subsequently give a rousing speech to the assembled ship's company. Nobody was noticeably roused; it was too near

tot-time and *Sheffield*'s galley had promised toad-in-the-hole. In the event, as Bungy Williams complained, 'there was too much 'ole and not enough bleedin' toad'. During that afternoon the Prime Minister was briefly seen several times as he swept past in the CinC's barge, raising his yachting cap or brandishing a cigar, to and from the flagship, or *Duke of York* or the new *Anson*. Ashore, all football pitches and the officers' nine-hole golf course were unfit for play.

The distribution of action casualty stations had been reorganized in accordance with a recent Admiralty Fleet Order. The main operating theatre would still be sited in the wardroom officers' bathroom flat with an auxiliary station on the Marines' messdeck, while four First Aid posts were situated in easily accessible points elsewhere. The general feeling that *Sheffield* and her associates were being prepared for something unusual was reinforced by two weeks of sea exercises with an emphasis on bombardment. When the rum came down each day there was speculation on second fronts and commando raids. The weather was foul, with gale following gale necessitating steam being maintained and anchor watches in harbour. Nobody was very sorry on 20 October when the cruiser steamed for the Clyde with Harcourt aboard and *Jamaica* in company. In passing, one projectile from each 6-inch turret was fired at Stack Skerry. 'A' turret was over but the other three scored direct hits.

That finished, the sailors turned their attention to polishing shoes and pressing blue jean collars. There could be shore leave tomorrow, at least for the off-duty watch, and most would make for Glasgow, Sauchiehall Street and Argyll Street, the officers more likely for the Tontine Hotel in Greenock to telephone wives and sweethearts.

When the two ships arrived in the Clyde, Treseder recalls, 'it was immediately obvious that tremendous events were at hand. The Clyde was full of troopships, merchant ships and warships of every type and size. There remained

Left: On 26 October 1942, off Belfast, *Sheffield* embarks 614 men of the US 135th Regimental Combat Team and 49 RN and RM personnel for Operation 'Torch' – the North Africa landings.

no doubt that something big was afoot – *but where*?' That evening, while *Sheffield*'s watch ashore was filling every unforgiving minute with sixty seconds' worth of whisky drunk, while Hitler was ordering the execution of all British commandos taken prisoner and the Russians were beginning a massive counter-attack in the Stalingrad sector, Rear-Admiral Harcourt and Captain Clarke attended a conference in *Bulolo*, now a Combined Operations headquarters ship. Twelve very large Royal Marine Commandos with submachine-guns, festooned with grenades and jungle knives, climbed aboard *Sheffield*, led by a small Lieutenant who sported a bright red beard. The Admiral and the Captain returned, thoughtfully uncommunicative, and finally an ammunition lighter nudged alongside. It all added up, the older hands agreed – but, when pressed, only sucked their teeth and sniffed knowingly, their eyes distant. A shore-going libertyman, in addition to a rubber condom, could now draw a small squeeze-tube of bactericidal cream, to be injected into the eye of his penis before or after (but preferably in anticipation of) a sexual exchange in Govan's blackout or an upper room in Paisley Road West. To the Surgeon Commander's relief, *Sheffield* departed Greenock on 24 October followed by *Jamaica* and the old carrier *Argus*. Astern, hundreds of ships were cram-packed with troops, American and British, crowding upper decks, ladders and boat-decks, jostling to look from the port-holes of airless troopdecks below.

Exercises were briefly shared with *Argus* before *Sheffield* parted company; the ship was proceeding to Belfast, Clarke explained, but he would not be granting any leave. The plot thickened further when the Commander divulged that, in

Belfast Lough, six hundred American troops were to be embarked and would be carried as passengers for two weeks. At midday the BBC announced a massive offensive by the Eighth Army at El Alamein, and now everybody on the messdecks knew where they were going. Bungy Williams said he had always known it right from the soddin' start.

Sheffield anchored twelve miles from Belfast at 1600, and during the following forenoon took aboard a large quantity of bedding and thirty-eight additional Carley floats. By the time the hands paused for Stand Easy it had become known that *Sheffield* was to provide anti-surface close protection for a large and fast British convoy to Gibraltar in the first instance and then escort a special assault force into the Mediterranean, but for what purpose could only be guessed at – and was, repeatedly.

It was all a little bizarre. No mail would leave the ship and there would be no communication with shore of any kind. Clarke would have been horrified had he known that, during the previous night, a Gunroom crew had smuggled Midshipman Tom Erskine ashore to a light tower for a clandestine meeting with his father.

Early in the afternoon of the 26th the small transport *Duchess of Abercorn* tied alongside and the Americans clambered aboard with a total disregard for the First Lieutenant's paintwork. They were a special detachment of the 135th Regimental Combat Team commanded by Colonel T. Swenwick, USA, which had been rehearsing a landing procedure for only eleven days at Sunnylands Camp in Carrickfergus, Ulster. Most of them were country boys from the Middle West and gave passable imitations of

John Wayne in expressing determination to come to grips with 'the Krauts' – which no doubt impressed the girls in Carrickfergus but did not fool Captain Clarke, who was viewing the prospect of an overcrowded ship with some concern.

'The addition of six hundred and seventy bodies to an already overcrowded cruiser for a period of thirteen days did not commend itself to me or my officers; the Commander and the First Lieutenant in particular were presented with considerable problems . . . the Americans' experience of the sea was limited to one trooping voyage across the Atlantic, and they would doubtless be seasick. They had never been aboard a warship before, which led one's mind to fire hazards, gun-shock, falling overboard, losing their gear and being quite unaccustomed to the highly disciplined routine enforced on a warship in dangerous waters. These matters also face masters of troopships, but in *Sheffield*'s case there was the added need to fight the ship at immediate notice, and I anticipated such a possibility with concern. With the best will in the world, our six hundred bewildered passengers, battened down between decks, would be bound to get in the way, to put it mildly . . .'

The entire afternoon and evening were absorbed in siting the Americans into their unfamiliar quarters. Their allocated spaces quickly became tangled sprawls of bodies and bedding, crap games, Crown & Anchor and poker schools. 'For twelve days', records Lucas, 'the output of our fresh water condenser was limited, so clothes-washing was forbidden and baths permitted only sparingly, on certain days. All meals were served in two instalments; the galleys could not otherwise cope, and sentries were placed in gangways to enforce queue discipline.'

As the American officers clattered into the wardroom ante-room, '*Sheffield* seemed as full as an egg', said Shipwright Lieutenant Pack, 'and orders were given to close all officers' wine privileges.' The wardroom was dry until further notice. The First Lieutenant, Alex Hobson, also remembered the difficulties of that period, when it was impossible to walk along the main deck without interrupting a gambling school or treading on sleeping men. Hopelessly he tried to 'keep the messdecks and flats in some kind

of order, to get the bodies out of the hammock nettings every morning, to get them to a sleeping billet at night, to persuade them to fall in for Abandon Ship stations each forenoon . . .'

Sailing at 0400 on 27 October, *Sheffield* joined the convoy four hours later off Malin Head. Thirty-eight merchant ships were carrying a hundred thousand men and their equipment. The escort was small, consisting of only one destroyer, *Clare*, the cutters *Walney* and *Hartland*, three sloops – *Ibis*, *Enchantress* and *Biter*, with *Sheffield*, were the only major warships in company, but, of course, there was massive cover beyond the horizon, and Operation 'Torch' was in motion.

The convoy was already formed up into ten columns, each of four ships, with the Commodore in *Largs* and Rear-Admiral Sir Harold Burrough, flying his flag in the HQ ship *Bulolo*. A stiffening north-easterly was whipping up the sea as, bunting streaming and escorts whoop-whooping, the armada turned southward, steaming 300 miles clear of the coast of Ireland, towards the Azores.

Column 1: *Orbita, Letitia, Zeeland* and *Mooltan*.
Column 2: *Reina del Pacifico, Tegelberg, Royal Scotsman* and *Royal Ulsterman*.
Column 3: *Largs, Durban Castle, Duchess of Bedford* and *Warwick Castle*.
Column 4: *Glengyle, Monarch of Bermuda, Llangibby Castle* and *Derbyshire*.
Column 5: *Batory, Queen Emma, Princess Beatrix* and *Ulster Monarch*.
Column 6: *Bulolo, Sheffield, Biter* and *Ettrick*.
Column 7: *Samuel Chase, Thomas Stone, Leedstown* and *Almaach*.
Column 8: *Strathnaver, Otranto, Winchester Castle* and *Exceller*.
Column 9: *Keren, Awatea, Sobieski* and *Cathay*.
Column 10: *Karanja, Viceroy of India, Marnix de St. Aldegard* and *Dempo*.

During the first two days of the passage southward the sea was untidy without being particularly bad, but enough to prostrate many of the passengers, and a nuisance when *Sheffield* refuelled several of the smaller escorts, transferring a total of 830 tons of oil. Conditions, however,

Right: Thirty-eight troop transports, carrying 100,000 men and their equipment, are shepherded through an untidy sea by *Sheffield* and a number of smaller escorts. With no interference from the enemy, the Americans felt cheated.

Left: Dawn, 6 November 1942. 'There were ships everywhere,' says a *Sheffield* officer, 'as far as eye could see – merchant ships, troopships, landing ships and warships. For those who had served with Admiral Somerville in the early days of Force H, this was a dramatic event, one we had all been waiting for since September 1939.'

improved, and the Americans recovered, sufficiently to watch, visibly impressed, a display of unarmed combat by the Royal Marine commandos. The sun grew warmer, with occasional rain, and on 2 November a general signal was received from Admiral Sir Andrew Cunningham, Allied Naval Commander of the Expeditionary Force, Operation 'Torch'.

'We are setting out on a great enterprise which, in my opinion, if it meets with complete success will exert a profound influence on the future course of the war. We have been entrusted with the safe conveyance of a large army and their support when they make their landing. It is one of our proudest naval traditions that when we work with the Army we never let them down.

In this case, an even heavier responsibility rests on us, as a large proportion of the soldiers who are depending on us are those of our great ally, the United States of America. I feel that it is unnecessary for me to call on you to make every effort; I know that every one of you will do your utmost to bring success in this great adventure. Andrew Cunningham, Admiral.'

This told *Sheffield*'s crewmen little more than they already knew, but Clarke was unable to enlighten them further because the ship, having oiled several others, was herself running low and must now detach from the convoy and proceed briefly to Gibraltar for replenishment. Early on 5 November 1942 *Sheffield* steamed into the familiar harbour to tie alongside *Rodney*, with only seven tons of fuel remaining from her full stowage of two thousand. Despite the urgency, Clarke had not dared to push the cruiser faster than 22½ knots.

The anchorage was impossibly crowded with vessels of every description, and, for security, the Americans were allowed on deck only if disguised in borrowed seamen's overalls or Marines' uniforms. The spectacle of one of H.M. ships with, apparently, hundreds of additional crew, strolling on deck and chewing gum, smoking, sun-bathing or lolling over guardrails generated considerable interest in *Rodney*, but it was accepted, by powerful rumour not disputed by anyone, that *Sheffield* was full of survivors. Oiling completed, the cruiser slipped and proceeded to sea at 1935, joined by *Argus, Avenger, Scylla, Charybdis* and three destroyers, to rejoin Convoy KMF.1, which had already passed through the Straits. The great Rock they knew so well faded astern, and in an hour had gone.

Now Clarke could tell his crew, and reveal to the Americans, that Operation 'Torch' – the Allied invasion of Vichy North-west Africa – had begun, from Casablanca in the west to Algiers in the east. *Sheffield* was a component of an inshore covering force for the landing of a picked detachment who would guard, and prevent sabotage to, harboured ships and port installations. The force, now aboard *Sheffield* and code-named Terminal Force, would first be transferred to destroyers; the landing would be effected during the early morning of Sunday 8 November. It was not known if the Vichy French troops ashore would resist, but cover to seaward would be provided by Force H – *Renown, Duke of York, Rodney, Victorious, Formidable, Furious*, three cruisers including *Sheffield* and seventeen destroyers.

The sun rose on Friday 6 November to reveal an unforgettable scene to *Sheffield*'s men at dawn action stations. 'There were ships everywhere', says Treseder, 'as far as the eye could see – merchant ships, troopships, landing ships and warships. For those who had served with Admiral Somerville in the early days of Force H, this was a dramatic moment, one we had all been waiting for since September 1939.'

During the forenoon the convoy KMF.1 divided, with part committed to a landing at Oran (Centre Force), while the remainder (Eastern Force), including *Sheffield*, continued on course for Algiers. Unbelievably the miles of ships seemed, so far, to have been unobserved by the enemy, a circumstance for which the British were grateful

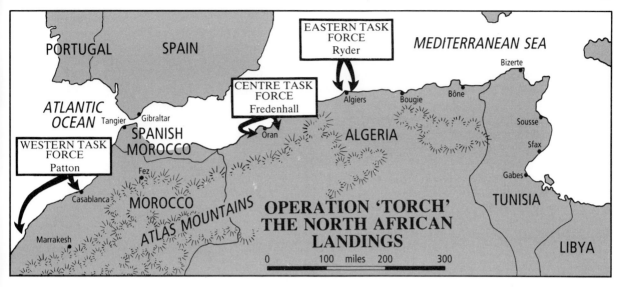

PORTUGAL SPAIN

MEDITERRANEAN SEA

EASTERN TASK FORCE
Ryder

ATLANTIC OCEAN

Bizerte

CENTRE TASK FORCE
Fredenhall

Algiers   Bougie   Bône

Tangier   Gibraltar
SPANISH MOROCCO

Oran

ALGERIA

Sousse

Sfax

WESTERN TASK FORCE
Patton

Fez

Gabes

Casablanca   MOROCCO

TUNISIA

Marrakesh   ATLAS MOUNTAINS

OPERATION 'TORCH'
THE NORTH AFRICAN
LANDINGS

LIBYA

0   100 miles 200   300

while their American passengers appeared to feel themselves cheated. They listened to the radio bulletins on the elections in the USA and argued about Thomas Dewey and Wendell Wilkie. The communiqué from Cairo said: 'During the night our troops made a further advance and took a number of German prisoners. Counter-attacks against our new positions were beaten off with losses to the enemy,'– to which the G.I.s from Illinois and Missouri responded, 'Yew ain't seen nuthin' yet, Buddy.'

Between 1615 and 1720 on the 7th the destroyers *Malcolm* and *Broke*, stripped of all non-essentials and looking fit only for a breaker's yard, eased alongside and took off the entire American combat force with, in addition, a party of RN officers and ratings –explosives experts – who wore American uniforms. The plans for the landings in French North Africa had been conceived in the hope that Vichy forces, government officials and the civilian population would not resist an American landing, but it was too much to expect, after Mers-el-Kebir, Dakar and Madagascar, that British forces would be welcomed with wine and flowers. The upper decks of *Malcolm* and *Broke* were impossibly crammed with men and equipment as they let go their lines and fell away into the night, disappearing into the deepening darkness. And there were still nine hours to go. *Sheffield*'s main deck was suddenly very empty and weirdly quiet, scattered with occasional, abandoned items of clothing, Baby Ruth and chewing-gum wrappers, nickels and dime coins which had rolled under coamings. The ship, having suppered, went to night action stations; they would be off Algiers soon after midnight. Few below flag rank could guess at the immensity of the operation or its implications. From the messdecks' limited viewpoint anything was likely to evolve; the men could only resign themselves to the philosophy that what was going to happen was going to happen. This was the stage of the film, Bungy Williams recalled, when Clarke Gable was embracing a submarine perioscope in Tokyo Bay while

Doris Day, back in Pensacola or Santa Monica, watched a clock bleedin' ticking and ticking . . .

Just before 0100 on Sunday 8 November the hands went to action stations. The night was warm, calm and quiet, with hardly a ripple on the sea. Southward was a speckle of shore lights, presumably of Algiers, and a blue-white pencil of a searchlight probed skyward. The assault programme called for landings by the U.S. 168th Combat Team in the Bay of Sidi Ferruch at 0200 and a similar action by the British 11th and 36th Brigades on the beaches north-east of Castiglione. When these operations had been successfully completed, *Malcolm* and *Broke* would force an entrance into Algiers harbour.

Gunfire could be heard from shoreward and several parachute flares were drifting down beyond Algiers. *Sheffield*'s turrets were turning. At 0220 situation reports received were indicating that the Americans had landed unopposed although losing most of their assault craft in the surf, while at Cap Matif the British were also ashore but were under heavy fire. The Algiers landing force began closing on the harbour, and *Malcolm* led *Broke* in their high-speed dash shoreward.

The Vichy forces ashore, however, had been alerted, and the two old destroyers (both were legacies of the First World War) were immediately met by a blinding flare of searchlights, and *Malcolm*, almost immediately hit in three boiler rooms and reduced to four knots, turned away to effect repairs, counting eight dead and twenty-two wounded. *Broke* also missed the boom but circled for a second attempt in the face of heavy-calibre machine-gun fire. It was not until 0520, with daylight, that this gallant old warrior smashed through the boom and screeched alongside the Quai de Falaise on Môle Louis Billiard, to empty her Americans ashore. But a detachment of French sailors, manning a casemate battery, hammered shell after shell into *Broke*. Here was a chance to avenge Mers-el-Kebir. At 0900 the destroyer, shredded by gunfire and every deck filled with dead and crawling wounded, choked by smoke, threw off her ropes and escaped seaward, leaving 200 Americans fighting for their lives. Even as she withdrew, *Broke* was hit again and again, and the Hunt-class destroyer *Zetland* moved inshore to cover the retreat by smoke.

The American troops landed were pinned down on the dock by machine-gun fire, but, says the official U.S. report, 'it was noted that the French were shooting more to restrain than to kill. Ultimately the Americans were surrounded and led off to a French military prison.' Their detention, however, was to be brief.

Meanwhile the only two French submarines in Algiers, *Caiman* and *Marsouin*, left harbour to attack the invasion fleet. The words Honour, Country, Valour and Discipline were emblazoned in gold on the quarterdeck of every French warship. Unfortunately the sortie was observed and reported by *Broke*, staggering seaward on one boiler. Depth-charged and bombed all day, the frustrated submarines finally made their escape under cover of darkness and limped into Toulon. *Broke* was taken in tow by *Zetland*, and might have been saved, too, if she could have been beached. The extent of her damage, however, was not fully appreciated, and she foundered in a rising sea next morning on the way to Gibraltar.

The R.N. boarding parties landed from *Sheffield* to prevent sabotage to port facilities were more successful, and were quickly seizing a number of moored ships. One party, finding itself separated from its objective – a large freighter – by a dockyard basin, hailed, in French, a launch passing in the darkness and were ferried by its startled crewmen to effect a quick capture.

Since the first shots of the action the Inshore Covering Squadron had been idling, waiting for orders to bombard and trying to piece together a coherent picture of events from intercepted signals on Broadcast CN. The dawn had been humid and sweaty, and the hands stood down, piecemeal, for a breakfast of a shrunken and calcified wafer of bacon and a half-slice of flinty fried bread. The BBC was announcing Allied landings in Algiers, Oran

and Casablanca, and even that Algiers had surrendered. Nobody in *Sheffield* knew about that, and nobody had known that Admiral Jean Darlan, Vice-President of Vichy France, was in Algiers, just over there beyond the smoke-hazed shore-line. *Sheffield*'s AA gun-crews searched an empty sky, unaware that an acute petrol shortage had grounded all Vichy French aircraft. At 1130 'Up Spirits' was piped, and, a half-hour later, 'Cooks to the Galley; Hands to the Mess for Rum.'

By noon further ships had begun to crowd off shore, and several flights of RAF fighters, flying fast and low, passed over the port, inland, suggesting that the Maison Blanche and Bleda airfields had been taken. At 1500, however, *Sheffield* was ordered to engage and silence a French naval fort to the eastward of Cape Matifu which was still impeding the advance of British troops and had already knocked out forty-five landing craft on the beaches. The cruiser hoisted 'Disregard my movements' and pulled out of line, increased speed to 26 knots and closed up 6-inch gun crews. Off Matifu the range was closed to 10,000 yards. It was late afternoon and conditions were superb, the day's heat cooling, the mirror-calm sea peeling away like torn blue silk from the bows.

And this was a target that could not run away. It was almost unfair. Gun-ready lamps glowed red in the DCT and the Director Layer waited for the order 'Shoot' from the Gunnery Officer, Orford Cameron, who, in turn, awaited the instruction to open fire from Captain Clarke.

'The fort is hoisting a white flag,' someone shouted, to everyone's frustration, and *Sheffield* withdrew with *Bermuda*, similarly committed. Fort Lempereur, the key to the western approaches to Algiers, it was reported, had ceased resistance at 1715, which presumably meant that all was over bar the shouting, but as dusk closed, and just as Clarke was about to revert to defence stations, action alarm bells were hammering and Savoia-Marchetti torpedo-bombers were scything in from seaward. There is uncertainty with regard to numbers; Treseder says 'about a dozen', and Lucas recalls 'at least sixteen', while the

Left: Early on 8 November *Sheffield* closes on Algiers, transfers her landing force to the destroyers *Malcolm* and *Broke*, which race for shore. But the Vichy French defenders have been alerted.

log remains cautiously uncommittal. Both cruisers were steaming at 25 knots, and it was at this time that a shell burst over *Sheffield*'s forecastle with shrapnel puncturing the steel deck in many places and damaging kit lockers on the main deck below. Most blamed a low-angled AA shell from *Bermuda*, but Treseder, in the Air Defence position, was convinced that a projectile from the centre gun of *Sheffield*'s own 'A' turret had burst prematurely. There were no casualties, and the attack was driven of without further damage.

The next two days, 9th and 10th, with *Sheffield* cruising off shore, were uneventful except for an air attack on each evening. Some miles to seaward the sloop *Ibis* was hit and sunk, while *Argus* suffered a very near miss. BBC bulletins – the only consistent source of information on what was happening merely a dozen miles away, announced that Admiral Darlan, in Algiers, had called on all French forces in North Africa to lay down their arms, which might mean, Bungy Williams said, that he would get some dhobeying done in the bleedin' Dog Watches. In five days, in Egypt, the British had smashed four German and eight Italian divisions, capturing 30,000 men including nine generals. Berlin described the Allied landings in North Africa as a shameful breach of international law, adding: 'With distaste the world is watching this conflagration being brought down to the level of gangsterdom. Needless to say, in this fresh crime the principal war criminals, Roosevelt and Churchill, are again united.'

During the evening of 10 November *Sheffield*, patrolling some 30 miles north of Tipasa, was ordered to take a convoy of three fast troop transports – *Cathay*, *Awatea* and *Karanja* – onward to Bougie, 110 miles eastward of Algiers. The French Fleet had so far made no effort to intercept the Anglo-American invasion convoys. Nor, more surprisingly, had the Italians, but the Allied build-up in Algeria was slow; the Germans were already flying reinforcements into Tunisia, and within hours would be pouring troops into the unoccupied areas of France. Now, the race to seal off the ports of Bizerta and Tunis, and so deny sea-borne supplies

to the Axis forces, had begun. In twenty-four hours a second convoy would leave Algiers to land troops at Bône, forty miles beyond Bougie.

Increased enemy air activity had been reported, and the route would be well within bomber range, but the run would be in darkness. It was not the enemy, however, that would bring *Sheffield* very near to disaster.

Transports and escort, under Rear-Admiral Harcourt, formed up at dusk in the Bay of Algiers and moved off eastward, keeping well to seaward of the 100-fathom line. Shortly before 0400 the convoy turned southward towards the flat, featureless shore hidden by the night.

'*Sheffield*, who had been leading the columns', Captain Clarke wrote, 'was now ordered to disengage to seaward. It was a pitch dark night and I was reluctant to drop back through the convoy because of one troopship which had been late at the start, and who was by then somewhere astern, closing up. Instead, I increased to 22 knots and disengaged ahead by means of a large sweep to the eastward [i.e., to port] and outside the dispositional area of the anti-submarine screen on the eastward side.'

What Clarke did not know was that one of the eastward screen, the mine-sweeping sloop *Cadmus*, of 850 tons, had lost touch on the turn to southward and was now coming up at full speed in order to regain her station. *Sheffield* and *Cadmus* were closing each other at a combined speed of 38 knots.

'At 0410 I suddenly saw a water disturbance close to and dead ahead of the ship, and in a few seconds it became evident that it was the bow wave of another ship on a precisely opposite course to ours. To have put the helm over would have achieved nothing; it might even have made matters worse. In a matter of moments the hull of *Cadmus* – for she it was – disappeared from view under the port bow. There was a scream of metal against metal, and then she vanished astern.'

No reason is offered for the apparent failure of surface-search radar to recognize the approaching danger. OA Lucas remembers that 'there was a heavy crash as [*Cadmus*]

Right: Later that day a dozen fast-flying Italian aircraft attack *Sheffield* and *Bermuda* from low level, and *Sheffield*'s fo'c'sle is drenched with splinters which, however, may have resulted from the premature burst of one of her own 6in shells. There are no casualties, and the cruiser's luck holds good.

rammed us aft of the hangar deck. She scraped right along our port side, tearing off various parts of our upperworks and rails, demolishing the vegetable store and scattering potatoes all over the upper deck.

I expected to get news of a sinking sweeper and a badly ripped cruiser. Yet, extraordinary as it was, all that *Sheffield* suffered materially was a split side-plate in the bridge superstructure, the loss of the port seaboat and davits, and some distortion to the side plating. The ship was still fully serviceable. *Cadmus* in her turn had a crescent-shaped piece out of her stem and a flooded forepeak, but nothing else. Although she required docking in due course, she was able to carry out her sweeping duties that day in Bougie Bay.'

It soon became apparent, however, that a young stoker was missing from a party of engine-room personnel who, coming up from below after the Middle watch, were enjoying a few minutes of fresh air on the hangar deck when the collision occurred. The body of Stoker A. Spong was found at the end of the catapult.

The ships steamed into Bougie Bay before dawn, and at first light a signal flashed by the Vichy shore authorities indicated that the British should enter harbour, but Harcourt was not to be rushed. He first had the bay swept for mines and then sent a destroyer to reconnoitre the harbour. Only then did he allow *Cathay, Awatea* and *Karanja* to enter and begin disembarkation. Almost immediately several enemy aircraft were sighted, and were warned off by AA fire. The sepia-coloured coastline, stippled with green vegetation and palms, stretched emptily to east and west. The undistinguished harbour accommodated a few small and shabby freighters, native fishing boats, a coastal brigantine, a rusting water-boat, and several French naval launches whose crews stared unemotionally. A tricolour flew over a signal station, and the jetty was thronged with soldiers and civilians, both French and Arab. Concrete blockhouses covered the harbour and the bay to eastward, and there were 40mm anti-aircraft batteries in a number of sand-bagged locations.

With Bougie assessed safe, and with further transports expected, *Sheffield* and *Bermuda* weighed during the late forenoon to return to Algiers; at 1530 the burial of Stoker Spong was conducted by Chaplain Synge and attended by all men who could be spared from defence stations. As gulls wheeled overhead the men drew off their caps. The Chaplain, his white surplice flying, spoke the sailors' psalm: 'They that go down to the sea in ships, and occupy their business in great waters . . .' The service had hardly concluded when aircraft were reported approaching from the north-east, and the cruisers increased speed in anticipation of combing the tracks of enemy torpedoes. The bombers, however, were less interested in moving targets that could hit back than the tethered transports off Bougie.

A few hours later Clarke was able to tell his crew that all three troopships earlier escorted to Bougie had been sunk as they tried to get their troops ashore. The survivors

from the P&O *Cathay* had been taken aboard the British India *Karanja*, which in turn was set ablaze and ordered to be abandoned. In the meantime the P&O *Strathnaver* had disembarked her passengers while under attack, and she now picked up the desperate survivors from both *Cathay* and *Karanja*. As *Strathnaver* had steamed away from Bougie, making for the comparative sanctuary of Tangier, she passed the B.I. transport *Narkundar* going into Bougie Bay. Shortly afterwards *Narkundar*, too, was reported sunk by enemy bombing.

First turn of the screws, all debts paid. Anything that happened after departure was probably best not thought about, although, as Bungy Williams observed, 'them Pongoes 'adn't even got started; they might as well 'ave stayed at 'ome and listened to it on the wireless'.

Algiers was regained by evening. The roads were now crowded with ships off-loading troops into lighters, guns and tanks, film camera crews and PX stores, while Dakota cargo aircraft flew overhead, shoreward, to sink from sight, almost every minute. The tidal waters floated with all the inevitable flotsam of a military landing – broken cartons, bottles and Spam tins, creeping oil and kitchen refuse. The breeze from shore was stickily warm and smelling of dust and that vague but ubiquitous fried-onions reek that is met consistently east of Gibraltar. Amplified music from an American freighter, with Deanna Durbin trilling 'O My Beloved Father', could be suffered from six cables distant. *Sheffield* was not to loiter, but was to pick up a slow convoy of empty merchant ships returning to Gibraltar. *Sheffield*'s crew had still not experienced the promised Casbah with its curvaceous and bangled slave-girls, allegedly awaiting rescue by a handsome Ordinary Seaman in a No. 6 white suit and seven-bell shore leave; but perhaps an invasion did not present the ideal environment for achieving an 'up-'omers' relationship. Gibraltar was more certain, if less exotic.

The next day was Friday the thirteenth. Far astern the destroyer *Clare* depth-charged an Asdic contact for hours, and a few distant approaches by enemy aircraft were shrugged off. Midshipman Joe Honeywill, promoted to High Angle Principal Control Officer (Starboard) was sufficiently frustrated to complain that 'it happened when we were at defence stations; poor old O. G. Cameron was PCO and we sighted a German aircraft in an excellent position on the starboard bow . . .'

It was young Honeywill's great moment. He could almost feel the touch of a sword on his shoulder and a voice saying, 'Arise, Sir Joseph Honeywill . . .'

Nothing happened that way. The 4-inch gun crews were alerted, he recalls, 'and then, unbelievably, I heard the broadcast: "Alarm Aircraft PORT". So the crews manned the port 4-inch batteries. Too late – no rounds were fired and I missed my sole chance of firing the 4-inch system after many, many long hours closed up. Such is life; I will say no more.'

15

'I vill now seeng "It is Snowing"'

GIBRALTAR, like Algiers, was crowded with ships, including heavy units of the Mediterranean Fleet and several cruisers briefly drawn from Arctic duties to screen the North African landings, and which must have been basking in the sunshine that warmed their weather-worn hulls. *Sheffield* secured to buoys, and there was the usual flurry of collar-pressing and pipe-claying. Considerable advice on the merits of bars and brothels was extended to those who had been aboard only since July, and speculation raced through the messdecks when, at 1130, a fast barge came alongside and Admiral Sir Andrew Cunningham, Allied Naval CinC, climbed to the quarterdeck, but he departed twenty minutes later.

'D'yer hear there? There will be no shore leave. The ship is under sailing orders. Special sea dutymen will close up for leaving harbour at 2100 in company with *Jamaica*. The Admiral will transfer his flag to *Bermuda* before departure.'

It was going to be Malta, this time for certain, said the messdeck pundits. Malta, Grand Harbour and the Gut, Blue Labels and Anchor Ale in the Gyppo Queen, Marsala at one-and-six a bottle, a urine-reeking mattress in Jim Irish's or, less likely, an equally unwashed middle-aged tart in Toni Bajada Lane. In the end, a horse-drawn gharri back to Customs House Steps . . .'

Sheffield, accompanied by *Jamaica*, slipped at 2118, to turn westward into a slate-grey November Atlantic, and when special sea dutymen had secured, Clarke spoke to his crew. The ship was bound for Scapa Flow.

Of course, Bungy Williams had suspected it all along. It stood to reason. And the damage suffered from the shell-burst at Algiers and the collision off Bougie could mean dockyard attention and home leave. In the event, the shrapnel holes in *Sheffield*'s forecastle were quickly patch-welded by Pack's shipwrights, and when the ship reached Scapa Flow on 20 November the damage sustained in the collision with *Cadmus* was taken in hand by workmen from the shore base. 'There was some disappointment,' says Pack, 'but the damage was not sufficient to justify the withdrawal of a cruiser from the Fleet, and subsequent events were to prove the point.' In Bungy William's opinion, it was bleedin' diabolical.

It was still the same old bloody Scapa, the same drizzling rain, puddled football pitches, the same crowded beer canteen. One modest improvement was the availability, through American forces channels, of films from the USA that were not yet on general release in Britain, and during the next three weeks, anchored in the grey Flow, *Sheffield*'s company would watch *The Magnificent Dope* (which, Bungy Williams conceded, was not the life story of the Master-at-Arms), *Yankee Doodle Dandy*, and Bing Crosby's *Holiday Inn*. There was mail again, almost daily, but the Home Service and the Forces Programme of the BBC were the sole sources of general news in the absence of newspapers. Sporting news was eagerly devoured, despite lack of continuity and, anyway, football had lost most of its partisan flavour. There was an irrepressible hope that, at some time, Britain would produce another heavyweight boxer to challenge the all-conquering Joe Louis.

On arrival in Scapa Flow, *Sheffield* had been twenty-seven days without a night in harbour. Many officers and men were showing signs of extreme fatigue, and demands on the Captain had been particularly severe. The three weeks to follow were to be spent in 'technical and tactical improvement', either within the Flow or outside, involving main armament firing, night encounters and oiling at sea. It was a strenuous routine but free of the debilitating mental strain of an operational commitment, and most men were enjoying eight hours of sleep at least one night in four.

On 13 December the cruiser was ordered to land both aircraft and replenish provisions and fuel to full capacity. Everyone knew what that meant, or said they did, and sniffed and nodded darkly when, on that day, Rear-Admiral 'Bob' Burnett and his staff were embarked. There was a general re-allocation of officers' accommodation to which Hobson, the First Lieutenant, was accustomed, but – 'How I hated to turn out of my cabin every time we had an Admiral on board!'

Burnett, at this time, was Rear-Admiral Destroyers (more usually referred to as 'RA.D'). He was by training and instinct a small ships' officer – Salt Horse – a physical fitness enthusiast, a keen boxer and a fencer. Immediately prior to the outbreak of war he had been the Commodore of RNB Chatham, a somewhat irrelevant distinction, but he was now probably the most experienced flag officer in the business of Arctic convoying. Treseder writes that 'he [Burnett] was the beau ideal of a sailors' Admiral. The men loved him, and would willingly have gone to hell and back for him,' – but this is an expression born of the delusion of

Left: Ordered back to Scapa Flow, *Sheffield* finds herself chosen to fly the flag of Rear-Admiral 'Bob' Burnett, for further Arctic service.

Right: One element of the crew that doesn't care where the ship is going: the Boy's Division after Sunday Divisions in Scapa. The Royal Navy was the only fighting service with under-eighteens in full battle involvement.

so many officers that they were loved by their ratings, who would gladly lay down their semi-illiterate, Clapham North lives for a high-born graduate of Dartmouth. Burnett was simply recognized as an efficient commander who, by guess or by God, had avoided the disastrous situations which, in the barracks canteens of Devonport, Portsmouth and Chatham, froze all conversation when the name Bonham-Carter was mentioned.

At 0515 on Monday 14 December, in the dark rain and cold, *Sheffield* departed Scapa Flow, the last mail closing during the previous evening, and eight hours later anchored in Loch Ewe on the Scottish north-west coast. Here, on the following forenoon, Burnett and Clarke shared a convoy conference with the masters of the sixteen ships of JW51A. This was half of the first of a new series of convoys to Russia (the other half was JW51B, to follow a week later) which, it was hoped, could exploit the darkness of the coming Arctic winter. The covering warships, Force R, would comprise *Sheffield* with RA.D. aboard, *Jamaica*, and the

destroyers *Musketeer* and *Matchless* – although subsequently *Musketeer* would be substituted by *Opportune*. Burnett, the Admiralty ordered, was not normally to steam nearer than 50 miles from the convoy unless acting on Intelligence of enemy surface forces, and on ensuring the safe passage of JW51A and JW51B through the most dangerous part of the route, from the longitude of Bear Island eastward, would then cover the return of Convoys RA51 and RA52, already unloaded and waiting at Murmansk.

There was a dank mist in the North Minch that shrouded the ragged coastline; everything above deck was sodden. It was unfortunate that, earlier in the war, all insulating metal sheeting on the inner face of *Sheffield*'s hull had been removed to facilitate access to splinter holes suffered from shell and bomb near misses. This meant that warm moist air within the ship was brought into direct contact with the freezing hull plating, to condense and form ice over the entire inner surface of the ship's hull as soon as the temperature dropped.

And Clarke, returning aboard, told his ship's company: 'You've all been singing and whistling "I'm Dreaming of a White Christmas". Well, you are going to get it.'

In addition, each half-convoy had its own close escort of a flotilla of destroyers and a clutch of minesweeping sloops, while a distant screen loitered between Jan Mayen and Bear Islands – the new battleship *Anson* (Admiral Sir Bruce Fraser), the cruiser *Cumberland* and the destroyers *Forester* and *Impulsive*.

'As regards the enemy,' says Captain Clarke, 'it was known that he had lately reinforced his forces in northern waters and he would probably have one pocket battleship, *Lützow*, one 8-inch cruiser, *Admiral Hipper*, one 6-inch cruiser, *Nürnberg*, and a flotilla of Fleet destroyers – and these apart from submarines based on Altenfiord and other anchorages, all of which could be employed against us.'

Sheffield left Loch Ewe at 1335 on Wednesday 16 December, and by noon on the following day had steamed 435 miles to rendezvous with *Jamaica*, who carried not only the flagship's final consignment of incoming mail but also both ships' Christmas turkeys, of which *Sheffield*'s share would be transferred as soon as practicable. As the ships steamed northward, it grew progressively colder and the weather worsened, which, Clarke mused, was perhaps not a bad thing.

'In the conditions of mid-winter it was improbable that the enemy could use aircraft to any great extent, and it was likely that the effectiveness of U-boat reconnaissance would be circumscribed. Nevertheless, the fact remained that our ships would have to pass south of Bear Island, because of the ice, and that patience and a liberal use of submarines ought to give him the warning he would like to have. An additional advantage to the enemy was that he would have no fuel worries, so close was he to his base, while with us it would be an ever-present concern. Reliance on fuelling from tankers at sea could not be accepted. On more days than not the weather precluded this – apart from the fact that fuelling at the limited speed necessary was an extreme hazard in U-boat infested waters. The only dependable plan was one in which the fuelling of escorts took place at the termination of each run. A cruiser such as *Sheffield* consumed eight tons an hour at 17 knots, but thirty tons an hour at 30 knots, so that operational speed was a matter for constant consideration. If the total capacity of the ship was 1,900 tons of usable fuel, it was evident that she could not steam at high speed for very long.'

Approaching Seidisfiord, where fuel tanks were to be topped up, the four warships ran into fog which progressively thickened until Burnett decided that entry was inadvisable. The destroyers, whose need was the greater, were ordered to remain off shore until visibility improved, to oil, and then rejoin *Sheffield* and *Jamaica*, proceeding north-eastward towards the main covering area.

'On the 22nd December', Clarke resumes, 'we reckoned the convoy was abreast of Bear Island, and for the next forty-eight hours we held our breaths while we steamed to and fro across that twenty degrees of longitude, 10°E to 30°E, keeping generally some 50 miles south of the convoy track. There was too much moon for our liking, but silence continued to prevail.'

The ships were at second state of readiness, an unpleasant requirement for men in exposed positions; the sea was calm but temperatures were well below freezing. 'Except for sheepskins for the upper-deck hands,' recalls Paymaster Commander R. Q. Pine, 'the only special clothing issued was of thick woolly pullovers and long underpants. I dislike wool next to my skin, and on receiving my issue I vowed I would never wear them – but how glad I was to do so when the temperature dropped to minus 17 degrees Fahrenheit. I kept them on for three weeks, night and day.'

By 23 December the half-convoy JW51A had passed through the sensitive zone, and the two cruisers, low on fuel, turned towards the Kola Inlet. On *Sheffield*'s previous visit the cruiser had called Murmansk radio station from only five miles for one hour without a response, and had finally achieved contact on H/F via Whitehall W/T in London. This time there were no frustrations other than the unheralded approach of an aircraft which, in seconds, retreated pell-mell in the face of the cruisers' explosive barrage and was subsequently identified as Russian. Clarke was unrepentent. 'Unidentified and unannounced visits by aircraft on HM ships in war are liable to get just that treatment, I'm afraid. We don't wait to see if it intends to drop a bomb.'

Sheffield's log records that, on Thursday 24 December 1942, at 1148, the ship anchored in Vaenga Bay, having steamed 406 miles since the previous noon, and took a Russian oiler alongside. The forward messes, unimpressed by either the miserable landscape or the dirty tanker alongside, applied themselves to their midday rum, getting down the mutton stew and alleged dumplings from the galley, and establishing rights to mess-stools and locker-tops for the afternoon's make-and-mend. Flurries of snow were sweeping across the ship, and two of the convoy's escorting trawlers, frozen and choked with ice, tied up, their crews given the freedom of the cruiser's facilities. The Gunroom officers were invited aboard the Russian oiler, and the skipper took great pleasure, in halting English, in intro-

ducing a female member of his crew. 'We had not seen female flesh for months,' said Midshipman Honeywill, 'and the Russian captain was aware of it. After a few moments the lady was locked firmly in her cabin and remained there for the duration of the British visit.'

Christmas Day dawned drearily. Ice glazed the upper deck and bulkheads were predictably streaming with water. It soon began snowing again, but extemporized decorations were being hung in the messes, the turkeys were in the galley, and the Captain was presented with a giant Christmas card signed by every member of his crew. Clarke's traditional forenoon tour of the messdecks was shared by the Admiral. There was an issue of muddy beer, earlier transferred in casks from *Jamaica*, and this, laced with the rum ration, had just been consumed when, totally unannounced, the Russian Northern Fleet choir and concert party swarmed aboard, having already boarded the destroyer *Faulknor* and consumed all her wardroom's whisky.

It was bitterly cold. On the quarterdeck watchkeeping in the open was abandoned after the bugle froze to the Marine bugler's lips and the Quartermaster had an ear frost-bitten. An ordnance artificer, working on a pom-pom, became so rigid with cold that, says Cameron, 'he was carried below looking like a U-tube, and could not straighten out until he was warmed up'.

The Russians ate and drank everything within reach, but they also sang and sang – two performances for ratings and a third for the wardroom (after having dinner) and a concluding concert aboard a dazed *Faulknor* after midnight. Above decks a blizzard howled. Pine remembers one of the singers announcing, with a charming smile: 'I vill now seeng It is Snowing,' and there was 'an awkward scene', the First Lieutenant recalls, 'when a Russian party emerged from the P.O.'s mess dressed up as Hitler and his senior associates and behaved obscenely.' It simply wasn't British. 'It was difficult to get rid of the Russians once they had wine in them, in particular the concertina player. They seemed

Left: Russia again? *Sheffield* pushes northward into the Arctic gloom, escorting the half-convoy JW15A – a photograph taken from the cruiser's anti-submarine-patrolling Walrus.

Right: The temperature falls to minus 17°, but the sea is calm. The Paymaster-Commander confesses to wearing his long woollen underpants night and day, for three weeks.

Right: *Sheffield* anchors in Vaenga Bay on Christmas Eve and begins to clear away clogging, frozen snow. A Russian oiler is alongside, and the men of British escort trawlers come aboard for hot baths and hot food.

Right: Christmas Day off Vaenga. A blizzard howls above, but the Boys exercise their annual privilege of wearing officers' uniform (the youngest claims the Captain's) and manfully puff on Naafi 'Stinko' cigars. They are only hours away from the Battle of the Barents Sea.

determined to stay all night.' Treseder rugby-tackled a Russian officer brandishing a loaded revolver.

During the day there were several occasions of enemy air activity, one of which provoked *Sheffield* to respond, Clarke confessed, with anti-aircraft fire 'a bit wild and more in keeping with Guy Fawkes Day', but the Germans seemed content to remain to westward, over the Russo-Finnish lines. On Boxing Day, at 1500, CinC, Northern Russian Fleet and his considerable entourage, guests of Admiral Burnett, climbed aboard *Sheffield* to claim their share of turkey and whisky, presumably already recommended by the Red Northern Fleet Choir. Meanwhile the UK-bound convoy of emptied ships, RA52, had been assembled in readiness for the run westward. The second, incoming Russia-bound half-convoy, JW51B, was reported nearing the suicidal channel between Bear Island and the Norwegian coast, escorted by the 17th Destroyer Flotilla. The Home Fleet's heavy units, covering the convoy's earlier passage, was turning back to Scapa Flow for refuelling. This left the fourteen merchant ships escorted by five destroyers – *Onslow* (D.17, Captain Robert St. Vincent Sherbrooke) *Obedient*, *Obdurate*, *Orwell* and *Achates*, the corvettes *Rhododendrum* and *Hyderabad*, and the trawlers *Bramble*, *Northern Gem* and *Vizalma*. These, on paper, were no possible match for the German naval forces in northern Norwegian waters, which included *Tirpitz*, *Hipper*, *Lützow*, *Scharnhorst* and a dozen or more destroyers. Indeed, *Sheffield* and *Jamaica* could be considered hardly more than morale-boosting reinforcements. It was time, however, for Force R to play its part, and at 1400 on Sunday 27 December the two cruisers weighed.

Hubert Treseder, in a letter only four days later, would write: 'There was a strange atmosphere of urgency about this last day or two. It is uncanny how the sailors sense that something may happen . . .'

Despite the icy, unrelieved bleakness of the Kola Inlet, which normally the British departed at the first available opportunity, the next four days of ferocious north-easterly gales were worse. The two ships pushed their bows deep into white-lashing seas as snow and sleet drove over them, penetrating the thickest of clothing and freezing to numbness any momentarily exposed flesh. There were long periods during which it was impossible to prepare food. 'On one occasion', says Paymaster Pine, 'I went to the Commander's cabin and found him trying to warm up a piece of steak and kidney pie at his electric fire. There was a problem in getting watchkeepers' cocoa to exposed positions before it became cold, and this was solved by the shipwrights fitting a biscuit tin into a wooden box with an insulating airspace and a lid similarly made.'

There can be no better account of the Barents Sea action, from one perspective, than that of Captain Arthur Clarke on *Sheffield*'s bridge, with Admiral Burnett at his shoulder – an action that the British participants named the Battle of Cape Misery, the nearest point of Bear Island – until Whitehall decided otherwise. Says Clarke:

Above: Russian Red Fleet singers and dancers swarm aboard the British warships. They eat and drink everything within reach, then ask for more. They are difficult to get rid of, and one brandishes a loaded revolver.

'We smashed our way, sometimes reduced to 10 knots, past North Cape. Southward of Bear Island, on the second day, we turned about, assuming that we were some sixty miles south-west of the incoming convoy, and so back along our earlier course across the danger zone.

During the night of 30/31 December the weather rapidly improved, and early in the morning the Admiral hauled the cruisers up to the northward in an anticipated clearer sky during the so-called day, and in his anxiety not to be observed by a possible casual reconnaissance aircraft. There was already some suspicion that JW51B had been detected by enemy submarines passing the longitude of Bear Island, and New Year's Eve was to be a crucial day. The outward [JW51B] and homeward [RA52] convoys would not be far apart, and it was also unfortunate that the Admiral had felt compelled to detach our two accompanying destroyers to return to the Kola Inlet to refuel, but their further steaming value was limited; it was conceivable that, in certain circumstances, they might become more a liability than an asset.

On the run northward the sea subsided rapidly. It was still very cold and overcast, but we could begin to clear away the ice and snow on the upper deck, and conditions generally allowed free manoeuvrability again.

It was still quite dark at 0819, however, when we obtained a radar contact to the northward. Two contacts, to be accurate – and of a nature that suggested one large and one smaller unit. By our reckoning the Murmansk convoy must be a good deal further ahead, and this, therefore, was either a straggler with an escort or, more ominously, enemy surface ships.'

Clarke was only partly right. The two cruisers, unable to achieve a positional fix during the past four days of bad weather, were thirty miles northward of the convoy. The radar contacts ahead, however, were indeed those of two stragglers – the American freighter *Chester Valley*, which had lost touch during the earlier gales, and the armed trawler *Vizalma*.

'Speed was increased. Both ships immediately prepared for action, while settling down to track and endeavour to identify what the contacts were. At 0932, while still closing the unknowns, gunfire flashes were observed below the horizon almost due south of us. Could they be coming from the convoy? If so, it was either considerably south of its planned track and behind time, or we were badly out of position. Was the gunfire against aircraft, or was something more profound happening?'

The speeding cruisers were not to be left long in doubt. At 0947 a preliminary enemy report was received from D17 (Sherbrooke in *Onslow*) on Fleet Wave: 'Am being attacked by surface ships.' Minutes later *Obdurate* hammered: 'Three destroyers bearing 310. My position 73°36′N, 29°00′E.' In the cold darkness, thirty miles to the south-east, the convoy JW51B had been intercepted by a German surface force consisting of the pocket battleship *Lützow*, the heavy cruiser *Admiral Hipper*, and the destroyers *Richard Beitzen, Theodor Riedel, Friedrich Eckoldt, Z29, Z30* and *Z31*. Shortly after 0930 three enemy destroyers had opened fire on *Obdurate* and the Battle of the Barents Sea had begun.

'This was it,' resumed Clarke. 'The Germans were out. At least one convoy had been found, and even at this moment the work of destruction must have started. The Admiral turned his cruisers about, speed was increased to 31 knots. From the apparent distance of the gunfire, it seemed probable that we had forty or fifty miles to go – the best part of an hour and a half – during which time the enemy was free to do much as he pleased. But of what did the enemy consist? The chances were that the Altenfiord units had come to sea in full strength, and that could mean a pocket battleship with 11-inch guns, 8-inch and 6-inch cruisers, a flotilla of destroyers – not to mention the support of U-boats previously disposed. To hold the ring on our side were five destroyers, two corvettes and a trawler with the convoy, while to drive off the enemy were just two 6-inch cruisers, *Sheffield* and *Jamaica*. Behind us there was nothing; the heavy units were far away, refuelling.

As we drove south, a strange unnatural calm descended on all of us. I had broadcast the situation to the ship's company, as it appeared, and wished them all Godspeed. There was little or nothing more a Captain can do. Communications circuits were checked and re-checked, mountings were trained from side to side to ensure no impedance from the heavy icing in exposed positions. Chief Yeoman Fuller

hoisted our silken battle ensign – a gift from the ladies of Sheffield. The surgeons laid out the tools of their trade, and in every corner of my ship, many isolated and alone under firmly clamped hatches, men waited.'

'We felt the ship heeling over', says Treseder, 'as she started making a big turn to head for the sound of the guns. The decks began to quiver, and the whole ship throbbed as the engines worked up to full power. By then our battle ensigns were flying at yardarms. To those of us who were stationed on the upper deck, the whip and crackle of those huge flags, as *Sheffield* drove at full speed towards the enemy, were sounds none of us will ever forget. *Jamaica*, just 800 yards astern, was only just visible. Our great white wakes streamed away into the darkness. Now came a time of waiting. Smoking was forbidden on deck, so my lads decided on a brew of kye – the Navy's cocoa – very thick, very hot and very sweet. It did marvels in that terrible cold.'

'What goes on', Clarke asks, 'in the minds of those inevitably committed to battle with a superior enemy? Each of us who has experienced this situation will, in detail, answer differently, but perhaps all will admit of one thing; he was afraid. But not of the enemy – but of fear itself. For myself, there was first that sinking, churning feeling in the gut, followed by an icy detachment during which my thoughts rushed in on me. This was the moment when I must forget nothing I had ever learned. One personal lapse, one professional mistake, one omission or one error of judgement and I would fail. I glanced around me. There was the Admiral, looking just the same as usual; we all knew his reputation. My officers were trustworthy and experienced; there would be no failure there. And the men were hardened and salted by training and sea time. Each would be a credit to the ship. On the port quarter, her bow wave foaming dimly in the darkness, was *Jamaica*. Her Captain, Jocelyn Storey, and I had joined the Naval College together thirty-two years before. We knew each other, and that helped too.'

The two cruisers had worked up to thirty knots, and the next half-hour would pass very quickly; nobody seemed to notice the intense cold. They peered ahead with streaming eyes for the gun-flares on the distant, twilight horizon that were getting ominously larger every minute. Burnett had ordered his ships' course to be transmitted on Fleet Wave; it would encourage Sherbrooke's escort and simultaneously warn them that friendly ships were approaching from northwesterly. Burnett's orders were clear. He had to ensure the safe arrival of the maximum number of the merchant ships now presumably under attack and also cover the continued passage of the homeward-bound convoy, which must now be to eastward of the battle area. If *Lützow* and *Hipper* were indeed running wild ahead, then the two cruisers were outclassed. They were welterweights drawn into a heavyweight contest. Burnett *must* achieve surprise merely to avoid his own destruction, let alone drive the enemy off. Steering roughly south-east, of course, he would enjoy the advantage of having such light as existed behind the enemy. The British would be presenting an end-on profile

to the larger ships, and they were certainly more hardened to the conditions prevailing. Finally, the Germans could not be certain that *Sheffield* and *Jamaica* were not just the outriders of a following, heavier force, and would be consequently apprehensive.

These and several other possibilities raced through the thoughts of the men in *Sheffield* – Burnett, Clarke and the Navigator, Back, on the bridge, Cameron in the DCT, Treseder in the Air Defence Position, Marine Thorndyke, gunlayer on the starboard side, Chief Stoker 'Geordie' Burdett, boiler room duty, his ears deafened by the screaming fans, Hobson, Principal Control Officer, with his battery of telephones on his bridge platform, and Shipwright Pack and his damage control party below, waiting and listening.

It was just after 1030 that radar reported a surface contact almost dead ahead, then added that a couple of smaller

---

Left: The armoured cruiser *Lützow* was one of the attacking German force during the Barents Sea action.

Below: Accompanying her was *Admiral Hipper*, heavy cruiser. Between them mounting six 11in guns, eight 8in and eight 5.9in guns, these two warships completely outgunned the screening *Sheffield* and *Jamaica*, but they were irresolutely handled and their attack failed against the convoy's determined escort. She is seen here pre-war before the addition of a funnel cap and a clipper bow, both of which altered her appearance noticeably.

contacts were in close company with the first. *Sheffield*'s 'A' and 'B' turrets came around to the bearing, barrels lifting against a sky continuing to pale. It was important that the cruisers held their fire until the intercept was identified and sufficiently visible by natural light for fall of shot to be spotted, or close enough for starshell to be used for the same purpose. *Sheffield*'s deck log recorded 32 knots, her nominal maximum. Below, turbine horse-power was climbing towards 80,000, steam leaks were hissing in the boiler room and the gratings underfoot vibrated.

'At 17,000 yards we could see something showing up against a vague horizon. According to the plot, the unknown was moving, more or less, at right angles to our line of advance, from starboard to port, and towards what we supposed would be the area of the convoy. Five minutes later the gunnery officer reported that he thought he would be able to see our shell splashes, and during that time it had become evident that we were closing a large, single-funnelled warship – not, we knew, one of ours, and almost certainly therefore *Hipper* or *Lützow*, apparently with at least two destroyers in company.

I asked: "Permission to open fire, sir?" The Admiral nodded, and the order was passed. There was a pause of perhaps two seconds, and then the fire gongs tinkled – and the first salvo broke the spell. Instantly, *Jamaica* followed suit, and into the dark sky sped our shells, their tracers describing the seemingly so leisurely arcs towards the target. The battle had begun, but was this the only enemy? If not, where in the darkness were the others? How far and in what direction was the convoy? Had it scattered or not? What had happened to its escort?'

With the benefit of being able to consult both navies' records, it is interesting at this stage to examine the events taking place elsewhere in the darkened theatre into which *Sheffield* and *Jamaica* were racing, and of which neither Burnett nor Clarke would know very much until several more days had passed.

On the morning of 31 December 1942, the Murmansk-bound convoy JW51B had passed the longitude of North Cape and was nearing the time at which it would turn southward on the last leg of the run to its destination. The convoy, however, had been blown considerably off course by heavy weather, and Burnett – who had hoped to be fairly close to the westward of JW51B, had in fact *passed ahead of the convoy* during the night of 30/31 December, and was well north of it when the half-grey dawn broke on that vital day. Two of the fourteen merchant ships in the convoy were still out of touch with the main body, following the earlier gales, and it was one of these, *Chester Valley*, with the armed trawler *Vizalma* standing by, with which *Sheffield* and *Jamaica* had made radar contact at 0819.

Quite separately, at 0830, *Obdurate*, one of the five destroyers with the main body, vaguely sighted three ships passing across the wake of the convoy. An hour later these opened fire, and *Obdurate*'s subsequent enemy report was pounced on by *Sheffield* and *Jamaica*. Captain Sherbrooke, senior officer of the escort, in *Onslow*, ordered *Obdurate*, *Orwell* and *Obedient* to join him, and turned towards the gunfire. This left one destroyer, *Achates*, and the three smaller escort vessels, *Rhododendrum*, *Hyderabad* and *Northern Gem*, to lay a smoke-screen between the merchant ships and the enemy attack.

Ten minutes later, at 0940, Sherbrooke sighted another and more formidable opponent in the shape of *Admiral Hipper*, of 14,000 tons and mounting eight 8-inch and twelve 4.1-inch guns, thus lethally superior to anything Sherbrooke's ships could muster. That was bad enough; Sherbrooke did not know there was worse to come. Only a few miles away was the light battleship *Lützow*, armed with six 11-inch, eight 5.9-inch and six 4.1-inch guns, capable of severely mauling the convoy, its escort *and* the two cruisers closing. The six accompanying German destroyers were all faster and more powerful than their five British counterparts.

What followed, however, was a remarkable fighting performance on the part of the British destroyers which were to hold the enemy at bay for almost two hours. The action was intermittent, largely because of the hesitant tactics of the enemy, who were dreading torpedo attacks and seemed to see torpedoes in every white-crested roller, sometimes hiding in smoke and sometimes firing in the direction of the convoy. It was plain that Hitler's extreme caution, his fear of losses, and his warning to Grand Admiral Raeder, the German Navy's CinC, that his ships 'must not accept any undue risks' weighed heavily on the commanders at sea, dampening their initiative, but this must not be allowed to detract from the brilliant defence fought by the British destroyers on 31 December; they spurned no opportunity of returning fire whenever conditions allowed, or of exploiting the tactical menace of their torpedoes to keep the enemy in a constant state of vacillation.

Shortly after 1000, however, the enemy made a determined effort to dispose of the flimsy barrier between it and the convoy. *Onslow* was badly hit and Sherbrooke severely wounded. The British defenders were forced briefly to withdraw, but *Hipper* and her destroyers were reluctant to press home their advantage despite the knowledge that *Lützow* and more destroyers were closing from south-eastward.

Meanwhile *Achates*, left with the convoy, had twice received the attention of *Hipper*'s guns. On the second occasion, at 1115, she suffered devastating damage. Her Captain and forty others were killed, her speed reduced to 15, and then 12 knots. Notwithstanding, *Achates* continued to cover the retreating convoy with smoke, finally to sink, at 1330 – still making smoke; 81 of her crew (totalling 138) were dragged from the icy black water by *Northern Gem*.

Earlier, at 1036, *Hipper* had also stumbled on the minesweeper *Bramble*, of 875 tons, and, in the poor light and scurrying snow, mistook her for a destroyer. The little ship, armed with a single 4-inch gun, had just time to hammer off a brief enemy sighting report before the German's 8-inch shells were tearing up the sea around her. Miraculously,

Above: Lieutenant-Commander Eric Back, *Sheffield*'s Navigation Officer, whose calm calculations in action, and in darkness, did much to help Admiral Burnett win one of the most heroic and far-reaching naval actions of the war.

twisting away at her maximum 17 knots, *Bramble* was still afloat after six minutes of shelling. Vice-Admiral Oskar Kummetz, aboard *Hipper*, was anxious to resume his attack on the convoy, and signalled *Friedrich Eckoldt* to detach and finish off the 'destroyer' that was obstinately refusing to sink.

At 31 knots *Sheffield* and *Jamaica* were pounding towards their Target B (having abandoned their first radar contact as probably less relevant than the attack on the convoy reported by *Onslow*) and at 1125 *Sheffield*'s log records: *1 CR and DD in sight bearing 205 degrees. Opened fire at CR. CR returned fire. Observed hit(s) on CR.*

Pencilled by a nervously excited midshipman of the watch, with the noise of his ship's broadside stinging his eardrums, the entry is understandably superficial. Captain Clarke, however, on *Sheffield*'s bridge, remembered the moment well.

'Our opening salvoes, heard and seen by the destroyers on the other side of the enemy ships, had naturally a very heartening effect. We had been expected, but when was speculative, and I can imagine that the time must have dragged in anticipation of much-needed help. Those same salvoes must have been a shock to the Germans. (Moral: Always keep a good lookout on the disengaged side in battle.) At least a minute passed before we observed the first ripple of orange flame from her turrets, and in that time both of us had clearly achieved hits. As the enemy opened fire, she began to circle, and her accompanying destroyers made smoke.'

The shipwright officer, Pack, with his party mustered forward on the main deck, recalls that, 'when the action started, a rating came below and began the rumour that spread quickly among the forward damage control parties that *Tirpitz* was attacking the convoy, and those of us who had experienced the accuracy of *Bismarck*'s salvoes were not too happy. Then there were some unusual crashes from forward, and it seemed that the ship had been hit.

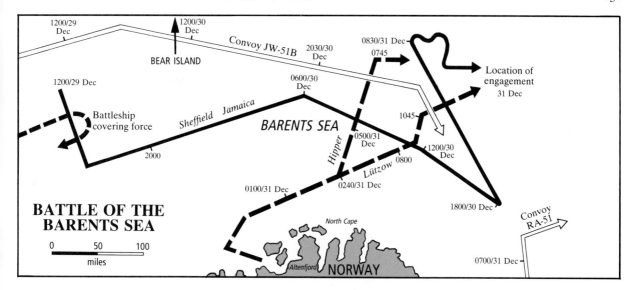

A Petty Officer Wireman with a bloodied head came staggering through the watertight door near the Sick Bay. A hurried investigation showed that no damage had been sustained, but the concussion of the forward turrets, firing at their lowest depression, had caused the unusual noise, and a heavy Nife secondary lamp had jumped off its hook, striking the Petty Officer's head.'

And the Germans had been caught completely by surprise by the sudden intervention of Force R – and, indeed, initially decided that *Sheffield* and *Jamaica* were destroyers. *Hipper* was hit in No. 3 boiler room, which began to flood, and in her hangar, which caught fire. At 1137 a confused Admiral Kummitz ordered a general withdrawal to westward, *Hipper* wheeling to starboard and her destroyers vomiting smoke. The extent of German disarray is illustrated by a radiotelephone exchange between the captains of *Hipper* and the destroyers *Friedrich Eckoldt* and *Richard Beitzen*.

Hipper from *Eckoldt*: 'Cruisers and destroyers in sight bearing 300 degrees. Is it you?'

Hipper from *Eckoldt*: 'On what bearing are you in relation to the convoy?'

Eckoldt from *Hipper*: 'Am north of the convoy.'

Hipper from *Eckoldt*: 'You are firing at me.'

Eckoldt from *Beitzen*: 'No. Those are British cruisers.'

When *Hipper* turned away, Burnett had ordered *Sheffield* and *Jamaica* to conform in an endeavour to maintain the hitting rate. Unfortunately it required very little smoke, in the poor light prevailing, to wreck observation, and although the range was now down to a lethal 8,000 yards, the cruisers were having to check fire. It was this pause, at 1145, however, that allowed *Sheffield*'s lookouts to sight a low dark object fine on the port bow and about three miles distant, which would otherwise have remained unnoticed through the welter of gunsmoke. It was evidently a destroyer, but whether German or British impossible to decide; the cruisers had no knowledge of the convoy escorts'

disposition. If the sighting was German, she was ideally placed for a torpedo attack, and with all guns shifting target, *Sheffield* turned her bows.

'At 31 knots', says Captain Clarke, 'the range closed with remarkable rapidity. In one minute we felt fairly certain that the ship was no friend of ours. With the Director Gunner's finger on the trigger, we made the battle challenge. (This is the only occasion of which I have heard of the battle challenge being made at night.) The reply, a triangle of white lights, was unrecognizable, and a salvo of six 6-inch shells was sent on its way at a range of 4,000 yards. The shells, at an almost horizontal trajectory, roared towards the point-blank target.

It seemed that certainly half the salvo hit, I could see sparks of penetration, followed by the flame and smoke of detonation. Each successive salvo equally found its mark. On opening fire I had agreed with the Admiral that in the last resort I should try to ram the enemy, but it became clear in a matter of two minutes that such an extreme step would be unnecessary. As we swept down on the target she was disintegrating under our eyes, and with a *coup de grâce* from our close-range weapons as we passed her at a few hundred yards, followed for good measure by a couple of salvoes from our after turrets, *Friedrich Eckoldt* was left, a horrible and smoking ruin, to sink astern.'

For *Sheffield*'s gun crews it was a rare bonanza. Marine 'Doddie' Thorndyke was the gunlayer of S.2 4-inch mounting, and he would never forget watching the German destroyer so close to the starboard side and sliding aft. 'I was ordered to slip my guns into local, and managed to get off eighteen rounds at blank range. I could see boats being lowered, and also men moving the torpedoes, but our pom-poms took care of those. The shells were certainly passing right through these men. I could also see men jumping off the stern, and the skipper was silhouetted against the flames around his bridge. She drifted astern like a grand fireworks display, and all her smaller guns were going off.'

Sheffield's log, as before, wastes few words, recording simply, at 1145: *1 DD (Maas class) on fire from repeated hits from 6-inch, 4-inch and pom-poms. Last seen burning, stopped and sinking. Position 73°22'N, 30°34'E.*

For a brief period *Jamaica*'s guns seemed to be widely off-target, but Clarke suddenly realized that she was firing across *Sheffield* at a second and more distant destroyer, subsequently identified as *Richard Beitzen*, which, however, now turned away south-westward into the swirling murk.

So far Burnett was only sure that he had stumbled into *Hipper* and two, perhaps three destroyers, and that the Germans had been caught napping, but he was also cognizant of the enemy forces in northern waters, and it was very likely that there were more, perhaps even heavier, German units in the vicinity than those seen. He turned the two cruisers westward in pursuit of *Hipper*. On *Sheffield*'s bridge, Clarke recalls, Eric Back coolly devoted his attention to fixing the ship's position by the stars.

'Half an hour after our turn to the westward in pursuit, we sighted a division of enemy destroyers broad on the port bow. They formed a definite torpedo menace. The director tower was put on the bearing and fire was ordered. To our dismay on the bridge, the first broadside passed high over the attacking enemy, clearly indicating that some error had occurred.'

There was indeed an error, but a simple one. Clarke, on the bridge, had given the target bearings correctly but without specifying that the target consisted of destroyers. The director tower had obediently ranged on the bearing indicated, only to observe with their loftier and more high-powered instruments something the bridge could not see – a much heavier enemy unit several thousand yards beyond the destroyers and on precisely the same bearing.

The DCT had assumed the larger – and to them the only – target as the object of Clarke's intentions, and had fired accordingly. *Sheffield*'s log is also a little confused:
1206: Closing CR and DD bearing 255 degrees.
1226: Challenged.
1228: Opened fire on DD and DD returned fire. DD appears to be a cruiser. Nürnberg? Hipper *in sight and has opened fire on us.*

It was in fact *Lützow* that had first flashed the challenge 'LLL' in the direction of *Sheffield* and *Jamaica*, believing, and wishing to confirm, that the two ships were German destroyers. Playing for time, Clarke had told the Chief Yeoman, 'Tiny' Fuller, to signal the same challenge back, to which *Lützow* dutifully replied: 'GGG'. The British cruiser's shells, however, were already on their way.

It was a critical moment. Burnett's cruisers were under threat from anything up to thirty torpedoes and simultaneously under long-range fire from both *Lützow* and *Hipper*. There was little that Clarke could do about the shellfire, and he gave his attention to preparing for an enemy torpedo attack.

'I remember noticing with some apprehension the columns of water which surrounded *Jamaica* and, curiously enough, I was afterwards told that those in *Jamaica* were equally concerned about the ordeal we appeared to be undergoing. Neither evidently appreciated that what was happening to their consort was also happening to themselves. It is clear that both ships were more than ordinarily fortunate in escaping damage at that stage . . .'

Treseder, in the Air Defence Position, had an excellent if somewhat hazardous view of the proceedings. 'Once action was joined with the German heavy ships', he says, 'the main task was to keep the lookouts on their job, especially on the disengaged side. The shells from our own guns could be seen

Left: In the confusion of close-range battle, the big German destroyer *Friedrich Eckoldt* (*Z.16*) stumbles within range of *Sheffield*'s expert guns, and within two minutes is left 'a horrible and smoking ruin, to sink astern'.

Right: The battle is over and won. Well-pleased, Rear-Admiral 'Bob' Burnett and Captain A. E. Scott-Moncreiff share the bridge of the destroyer *Opportune*, in company.

bursting on the enemy, and with each series of flashes one could hear loud cheers from all exposed personnel at the AA guns and close-range weapons. The enemy was firing some sort of shrapnel that showed as black patches drifting past the ship, about twenty feet above us. The enemy shot seemed to be falling in our wake. Their ranging was very acccurate but their estimate of our speed must have been about one knot short. *Sheffield* by this time was going at a tremendous speed; I remember being told that the engineers had generated some 5,000 more horse-power than had ever been attained before.'

For something like twenty-two minutes the two British 6-inch cruisers fought the pocket battleship and 8-inch heavy cruiser, toe to toe. Burnett was pushing his luck, but he was that sort of commander, and, fortunately for him, prevailing because – by Rader's own confession – the German gunners were total amateurs at fighting under Arctic conditions and their commanders were tactically outclassed. The German Grand Admiral's honesty is gratifying, but loses sight of the fact that both sides collided under weather conditions foul for both, and both were equally unaware of the other's strength. It was the British, however, who recovered first and immediately took positive action, i.e., attack was the best defence, while the Germans, never confident, floundered, seemingly anxious only to get to hell out of it.

It seemed impossible that the two cruisers' good fortune could continue much longer. Avoiding action was imperative if the enemy's torpedoes had already been fired, and every second would count. Burnett ordered the turn-away at 1246, at which time *Sheffield*'s log observed that the enemy had also altered course and the range was opening rapidly. At 1347 all contact with *Lützow* and *Hipper* was reported lost.

'The question was what to do next,' says Clarke. 'The enemy's major units were out of range, but any sensible admiral would have placed his destroyers between himself and us, and as far as we knew there might be as many as six. The full effect of the Arctic night was rapidly approaching. We could continue to try to shadow the retiring enemy, making all possible use of our limited radar [*Jamaica*'s surface warning radar was out of action from gun blast, while *Sheffield*'s operators, in those days working in semi-exposed positions, were almost crippled from cold] and in so doing risk the danger of co-ordinated destroyer attack. It was a risk not to be lightly disregarded, despite the remarkably poor show they had put up so far. Any destroyer captain would say that our situation was a gift of heaven to him.

Moreover, the real strength of the enemy's major surface force was still unknown to us, and this uncertainty had nagged at my mind all day. We were already more than 40 miles from the nearest of the two convoys and drawing further away. Shadowing the located enemy would have its point in confirming their continued retirement, but could lead to no interception, for none of our own surface ships were sufficiently westward to dispute their return to Altenfiord.

The Admiral reluctantly decided to abandon the chase and return to the vicinity of the convoys lest a third major enemy warship, for instance, *Nürnberg*, was also out and inclined to show more enterprise than her fellows.'

It was not an easy choice to make, and might well have been criticized by the fire-eating elements in Whitehall, but Burnett's overriding responsibility was the defence of the convoys, more important than a pell-mell chase that would almost certainly prove futile. The cruisers' remaining fuel, in any case, had been seriously depleted during the high-speed action, and would permit of little tactical freedom in any emergency.

During the last night of 1942 the two cruisers remained close to the westward of the homeward bound RA52 convoy; the spectral *Nürnberg* did not reveal herself, and it was later established that she had not been at sea during this period.

The quarterdeck bell struck sixteen at midnight, but the men on deck, with numbed faces and blue lips, shrugged themselves into their hooded coats, stamped their cold-aching feet as Arctic sleet, driven by a Force 8 gale, tore at the plunging ships. By dawn exhaustion and cold had reduced almost everyone to stumbling half-humans desperately trying to keep eyes open or talk sensibly. The gale had stove-in several scuttles and icy brine was swilling over feet in the forward messdecks and the recreation space, but nobody seemed to want to do anything about it.

Friday 1 January 1943: Noon position 73.21N 30.24E. 501 miles steamed.

The two cruisers' avoidance of serious damage was little less than incredible. *Sheffield*'s sole battle casualty was a signalman slightly wounded by a flying splinter. Shell fragments had punched a number of holes in the funnels and upperworks; Clarke was annoyed to discover, in his cabin aft, a flood from two small holes just above the waterline. 'The carpet', he lamented, 'never quite recovered.' A three-inch shell fragment had sheared through a multi-phone panel in the centre of the bridge and must have passed within inches of the Captain, the First Lieutenant and the Navigator, yet none of them knew of it at the time. 'It just goes to show', mused Clarke, 'how a reputation for nonchalance can quite unwittingly be gained.' Alex Hobson, the First Lieutenant, was still on the bridge while, below, the W/T Office was reading the Admiralty's lengthy half-yearly promotions broadcast, and it was Burnett, on the voice-pipe, who congratulated him on his promotion to Commander.

Self-inflicted damage was more serious, largely from the blast effect of point-blank full charge broadsides, fired on extreme bearings. (*Sheffield* had fired 583 6-inch projectiles.) Some upper-deck cross beams were split, a number of between-deck stanchions had cracked, and, under the quarterdeck, electrical circuitry had suffered damage. None of this was immediately serious, but could become so if aggravated by further low-angle fire from the turrets.

On the first forenoon of 1943 the ships' companies were still clinging to their action stations, having been closed up for 58 hours. A vicious black sea was running, a freezing Force 8 gale made nonsense of duffle coats, football shirts and long underpants, while the off-duty men, below, fought a fatiguing battle with buckets and squeegees to clear the messdecks of icy, muddy water. Steaming westward, the ships had passed beyond Bear Island and were giving the Norwegian coast a wide berth. Nobody was yet sure who or what they had fought in the Barents Sea, or what had been the result. The BBC's long-distance broadcasts were battered into incoherency by screeching static, and even the admiralty's non-stop broadcasts HD (78 kc/s) and BN (107 kc/s) in Morse cipher, needed double-banked operators. The messdecks were loud with blaspheming argument as the reheated, crusted bacon hash and repeatedly re-boiled potatoes were excreted onto plates. The overflowing gash buckets were emptied into the lee side chutes by every mess OD, and the Naafi dry canteen opened for the sale of cigarettes, nutty and OK Sauce. Rum was piped, thank Christ, and at 1430, when the relieved forenoon watchkeepers had eaten, the ship was reduced to Quarters Rest.

Speed was reduced to 10 knots in the teeth of a blizzard of snow and sleet. The cold was intense, and the Ordnance Artificer, Lucas, noted that the inch-thick armour that fronted the AA guns had been reinforced by five inches of ice. With difficulty the ship entered Seidisfiord at 0400 on Monday 4 January, only to fuel and depart again during the following forenoon for Scapa Flow. The Fleet anchorage

Left: *Sheffield* (looking aft) heads for home through rough seas after the Russians had declined to believe that a German squadron had been engaged in seas made safe by the glorious Soviet Navy, and the welcome afforded by CinC Home Fleet, Sir John Tovey, is less than generous.

was reached on the evening of the 6th, and lower deck was cleared to receive the CinC, Admiral Sir John Tovey.

It was only now that the full details of the Barents Sea action were being learned. As a battle, Clarke would write later, it was at first sight disappointing; the enemy was not annihilated, and the events of 31 December were really a series of sporadic and short-lived engagements rather than a continuous hammer-and-tongs exchange. Says Clarke . . .

'As it was, the Germans lost a modern Fleet destroyer, which was carrying the senior officer of the flotilla; *Hipper* was so badly damaged that she had to return to Germany and would take no further part in the war. Most important, however, the Germans had failed to intercept a single merchant ship.

The British had lost the minesweeper *Bramble*. Her meeting with the enemy was quite fortuitous. None of her complement survived to record what happened, but her end must have been swift. *Achates* made a sacrifice of outstanding value, and her loss must be recognized as the price which had to be paid for continued convoy immunity.

No other British ships were sunk or damaged beyond repair. The story might have been different if the German major units had been prepared to be truly offensive. By the law of averages a few more enemy salvoes must have resulted in hits; it does not take many 11-inch or 8-inch high-explosive shells to bring a cruiser to a standstill. Once our mobility had been circumscribed, the enemy would have been free to make another onslaught on the convoy, and subsequently to dispose of the cruisers at leisure.'

Clarke does not mention that the badly damaged *Onslow* had limped into Vaenga on New Year's Day, having buried seventeen dead at sea and now to transfer twenty-three wounded into Russian shore quarters that were appallingly ill equipped and unheated. Little *Northern Gem*, too, had berthed, filled with wounded and survivors from *Achates*. All were regarded with indifference by the Russians, most of whom refused to believe that major German warships had been encountered in an area so valiantly defended by the Soviet Navy.

The German failure was to have an explosive effect on the German High Command. Hitler, enraged, at first threatened to have all the Navy's big ships scrapped, use their guns and armour in his Fortress Europe scheme and consign their crews to more active roles – despite the fact that he had earlier ordered no unnecessary risks to be taken. In the event the ships were retained, but for the remainder of the war would be extremely reluctant to venture from their protected fiords. Raeder, Grand Admiral since April 1939, was replaced by Dönitz on 30 January 1943.

Admiral Tovey's address was not unanimously well received by the ship's company, shivering on the quarterdeck in a cutting Orkneys wind. He congratulated them on their performance in the Barents Sea action, although perhaps there had been an element of luck involved – and

he questioned the time apparently required by the DCT to change the target of the forward turrets. His own flagship's company, the Admiral went on, were very jealous of *Sheffield*'s men; it was no pleasure to be tied to a buoy in Scapa Flow while the cruisers enjoyed themselves at sea. However, *Sheffield* had earned herself a home leave, and he was ordering her to the Clyde for repairs immediately. It was only the final statement that generated a cheer from the men and a dutiful smile from the officers.

At 1300 on Saturday 9 January *Sheffield* tied to a buoy off a crowded Greenock under grey, drizzling skies. There was a wonderful off-shore smell of oil and steam, hemp and grime. During the passage from Scapa Flow there had been considerable speculation on the length of leave to be granted, but most agreed it would be lengthy; the Stokers' messdeck said three or four weeks, some optimistic suggested seven. The CinC, however, had already ruled that the ship must not be absent from the Fleet for longer than ten days, and, on arrival in the Clyde, Clarke announced 72 hours for each watch, with the Port watch getting away immediately. A special train had been ordered to convey Southerners non-stop to King's Cross. Leave passes and travel warrants were issued and the first leave party raced ashore. A ten days' docking was impossible; to be sure, on their return, there would be an extension of leave, and everyone would be back 'up the line' again. No dockyard could remedy Old Shiny's dozens of leaks and fractures, replace the catapult and all the turret pumps in only ten days. It would take *that* time, claimed Bungy Williams, for the dockyard maties to get their bleedin' crib games organized.

A period of leave measured in only hours, like Samuel Johnson's death sentence, concentrated the mind wonderfully. Not a single moment must be squandered on trivial activities. Older, married men would have chosen to spend every golden minute in the company of their immediate families; the world beyond the front door was unimportant. Younger blades, unhealthily deprived of any contact with the opposite sex, sought gratification, anywhere. So much, however, had changed – things like food shortages, and British Restaurants, the newspapers reduced to four pages, a shortage of childrens' shoes, and queues everywhere. The lighting in blacked-out railway carriages could now be switched on at a station, instead of being reduced to a small blue bulb. Passengers were urged to make sure the train had stopped at a station before alighting. The incidence of venereal disease had soared; treatment was compulsory, and refusal to submit to treatment was liable to three months' imprisonment or a £100 fine, or both. In London, thousands sheltered nightly in Underground stations, emerging with the chill dawn, dusty and yawning. Women were being urged to wash clothes in less water, which required less soap, but the sweets ration had been raised from three to four ounces weekly. The price of Scotch whisky had risen to an unprecedented 23 shillings per bottle.

16

'There are ten tons of manure on the port anchor . . .'

THE Port watch returned from leave on 12 January and the Starboard men departed immediately, only to discover, when they regained Dalmuir three days later, that John Brown's yard, unlike Palmer's on the Tyne nine months earlier, had met their completion date. There was no extension of leave, and a considerable number of ratings from both watches had not reported back aboard as the ship secured at Greenock for refuelling and then proceeded to sea. Not a few throats were choked on that evening of Sunday 17 January as the cruiser moved at slow speed through the lines of tethered merchant ships in the Firth of Clyde – sombre, silent shapes against a darkening sky – then turned northward into a stinging, salt wind. It had been futile trying to tell them, at home, what war in the Arctic was like, because it was beyond their domesticated comprehension. They nodded sympathetically, but hardship for them meant queues for buses, no oranges or elastic, the cheese ration, and only 66 clothing coupons to last a whole year. And Mrs Watkins had trod on her glasses in the blackout. Just fancy.

Never mind, they said, encouragingly. Now that Monty's defeated Rommel, it'll soon be over. And the Japs won't last – not with their rubbishy tin ships and their bad eyesight.

Sheffield passed through the Hoxa Gate and anchored in Scapa Flow at 1335 on 18 January – the same old bloody Scapa, panting drifters vomiting smoke, drizzling rain, sodden ensigns hanging limply on their halyards and gulls wheeling, crying, seeking the food refuse spilled from the warships, the distant strains of a band on the flagship and the bathroom sweepers frozen to immobility by Vera Lynn. The new battleship *Anson*, indecently pristine, was anchored in mid-Flow, flying the flag of the Second-in-Command Home Fleet, Admiral Fraser. Predictably, all football pitches were unfit for play, and the film showing at the Naval cinema on Flotta was *Escape to Glory*, featuring Pat O'Brien and Constance Bennett. Ship's Christmas cards were being sold off at half price by the bookstall.

The ship was already under orders. On the evening of 21 January the battleship *Anson* made a great business of weighing anchor, and *Sheffield* followed her into the open sea to rendezvous with four destroyers. Two further convoys were to be steamed to Murmansk, and Admiral's Fraser's force was providing the distant cover. For the men aboard all ships concerned this was a penance, three weeks of monotonous patrolling across that bitter expanse of Norwegian Sea between Iceland, Jan Mayen, Bear Island and Lofoten. Why anyone should want to fight over the possession of these latitudes was beyond the wildest speculation. Hell was not a fiery furnace. Hell was lethally cold, and it was positioned in *Sheffield*'s log at 72°38′N, 06°43′E on 25 January, but Hell could get worse. North-easterly gales drove freezing sleet and lashing rain. The temperature dropped to 9° Fahrenheit, or twenty degrees of frost; the coldest that *Sheffield* had ever logged. There was nothing to see from the bridge except long black rollers, white-slashed and steaming with icy spindrift; it was impossible to see where the sea ended and sky began. Men collected meals from the galley in pairs, for negotiating a ladder with a tray of stew needed more than one pair of hands or feet if the mess were not to be reduced to bread-and-margarine. And God help the rum bosun who reached his messdeck with an empty fanny, and said: 'Sorry. I was jes' coming past the Sick Bay, see – and all of a sudden . . .'

Almost two thousand miles later, on 27 January, the ships anchored off Akuryri, northern Iceland, for refuelling, a brief period of respite from the bruising weather, and a few hours of liberty for both watches. The small town – second largest in Iceland and with a population of some 4,000, was close to the Arctic Circle, but the sailors were pleasantly surprised to find macadamed streets and avenues from which the snow had been cleared, good shops and restaurants, and, after dusk, uninhibited lighting. If the Icelanders were not cordial, having always resented the Anglo-American occupation, they were at least polite; the British had money to spend. One extraordinary feature, Lucas recalls, was the large number of rats. 'They just played in the gardens and around the refuse bins as if they were domestic pets; I did not see a dog anywhere.'

Replenished, the warships departed Akuryri and its shops, lights and rats after three days, for a further week of heaving Arctic seas and shuddering cold. If the Germans were at sea in these conditions, Bungy Williams opined, then they must be just as soddin' solid as the nits in the Admiralty. And as for Bungy Williams, he was bleedin' chocker.

The sanctuary of Hvalfiord was gained on 4 February, where fifty Royal Marines, to their incredulous disgust, were landed for shore exercises and the bandsmen were given instruction in pistol-firing – which, it must be supposed, was a useful accomplishment for men usually employed in the collection of wounded during action. Meanwhile the BBC was telling of a German army surrendering at Stalingrad – but Stalingrad was far distant and nebulous. Hammersmith Broadway, Lime Street, Old Trafford and Bromsgrove Street were nearer to the forward messdecks. In Britain a poster displayed in hotels and public houses stated: 'Service personnel are informed that the authorities have threatened to place these premises out of bounds unless careless talk ceases.' The worst offenders, said the manager of a large hotel in a military area, were officers.

Anson and *Sheffield* left for Scapa Flow on the 8th, and on passage were required to represent an enemy force attempting to break out into the Atlantic, so that the RAF could practise interception. The sailors were not very enthusiastic. In the event the RAF's Coastal Command aircraft made their sighting off Greenland, and destroyers ordered out from Scapa Flow, equally unimpressed, were deployed to intercept and shadow the 'enemy' until a theoretical squadron of Home Fleet battleships arrived to do battle.

Sheffield's anchor crashed into Scapa Flow's sullen waters, sending the gulls screaming, at 1620 on 11 February. The forecastle party was dismissed, quarterdeck watchkeepers mustered, and the quartermaster's pipe shrilled. The ship's library, in the chapel, would be opened between 1800 and 2000. Tombola would be played in the recreation space and the evening's film, in the hangar, was *Chad Hanna*. Then, only seventy-five minutes after

securing, a launch nudged alongside the after ladder and Captain Charles Addis climbed to the quarterdeck. He was to assume command of *Sheffield* at 0900 on the following day.

Sailors have always regarded new commanding officers with a degree of apprehension amounting sometimes to ill-disguised resentment. Clarke, for instance, had relieved a highly-regarded Larcom sixteen months before. He had never been a fire-eating, belligerent sailor with a butcher's bill to prove it, but rather a quiet, calculating tactician who balanced potential gains against the probable damage to his ship and losses among his crew. 'His unfailing courtesy to every man', recorded Treseder, 'won him the respect and affection of everyone from the most senior to the ship's boys.' Clarke had welded ship and people into a superb fighting machine, and his successor, Charles Thornburn Addis, second son of Sir Charles Addis, sometime Director of the Bank of England, had a great deal to measure up to in the opinion of *Sheffield*'s company. They would have their eyes on Addis, and no flannel.

And he had been aboard only a few hours when a Force 8 gale tore savagely across the Pentland Firth, whipping up the Flow and rocking the warships at anchor. All small boat traffic was suspended, and for three days Clarke was marooned aboard, mildly embarrassed at being obliged to stand idly while Addis contended with dragging anchors, a hazardous drift and finally a change of berth under steam. Clarke managed to get away at noon on the 14th, almost unnoticed, in a drifter, to catch the ferry for Scrabster on the mainland, then London and leave. 'I was beyond words,' he said about his hurried departure. 'It was a terrible wrench to leave a ship which had been my beginning and end of life for so long and my faithful companion in triumph and

Right: On 12 February 1943 Captain Arthur Clarke (right) is relieved of his command. He will be appointed Chief of Staff to the Governor of Malta and to CinC Med. Commander M. L. St. L. Searle (left) has only a few more weeks to serve in *Sheffield*.

vicissitude. As I last saw her, she lay firmly straining at her cables, steam up, boats secured for sea; all set for further ventures. I felt very miserable.'

Some weeks later Clarke flew to Malta to become Chief of Staff to the Governor and Commander-in-Chief.

When a new officer assumes command of a ship there is frequently a temptation to test his depth of humour, to ascertain just how far one could go before tolerance wilted, and Addis was tested very early. *Sheffield*'s new berth was considered to be still too near to Flotta, and she was ordered to move further into the centre of the Flow. This was done without difficulty, but when the ice anchor was hove in, and came into sight, it was seen to be foul, enwrapped with several fathoms of sodden manila. The Gunnery Officer, Cameron, cable officer at the time, reported to the bridge by telephone: 'There are ten fathoms of manila around the port anchor.' On the bridge, this was reported to the Captain by the midshipman as 'there are ten tons of manure on the port anchor, sir . . .'

Despite the whine of the wind, the silence was like torture. Addis's face was expressionless, his eyes coldly angry. Everyone froze, terrified. The humorous midshipman, glancing around for approval, found none; they were all suddenly interested in the nearest bulkhead, and the Captain had neither moved nor spoken, but stood facing forward, rigidly, his hands behind his back. Then someone cleared his throat desperately, and the midshipman prayed that he could be anywhere except here. It hadn't worked out. He had been so brave in the Gunroom over the breakfast haddock. It had sounded funny then, even if the steward had shaken his head warningly. Now, in his hand, the telephone was like a piece of frozen cod.

His nerve broke. 'Ten fathoms of manila rope, sir,' he croaked, 'around the port anchor.' Never again, he swore. Never again.

By the evening of 16 February the weather had moderated sufficiently for *Sheffield* to weigh and proceed without further incident, bound for Seidisfiord. Addis did not know it, but the annoyances of Scapa Flow were as nothing to those he was about to experience. In his first week of command he was steaming his ship towards the Great Storm of February 1943, the worst recorded in those waters.

During the first few hours, however, there was nothing worse than a Force 7 south-westerly – only an irritation to a 10,000-tonner. By midnight, off Cape Wrath, the swell was getting nastier, and the ship's company was warned to prepare for rough weather. Mess lockers were lashed, deadlights and hatch-clips tightened, and everything above and below capable of movement secured accordingly. The weather continued to deteriorate, and by the afternoon of the 17th the wind was around in the west and blowing at Force 10, a 'Whole Gale' on the Beaufort Scale with a velocity of 48–55 knots.

And it got steadily worse. By evening Addis had decided to heave to, and at midnight, with the ship labouring, it was reported that the Asdic dome had been damaged and the compartment flooded. During the Morning watch the starboard whaler, five Carley floats and a heavy accommodation ladder were wrenched away and lost, and at 0600 a blizzard of hail was driving from westward. At noon on the 18th the ship's position was logged as 60°45′N, 14°28′W, estimated speed 5 knots.

'It is difficult', wrote Treseder, 'to even try to describe this terrible storm. Over the previous nineteen years I had been ashore for less than fifteen months. I had experienced hurricanes, typhoons and cyclones; I had seen the huge swell and seas between the Cape and Australia, but never had I seen such a sea as this.'

At 1500 the second whaler was smashed and the Asdic dome carried away completely. A later examination would

Above: Captain Charles Thorburn Addis relieves a highly regarded predecessor and assumes command of a crack cruiser manned by a highly professional and critical crew. And he is about to steam *Sheffield* into the great Storm of February 1943, the worst ever recorded for the North Atlantic.

show that the paravane towing wires had crossed under the keel and torn off the assembly.

Seen from the bridge, some 78 feet above the waterline, the sea was coming at the ship *above eye level*. Beyond followed even bigger and more terrifying seas, with the gale whipping off the tops of the approaching mountains and filling the air with blinding, lashing spray. The endless screaming and screeching of the weather was exhausting, and the constant, buffeting motion numbed the body and senses.

Below, conditions were indescribably chaotic, particularly on the forward messdecks. Inches of dirty water swilled backward and forward, floating with clothing, messtraps and ruined provisions; the entire structure creaked and groaned with every shock of the sea. The atmosphere was becoming increasingly foul, the heads reeking of vomit and excreta regurgitated by the latrines. The seasick suffered the torments of the damned, and sleep was impossible.

Addis was nursing his ship, which would only just handle. By dawn on the 19th the gale was back to north-westerly, Force 11, and the barometer had fallen to 960 millibars. Any movement from one part of the ship to another was hazardous. Without warning, ladders and decks underfoot would simply drop from under as the ship pitched, or, equally unpredictably, soar upwards like some fairground amusement – except that nobody was amused. The prize could be a broken limb, crushed ribs or a fractured skull, and for the raw hands who had joined the ship at Greenock, this was a nightmarish experience.

Just before 1100 the Gunnery Officer, Orford Cameron, was on the bridge, looking down at the forward 6-inch turrets, when the ship seemed to miss her step and then plunge her bows deep into an enormous swell. The forecastle disappeared under a green sea, and *Sheffield* shuddered as if hit by a massive fist. Slowly, laboriously, the bows lifted towards the savage mountainscape ahead, and hundreds of tons of foaming water surged aft. From above, Cameron

stared through the blizzard of spray that hit the bridge like white grapeshot. There was a gaping hole in the roof of 'A' turret, which, like its companion, had been trained on the starboard beam to avoid damage. Now, unbelievably, the sea had punched in the side of the turret and lifted off an entire one-third of the armoured roof, of 1¾-inch steel, flinging it like matchwood over the port side.

Damage control reports were demanded immediately, and the Warrant Ordnance Officer, Higgie, went down at once to train 'A' turret in power until its sound side faced forward. Thankfully only three men of the twenty-seven in the gun-house were hurt – one with a broken jaw and nose and two with severe bruising.

All relevant hatches had been closed within seconds of the mishap, but already the forward damage control sentry had reported to Pack that the cable locker appeared to be flooded. Pack struggled forward to discover that not only the cable locker but the flat above right up to and above the hatch on the capstan engine flat had been waterlogged; the watertight covers over the naval pipes, or chain pipes, to the cable locker, had been torn away. He estimated that between 200 and 300 tons of flood water had entered the ship's fore end. The after damage control party reported five depth-charges lost. Bungy Williams said never mind the bleedin' depth-charges. Was the soddin' rum safe?

All pumps, including the war issue emergency mobile pumps, were ordered into action. At noon, in position 63°25′N, 15°43′W, a hurricane of Force 12 was logged, and shortly afterwards the Meteorological Officer reported that the wind speed had gone off his Beaufort Scale and, anyway, the anemometer on the foremast had been blown to pieces. Above, the canopy of ragged black cloud was being driven at frenzied speed towards the horizon, hidden beyond the spindrift of rolling ocean.

During the early afternoon Treseder had stretched himself wearily on his bunk, head aching and eyes red-sore from peering through binoculars, but was suddenly alerted by

Left and right: The seas get bigger and bigger. Everything that might spill or move is fastened down. Looking ahead from *Sheffield*'s bridge – there comes the first giant roller that the ship is going to ship green . . .

. . . and for a sickening moment the bows go down, and down, and down – but – bless her – she comes up, and the sea shivers over her, tearing, destroying. Even the big guns must be traversed to port or starboard to reduce the sea's hammering blows.

Right: The storm is sufficiently powerful to gouge off one third of the armoured roof of 'A' turret and punch in the turret side, destroy fo'c'sle vents and wrench open a four-inch crack in the deck of the Admiral's sea cabin, tear off the Asdic dome and flood flats and passage-ways.

Far right: The storm tears away a 32-foot whaler and smashes it to matchwood.

what he though was a 4-inch gun firing. He snatched up his life-belt and helmet and climbed hastily to the bridge, but the soaked watchkeepers knew nothing of any gunfire, only that the ship had again rammed her bows into a heavy sea, which had cannoned into the bridge structure and exploded high over the compass platform. A search for damage revealed that, in the Admiral's sea cabin, the deck plating had suffered a four-inch crack, and shipwrights began work immediately to prevent it spreading.

By early evening, thankfully, the wind had begun to moderate, reducing to westerly Force 8 by 2000, so that Addis was able to resume course for Iceland. At 2042 speed was increased to 15 knots and, a few minutes later, to a tentative 18 knots. There was a cheer from the exposed hands as a long-awaited belch of smoke lifted from a funnel. An exhausted Addis went below. On the messdecks, the task of clearing up the flooded squalor could now begin, and the galley could flash up cookers. The pumps were still working hard, but by midnight the wind had dropped to a mere Force 3, with only a slight sea running. It seemed impossible that, only a half day earlier, the cruiser had been fighting for her survival. At 0900 on Saturday 20 February, *Sheffield* anchored in Seidisfiord with a make-and-mend piped from noon.

There was no possibility of Old Shiny, in her damaged condition, being involved in strenuous Arctic convoy duties. An inspection of 'A' turret's damage revealed that, quite apart from the roof, the surrounding structure and the trunk had been damaged or distorted, and the three guns were totally inoperative. A temporary covering of planking and canvas was rigged over the gunhouse; the entire turret

would have to be replaced – and that meant a UK dockyard. A joyful Bungy Williams, at tot-time, declared that there was Someone Up There who poked down a soddin' finger when church-going blokes like himself were deprived of bleedin' leave.

Less happily, a later-arriving destroyer transferred to *Sheffield* twelve ratings under escort, absent without leave when the cruiser had departed Greenock seven weeks before, and now charged under KR668. They trooped aboard, some lacking collars or caps, most with eyes lowered but two or three still cheerfully unrepentant. Their erstwhile mess-fellows regarded them, mustered outside the Regulating Office, with a mixture of disesteem and sympathy; there, but for the grace of God, could go any man. It was unlikely that any plea of mitigating circumstances would serve any purpose when they were arraigned before the Captain. Wartime disciplines prevailed, and they had been pointedly warned, before going on leave, that *Sheffield* was under sailing orders. In the event, Addis 'stood over' all cases, which meant that he regarded all defaulters as deserving more than 28 days' detention – the maximum he was permitted to prescribe – and so requiring a decision from the CinC which would be promulgated in due course.

The elements were determined to pursue *Sheffield* even into the sanctuary of Seidisfiord. During the night of 21/22 February a vagrant gale sprang, snarling, on the anchorage, and *Sheffield*'s sister, *Glasgow*, was dragged ashore, to ground. It all went to show, as Bungy Williams observed, that yer weren't even safe in yer bleedin' 'ammock. *Glasgow*, however, was towed off and refloated, little the worse, during the afternoon.

Left: A party of *Sheffield*'s a young Royal Marines prepares for shore-going in Greenock. The names pencilled on the reverse of this photograph are Larry and Eddy (rear), Jack, Eddy, Doddy, Rocky, Ted, Taff, Blondie.

Considered fit for sea, *Sheffield* weighed and proceeded at 0839 on Wednesday 24 February, bound for the Clyde, Glasgow Central and all points southward thereafter. A Force 9 gale snapped at her heels for four hundred miles, but nobody cared now. The weathered cruiser anchored off Greenock at 1445 on the 26th. It was not raining, and a bleak sun tried valiantly to push finger through cloud and industrial smoke. Someone said he could smell fish and chips already.

'As the ship moved up the Clyde to Dalmuir', writes Shipwright Lieutenant Pack, 'the absentees were mustered on the quarterdeck, lower deck was cleared, and their commitment warrants were read aloud by the Captain. The defaulters had all been sentenced to lengthy detention.'

'Now, therefore, I, the undersigned Captain Charles Addis, Royal Navy, do hereby in pursuance of the Naval Discipline Act, and all other Acts and powers enabling me in this behalf, order that the said rating shall be, as soon as practicable, committed to a Naval detention barrack, to undergo his said sentence according to law . . .'

Meanwhile, *Sheffield* had de-ammunitioned with that incredible speed only possible when men are about to go on leave. The ship, refitting, would remain at Dalmuir for the next three months, and during that period Commander M. W. Searle was relieved. An outstanding sailor, he had been dubbed 'Frankenstein' by the ship's junior officers because of his unflagging pursuance of their improved efficiency, and described by Captain Clarke as 'a gift from heaven to me'. Everyone mourned the departure of Searle (subsequently Rear-Admiral M. W. St. L. Searle, CB, CBE) and were comforted only when learning the identity of his successor, Commander Geoffrey Sladen, already awarded the DSC, and DSO and Bar for his courage and skill in command of the submarine *Trident*.

Sheffield was about to be stripped of her aircraft catapult, although retaining the two cranes. With the introduction of escort carriers, surface-search and gunnery radar, and shore-based long-range aircraft, the low-performance reconnaissance seaplanes with which battleships and cruisers were provided, and which still required to be hoisted inboard, had become of little use except for collecting mail, and might now with advantage be dispensed with. The hangars were blanked off, and an additional number of twin Oerlikon mountings installed. Finally, a complete change of paintwork was imposed, so that the second leave party, returning during the first week in June, could hardly recognize the vessel that lay in the Dalmuir basin. Several officers had been sent away on courses, Pack had departed, and Treseder discovered that he had been appointed Damage Control Officer.

Press, radio and consequently the civilian public seemed convinced that the tide of war had turned at last. All organized Axis resistance in North Africa had been crushed, and the battle of the North Atlantic was swinging in favour of the British; during May alone forty-one U-boats had failed to return to their bases. RAF bombers had breached the Eder and Möhne dams. Newspapers confidently predicted, with maps, that the next stage of operations would involve landings in either Sicily, Sardinia or Italy – a pretty safe bet – which would be the curtain-raiser for the Second Front. The war in the Pacific, from which the British had been almost totally expelled, enjoyed only scant news coverage.

Weather decks, messdecks and flats were littered with dockyard refuse and uncomfortably silent. A miscellany of stores arrived daily: powdered eggs, aerial wire, potatoes, solid cocoa, insulating tape, drums of G10 and B55 paint, tinned tomatoes and Nestlés milk, soft soap, sacks and sacks of flour. On 6 June the shore power lines were disconnected and the familiar hum of the ship's own generators announced that Old Shiny was alive and well and ready to go. Fresh drafts of ratings had travelled up from Chatham, all Hostilities Only personnel and seeming younger than ever; among the executive officers only the Captain, the Commander, four Lieutenant-Commanders and one Sub-Lieutenant held regular commissions. All others were of the RNVR.

The reek of acetylene had not been completely flushed from below decks when *Sheffield* carried out degaussing runs off Arran. Ammunitioning and storing were completed, and on the 11th the cruiser slipped for Scapa Flow, intensively drilling guns crews on passage.

The problem, as Bungy Williams explained to a new coterie of fresh-faced Ordinary Seamen, was where Old Shiny was going next. There was Western Approaches and the Black Pit of the Atlantic, or there was the Russian run and the white-shot hell of the Barents and Bear Island. The German U-boats hunted in packs, and the American Navy, Bungy said, was still fighting the war like it was a Hollywood film, but the merchant ships being sunk were almost all British. In the Mediterranean, now, convoys could steam from Gibraltar clear to Egypt without interference. Two years ago, said Bungy, sniffing reminiscently, it was bleedin' different, mate. Blokes coming to sea these days was having it like Butlin's . . .

Of course, he added wistfully, some ships did seem to get quiet numbers – like keeping an eye on interned enemy vessels, not to mention Carmen Miranda, in Rio de Janeiro, or fat black parties with rings in their noses in Simonstown.

During the thirty days following arrival in Scapa Flow, *Sheffield* steamed almost three thousand miles in working-up her crew to an acceptable standard of proficiency, and CS10, Rear-Admiral Burnett, pronounced the ship ready in all respects after proving exercises on 22 July. Four days later the cruiser arrived in Plymouth Sound and secured to a buoy. The weather was warm, the sea twinkling silver in the sunshine, and the distant Hoe beyond Drake's Island was an inviting haven after the grey bleakness of the Orkneys, but the Chatham men were not yet to tread the streets of the West Country base, home of the rival Devonport Division.

Left: In mid-1943 *Sheffield* was operating in the Bay of Biscay, screening south-bound convoys making for Sicily. Air attacks were becoming fewer. Here, a long stick of heavy bombs falls well to starboard of the cruiser, where crew watch anxiously as an escort carrier (left of picture) survives unscathed.

At 2030 special sea dutymen were piped to muster, and fifteen minutes later *Sheffield* had slipped and was nosing past Penlee Point and Rame Head, steering south-westward.

It *must* be the Mediterranean, Bungy Williams told his junior disciples – as he had predicted in the first place and they all nodded as they peeled the potatoes. And there was not much that he, Bungy Williams, did not know about the Mediterranean – like that whore-house with the lace curtains in Line Wall Road, Gibraltar, or Fat Mary's upstairs, just off Old Bakery Street in Valletta. Needless to say, he, Bungy Williams, was prepared to be guide and consultant to all Ordinary Seamen who, having drawn the pay arrears held in credit during training, desired to be introduced to the steaming delights of the near-Orient, the mysteries of women and the true meaning of love. There would be a five nicker bone fide deposit for a start.

The old hands in the Bear Pit – the stokers' messdeck – had reintroduced Crown & Anchor facilities in the bathroom flat. A lucky lad could win a hundred pounds easy before the ship reached Gibraltar. Nobody won a hundred pounds, and the ship never reached Gibraltar. *Sheffield* steamed and counter-steamed across the Bay of Biscay, well to westward, screening several south-bound convoys, presumably bound for Sicily. There was a flurry of excitement on the 29th when several enemy aircraft made a tentative approach, but their hastily dropped bombs fell wide of any ships before the barrage drove them off. Later that day *Sheffield* turned back for Plymouth with a defective boiler, her new hands having achieved four days of foreign service and, briefly, smelled cordite. Securing during the evening of Saturday 31 July, the cruiser was subsequently ordered up the Hamoaze to Devonport Dockyard.

This was new territory for even the older Chatham hands. Unlike the Medway dockyard, limited to cruisers and below, Devonport – more familiarly known as 'Guzz', was a base for capital ships – a vast complex of dry docks, slipways

and basins that could easily baffle a light cruiser man. The fine arches of Albert Gate opened into Devonport's Fore Street, razed by enemy bombing and now accommodating a single cinema screening *Hellzapoppin*, the Salvation Army canteen and Miss Agnes Weston's hostel, Bernard's Naval Tailors, several decrepit public houses clinging tenaciously to solvency and, in nearby Morice Square, the Devonport Fleet Club, which rented clean beds to sailors for four shillings nightly, breakfast extra. Twenty minutes' walk away, however, was Plymouth's Union Street and George Street, more pubs and shore patrols, servicemen's canteens, cinemas and a shabby little theatre, sleazy tarts wheedling, fish-and-chip shops, a tattooist. London was too remote to be reached during a few hours of shore leave, but those midsummer evenings in Plymouth would be long remembered – not least for the 'tiddy-'oggie', the West Country's hot meat-and-potato pasty that would be many a sailor's supper on his unsteady walk back to the dockyard. And it was here that Orford Cameron left the ship, and Hubert Treseder became First Lieutenant.

One of Treseder's first projects was extremely unpopular. He arranged for the entire ship's company to pass through the demanding RN Fire Fighting School in Devonport, where everyone fought chemical, electrical and monstrous oil fires, and were compelled to negotiate, in complete darkness and asphyxiating smoke, a tortuous simulation of a ship's compartments and passageways. There was further punishment for *Sheffield*'s Royal Marines. They were taken off to the Devon hinterland for ten days under canvas, involving, writes Colour-Sergeant C. F. Smith, '. . . unarmed combat, heavily loaded equipment, strenuous exercises and tactical training. You should have seen them sweat. During leisure hours, rabbit shooting for the pot was a popular pastime, augmenting our tinned meat ration, and meant snooping from shrubbery to shrubbery . . .' Freshly shot rabbit could hardly fail to be an improvement on corned beef, canned silverside, baked beans, and poor quality sausages and cheese, but sniping at small game with Lee-Enfield rifles, lethal at two miles, was an occupation of doubtful wisdom in an English countryside. Meanwhile, in Devonport's barracks cinema a film by the Crown Film Unit, *Coastal Command*, was being screened, and Rome Radio had claimed that 'the gallant men of the Italian Navy are continuing to defend their Motherland'. The Italian Navy was only two weeks away from its surrender to the Mediterranean Fleet.

The ship was at sea for the first week of August, with RAF officers aboard, exercising in fighter direction while patrolling west of the Bay of Biscay. These were sunshine days with the war distant. British and American forces had overrun Sicily and King Victor Emmanuel had dismissed Mussolini. The Russians seemed to be advancing almost everywhere, and Germany was being pounded by round-the-clock bombing. It was almost indecent to be so far from the scene of action and merely playing games with the local air patrols, although the RAF types who were not seasick regarded the exercises with square-jawed Biggles determination. *Sheffield* was back at her Plymouth buoy by 7 September for three days, and again on the 18th. The men were developing a fondness for the Devon base and a respect for the Wren crews of the trot boats who, no matter the time or weather, brought their craft alongside with mail, or to take off or return libertymen. The boat girls, however, were totally indifferent towards amatory proposals. Accommodated in the shore establishment HMS *Impregnable*, it would not be surprising, Bungy Williams claimed, if they all wore Admiralty pattern galvanized knickers.

The idyllic period of release, of daily shore-going, boozing, kissing and groping at warm bodies in the half-dark of Devonport Park had to come to an end – and it did, on 20 September. All leave was cancelled and a lighter from the magazine at up-river St. Budeaux tied alongside to transfer bombardment shell. The ship was under sailing orders.

Well, British troops had landed at Reggio, mainland Italy, in force, two weeks before (and in fact Italy had already surrendered to the Allies, but this meant little while the Germans under Kesselring held all the defensive trump cards).

When the swollen-eyed Wrens of the duty boat reached the jetty steps before dawn on Tuesday 21 September, the cruiser had gone. The girls passed cigarettes, shrugged themselves into their scarves and collars. *Sheffield* yesterday, something else tomorrow – sailors and stokers, marines, boy officers promising, promising, sincerely explaining that *he* was different from the others, but, in the end, they were all the same . . .

Sheffield had slipped at 0400, and, clearing the Lizard, Addis turned to 240 and called for speed. That, pronounced the messdeck pundits, spelled Gibraltar and the Mediterranean in a hurry. By noon the cruiser had steamed 214 miles. Decks were beginning to vibrate underfoot, and an apprehensive Treseder watched the recently painted funnels begin to blister. But there was to be no reprieve. 'The next day's run', he lamented, 'from noon 21st to noon 22nd, is one I'll never forget. We steamed 710 nautical miles.'

The Allies had made three amphibious assaults on the Italian mainland, Addis told his crew. One was across the Straits of Messina, the second at Taranto and the third, Operation 'Avalanche', had landed General Mark Clarke's Fifth Army (the British X Corps and the American VI Corps) at Salerno. It was this latter operation that had been almost dislodged by heavy German counter-attacks, and although the beach-head had now been consolidated, the troops ashore needed help. Offshore bombardment ships, however, had already been attacked by a new enemy weapon – glider bombs. The British cruiser *Uganda* and the American *Savannah* had been seriously damaged, as had the veteran battleship *Warspite*, and the US destroyer *Rowan* had been sunk by a torpedo-boat.

So that, then, was the reason for the hurried embarkation of bombardment shell, followed by thirty hours of pounding at 30 knots. Oddly the Army still maintained a naïve faith in naval bombardment when the Navy, in honesty, had far less, although resignedly were always game for another try. It had been demonstrated during the First World War, confirmed repeatedly in the present war so far, and was to be proven again during the Normandy landings, yet to come, that sea-borne bombardments, particularly against an enemy who knew his business, were far less effective than all the noise and smoke suggested, while the ships, of necessity moving slowly and sometimes anchored, were tempting targets for fortified or mobile shore batteries, aircraft or torpedo craft.

Astern of *Sheffield* the sea tumbled like snow, her white wake ribboning away for hour after hour as she hammered southward. There was no need for zigzagging. Amidships, below, passageways were warming uncomfortably; stokers in the boiler-room wore nothing under cotton overalls except a sweat-rag around the neck. There was small demand for hot soup or cocoa, and BBC reception grew progressively more difficult to comprehend. During the forenoon of 23 September the distant shape of Gibraltar, a grey lion couchant, could be seen ahead through a hazy sea mist, and at 1130 the ship passed between the South and Detached Moles.

Already warned that there could be no leave, the men thronged the upper deck. The anchorage was crowded to capacity with British and American warships and freighters, and alongside the resident depot ship, *Maidstone*, were submarines of the 8th Flotilla and several others flying both Free French and Italian ensigns. Westward across the bay could be seen the white clutter of Algeciras in neutral Spain and, nearer, La Linear. The great fortress rock climbed skyward, its lower levels terraced by Gibraltar's streets and houses, the Moorish castle with its ludicrously huge Union flag, and, at harbour level, the jetties, trees and low buildings of the naval base, HMS *Rooke*.

Gibraltar Radio, repeating BBC bulletins, was claiming that Sardinia had surrendered to a small British force after evacuation by the Germans, while, in Italy, the enemy was withdrawing northward from the Salerno beach-head.

At 1830, a dockyard cutter lifted the slip hawser from the buoy and *Sheffield*'s funnels belched black. The thousand miles to Malta was steamed at an average of 27 knots, and the cruiser was met off Fifla Island by a tug, to be led through the searched channel, past Ricasoli Point and into Grand Harbour. The island had survived, but at savage cost. Anchorages were littered with sunken hulks, and the dun-coloured streets of Valletta, Floriana and Sliema were clogged with rubble. At noon on 25 September *Sheffield* berthed on the port side of the battleship *Rodney* and began to offload mail. Mary's Bar, the Dreadnought and the Movement Inn were still in prosperous business on Lascaris Wharf, and if a libertyman ventured further by the Barracca Lift or a horse-drawn gharri, he ran the gauntlet of the Silver Star, the Regal and the Red Rose, the Egyptian Queen, the Mae West, the Bing Crosby, the Wheel of Fortune, all of which under one name or another and over several generations of sailors, had applied themselves expertly to providing exactly what the shore-going sailor wanted – food on a clean plate, booze in plenty and the company of buxom, teasing females (but far less frequently for a sexual relationship than was popularly suggested or the sailor pretended) and finally a mattress in a crowded, dank and urine-reeking doss-house in which he could sleep until the first boat took him from Custom House Steps next morning.

Addis's orders required him to take *Sheffield* on to the Salerno area, where, although there was now less enemy pressure, the Army was still asking for supporting fire. Both British and American cruisers, under aircraft control, had been in continuous action and the expenditure of ammunition had been immense; *Mauritius*, for example, had fired one thousand 6-inch shells on 13 September alone. *Sheffield* would relieve *Orion*, whose guns needed re-rifling, and this time would land an officer of the Royal Artillery with a portable radio, who would find a suitable elevation from which to transmit fire-control instructions.

And there was a new development, Addis was warned. The Germans, who were very much alive and spitefully kicking, were employing a new glider bomb, radio-directed from Dornier aircraft and launched from 18,000 feet, achieving a velocity that made any defensive AA fire useless. One of these bombs had already hit *Warspite* and penetrated every deck, going out through her keel. She had taken on 5,000 tons of water. The Italian battleship *Roma* had been sunk on her way from La Spezia to Malta to surrender, and, off Salerno, the cruisers *Uganda*, *Savannah* and *Philadelphia* had been seriously damaged. The high-flying controlling aircraft were beyond reach of gunfire, evasion was almost impossible, and the heaviest of armour had proved inadequate.

Grand Harbour was still wreathed in morning mist and silent at 0500 on the 27th when *Sheffield* slipped from *Rodney* and eased past congested shipping, Fort St. Angelo and the breakwater to the open sea. Two days later, aboard *Nelson*, General Dwight D. Eisenhower and the Italian Prime Minister, Marshal Badoglio, would sign the final Italian surrender document. Meanwhile, pursued by dolphins, *Sheffield* steamed northward and, fifteen hours later, anchored in the Gulf of Salerno.

From seaward there was little evidence of the near disastrous landings of three weeks earlier except for the LSTs and other landing vessels anchored offshore. The trooper *Devonshire* was departing, having disembarked her troops, and several fighters, flying fast and low over the port area, were tracked by *Sheffield*'s guns until identified as USAAF Lightnings. It was a fertile coastline with, beyond, the Appenines climbing to an azure sky. The Germans under Kesselring had withdrawn to their Gustav Line, which spanned the narrow 'ankle' of Italy, and from hereafter the Allies' progress would be reduced to a slogging crawl. German propaganda leaflets showed the Italian mountain ranges armed with grinning jaws that waited to devour the approaching Americans and British. '*The mountains and valleys of sunny Italy*', said the caption, '*want to see you.*' German-controlled Rome Radio was still boasting of the evacuation of Sicily by more than 100,000 Axis troops: 'Despite being outnumbered twenty-fold, the heroic German rearguard made it possible for the Axis troops to withdraw from Sicily to the mainland of Italy almost unhindered and with their weapons and equipment, nearly 10,000 lorries, 17,000 tons of ammunition, fuel and other supplies as well as more than 4,000 wounded. At the same time hundreds of American and British tanks and heavy weapons have been destroyed, many thousands of troops forced to surrender . . .' The stinging annoyance was that, give or take an element of chauvinism, the Germans were about right.

The Army's Forward Observation Officer, Bolland, was put ashore with his radio and support team. Army wireless operating was regarded as a joke by the Navy's W/T Branch, and the gunnery control frequency would have to be manned by seasoned operators who could make sense of anything from farmyard noises to Siamese funeral music. In the event, *Sheffield* began firing during the forenoon of 28 September.

By this time the assault phase had long passed and British troops were advancing on Naples, some thirty miles north-westward, and against targets like field batteries and tank concentrations, sometimes ten miles inland, the cruiser's fire was far more effective than against fortified emplacements, and if necessary *Sheffield* could lay down saturation fire of up to ninety 6-inch projectiles a minute.

A request for fire support might be received at any time, and from the ship it was possible to watch the flight of the shells as they floated almost leisurely over the Calabrian coastline. On one such occasion Paymaster-Commander

Above: Off Salerno to provide supporting fire to Allied forces ashore, *Sheffield* closes up gun crews. On her compass platform the Chief Yeoman of Signals; Fuller; Captain Addis and Commander Lumsden have the company of two Army liaison officers, one of whom, leaning lazily on the binnacle, is about to be rudely awakened...

Right: . . . by the ear-shattering concussion of a 6in salvo directed against Kesselring's stubborn resistance in Calabria. *Sheffield* was only one of several RN warships involved; others included the old battleships *Warspite* and *Valiant*, the monitors *Abercrombie*, *Roberts* and *Erebus*, and the cruisers *Aurora* and *Penelope*.

Pine had gone ashore to purchase fresh vegetables and fruit when *Sheffield* opened fire on an inland enemy, to whom devastation and death were only seconds away. The local people were totally unconcerned by the shells screaming over their heads but, to Pine's amazement, all ran for shelter when a hail-storm started.

Others managed to get ashore briefly, on various pretexts, but perhaps wished they had not, for they could see for themselves the shambles that had resulted from the earlier bombardments by *Valiant* and *Warspite*, the monitors *Abercrombie, Roberts* and *Erebus*, the cruisers *Aurora* and *Penelope*. Trees were broken and olive groves devastated, houses torn to ruin. Burnt-out tanks and their charred occupants remained in the fields among the stinking, bloating corpses of farm animals, and the graves of the fallen were everywhere. The sailors told of abandoned helmets clogged with brain tissue, boots that still hugged a severed foot – and yet, among all this, the Italian farmers worked as if nothing of note had happened. After dusk the local entrepreneurs would quietly bring their small boats under the anchored *Sheffield*'s forward scuttles to barter bottles of indigenous brandy for items of clothing and footwear, lowered on a string. The brandy, variously flavoured, was a punishing alcohol best drunk, Bungy Williams advised, lying on the deck to avoid falling or, better, already in a hammock; it was a superb four-star paraffin, to be ranked not far below methylated spirit, Brasso and anti-fouling paint.

Naples was taken on 1 October, and on the 5th, her support being less frequently required while, at the same time, her ammunition stocks falling, *Sheffield* withdrew first to Augusta in Sicily and then to Malta for replenishment. The inner reaches of Grand Harbour were still occupied by surrendered Italian warships with unpronounceable names, their crews lounging indolently and still flying Italian ensigns. In Barrow-in-Furness, the BBC reported, eight thousand Vickers-Armstrong workers were on strike for increased pay, and already 900,000 hours had been lost. Four days later the British cruiser was anchored in Naples Bay with AA gun crews closed up and asking if there was any justice in this world. Ashore, beyond the coast-hugging railway, white dust rose in clouds as the Army's camouflaged columns of trucks, carriers, tanks and Jeeps rumbled northward. On that day, Wednesday 13 October, Italy declared war on Germany. *Sheffield* steamed 136 miles southward to Taranto, where more Italian warships were moored, but with no interest in any activity that might take them to sea; for the Italian Navy the war was over and, that being so, both officers and men considered that they should all now go home. 'My Government', Premier Badoglio had promised Eisenhower, 'will be proud to march with you on to inevitable victory,' but nobody had explained this to the Italian Fleet.

The Italians had been ordered to return a small Greek patrol boat to a Lieutenant of the Royal Hellenic Navy who had taken passage in *Sheffield*, but when the boat was brought alongside it was found to be in a filthy condition and completely stripped of all fittings. The Italians did not need to understand much English to realize that Commander Slader's expletives meant big trouble. The boat was hurriedly taken off and, when returned several hours later, had been thoroughly scoured and refurbished.

Ashore, the fighting had moved slowly northward through roadless, mountainous terrain that strongly favoured the defensive and now made even more difficult by rain, snow

Left: During a few days of relaxation in Taranto, surrendered by the Italians, *Sheffield*'s men stage a concert-party for themselves in the starboard hangar, featuring the Silversmiths' Band, bawdy songs and false whiskers.

and ice. The American Fifth Army had collided with Monte Cassino, and in mid-November the Allied commander, General Alexander, called for a halt along the entire front for rest and regrouping. *Sheffield*, with no employment, departed Taranto and secured in Grand Harbour during the forenoon of the 9th. Watchkeepers' leave was piped from 1330, and that evening, in the starboard hangar, Nöel Coward and his grim-faced actor-heroes of *In Which We Serve* had the ship's company guffawing, but at Naval HQ Captain Arthur Clarke, Chief of Staff, had a few tongue-in-cheek surprises for Old Shiny, the ship he had commanded eleven months before.

On 17 November the cruiser embarked a number of passengers among whom were several naval veterans of the First World War, still serving. Among them was Admiral Sir Featherstone-Meade, who, recalls Surgeon-Commander John Foulkes, 'was a very sick man who had volunteered to replace his son, taken prisoner', and had been given command of a team of similarly elderly sailors in ferrying a number of small wooden minesweepers from the USA to the Mediterranean. *Sheffield*'s First Lieutenant, Treseder, had made 'elaborate arrangements for this distinguished party to be accommodated in the Wardroom, but most of them preferred to be in the Chiefs' and Petty Officers' messes. They were all over seventy; they had medal ribbons covering the campaigns of the past fifty years.'

The Commander, Slader, had given his own cabin to the sick Featherstone-Meade, and that same morning (18 November) *Sheffield* steamed free of Malta and steered westward, not to Gibraltar but to a buoy off Mers-el-Kebir, in drizzling rain on the following day. Thirty minutes after securing, bosuns' pipes were shrilling and Admiral Sir John Cunningham CinC, Mediterranean, was embarked with several staff. This meant the surrender of Captain Addis's cabin, and the Captain would normally have transferred to Slader's, but this was now occupied by the sick Featherstone-Meade. The complication had not been solved when, that evening, Featherstone-Meade suffered a coronary thrombosis.

Notified, Addis took the Surgeon-Commander, John Foulkes, to Cunningham, who was told that drugs for the treatment of heart diseases were not routinely carried by warships. Cunningham sympathized. 'Of course, the Navy doesn't cater for old gentlemen. I take off my cap to old Featherstone-Meade.' He pondered. 'Now, Doc – sit at my desk; there's a paper and pencil. Write down the name of the drug you want, and I'll send ashore for it.'

Foulkes pencilled the name of the drug he wanted – *Cardiozol Ephredine* – and Cunningham's eyebrows rose. 'I've never heard of it.'

The surgeon shook his head. 'That's not surprising, sir. It's made by a German manufacturers, Schering & Company –'

'Good God, Doc –' The CinC was incredulous. 'Are you expecting me to ask the enemy for a drug to save a British Admiral?' He and Addis laughed at each other.

'However', Foulkes recalled, years later, 'We did get an American equivalent of the drug I had specified, and the conclusion was that we got old Featherstone-Meade safely home. It was not for a long time after that I eventually read his obituary.'

The following morning the new and gleaming American battleship *Iowa*, with three escorts, steamed slowly into Oran harbour and secured. Aboard her, it was learned, were President Roosevelt and an entourage of senior US officers, including Generals Marshal and Arnold, and Admirals Leahy and King, on passage to a yet undisclosed destination, later known to be first Cairo and then Tehran.

The great warship, of 44,560 tons and massively turretted, lay long and low in the water close against the fortified breakwater, her clinically clean boats with crews in immaculate whites riding alongside. The British cruiser men, feeling shabby but unashamed, did not know that *Iowa*, like *Sheffield* eighteen months before, had just narrowly missed being torpedoed by one of her own escorting destroyers.

On 14 November, 350 miles eastward of Bermuda, USS *William D. Porter*, in company with *Iowa*, was engaged in torpedo drill and had aimed at the battleship's No. 2 magazine, when her third tube suddenly vomited a live, fully armed torpedo which, incredibly, *had been left unnoticed since the destroyer's previous combat patrol.* 'Had that torpedo hit the *Iowa*,' recorded the President's log, 'with her passenger list of distinguished statesmen, military, naval and aerial strategists and planners, it could have had untold effects on the outcome of the war and the destiny of the country.'

By the grace of God the torpedo exploded in the wake of *Iowa*. General Henry Arnold, USAAF, could not resist asking Admiral Ernest King, USN: 'Tell me, Ernest, does this happen often in your Navy?'

During the afternoon of 20 November, Cunningham struck his flag and transferred, and *Sheffield*, at 1815, steamed westward, pausing at Gibraltar for fuel, then continued into the Atlantic. An uneventful passage brought the cruiser off Plymouth, where passengers were put ashore and Addis conceded three days' leave to each watch with the warning that the ship was under sailing orders. Many of the men, released, made a dash for North Road Station and a train for Paddington, while others, with homes too distant, reserved hostel beds in Devonport, consoling themselves that Christmas was only a month away, when there was sure to be a more generous allocation of leave. Nothing of consequence was going to happen to Old Shiny during the few closing weeks of 1943.

But something was, and *Sheffield*'s sunshine, lotus-eating interlude had ended; the war in the Arctic had not.

17

'Over a seaman's grave no roses bloom'

BY TUESDAY 7 December *Sheffield* was secured to a buoy in Scapa Flow, a somewhat ominous venue. The men had been hoping, wistfully, for a return to the Mediterranean, but such a prospect was frozen completely when, on the following day, Rear-Admiral Burnett climbed to the quarter-deck and announced that he had specifically asked that *Sheffield* should join *Norfolk* and his own flagship *Belfast* in an operation to cover a convoy to Russia, JW55B. It was more than likely, he added cheerily, that the three cruisers would see some action; the German battlecruiser *Scharnhorst* was known to be lurking in northern waters. And, of course, it meant Christmas in the Barents Sea.

Bungy Williams hoped that other soddin' flag officers didn't begin specifically asking for *Sheffield* – like Admiral James Somerville, for instance, now commanding the Eastern Fleet. There was an atmosphere of gloom throughout the ship, not lightened by the cold bleakness of a December Scapa Flow, and relieved only briefly by the visit of the actor, Bernard Miles, on the 10th. He entertained the ship's company in the starboard hangar and, says Treseder, 'gave one of the finest one-man shows that most of us had ever seen, his only prop being a large cart-wheel. Not only did he make us laugh – and *Sheffield* desperately needed laughter – but his sketch of a Chelsea pensioner brought many almost to tears. Mr. Miles probably never knew how he had lifted the wilting spirits of an entire ship's company with his wonderful performance, and I have never forgotten him . . .'

On 12 December, shortly before midnight, the three warships slipped from their buoys and slid quietly from the Flow. The heavy cruiser *Norfolk*, of course, was a seasoned Arctic warrior, but *Belfast*, mined during November 1939 and docked for three years, rebuilding, was an unknown quantity as a fighting unit. In accordance with earlier practice the trio paused to top-up fuel tanks in Seidisfiord, and then pressed on northward into the bitterly cold and unreal Arctic half-light.

Five days later, during the first hour of 20 December, the three cruisers anchored in the Kola Inlet, having steered as far north as 73°33'N. Later on this same day the homeward-bound convoy RA55A slipped from the Kola while JW55B sailed from Loch Ewe, bound for Russia, each with ten escorting destroyers. *Sheffield*'s crew would

have rather been anywhere in the world other than the dark and freezing Russian anchorage, but, with her two sisters, she remained. The sombre film *Wuthering Heights*, in the draughty starboard hangar, did little to raise spirits, nor the prospect of another Christmas in this wretched place. 'This is where we soddin' came in,' said Bungy Williams. 'We saw the bleedin' Russian Choir three times last year.' And this time there would be no turkeys, only pork with boiled and baked potatoes, boiled peas and a doubtful apple sauce. The waters of the anchorage were thinly skinned with ice that entrapped all jettisoned mess refuse and excreta, and much else, both revolting and puzzling. Nobody could offer a convincing explanation for the frozen condoms in an environment so totally devoid of women – and, as Bungy Williams so shrewdly observed – where both sailors and brass monkeys would find their frost-bitten libido unequal to even the most ardent female invitation.

The time was approaching for the cruiser squadron to proceed to cover the incoming convoy, JW55B, and the three ships slipped early in the afternoon of 23 December. Vaenga Pier disappeared in the ice haze astern as weather reports predicted strong westerly gales. The home-going vessels of RA55A, three days to westward, would by now be under the protective surveillance of Admiral Sir Bruce Fraser, at sea in the battleship *Duke of York*, accompanied by *Jamaica* and the destroyers *Savage*, *Saumarez*, *Scorpion* and the Norwegian-manned *Stord*, but the Russia-bound convoy, JW55B, was entering the Barents Sea and the area of greatest peril.

Burnett, in *Belfast*, had ordered his ships to action stations during the evening of Christmas Eve, in which state they remained throughout the night and during Christmas Day, reduced to action meals as the ships nosed through long, slow rollers cluttered with ice rubble, the wind rising. Chaplain John Higgins recalls that, during the day, Addis permitted each watch, in turn, to stand down for one-hour periods so that they could eat in comfort and, if they wished, attend a brief Communion service in the hangar or, for bridge personnel, the Captain's sea cabin. A warning had been received on area broadcast that an enemy force had departed Altenfiord on the 25th, but there were no details. Fraser had confessed to a strong hunch that Rear-Admiral Erich Bey would take his last serviceable capital ship, *Scharnhorst*, to sea in an attempt to disrupt the flow of British and American war supplies that contributed so vitally to the relentless deterioration of German fortunes on the Eastern Front.

And if *Scharnhorst* did come out, intending a quick massacre of a British convoy and an equally quick retreat to sanctuary, then Fraser was going to nail her.

Around noon, in position 74°15′N, 25°29′E, Captain Addis spoke to *Sheffield*'s company. *Scharnhorst* was out, running berserk, accompanied by six heavy destroyers, steering northward from North Cape, which meant that the German commander meant to intercept JW55B somewhere eastward of Bear Island.

Scharnhorst mounted nine 11-inch guns in three turrets, twelve 5.9-inch and fourteen 4.1-inch guns in addition to light AA armament and torpedo tubes, so that Burnett would have uncomfortable odds against him. The German ship, with her sister *Gneisenau*, had enjoyed a successful war, in 1940 sinking the AMC *Rawalpindi*, the aircraft carrier *Glorious* and the destroyers *Acasta* and *Ardent*, followed by twenty-two merchant ships in 1941. The following year *Scharnhorst*, *Gneisenau* and *Prinz Eugen* embarrassed the British by their audacious dash from Brest to Wilhemshaven, although, in the event, this was to prove a strategic error on the part of the Germans. All were regarded as lucky ships, but now parted from her twin. *Scharnhorst*'s luck was beginning to drain, and the Home Fleet's CinC, Sir Bruce Fraser, was hoping to show that luck would never long prevail against judgement based on experience, seamanship and professional anticipation. Within hours of leaving Altenfiord the trap had snapped shut behind Admiral Bey in *Scharnhorst*.

Burnett's cruisers were observing zone two, or 'B' time – two hours ahead of Greenwich Mean Time. During the night of Christmas Day (or, more accurately, the early morning of Boxing Day) the southerly wind rose to Force 7, bringing snow and then frozen, slashing rain from Lapland, but by 0800 had fallen to Force 3. Ahead of *Sheffield* were the diffused shapes of *Belfast* and *Norfolk*, repeatedly lost to sight in the snow-swirling half-darkness. Coffee and kye had come up from below, and on bridge, flag-deck and among the cruelly exposed gun positions, the heavy cups were clutched by hands numbed by icy, sodden gloves. The sky, when it could be seen, was a low roof of heavy cloud to which there was no end, and the sea was black treacle, rolling slowly, laced with white froth which clawed upwards at the ships as they passed. A man from below, in overalls, who ran for the refuse chute, did so with clenched teeth, praying that some bastard had not closed and clipped the door behind him. Descending to the main deck from below, the stale but luxuriously warm air embraced a man like a lover and held him close. After this soddin' war, they vowed, they'd not go nearer to the

sea than Southend Pier or the Woolwich Ferry.

At dawn – or what the clock said was dawn – the three cruisers were steaming westerly, positioned about 150 miles east of the incoming JW55B, which was now well within the interception zone. The homeward-bound RA55A, Addis explained to his ship's company, was to the westward of Bear Island and considered out of serious danger, although it had been sighted and reported by the Luftwaffe. Meanwhile, assuming that *Scharnhorst* was continuing northward from North Cape to head off JW55B, *Duke of York* and *Jamaica* were steaming fast from westward to get behind the enemy. If there was going to be any action, Addis concluded, it would be today. At 1025 Burnett ordered 24 knots while, far beyond the uncertain, black horizon, Fraser had ordered four destroyers of the now secure RA55A under Commander T. L. Fisher to retrace course and reinforce the escort of JW55B. *Musketeer*, *Opportune*, *Virago* and *Matchless* were on their way back.

'Down below', said Treseder, now Damage Control Officer, 'we had settled down to another Forenoon watch.' Communication circuits, pumps and switches had been checked and rechecked; there was little more the men could do, and they sat in a sullen group, smoking,' We could only wait. It was my first experience of action stations away from the guns, and I confess I did not enjoy those long hours of waiting and listening. Our role was completely passive unless or until the ship was damaged by torpedo, shell or weather. I hope my nervousness was not too apparent.'

On the darkened bridge nobody spoke or moved unless necessary; it was difficult to distinguish one hunched figure from another, and there were more important things to think about than conversation. A few cigarettes glowed red within cupped hands, and the Navigating Officer said, in a sepulchral voice, that the barometer was holding steady.

At 1052 the radar plot reported a contact bearing 272 degrees, thirteen miles, and, on the main deck below, Treseder felt the deck underfoot begin to vibrate as *Sheffield* increased speed. Seconds later, over the address system, the crew were warned. The size of the radar echo suggested that the squadron had run into *Scharnhorst*, and Admiral Burnett was moving the cruisers across the convoy, north-westward.

It was, indeed, *Scharnhorst*, and Bey was unaware of the British warships closing on him because bad weather had grounded all German reconnaissance aircraft. That same weather had also reduced the speed of his destroyers to ten knots. Bey had earlier ordered them to form a scouting line heading south-west as *Scharnhorst* continued northward, and they had now lost touch. Bey was not too concerned; he regarded the destroyers to be of little fighting value in bad weather. The first intimation of something going wrong

was a star-shell that burst suddenly and whitely overhead, and *Scharnhorst* was nakedly illuminated.

Sheffield's log records: *1104: 180 degrees 7 cables from Belfast. 1117: Formed line of bearing 160 degrees.* And it was at 1127 that Old Shiny reported to the Admiral: 'Enemy in sight.'

Scharnhorst was only 13,000 yards away, but visibility was filthy. Treseder recalls that, 'Minutes later we heard the 4-inch guns firing, and knew that they must be firing star-shell. We then heard that *Norfolk* had opened fire.'

Because Burnett had disposed his three cruisers in quarterline, only the 'County'-class cruiser *Norfolk* was able to open fire immediately with her 8-inch armament and, at six miles, obliterate the enemy's forward radar facility, although the British would not know this until much later.

It was superb shooting, and *Scharnhorst* had been blinded within three minutes of being sighted by the British. Bey immediately wheeled away southward with Burnett's cruisers in pursuit. Now, however, they were smashing their bows into a heavy sea – a black, heaving mountainscape from which sheeting spindrift lifted. Blizzards of vicious spray drenched forecastles, and *Sheffield's* hull was shuddering with every blow. Twenty-four knots

was too much for this weather, while *Scharnhorst*, of 34,840 tons, was still able to maintain thirty, and was disappearing rapidly in the white-shot murk ahead.

Sheffield's navigator, Lumsden, had by some means established the squadron's position as 73°50'N, 22°08'E, and had even logged the ship's mileage since the previous noon as 452.4. 'After this brief contact with the enemy', Lumsden also recorded, 'Admiral Burnett decided that he could not keep up with such a heavy ship in the sea then running, that in continuing to chase he might allow the enemy to outdistance him and then still reach the convoy. Accordingly he turned his cruisers to the north-west and made off to a new position in anticipation of the enemy's new line of approach, which he judged would be from the east.'

Burnett had anticipated correctly; Bey circled eastward and then steamed north-east, calling for his errant destroyers to locate the convoy. He had now received Intelligence of another surface force to the far south-west, closing, but could not guess what this might be, while his own destroyers, deploying in search, were drawing even further away from him.

Meanwhile, at 1230, Burnett's three cruisers had been joined by the destroyers *Musketeer, Opportune, Virago* and

Above: The German battlecruiser *Scharnhorst*, of 34,840 tons, and her sister, *Gneisenau* had been dubbed 'Salmon & Gluckstein' by the Royal Navy. *Scharnhorst* had enjoyed a successful war until December 1943, when her luck ran out. Harried by Rear-Admiral Burnett's cruiser squadron, she was driven towards the guns of the battleship *Duke of York*.

Matchless, the senior officer of whom immediately flashed: 'Am awaiting your instructions to attack.' Burnett, a little puzzled because contact with the enemy had been lost, asked, 'Attack what?' – to which the intrepid destroyer commander replied, 'Anything that turns up.'

Burnett's predicament, if it could be described as such, was very similar to that of Somerville in 1940. Which should the commander of a screening force regard of greater priority – the safety of the convoy to which he was assigned or the pursuit and *possible* destruction of an attacking force? It is almost certain that Burnett did not, even momentarily, consider the possibility of clinging to *Scharnhorst* at all costs until Fraser's *Duke of York* came up (or did not). Burnett did not hesitate in opting for the convoy's safety; he could shrug off subsequent armchair criticizm, as had

Somerville, because in retrospect both proved right. Even so, had *Scharnhorst* escaped the trap that Fraser had primed, Burnett would have been crucified.

At 1409 the circling *Scharnhorst* was again being tracked by radar, and now the three British cruisers were re-positioned, in the Germans' path and ten miles ahead of convoy JW55B. Twelve minutes later *Sheffield* again reported: Enemy in sight, bearing 088 degrees.

Sheffield opened fire with her forward 6-inch guns at 11,000 yards, followed immediately by *Norfolk* and then *Belfast*, while *Scharnhorst* replied with her entire broad-side, concentrating on *Norfolk*, the opponent most likely to inflict crippling damage. In order to bring all nine 11-inch guns to bear, it was necessary for the German to alter course some 50 degrees to the southward. Two shells from an early salvo found *Norfolk*, silencing a turret, destroying her radar facility and starting a fire aft.

'But that brave ship', said Lumsden, on *Sheffield*'s bridge, 'kept well up with the battle during this critical stage and continued to engage with her forward guns while she fought the flames aft. *Scharnhorst* had now altered course again to south-west, turning her guns on *Sheffield*, who was straddled but only superficially damaged by splinters. It was beginning to get dark.

The scene was majestic. All ships were using tracer, shell, and these could be followed from muzzle to target when fired by our own ships, and from the enemy's guns to the highest point of their trajectory as they came towards us, then disappearing until their huge splashes erupted in the sea. The British shells could be seen, neat groups of speeding death, and hits on the enemy were being observed from early in the action, which lasted seventeen minutes. *Scharnhorst* turned away at 1440 to the south-east, frustrating the efforts of our destroyers, a mile ahead of the cruisers, to position themselves for a torpedo attack.'

Several things were worrying Bey. He had regained communication with his five destroyers and ordered them to return to Altenfiord, where he expected to join them in due course, but he had been roughly handled by the three British cruisers, and it was likely that *Scharnhorst* would suffer even greater damage if he persisted in closing the yet unseen convoy. Finally there had been that aerial recon-naissance report of an unidentified group of ships far to the south-west, which might – if it were not just a Luftwaffe fantasy – impede his withdrawal to sanctuary. Bey decided that, this time, discretion was the better part of valour; tomorrow was another day. He turned for base, calling for his ship's best speed, which was significantly better than anything the yapping British cruisers could achieve in the prevailing heavy seas.

Bey was right, but too late. Had he decided to abort his operation as soon as the British cruisers had intercepted him, four hours earlier, he might have squeezed free before the jaws of Fraser's trap snaped shut. Now, Burnett's cruisers needed only to snarl at the heels of *Scharnhorst*, keeping her moving, because from the opposite direction the battleship *Duke of York*, the cruiser *Jamaica* and four destroyers were closing.

Between the two British groups Bey was about to be lethally sandwiched.

For the next three hours Burnett's cruisers followed *Scharnhorst*, maintaining a commendable 27 knots, shadowing by radar and keeping out of gunnery range as the enemy battle-cruiser headed for the Norwegian coast. It was now completely dark although only late afternoon. Fortunately the sea had eased, and *Sheffield*'s galley was issuing action meals.

By 1800 it was anticipated that, at any moment, *Duke of York* would be in radar contact with *Scharnhorst*, and a resumption of action was imminent. This time, Treseder was musing, Old Shiny might not survive unscathed; the effect of 11-inch projectiles on the cruiser's modest armour would be devastating. There was some consolation in the knowledge that all his men had been through the tough fire-fighting school in RNB Devonport, and subsequent repeated drills had ensured that they were familiar with the complexity of valves for flooding and ventilation in darkness, and could make their way over obstacles, blindfolded, from one end of the warship to the other.

At 1806 disaster struck. Investigation of a sudden and intense vibration aft accompanied by 'a very expensive noise' revealed that *Sheffield*'s port inner propeller shaft had stripped its gearing. In seconds the cruiser, an efficient and lethal fighting unit, had become a hamstrung cripple.

Addis reduced speed immediately to 8 knots so that engine-room personnel could lock the ruined shaft – the same that had been so seriously under strain when the ship had struck a mine twenty-one months earlier, although whether or not that circumstance was a contributing factor towards the present collapse was beyond assessment. Right now, nobody cared a monkey's. There were *Norfolk* and *Belfast* increasing speed to close *Scharnhorst*, their guns lifting and sniffing at the enemy, while somewhere out there in the snow-spitting darkness were *Duke of York* and *Jamaica* – not to mention those wild-cat destroyers that never did anything according to the book – about to erase from the German Navy's shrinking list of warships the name of *Scharnhorst*, and at this crucial moment *Sheffield* was slowing to a walking pace, wallowing, out of the hunt.

Thirteen frustrating minutes passed before the engine-room could report that the ship was ready to proceed at moderate speed, and Addis increased to 22½ knots by 1820. *Sheffield* was out of the action, but ahead, in the darkness, a trio of star-shells flared. *Belfast* and *Norfolk* were in contact again with the enemy, and *Duke of York*, at last, had come into contention. At 1850 the rumble of heavy guns came from southward. *Scharnhorst* had been surprised for the third time, and *Duke of York* and *Jamaica*, having stalked the German by radar for the previous thirty-three minutes, had opened fire at 12,000 yards.

Scharnhorst twisted desperately to eastward, Bey calling for his ship's emergency full speed. She was capable of outpacing all of her pursuers, but her escape route was blocked, and there was no sanctuary for her eastward. Bey was compelled repeatedly to swing to starboard so that his six forward guns could bear. Both *Norfolk* and *Belfast* fired, but they could not keep within range as *Scharnhorst*'s speed progressively increased. *Duke of York*, too, in her first action, was experiencing trouble. Scorching gases from her after guns, on their extreme forward bearing, were searing down deck ventilators, to burn out the wardroom.

The battleship, however, although herself straddled, was dictating terms, and her 14-inch projectiles were hitting with cruel effect. *Scharnhorst* was hit near her forward triple turret, which jammed, and her second forward turret was also out of action for a time. A third shell struck amidships, but she was still opening the range.

Her course, unfortunately, was taking her nowhere; ahead, eastward, there lay only an icy void. Time and weight of metal were now on the British side, and there remained for the Germans the choice of scuttling or of going down fighting to the last. To her credit, *Scharnhorst* chose the latter. So many of her predecessors, including *Graf Spee* and *Bismarck*, and many other German warships during both wars, when frustrated, chose petulantly to scuttle and then, subsequently, claim that they had not been outfought; the ship had taken its own life. It was a philosophy totally foreign to the British at sea, who did not regard themselves as very heroic but to whom scuttling was tantamount to shameful suicide, and never ceased to be surprised at the arrogance of German survivors dragged from a freezing sea who seemed to feel that sinking their own ship was something to crow about.

Duke of York had been hit several times, but the superficial damage sustained was quickly controlled. In *Sheffield*, struggling to keep up with the exchange, Lumsden was impressed.

'The flagship, *Duke of York*, was plunging forward to seize an opportunity for which the whole Home Fleet had tirelessly waited throughout four long years of war, firing a full broadside of her fourteen-inch guns, the great flashes emphasizing her tremendous power. The moment will live long with all who had spent anxious hours working and waiting for just this fiery thunder that heralded the destruction of the foe . . .'

Not of Shakespearean quality, but conforming to that commonly shared desire of hardened yet war-weary sailors, irrespective of rank, to address poetry to the clouds, or shout obscenities at God and, later, thank him with hymns, or laugh or cry, or stand silently with clenched eyes – for if *Scharnhorst* could be destroyed this day, Sunday 26 December 1943, Germany's surface challenge would be broken. The monster *Tirpitz*, seriously damaged, lay in Altenfiord and would never be allowed to leave, while

Cruisers re-engage Scharnhorst

BEAR
ISLAND

0 50 100
miles

1221

Convoy JW-55B 0630 0700

Cruisers Norfolk,
Sheffield and Belfast

0929
Cruisers engage
Scharnhorst

Cruisers
shadow
Scharnhorst

ARCTIC OCEAN

Duke of York, Jamaica
and 4 destroyers

1650

1945
Scharnhorst
sinks

Scharnhorst and 5 destroyers

Duke of York and
Jamaica
engage Scharnhorst

North Cape

**BATTLE OF THE
NORTH CAPE**

Altenfjord NORWAY

Gneisenau was little better than a shell in Gotenhafen. *Prinz Eugen* had been relegated to training duties in the Baltic, and there was little else that mattered.

Lumsden writes that at 2024 *Scharnhorst* was damaged aft and her speed reduced to 20 knots by flooding, although it is unlikely that she was, in fact, slowed that much. The German official account records that their ship was 'slowed slightly', and this would seem to be correct, because *Duke of York* was still unable to reduce the ten miles by which she trailed her adversary, and just afterwards both vessels ceased firing. Shortly before 2100 Admiral Fraser ordered his four accompanying destroyers ahead to place themselves favourably for a torpedo attack on the enemy. This they did, overhauling only with difficulty against the sea and assuming positions on either bow of *Scharnhorst* – *Savage* and *Saumarez* to the north, *Scorpion* and *Stord* to southward. The northerly pair were immediately engaged by the battle-cruiser's secondary guns.

Intent on the two destroyers to port, *Scharnhorst*'s lookouts did not observe the pair to starboard until they had closed to within 3,000 yards. The battle-cruiser wheeled desperately to avoid the sixteen torpedoes launched in her direction, but just too late. One struck her amidships, and, before damage could be fully assessed, the destroyers to northward also attacked, and three more torpedoes smashed into her. With a boiler-room wrecked, *Scharnhorst*'s speed dropped to 8 knots.

Saumarez was limping away, damaged and out of the battle, but she would live to fight another day. In *Scharnhorst*'s smoke-filled engine-room, the artificers worked crazily, but with every passing minute their ship's already cobweb thin hopes of surviving this ill-conceived sortie were evaporating. By 2100 *Duke of York* and *Jamaica* had come up and re-opened fire at 10,400 yards. Burnett's *Belfast* and *Norfolk* were coming within range, and even frustrated *Sheffield*, achieving 22¾ knots, had come close enough

to see Burnett's four destroyers plunging away to join those already attacking *Scharnhorst*. The sea was punishing, the Arctic night black and freezing. Icy air inhaled incautiously clawed at the lungs, to set a man gasping and coughing. Ahead in the sullen void there were more star-shells.

Scharnhorst's engineers had achieved near miracles; their ship had worked up to 22 knots, but it was not going to be enough. The remaining four destroyers, in company with Burnett – *Musketeer*, *Opportune*, *Virago* and *Matchless* – had been unleashed, and at 2142 they closed on their running enemy, while *Jamaica*, *Belfast* and *Norfolk* also made ready to attack with torpedoes.

German records state that *Scharnhorst* was struck by 14 to 15 torpedoes and hit thirteen times by 14-inch shells. If this is so, then the quality of her armour and her damage control efficiency must have been phenomenal. Certainly she was in a desperate condition during the thirty-six minutes of the final action. Fires raged unchecked through her lower decks and there were ragged, charred holes in her sides. Scalding steam hissed from dozens of fractured pipes, while ladders and doors were twisted and buckled. The casualty stations were like slaughter-houses, crowded with maimed; medical orderlies crawled among the chaos, administering morphia. There was acrid, yellow smoke everywhere. Admiral Bey had already transmitted a signal to Adolf Hitler, promising to fight to the end, and now the end was very near.

At 2145 two massive, internal explosions rocked the battle-cruiser, heard by every British ship, including distant *Sheffield*. 'Explosions and fires ravaged the doomed ship,' a German officer wrote later,' but each gun fired until it was shot out. Then *Scharnhorst* settled, listed to starboard, rolled over and sank. The British destroyers and cruisers rushed into the cloud of smoke that marked the passing, but the icy waters silenced those who gave one last cheer for their ship and started to sing 'Over a seaman's grave no roses bloom.' Of *Scharnhorst*'s 2,000 crew, only 36 survived.

Sheffield had arrived just too late to make a final contribution, but, as she passed over the position of *Scharnhorst*'s sinking, floating with filthy scum and scattered with broken flotsam, there rose a macabre rumbling from deep below the keel. 'It was a very eerie and melancholy sensation', recalled Marine Thorndyke, 'when we steamed over the grave of *Scharnhorst* and heard the terrible explosions going on under water.'

Belfast was sighted at 2300, and eleven minutes later *Sheffield* had taken station astern of *Norfolk*. Before midnight all ships had thankfully secured from quarters and had resumed cruising watches, on course for the Kola Inlet.

The anchorage was reached at 1730 on the following day, Monday 27 December, and an hour later the bosun's pipe shrieked over the address system:

'D'yer hear there? By order of the Commander-in-Chief. Splice the Mainbrace. Up Spirits. Hands to the mess for rum.'

'There's time', Bungy Williams soliloquized, 'when yer wish yer could bleedin' join up for ever.'

The next day, 28th, dawned chill and miserable, and Guard and Steerage, the watchkeepers, were left undisturbed in their hammocks until 0700 unless they impeded a gangway or ladder. There were cornflakes, then sausage and egg for breakfast, reminding everyone that today was the ship's postponed Christmas. At 1115 lower deck was cleared for a thanksgiving service on the quarterdeck, the duration of which the chaplain sensibly limited to fifteen minutes, following which Admiral Burnett, equally brief, spoke to the ship's company. He, like the chaplain, was aware that a man's more sentimental responses tend to be blunted by a freezing wind that penetrated clothing and numbed extremities. If Jesus had delivered his Sermon on the Mount to a gathering on the shore of the Barents Sea instead of the sun-drenched Sea of Galilee, perhaps Christianity would have survived no further.

Sheffield's belated Christmas dinner of roast pork, boiled and roast potatoes, peas, then Christmas pudding, was followed by a make-and-mend afternoon during which almost every off-duty man slept. *Duke of York* had passed up the Kola Inlet to Murmansk, where she was formally visited by the CinC of the Russian Northern Fleet, Admiral Arseni Golovka. The largest vessel under his command was a destroyer; the few remaining capital ships of the Soviet Navy were all of pre-1914, Tzarist vintage, and had for long been confined to the Baltic or the Black Sea. Golovka admitted to being 'powerfully impressed' by the British battleship, and particularly admired the ship's bakery. He was given a sackful of buns to take away with him.

A few days later, proceeding homeward, *Duke of York* passed through the area of the recent battle, and Admiral Sir Bruce Fraser ordered a guard of honour and a wreath dropped into the sea in salute to the dead of *Scharnhorst*.

Burnett's squadron left Vaenga at 2300 on the night of the 29th. Day or night, it was pretty much the same. Averaging 25 knots, the ships achieved Scapa Flow without mishap during the first hour of Sunday 2 January 1944.

'D'yer hear there? Both watches will muster as usual at 0815. Mail issue will be piped at 0930. There will be no Divisions, but a Church of England service will be held in the starboard hangar at 1015. Roman Catholics and Free Churches may proceed ashore at 1000, dress Number Twos. Cigarettes and pipe tobacco will be issued at 1100 in the Office Flat. All messes should return trays to the galley immediately. The film tonight will be *Road to Zanzibar*, featuring Bing Crosby, Bob Hope and Dorothy Lamour. Normal Sunday routine will be followed after midday . . .'

Since the first day of the war the Navy had steamed thousands upon thousands of miles in trying to nail down the elusive *Scharnhorst* and *Gneisenau* – dubbed Salmon & Gluckstein – and now it was done. Winston Churchill telegraphed the Commander-in-Chief: 'Everything comes to those who know how to wait.' He was content that, now, the Admiralty could release battleships and aircraft carriers from the Atlantic-Arctic theatre for the offensive against Japan. He wanted a modern British Pacific Fleet to balance the massive American investment in the South Pacific which, sooner or later, would roll like a tidal flow over hitherto British possessions. A realistic British presence east of Colombo was necessary as soon as possible; if the Americans occupied Hong Kong, Singapore, Borneo and Sarawak first, they might prove difficult to dislodge.

Scores of congratulatory signals were being received by the Commander-in-Chief and by ships that had participated in the successful action against *Scharnhorst*, some of them from the unlikeliest of sources.

From the War Cabinet, London: Hearty congratulations on the tenacious defence of the convoy and the brilliant pursuit and sinking of the *Scharnhorst*.

From President Roosevelt: The sinking of the *Scharnhorst* has been great news to all of us. Congratulations to Home Fleet.

From Marshal Stalin: We in Moscow are thrilled by your magnificent achievement. Congratulations to you and all.

From CinC, Mediterranean: Heartiest congratulations on your success.

From CinC Eastern Fleet (Admiral Somerville): Hearty congratulations on your grand party where a good time was had by all except the Hun.

From V.A. Malta (Admiral Bonham-Carter): Heartiest congratulations. Your prophecy on my departure has not taken long to come true. I am very envious.

From CinC, Royal Norwegian Navy: Congratulations. Am very pleased to hear that you are satisfied with *Stord*'s behaviour.

From CinC, Greek Fleet: Please accept my heartiest congratulations on behalf of officers and men under my command for gallant action off North Cape.

There were many, many more from high-ranking officers of all services, statesmen and civic leaders – and some from humbler but equally sincere well-wishers.

From Sheffield Sea Cadet Corps: Sheffield Sea Cadet Corps send their congratulations on your recent brilliant achievement together with best wishes for 1944. Cadets greatly inspired, would be greatly thrilled if you could come and tell us about action.

From Children of Notre Dame High School, Sheffield: Well done, God bless and prosper you all, your proud and happy children of Notre Dame School, Sheffield.

Sheffield remained in the Flow until 22 January, when she steamed down to Liverpool, to secure at Princess Stage, and three days later moved to Birkenhead to Cammell Laird's No. 6 Graving Dock for repairs to the port inner shaft. With Captain Addis temporarily in hospital, Commander Sladen assumed command as Acting Captain with Lieutenant-Commander Treseder his Executive Officer.

18

'The ship is to prepare for service in the Pacific'

JANUARY 1944. Russian tanks were grinding remorselessly westward, and the Germans, stumbling back, were beginning to smell defeat. In the Pacific, too, American operations were gathering momentum, but the Japanese were resisting ferociously by land, sea and air. General Dwight Eisenhower had been appointed Supreme Commander, Allied Expeditionary Force (SCAEF) in anticipation of the Second Front, which must surely be undertaken during 1944.

Britain seemed to be crowded with Americans with their Hollywood 'B' movie vocabulary and gauche behaviour. They had been welcome at first, if not always for the right reasons, but stresses were beginning to show in their personal relationships that could not always be resolved by bromide platitudes about 'our common heritage'. In thousands of Nissen huts and tents from Iceland to Burma lectures by the Army Bureau of Current Affairs described something called a Beveridge Plan, which, in turn, evoked a vision of a post-war Britain in which poverty and unemployment were abolished for ever. A report from Stockholm described a 'flying rocket bomb' developed by the Germans, which was towed into the air by plane for release, when a special propellant sent it to a height of up to five miles before it began to glide towards its objective. When exploding, the missile emitted a huge orange and blue flame, and inflicted damage to a radius of 400 yards.

The ship emerged from dock on 8 February to anchor in mid-river. The Mersey in February was mud-coloured, greasy, the sky overcast and always threatening rain. A haze of coal smoke lay over Liverpool, tangy in the nostrils. A gift of 100,000 cigarettes from the Sheffield Newspapers War Fund had been received, a hundred for every man. The City's concession justified three illustrated feature articles in the *Sheffield Star* – more recognition than the ship had received since her launching in 1936. In return, *Sheffield*'s Canteen Committee voted £25 towards the endowment of a cot in the ship's name in the City's Children's Hospital. The City increased the sum to £50, whereupon *Sheffield*'s Canteen Committee, mildly stung, approved the allocation of an annual amount to maintain the cot until the end of 1946.

Correspondence regarding the children's hospital cot would be exchanged until the end of 1944, by which time everyone would be thoroughly tired of the subject and wishing that *Sheffield* had chosen a simpler means of making charitable donations. Meanwhile, on 9 February, the cruiser had left the Mersey for Scapa Flow.

Only the national newspapers and the trades unions were exploiting the marginally improved war situation. The newspapers were already debating 'How we will Deal With the Germans' or 'The Empire must be Run on New Lines.' – with readers' views invited, while a wave of industrial strikes for more pay was sweeping like a tidal wave over the country. An Allied force had landed at Anzio, in Italy (Churchill's 'wild cat flung on to the shore . . .') and that presumably heralded the end of the Italian campaign. The Germans, in fact, had far from shot their bolt in Italy, while, at sea, if the surface threat had diminished, the U-boat offensive still had to be met. German submarines were being equipped with Snorkel, an air-intake accessory which permitted them to use their diesel engines at periscope depth, while radar countermeasures had been improved and heavier flak batteries mounted. Finally, Fortress Europe had to be stormed; ships and landing craft

Right: It is now 1944, *Sheffield* accompanies several small carrier task forces in North Atlantic sweeps for enemy shipping. From her bridge is a familiar sight – the distant escort carrier *Empress* (earlier the American mercantile *Carnegie*) flying off the last combat air patrol of the evening.

would have to disembark men on the most heavily fortified coastline of all time, and if the Dieppe adventure offered any yardstick, the losses could be horrendous.

And after all that, if one could think sufficiently far ahead, there were the Japanese to be reckoned with. The Americans were saying that an invasion of the mainland of Japan could cost a million Allied lives.

Sladen anchored *Sheffield* in Scapa Flow during the afternoon of 10 February 1944. It was on this day that fifteen Russian aircraft attempted a bombing raid on *Tirpitz* in Kaafiord. Only four located the battleship, and only a single one-ton bomb achieved a near miss, leaving the ship undamaged.

It becomes somewhat tedious to repeat that Scapa Flow was still the same old soddin' Scapa, as did Bungy Williams, who was himself frequently tedious. Another draft of ratings climbed aboard, brought from *Dunluce Castle*; a similar number of the existing crew had been ordered to pack bags, lash hammocks, and stand by for discharge to Depot. Several weeks of working-up could be anticipated before, presumably, *Sheffield* rejoined the 10th Cruiser Squadron for Arctic duties. The CinC, Sir Bruce Fraser, boarded during the late forenoon of the 11th, but departed ten minutes later without a glance at the paintwork and gleaming steel bright-work on which the hands had been working since dawn, and on the 19th the wardroom dined Sir Robert Burnett. Provisions were embarked, including Naafi stores – duty-free cigarettes, confectionery, toilet soaps, Brylcreem and toothpaste, bottled sauces, canned fruits – none subject to rationing, so that many men hoarded quantities of the more desirable purchases for taking home on their next leave. Junior ratings' bedding was scheduled to be aired on the upper deck, but the order was cancelled; mattresses and blankets would have come back below even damper than they had gone up. On Flotta the beer canteen was crowded with ratings from the fleet carriers and escort carriers that occupied the Flow's centre-line of anchorage berths, the corrugated iron cinema was screening *Escape to Glory*, featuring Constance Bennett and Pat O'Brien, while all football pitches were unfit for play. Vera Lynn screamed *We'll Meet Again* repeatedly from the messdeck loudspeakers, and Bungy Williams was suffering from athlete's foot.

Sir Andrew Cunningham had been First Sea Lord at the Admiralty since 15 October 1943, not entirely with Winston Churchill's approval; Cunningham promised to be far less compliant than his predecessor, Sir Dudley Pound, who had survived his retirement by only six days.

It was an unpleasant surprise to all the armchair pundits in Whitehall to learn that *Tirpitz*, only three weeks after the Russian air attack, had been exercising at sea. The experts had claimed that the German monster could not be battleworthy until she had been docked in Wilhemshaven or Kiel for repair and refitting, and there was no possibil-

ity of her undertaking a thousand-mile passage, probably under tow. Neither Navy nor RAF would allow another *Scharnhorst/Gneisenau* dash for sanctuary; too many heads had rolled on that earlier occasion. But now, if *Tirpitz* were indeed preparing for sea, and was about to be turned loose like her twin, *Bismarck*, the Allies' European time-table could receive a nasty jolt. The German battleship's mere existence had provoked the PQ17 convoy disaster in 1942.

The problem was that the RAF had no UK-based bombers capable of carrying a sufficiently heavy bomb-load to Altenfiord and return, and while the Navy's carriers could get nearer to the target, the load capacity of their Swordfish and Albacore aircraft was inadequate, which was why *Tirpitz* had remained so long unmolested. Now the Fleet Air Arm had been equipped with Fairey Barracuda torpedo/dive-bombers with a load capacity of 1,640lb, and plans for an attack on *Tirpitz* had been finalized some weeks earlier.

During the remainder of February and through most of March, *Sheffield* was intensively exercising, and on the 29th Captain Addis resumed command. An RFA was alongside, and the carriers in the Flow were taking on Avgas, but there was little to suggest that an operation was about to be mounted. A number of the ship's company had been issued with four inches of coloured ribbon, representing the 1939–43 Star (the medal was not yet available); the BBC announced the death of Major-General Orde Wingate in Burma, while it was conceded that the campaign to capture Monte Cassino in Italy was a 'temporary failure'.

Early on Tuesday 30 March 1944 the ship was warned of departure; the mail closed and Bernard's and Flemings' representatives were halted at the ladder and politely requested to come back next week. Ladders were raised, booms secured and boats hoisted inboard. Forward, dinner was liver with a whisper of bacon hidden under a brown sludge, and boiled potatoes. Bread had been freshly drawn from the bakery, but most of the semolina pudding was consigned to the messdecks' 'gash' buckets and subsequently to the duty refuse chute on the starboard side amidships. The seagulls rejoiced. This, it was supposed, was going to be just another series of exercises, of torpedo attacks against another ship's wash, smoke-screens, AA shoots at a slowly towed drogue, and that probably meant messdecks drenched with dust from the ventilation trunking and the sugar fouled. At 1800 the address system hummed.

'Cable party to muster forward. All hands not in rig of the day clear upper deck. Close all scuttles and watertight doors. Special sea dutymen close up. Stand by for leaving harbour.'

The sharp edge of Operation 'Tungsten' was represented by the fleet carriers *Victorious* and old-timer *Furious*, between them embarking more than forty Barracudas, supported by four escort carriers, *Emperor, Pursuer, Searcher* and *Fencer*, additionally fielding forty Corsairs, Wildcat and Hellcat fighters. *Fencer* was intended for an anti-submarine role with Swordfish. Practice bombing runs had already been carried out in Loch Eriboll, an hour's steaming from Cape Wrath, against a battleship protected by a smoke barrage, and the aircrews had pared down the time factor for each strike to a mere one minute.

Two of the operation's principals, the battleship *Duke of York* (flying Admiral Fraser's flag) and the carrier *Victorious*, were already at sea as components of the distant screen for convoy JW58, bound for the Kola, but the remainder of the force was free of Scapa Flow by nightfall of Thursday 30 March, reduced to minimal steaming lights and heading north-easterly at 18 knots into a cold but calm night with the stars showing like silver confetti. By noon 31st the ships had covered more than 300 miles and all was quiet.

It was intended that all carriers and escorts should rendezvous 250 miles north-west of Altenfiord, and this was achieved on 2 April in position 70°04′N, 07°13′E; the combined force was steaming for Point Oboe, the position on the chart, 120 miles north-west of the target, from where the attack sorties would be flown. Throughout the Dog watches the aircraft were given their final checks and flight-deck machinery was tested. Ten Barracudas were loaded with a single 1,600lb armour-piercing bomb, twenty-two with three semi-armour-piercing bombs of 500lb, and ten with one 600-pounder for under-surface blasting. The aircraft for the first detail were positioned for take-off and all pilots had been briefed by their Commanders (Air) before being told to take advantage of an early night.

They were roused from sleep at 0130 on the 3rd, Monday, to be served an egg-and-bacon breakfast and, at 0345, mustered for their final briefing. At fifteen minutes the crews were piped to man their aircraft, and at ten minutes the order was given to 'man the chocks, stand clear of propellers, stand by to start up'. At five minutes the carriers began to turn into the wind with, on every flight-deck, the aircraft directed into a queue in the pre-dawn darkness behind the flight leader. At 0415 precisely the first strike lifted off, and Barracudas, Corsairs, Hellcats and Wildcats jockeyed into formation, telling off their call-signs on low-power H/F before turning away southward at little above sea level to avoid radar detection.

It was a superb morning, with the sky blue and cloudless, the sea calm. Twenty miles from the Norwegian coast the aircraft climbed to 8,000 feet to negotiate the mountains that could be seen glowing pink in the dawn sunlight ahead, and just before 0530 *Tirpitz* was sighted below, at the head of Altenfiord.

The aircrew had been warned to expect fierce fighter opposition, but the sky over the fiord was empty, so the massive TARCAP – Target Combat Air Patrol – could be released from its escort role to smother the enemy's AA and radar capability with cannon-fire. The Barracudas came in at well below 3,000 feet to release their bombs, of which nine struck home, and then climbed away, leaving *Tirpitz*

hidden under dark brown smoke and on fire aft. One Barracuda was missing.

The second sortie had just taken off from the strike force and was heading coastward, firing brief testing bursts from machine-guns. The sun was rising clear of the mountains ahead and flashing silver on the perspex cockpit cowlings as they rose and fell. From 8,000 feet the white valleys and escarpments below were pristinely beautiful. There was no flak yet, no movement.

Tirpitz had been in the process of departing her anchorage for speed trials when the first attack caught her totally by surprise; she had a hundred dead and two hundred wounded. The tugs had been sent away and the battleship was moving back to her earlier berth where she could get down her casualties and, in addition to her own armament, she would be under the cover of the shore smoke-generators and other ships' AA fire. Too soon, however, at 0529, the second British strike pounced.

This time *Tirpitz* was ready and, although shaken, her crew fought back. The ship's gun crews were not helped by the rolling blanket of protective smoke which also hid the incoming British fighters, gunning decks and control positions. The second attack scored four more hits with a second Barracuda lost, and *Tirpitz* was no longer battleworthy, her casualties totalling 122 dead and 316 wounded, including the Captain. It would be learned later that no bomb had penetrated the battleship's armoured deck, presumably because the attacking aircraft had failed to remain above 3,000 feet when releasing their bombs, as ordered, to ensure sufficient penetrative momentum. Even so, the operation was considered satisfactory; *Tirpitz* had been hurt, and would need six months to repair her damage. The carriers, with their escort steaming north-easterly, landed-on their squadrons and turned about for home.

Aboard *Sheffield* feelings vacillated between disappointment and relief. The Home Fleet's most experienced radar guard, the cruisers's role had been one of watching and listening for Luftwaffe threats from Bardufoss or some other Norwegian airfield, but the enemy had kept his head down. Scapa Flow was regained at 1620 on 6 April, and on the following day Hubert Treseder left the ship. There was shepherd's pie for dinner (which included, Bungy Williams claimed, certain unmentionable parts of the shepherd's dog) and the 16mm film projector broke down four times during the screening of *That Night in Rio*, intermittently featuring evocative Alice Faye and only slightly less evocative Don Ameche.

At this time, far beyond the knowledge of anyone in *Sheffield*, there raged a high-level dispute over the necessity for further naval air attacks on *Tirpitz*. The First Sea Lord, Cunningham, demanded that more sorties be flown as soon as possible; the enemy should not be given time to draw breath. It was a vintage Cunningham viewpoint. However, Fraser, CinC, Home Fleet, considered that the modest results achieved by naval aircraft, which were not designed for the task, did not justify the immense labour involved. Long-distance, inland targets were the responsibility of the RAF, which had bled the Navy white and allowed thousands of sailors to die while pursuing their strategic bombing programme over Europe. 'Tungsten', said Fraser, was not to be repeated – at least, not by the Navy.

Cunningham returned that, although he respected Fraser's views, the Admiralty's decisions must come first. This was, of course, an opinion that cut little ice among the officers and men at sea. Since 1939 warships had repeatedly been expected to make do with out-dated or inadequate aircraft, or to operate without air cover in enemy-dominated waters, and this time Fraser was digging his toes in. If the Admiralty presented him with a direct order to repeat 'Tungsten', he told Cunningham, then he, Fraser, would haul down his flag.

In the twentieth century admirals were no longer shot on their own quarterdecks *pour encourager les autres*, while the resignation of a CinC during wartime would have been extremely embarrassing. Cunningham himself was no stranger to both poor RAF support and unwarranted interference from the Admiralty, i.e., Churchill, but he was now the First Sea Lord, and Fraser's revolt could not be tolerated. 'I do not know what the underlying reason for (Fraser's) attitude is,' Cunningham recorded. 'To me a most untenable position to take up, but it may be that he resented very much being bludgeoned into 'Tungsten' originally and is determined to resist further pressure.'

Both men were determined to prevail, and in the end the tense situation was relieved by Admiral Sir Henry Moore, Second-in-Command of the Home Fleet, who took the carrier force to sea. On reaching the operational area, however, atrocious weather prevented any flying for several days until, his destroyers low on fuel, Moore was compelled to call off the whole thing and return to base. From every premise, honour had been served.

By this time, *Sheffield*'s company no longer cared. The cruiser had accompanied a small carrier group for a flying operation, 'Pitchbowl', east of the Faroes, but on 17 April departed Scapa Flow for the Clyde. On the 21st *Sheffield* moved into Scott's yard for a seventeen days' inspection and refit. There was evidence everywhere, now, that a massive amphibious offensive against enemy-occupied Europe was only weeks away. Warships, landing ships and assault craft of every description were leaving northern ports for the south coast, and every road southward crawled with trucks, tanks and guns. There was a clamp-down on information leaving the country, and the Government had imposed restrictions on diplomatic privileges; communications were censored, no code traffic was permitted and pouches were subject to inspection. The United States consul in Dublin had passed to the Prime Minister, Mr. de Valera, documentary evidence of the IRA's plans to co-operate with Nazi Germany.

In Burma the Japanese advance had been stopped at Kohima after a bloody two-weeks' battle, and in Bombay nearly a thousand people had been killed and twenty ships destroyed by an explosion of 1,300 tons of TNT in the freighter *Fort Stikene*.

Sheffield undocked on Sunday 7 May, refuelled, and was back in her old berth in Scapa Flow on the 10th. Consensus of opinion had it that Old Shiny, with her bombardment expertise, was a sure certainty for the invasion – thus the brief Clyde refit. Bungy Williams hoped it would be France. He hadn't tasted decent champagne since – well, he jes' couldn't soddin' remember – and the mind boggled at what a French party would do for a pair of Du Pont fifteen denier. Shave off.

It was during this month that the King was in Scapa Flow, visiting the Fleet, and on the evening of the 11th invited one officer from every warship in the base to dine with him in the Admiral's cabin of *Duke of York*. Surgeon-Lieutenant (D) J. F. Humphrey-Jones, *Sheffield*'s dental officer, was delighted to find himself elected to represent *Sheffield*. 'It was a unique honour', he confessed, 'and the King was a perfect host. Despite the dinner being served in May, Christmas pudding was served, as this was the *pièce de résistance* of the flagship's chef. The King was amused to find two sixpences in his portion, and asked for them to be washed for his two daughters.'

On the following forenoon less delighted detachments from all ships, in best suits and medals if any, were transported to *Furious*, to be inspected by His Majesty on the flight-deck. That evening *Sheffield* accompanied a small carrier task force out of the Flow and eastward. During the following four days the force would steam 1,418 miles and come very close to the Norwegian coast in a hunt for enemy merchant ships; the Luftwaffe chose not to interfere, but as a result of this sweep and another, a month later, the carriers' Barracudas and Fireflies would sink seven freighters and damage five.

Everything seemed rather easy. It was not that any sailor experienced deprivation when he regained his base without a blood-drenching confrontation with the enemy, it was simply that, after more than four years, he had grown to recognize that any lull in the long storm did not bode well. The Germans were too proud and disciplined to walk away from a war, and they were also cunning bastards; they had accumulated a lot of ugly shot in their locker, waiting and ready.

It was a quiet period for *Sheffield* in Scapa Flow – quiet, that is, save for the incessant chipping of paint hammers. Drafts of ratings were leaving and joining almost daily, and another litter of kittens had been born in the Royal Marines' office. The appearance of Spam, earlier in the war welcomed as an alternative to corned beef, was becoming as frequent. Many warships that had for so long frequented Scapa Flow were now gone, consigned to the Far East. *King George V*, *Indomitable* and *Illustrious* had steamed, while *Howe* and *Victorious* were soon to follow. Some would

Right: In amazement, *Sheffield*'s crew find themselves among the ice of the far North again, still seeking the last of the enemy's blockade-runners, but the Arctic is empty. Everyone has gone home.

remain for ever beneath some distant tropical sea, havens for shoals of angelfish and barracuda. *Prince of Wales* and *Repulse* lay under the South China Sea, *Dorsetshire* and *Cornwall* in the Indian Ocean, *Exeter* off Java. *Sheffield* was to be repainted in the same colours as before, except that the existing dark tones would now be light and the light areas reversed to dark. There was bleedin' times, Bungy Williams muttered darkly, and raised his eyes to the deck-head.

And it was one of those lulls that always seemed to precede a storm. Everyone knew that *Sheffield* would be up front when the Second Front shooting began. The Royal Marines' dance band was rehearsing in the forward recreation space. If a bunch of parties under Ivy Benson could do it, then so could *Sheffield*'s Royal Marine Band under Colour Sergeant Burrows. Unfortunately rehearsals were frequently interrupted by sailors and stokers who wished to demonstrate their tap-dancing expertise in company with Ginger Rogers, who always seemed to resemble a deck-mop, or crooning like Bing Crosby. The film in the chilly little cinema on Flotta was *The Roaring Twenties*, featuring Cagney and Bogart.

The sun rose at 0544 on Tuesday 6 June 1944 and the BBC's first news bulletin, announcing that massive Allied forces had landed in Normandy was received in *Sheffield* first in incredulous silence and then by hoots of disbelief.

That dawn, as the cruiser had swung slowly at her anchor and her men slept in their hammocks, the greatest single act of warfare in history – the invasion of Europe – had been launched. How was it possible to exclude Old Shiny, who had been given nothing better to do than daily exercises off the Orkneys? The crew drew their breakfast herrings in tomato sauce, boiled hot in their tins, and sat, arguing over tea-puddled mess-tables. Carrol Gibbons's music went unheard. An order for silence was shouted at both watches mustering at 0815, and the First Lieutenant seemed bemused. He would have agreed with Bungy Williams that 'having ter jes' listen ter it on the wireless' was an unusual role for *Sheffield*.

And it had not been an oversight. 'The naval forces which had previously assembled under the overall command of Admiral Sir Bertram Ramsay,' said Communiqué No. 2, 'made their departure in fresh weather, and were joined during the night by bombarding forces which had previously left northern waters.'

For several days it was almost painful to listen to further BBC news bulletins, and every newspaper was choked with correspondents' reports from the 'Liberation Front'. Reduced to merely paraphrasing the information conceded by Supreme Headquarters, newspapers were compelled to print 'human' stories – of British soldiers allowed only ten shillings-worth of French francs (which was totally untrue) and of a carrier pigeon flying one of the first reports of the invasion from Reuter's correspondent in France. There

Left: In Scapa Flow there is leisure time for another ship's concert; humour is forced. The war in Europe is approaching its end, but there is another yet to be concluded, in the Far East, and a million men must die, it is predicted, before the Japanese are finally crushed.

were many fabricated quotes – 'A shy Corporal from Carlisle gave me his parents' address. Tell them, he said, I'm thinking of them . . .'

For days the sky over Scapa Flow was overcast, with visibility poor, and a nightly sea mist, clinging to the sea, kept decks soaked and brightwork tarnished, while a light north-westerly wind scarcely ruffled the heathered slopes of Flotta, Lyness and Longhope. Several hundred Italian prisoners-of-war, taken in North Africa, laboured over the construction of a stone and concrete causeway – the Churchill Barrier – across Kirk Sound, through which Gunther Prien had taken *U47* to torpedo *Royal Oak*. On that day in October 1939 many of *Sheffield*'s younger sailors had been schoolboys in short pants. Was the war really in its *fifth* year?

With the English Channel and the Irish Sea sealed off by massive British surface and air operations, the German naval response to the invasion was choked at birth, and all U-boats were subsequently ordered to withdraw to their bases. Some of those bases, however, were in Norway, to which increasing numbers of German warships were retreating as the Russian advance threatened Baltic ports. It had been suggested that Adolf Hitler was preparing a 'Bavarian Redoubt', and, by the same token, there could also be a last-ditch stand in Norway. Moreover, convoys to northern Russian ports were continuing, while finally there were reports of a new and advanced class of U-boat, running on hydrogen peroxide fuel – subsequently identified as the Walter Types XVII and XXVI, capable of underwater speeds of 20 knots and 24 knots respectively. Sufficent numbers of such craft, if they did exist, could put the clock back sickeningly. Allied surface escorts would

be easily outrun by submerged U-boats, and that spelled massacre.

And so when *Sheffield* weighed at 0512 on 20 June, it was not to proceed southward towards the Channel, but north-west, first for a speculative sweep in Norwegian waters and then altering away beyond the Arctic Circle until, in Latitude 72, the cruiser's bows were pushing through the first rubble of pack ice. Save for a few passing flocks of birds, mostly tern, occasionally a pair of skua, the Arctic was coldly empty. Everyone, said Bungy Williams, 'ad bleedin' gone 'ome, and so should Old Shiny'. So Captain Addis turned *Sheffield* southward for the last time, to anchor again in Scapa Flow two days later, Sunday 25th.

Sixteen cruisers, in addition to battleships and destroyers, had supported the Normandy landings with bombardment fire along the entire fifty miles from Barfleur to Le Havre, and now, three weeks later and with the Allies well established ashore, most of them had returned to UK ports to replenish ammunition and await the unlikely possibility of enemy counter-attacks sufficiently massive to push the British and Americans back to the sea. There was no role in the Channel for *Sheffield*, but her company listened daily to radio reports of a new German weapon, a pilotless flying bomb which putt-puttered, deceptively fast, over southern England – where most of the Chatham-based men had their homes and families. They had assumed that, for the folks at home, the war's worst days were over; the Luftwaffe had been broken. But now there was this thing that the Americans had named a Doodle Bug. It was a crying pity, some sniffed, that a few of the missiles couldn't reach New York, but that was only being nasty to our trans-Atlantic cousins, who enjoyed the war by proxy and the courtesy of Ed. Murrow's broadcasts. And there had been secret enemy weapons earlier – the magnetic and then the acoustic mine, the human torpedo and the two-man submarine, the radio-controlled bomb launched from aircraft – but none of them had been directed against the civilian public. It was true that, with only rare exceptions, secret and freakish weapons did not win wars, but that fact was little consolation to those with upturned faces who heard the stuttering chutter of the approaching bomb suddenly cease, followed by that awful silence of long, long seconds . . .

There was a general tendency to forget that, even after the Germans were defeated – and they were still resisting savagely – there was yet another war to fight. No, men did not forget; they simply tried not to think about it, because it was to be fought on the other side of the world against an enemy to whom the concept of surrender did not exist. The Japanese.

The Americans in the Pacific had done remarkably well in their drive towards the Japanese homeland, but they would be the first to concede that, at this time, they had only gnawed at the edges of the enemy's defence perimeter, and every little atoll, every palm-tasselled strand of coral had cost the lives of good American boys. The Pacific war threatened to be a long and expensive purgatory, and if American boys were going to die in liberating erstwhile British, Dutch and French colonial possessions, then the USA would demand a big say in those territories' subsequent status.

The Royal Navy and United States Navy had ironed out most of their differences. They shared a common phonetic alphabet for use over R/T; the British had been persuaded to abandon Apples, Duff, Harry, Isaac, Orange, Tommy and Yorker in favour of Able, Dog, How, Item, Jig, Oboe, Tare and Yoke, but refused to countenance Left and Right rudder instead of Port and Starboard, or topsides instead of upper deck. Vessels were now Task Units and members of Task Groups, which, in turn, were components of Task Forces. The British inventions RDF and Asdic had become the Americanized Radar and Sonar, and words like 'antenna' and 'gasoline' were creeping into daily vocabulary. The British rating, however, still drew his midday tot of rum while the American was limited to Coke; alcohol was available in Royal Naval wardrooms, never in American.

By the end of the month *Sheffield* had steamed the 400 miles from Scapa Flow to Greenock, and then moved past Helensburgh into Gareloch. Any of the men, if pressed, would have confessed to an inner empty feeling, incomprehensible. This, for sure, was the end of something, but they could not say whether for good or bad. Something was going to happen. The messdecks were thronged with ratings transferring kit from locker to kitbag, packing suitcases and lashing hammocks for the long journey south, to Chatham and the penance of Royal Naval Barracks with its debilitating joining routine which required men to report at, in correct sequence, the Victualling Office, the Regulating Office, The Duty Watch Office, the Sick Bay for genitals' inspection, inoculations and vaccinations, the Gymnasium for kit inspection, the Drafting Office and finally the Pay Office. At sea, men might curse their ship as the worst in the Fleet, but in RNB they could think of little other than the prospect of getting back to sea, any sea, aboard anything that would take them away from this insufferable slum teeming with thousands of similarly disgruntled sailors who waited and waited, walking aimlessly or drinking undrinkable Naafi tea or carefully counting their coppers to ascertain the possibility of three hours of analgesic darkness in a Chatham cinema.

The Allied invasion of Normandy was progressing, not spectacularly but steadily. Caen had fallen to British and Canadian troops and the Americans had taken St-Lô. All German resistance in the Cherbourg Peninsular had ended. The Russians were advancing on all fronts, remorselessly, and in Burma the Japs were withdrawing through monsoon rain and mud. Saipan had fallen to U.S. forces, with the Japanese garrison of 27,000 being almost totally annihilated.

At home, squads of selected policewomen were being trained to deal with the growing problem of 'soldier-mad' girls, usually teenagers, who haunted barracks gates and pestered servicemen, preferably American, often living rough and frequently carriers of venereal disease. John Barkers of Kensington offered fully-fashioned fine lisle stockings at 4/3d and three coupons a pair (not more than two pairs per customer) in shades of Fawn, Medium Beige, Dark Suntan and Mole Beige.

Aboard *Sheffield*, all leave was terminated when the watchkeepers came off at 1130 on 17 July, and the last mail closed; the ship was under sailing orders. Messdeck rumours with regard to *Sheffield*'s future were as numerous as there were messes, but most of them pointed in the direction of the Far East. Bungy Williams warned his junior disciples to watch out for either Chinese stewards or Indian dhobey-wallahs. No, not soddin' Red Indians.

Routine orders were posted during the Dog watches and ended all speculation.

Routine Office 17 July 1944.
Sailing Orders for Tuesday 18th July.
1030 Prepare for sea. Hoist 1st Motor Boat and Pulling Cutters. Away 2nd Cutter with mail orderly.
1100 Mooring party of the Port Watch fall in in the Heads Flat. Harbour Close Range Weapons' Crew up 2nd Motor Cutter.
1115 Special Sea Dutymen and Skeleton Damage Control Parties to your stations.
1200 Slip and proceed to sea.
1400 Starboard Watch to Defence Stations. Lookouts and Close Range Weapons' Crews of the White Watch close up.
1600 Action Stations.
1700 Secure. Assume Second State of Readiness.
We shall remain at Second State of Readiness until 1200 noon Monday 24th July, securing again in South Boston Navy Yard, Boston, Massachusetts, U.S.A. The ship is to be prepared for operational service in the Pacific.

Sgd. G. M. Sladen, Commander.

19

'Drunken and licentious British, ravishing the daughters of Massachusetts'

FOLLOWING an uneventful passage, *Sheffield* entered the Charles River estuary to tie alongside the North Jetty of South Boston Navy Yard at 0805 on 25 July. Since the first day of the war, Old Shiny had steamed more than 236,000 miles, roughly equal to ten times around the world, and, the first warship to carry her name, had earned twelve battle honours. This was more than any other ship of her class, equalled only by the destroyer *Tartar*, and surpassed only by the battleship *Warspite*, the cruiser *Orion* and the destroyer *Nubian*, each of which had earned thirteen. Now *Sheffield* was to be made ready for service against the Japanese.

After the leisurely attitude towards work usually shown by British dockyard personnel, the Americans' alacrity was almost intimidating. Their planning staff climbed aboard immediately upon the ship's berthing, followed by an army of workmen who lost no time in stripping down defective items in readiness for replacement. Had this been Hebburn or Belfast the work force would likely have declared a strike for more pay or the ship would never leave the dock; and sod the war. Trades unions hadn't started the war.

Accommodation for the ship's company, including junior officers, had been provided in the USN Receiving Station, Fargo Barracks, a short distance from the dock, while officers above the rank of Lieutenant were directed to private accommodation by the U.S. Officers' Club Housing Agency. Only the duty part of the watch reported aboard daily; it was, as Bungy Williams conceded, like one of them films at the Odeon. Americans gorged more meat during one meal than a week's ration for a British family of five.

Sheffield's first requirement had been the complete removal of 'X' turret and the augmentation of AA armament. The dockyard workers were already removing turret gearing, but a searching scrutiny by both British and American inspectors revealed that the cruiser needed much more dockyard attention than had been anticipated if she were to be fit for the British Pacific Fleet. *Sheffield*, in fact, was a very tired lady. The Americans, between themselves, questioned whether she was worth refitting at all; United States dockyards were turning our new warships like popcorn – but they were too polite to say so. The refit continued.

Boston, architecturally, was surprisingly English – Beacon Street and Louisburg Square could have been in Chelsea, and the Boston Common area was more like Southampton. Facilities for golf, tennis and squash were excellent, and American service clubs extended membership to both officers and ratings.

Much warm-hearted generosity, however, was more than balanced by the hostility of a sizeable Irish-American faction, and *Sheffield*'s men were warned to avoid even the most casual political exchanges.

'The most extra-ordinary example of anti-British prejudice', recorded the Chaplain, John Higgins, 'was shown at a public ceremony, in Boston's central square, for the unveiling of a plaque commemorating the residents' hospitality to British servicemen during the war years. It was unveiled by Captain John Eaton (who had come from the UK to relieve Captain Addis). It was surprising, not to say discourteous, that the local authority chose to devote the first part of the ceremony to the reading of winning essays from a competition sponsored by the Daughters of the Revolution. The subject of the essays was *How We Drove Out the British*, and all were rich in descriptions of American patriotism and courage while simultaneously reviling British perfidy. It was only after enduring several of these offensive recitals that the Captain was able to climb to his feet and thank the Bostonians for entertaining us.'

War news was understandably predominantly of American interest, to which *Sheffield*'s men did not object although occasionally wondering if the presence of British troops in France was really necessary. In mid-August, apparently an American force, supported by French troops, had landed in southern France, and apparently Paris fell to the Americans on the 25th. American NBC reported Patton's tanks driving towards Germany, with no mention of British or Canadians, and the US First Army crossed into Belgium. Newspaper and radio bulletins covering the war in the Pacific and Far East referred exclusively to American activities; nobody in Boston would have believed that there was a British army fighting in Burma, or a British Pacific Fleet, and in due course Hollywood would confirm that the Burma campaign was indeed won by Errol Flynn leading the American Merrill's Marauders.

Meanwhile, many of *Sheffield*'s sailors were experiencing difficulty in making ends meet on their British pay, in spite of an increment of a few pence conceded by the Admiralty for the duration of the refit. 'Many of the ship's company', said Electrical Artificer Peter Standen, 'took on additional work ashore to augment their pay. It was usual to see men going ashore with overalls tucked under an arm, and so popular did the extra work become that the Union Jack Club in Boston maintained an employment exchange. The jobs taken were many and varied, and included dish-washing in hotels and restaurants, house-cleaning, chocolate-packing, waiting at tables and laundry work – in fact any of the tasks that Bostonians considered fit only for Negroes, or poor whites like the British. However, one Petty Officer trod the stage of the Boston Opera House as an extra during a visit by the New York Metropolitan Opera Company.'

In September *Sheffield* heard of the first V-2 rockets landing on London, and nervous excitement rippled through Boston at the thought of such missiles reaching the American eastern seaboard. What did reach New England during the 13th and 14th of that month was a tropical hurricane, the centre of which passed out to sea less than twenty miles from Boston and, ashore, wrecked buildings and vehicles, and tore down trees and telegraph poles but inflicted no damage on the docked cruiser. Several officers, including the Reverend John Higgins, were sent to Washington for cipher courses, and a new draft of ratings and Marines had arrived in New York in *Queen Mary*, then troop-carrying. By now the refit was well advanced. *Sheffield*'s main armament had been reduced to nine 6-inch guns in three turrets, but in addition to her original eight 4-inch HA guns and two quadruple pom-poms, she now had space to accommodate four quadruple 40mm Bofors guns as well as ten twin and seven single Oerlikon mountings. At last, almost too late, Old Shiny was carrying the sort of AA armament that she and her sisters had wished for so desperately off Norway and during those savage Mediterranean club runs to Malta. At last, the message had got home to some of those Whitehall warriors who had for so long insisted that aircraft were no match for properly handled warships, and that only greater resolution on the part of ships' commanding officers was needed to defeat the dive-bombers.

Tell that, said the United States Navy, to the Kamikaze pilots of Emperor Hirohito. And so say all of us, added *Sheffield*'s company.

Some of the men were beginning to appreciate the finer points of American football, baseball and basketball, none of which, however, attracted any permanent adherents. The first, they agreed, was only Rugby League in padding, the second an adult version of the schoolchildrens' 'Rounders', and the third was played in the UK by little girls in gym-slips. There was a slowly growing guilt complex, particularly among those who had wives and children in food-rationed, grey-bleached Britain, and a desire to depart this well-fed USA. American radio's syndicated news bulletins bayed angrily of two American GIs being shot by a ten-year-old German girl, an infamy that only demonstrated the diabolism of Hitler's Germany. Nobody

debated whether a Congressional Medal of Honor would not have been awarded to any American ten-year-old who shot two German invaders.

As the weather warmed, Bostonians began appearing in violently coloured T-shirts and baseball caps, and, the British observed, whether at work or leisure, walking, driving or watching a ball game, never seemed to tire of eating – hamburgers, pizzas, cookies, three-deckers, angel cake, cream cheese on rye with sauerkraut and ketchup, chilli, or dishes like Omelette Chasseur, which looked like something scraped off the floor of a farmyard. Policemen had paunches spilling over their waist-belts, while Rita's on Milk Street was allegedly the best little angel house on the East Coast and was patronized by the Mayor and the Assistant District Attorney.

Some of *Sheffield*'s more erudite took advantage of the tours organized by the *Boston Globe* newspaper which took in the Massachusetts Institute of Technology, the University of Harvard and the site of the Battle of Bunker Hill. The Bostonians were very sensitive about 1775, Paul Revere, and 'drunken and licentious British soldiery, crazed with alcohol', who smashed, slashed, burned, looted and, of course, ravished the fair daughters of Massachusetts. Bungy Williams said that he'd seen the film; 'Gary Cooper wore one of them comic 'ats with a tail down the back'.

On 14 February 1945 Captain J. W. M. Eaton had arrived in Boston to assume command. By now the Allied armies had driven deeply into Germany; enemy radio programmes directed at British and American troops had suddenly become conciliatory and wheedling. 'The British and Americans are both good guys – as are their opponents, the Germans. Why go on killing? It's senseless. Think of the good times we all had together in the piping days of peace. Why can't we all be friends again?'

Sheffield's ensign was lowered on 12 April. Franklin Delano Roosevelt, President of the United States longer than anyone, had died of a massive stroke at the winter White House in Warm Springs. On the following day lower deck was cleared, and five minutes' silence observed between 1605 and 1610. Among the men there was genuine regret; there was none who would not have acknowledged the debt owed to Roosevelt. He had been a true friend to the British and a magnificent ally. Nobody had heard of Mr. Hary S. Truman, but if he were only half the man his predecessor had been, then he would do well enough. And it seemed singularly unfair that within the next four weeks the German High Command would surrender unconditionally, and both Hitler and Mussolini would be dead.

Everything, now, was in the melting-pot. *Sheffield*'s refit had not been completed, and there would never be an explanation for the directive from Whitehall that terminated all work and ordered the cruiser back to Portsmouth. The American workforce trooped ashore with their lunchcans and Old Shiny's company returned to a daily routine of strong yellow soap, scrubbers and squeegees. At 0800 on 21 May the loudspeakers in every messdeck and flat click-clicked and a bosun's pipe wailed: 'D'yer hear there? Prepare for sea.'

Under way and turning south-easterly, *Sheffield* ran her measured-mile speed trials off Provincetown, Cape Cod, where the earliest English fugitives from religious intolerance had named their settlements Plymouth, Chatham, Cambridge, Taunton and Barnstable. The trials successful, the cruiser secured again alongside South Boston's North Jetty to prepare for final departure.

Passengers embarked for the UK included several recently acquired American wives of members of the ship's company, who were accommodated in vacated officers' cabins, with the officers so deprived transferring to the Gunroom. Also taken aboard for passage were three dozen English boys who had been evacuated to the USA earlier in the war. They were to be confined to the hangar deck under the supervision of the chaplain, Higgins, and Surgeon-Lieutenant Humphrey-Jones. The boys slept in hammocks in the port hangar and messed in the starboard counter-part. Humphrey-Jones would always claim that his penance was the reward of having provided the Paymaster-Commander, Pine, with a set of dentures which, although fitting snugly, turned the Paymaster's merest smile into a demoniacal grin. There had been a tiny but crucial error of measurement. Sick Bay P. O. Walley recalls that 'only the Wardroom were delighted. The Paybob had hitherto been of rather serious mien, not given to levity. Now, each time he entered the Wardroom, he had no choice but to grin like a lunatic.'

At 1330 on Monday 28 May *Sheffield* eased away from North Jetty to anchor in President's Roads. Only one rating among the entire ship's company had submitted a request to be assigned ashore in the USA because he wished to marry an American girl. As the same man, ten months before – when the ship had first reached Boston – had requested to be immediately returned to the UK because he had been about to marry an English girl, Captain Eaton declined the request.

During the evening of the next day, Tuesday 29th, the cruiser weighed and passed slowly out of the Charles River into Massachusetts Bay, and as the American shoreline grew indistinct astern, turned her bows to 080, homeward, and, to the satisfaction of the boys congregated on the hangar deck, increased to 28 knots. By the following noon *Sheffield* was 532 miles on passage, with CBS beginning to fade and BBC coming in strongly with Workers' Playtime and Variety Band-box, Dinah Shore singing and Reginald Foort on the organ. Already the end of the war in Europe had become visually apparent; the Admiralty and U.S. Navy Department had jointly announced that all merchant vessels in the Atlantic, Arctic and Indian Oceans should now 'burn navigation lights at full brilliance and need not darken ship'. War conditions applied only to the Pacific theatre.

Aboard *Sheffield*, as in any other ship that had been blacked out for almost six years, the lifting of restrictions was almost uncomfortable, and, momentarily, the sight of a distant vessel with full navigational lights, deck lights and port-holes twinkling could give a bridge officer a nasty jolt. But there were limits to the extent to which a warship could relax. Asdic watch was still maintained because not all of the U-boats of surrendered Germany had yet reported their compliance and reached an Allied port. Radar operators, too, maintained surveillance; it was becoming clear that this facility could be a valuable navigational aid in peacetime.

Another subject was occupying BBC programme time during *Sheffield*'s six-day crossing. There was to be a General Election, the first since November 1935, when a Conservative government had been returned with a majority of 247. Thus a very large percentage of the electorate had never voted, and although there had been a coalition government since May 1940, and several Socialist ministers had made valuable contributions towards the war's successful pursuance, it had been dominated by Winston Churchill and was generally regarded as having been Conservative. There was surprise and some annoyance, even in the Labour Party, that the coalition should not be allowed to continue until after the defeat of Japan, but Churchill bowed to the demands of the more insistent Left, assured by his own supporters that the Conservatives had little to fear. The election would be staged on 5 July, although the result would not be known for a further three weeks because of the votes of servicemen overseas.

Sheffield reached the Channel during the night of 4/5 June, and by dawn was following a slow thread of Dorset coast speckled with tiny lights. Then Hurst Castle slid past to port, Fort Warden to starboard, and at 0905 the cruiser anchored in Spithead. During the early afternoon she weighed again, and at 1440 secured alongside North Corner Jetty.

There was still much to be done before *Sheffield* could be considered fit for the Pacific theatre. Additional and advanced electronics were to be installed, including target acquisition radar, an improved air warning system, several barrage directors for both main and secondary armament, and an updated main gunnery equipment. Also to be added was a more sophisticated height-finding surface and air warning outfit and, not least, a number of American TBS radio trans-receivers. The ship's radar complement had been increased, and Communications personnel were being despatched to the Signals School in Petersfield for refresher courses.

In Portsmouth Dockyard, Bungy Williams described to the messdeck's younger element how the two stone lions crouched outside the Guildhall rose to their feet and roared every time a virgin walked past.

The Labour Party was fighting its election campaign largely on a programme of nationalization – of the Bank of

England, the coal-mines, road and rail transport, civil aviation and the steel industry. The Conservatives' tactics were based on Winston Churchill's reputation as a great war leader while simultaneously implying that a Labour government would impose a Gestapo-type control of the people, seize savings and dissolve all private ownership. To Churchill's bitter disappointment and Attlee's surprise the Labour Party was returned to power with a majority of almost 150. The people voted not so much for Social- ism and nationalisation, or against the Conservatives, but more from an eagerness to 'let someone else have a go'; they were weary of hardships and austerity. Moreover, the Labour Party's electoral machinery had been more efficient than that of the Conservatives, whose campaign had been negative by comparison. Churchill's war reputation was not

enough, and Servicemen were not convinced that he was necessarily the right leader of a post-war administration. 'I regret', said Churchill, handing in his resignation to the King, 'that I have not been permitted to finish the work against Japan. For this, however, all plans and preparations have been made, and the results may come much quicker than we have hitherto been entitled to expect.'

Those 'plans and preparations' of course, included the build-up of the British Pacific Fleet, which in May had consisted of *King George V, Howe, Indomitable, Victori- ous, Indefatigable* and *Formidable*, the cruisers *Swiftsure, Gambia, Black Prince, Uganda* and *Euryalus*, eleven destroyers, and would soon be supplemented by *Sheffield*. The BPF had already been in action, and both *Formidable* and *Indefatigable* had been slightly damaged during a Kami- kaze attack.

Nobody had expected a new Government to change things overnight, but any anticipation of *some* improvement was disappointed. Overtime was still taxed at ten shillings in the pound, rationing continued as before, and there was a severe shortage of all consumer goods. The first trickle of conscripted and time-expired men was being released

Below: it is not yet the Pacific for *Sheffield*. She is ordered to Boston, USA, for a dockyard refit and a mixed reception of generous American hospitality and vociferous Irish-American hostility. The refit is prematurely terminated by the surrender of Germany and, heading home, the elderly *Sheffield* lifts her skirts to a height of 28 knots. Ahead of her the lights of Europe are ablaze after six years of darkness.

from the forces, with priorities based on an age-plus-service formula. At the Admiralty, Mr. A. V. Alexander, having been briefly replaced by Brendan Bracken, was again First Lord; he was regarded as honest and sensible, if somewhat plodding. Cunningham was still the First Sea Lord.

Sheffield's company were being issued with tropical clothing, including coal-scuttle shaped topees. Parties of ratings were marched to R.N. Sick Quarters each forenoon, with paybooks, to have vaccinations and inoculations boosted. It was assumed that the cruiser would proceed to Sydney, Australia, via the Panama Canal, although there was another school of opinion which suggested that *Sheffield* would be routed eastward through Suez to join the Eastern Fleet and subsequently Mountbatten's operations against Japanese-occupied Burma and Malaya. In Bungy William's view the issue of topees pointed towards the Road to Mandalay where the Old Flotilla lay, about which, as a schoolboy in West Ham, he had sung songs on Empire Day. That had been in Ramsay MacDonald's time, and the Atlantic Fleet had mutinied. Meanwhile, there was a thing or two that Bungy Williams could tell the younger generation about them slant-eyed little darlings in their slit-up skirts . . .

The news on Tuesday 7 August that featured in every BBC broadcast and filled the front page of every newspaper stunned some, but left most people uncomprehending. One 'atomic' bomb had been dropped on a Japanese city, Hiroshima. The bomb, it was claimed, had an explosive power equal to 20,000 tons of TNT, which was roughly 2,000 times the blast power of the RAF's 'Grand Slam' – hitherto the biggest bomb yet used during the war. Well, that only meant that the 'atomic' bomb was a bigger and better bomb, which was a good thing, but hardly seemed to justify all this fuss, did it? Those who consulted their home encyclopaedias read that, if only atomic power could be harnessed, a walnut-sized piece of coal could drive *Queen Mary* across the Atlantic and back.

It was not until the next day, Wednesday, that the full horror was explained. Hiroshima, a city of 300,000 people (the size of Coventry or Nottingham) had ceased to exist. It had 'vanished in a vast ball of fire'. In Guam the crew of the aircraft that had dropped the bomb were being quoted. 'We dropped the bomb at exactly 9.15 a.m . . .' the observer, Parsons, said. 'After the missile had been released I sighed and stood back for the shock. When it came the men aboard with me gasped "My God" – and what had been Hiroshima was a mountain of smoke like a giant mushroom.'

Japan had been presented with an ultimatum: 'We will withhold further use of the atomic bomb for 48 hours, in which time you can surrender. Otherwise you face the prospect of the entire obliteration of the Japanese people.'

On 8 August Russia declared war on Japan. A second atomic bomb was dropped on Nagasaki on the 9th, and five days later the Japanese government agreed to surrender unconditionally.

With no warning until 8 a.m., Wednesday 15 August was declared VJ-Day and the first of a two-day public holiday. There was early chaos as hundreds of workers, in ignorance, queued for trains and buses that did not come. Housewives dashed for shops to form more queues, for bread, groceries, meat. Most shops opened for only two hours. In Manchester angry shoppers hammered on closed shop doors, and there was a severe shortage of cigarettes and beer in Liverpool. Fighting occurred in Leeds between queueing housewives and potential queue-jumpers. In London taxicabs stopped running and bus-conductors gave up trying to collect fares on buses crammed to the running-board.

Ships in Portsmouth harbour cancelled daily routines and piped a make-and-mend from midday. RNB shore patrols were doubled, but the city's streets were quiet until evening, when the first hastily built bonfires burst into flame on Portsdown Hill, and every moored warship began firing rockets and Very lights over the port's rooftops. The cost of pyrotechnics consumed during that twelve hours must have had the Director of Naval Accounts in Bath sucking his teeth in disbelief. Every Portsmouth bar was crowded to capacity with sailors, soldiers, Wrens and Waafs, and dozens of couples fornicated triumphantly on Southsea Common. Thousands of people joyously tore up their identity cards, food, clothing and petrol ration coupons. They would be sorry, for the rationing of many goods was to continue until July 1954.

Quite suddenly all urgency had evaporated, and dockyard pressure to bring *Sheffield*'s refit to completion died to a level of almost indifference after VJ-Day. There was no longer a Pacific war and therefore no need for Old Shiny. Half of the ship's company had become obsessed with their approaching release from the service, demobilization groups, financial gratuities and post-war employment. It was difficult for the First Lieutenant to generate enthusiasm for ship-side painting among men who were, they thought, only a few weeks away from discharge, civilian jobs, a Council house with a garden, and Social Security support for those who did not care to work. The national welfare blueprint was a programme for the ordinary people, and many could hardly believe in it. You got what you paid for. Give an idle man three pounds a week for remaining idle, they said, and he'll spent it on drink and gambling. Meanwhile, on 2 September, the USA demanded that in exchange for further financial aid Britain must liquidate the greater part of the Empire's economic policy; the objective was the opening for U.S. industry to feed products into the markets of the British Empire. The BBC terminated the broadcasting of American radio programmes for the AEF. London busmen decided to work according to rule in protest against the summer schedules, and pay talks between the railway unions and the railway companies had broken down.

Peace had returned.

20

'I don't think you know me; my name's Philip.'

THE end of any period of war is anticlimax. Battles make news, inspire books and films and generate powerful emotions, but when the captains and the kings and the brass bands have departed, the ships and men that remain are no longer the subjects of public interest and regard, and will not be acknowledged again until storm clouds gather elsewhere, and a fleet is ordered to Korea, or Suez, or the Falklands, when – as Kipling had already shrugged, 'But it's "Thin red line of 'eroes" when the drums begin to roll.'

Sheffield's men debated how long it would be for the executioner's axe to fall on Old Shiny, when so many fine ships were already being scrapped, but at 1100 on Wednesday 14 November Captain Kenneth Harkness climbed the after brow and picked his way among trailed acetylene hoses, clutters of scrap and puddles of rust-coloured water to assume command. *Sheffield*, having enjoyed an expensive refit, was not yet for the grave-yard; she was to be brought forward to enable her to serve as the flagship of the North American and West Indies Station.

The ship's silver, deposited for safety in the vaults of Dumfermline's Bank of Scotland just before the outbreak of war, was re-embarked. Harkness had been battling to have a wooden quarterdeck refitted – it had been removed in 1942 and replaced by a composition which, although more practical for war service, did not flatter the appearance of a peacetime flagship. In rejecting the Captain's request, one Admiralty department claimed that the weight of a wooden quarterdeck, added to that of all the radar and AA armament fitted since the ship was built, would be too much for the ship's stability. Another said that there was at that time no suitable wood in the UK, while yet a third insisted that the country simply could not afford such luxuries as new wooden decks, even for flagships.

Harkness's persistence, however, finally wore down resistance. In mid-November 1945 he received an exasperated signal: 'Approved to fit *Sheffield* with wooden QD.' For the Captain it was a Pyrrhic victory; the eight months taken by the dockyard to replank the quarterdeck meant a similar reduction of his 'time in command'.

During early March 1946 the CinC, Admiral Sir Geoffrey Layton, asked Harkness if *Sheffield*, still alongside, could stage a lunch party for HRH the Princess Marina, Duchess of Kent, who was visiting Portsmouth on the 14th to inspect the Wrens. The Duchess would, of course, be accompanied by Sir Geoffrey and Lady Layton, and it would be appreciated if an invitation could be extended to a Lieutenant Prince Philip Mountbatten, RN.

Captain Harkness was delighted, but had never heard of a Lieutenant Prince Philip. Layton explained that his guest was Prince Philip of Greece and Denmark, first cousin to HRH. It meant little to Harkness, but the CinC's patronage could not be questioned, and the nebulous Lieutenant was invited.

The great day arrived, with the quarterdeck ratings in No. 2's and lanyards. 'Minutes before the Royal limousine was due', recalls Harkness, 'I mustered my guests and all were present except this unknown Prince. I had warned the Officer of the Watch that if he saw a two-striper coming on board for the lunch, he ought to be piped over the side; apparently he was in command of one of H.M. ships.

The minutes ticked by and the OOW was certain that no Lieutenant had passed over the quarterdeck. In a state of near panic I again made a quick cast of the guests in the wardroom and, this time, found a good-looking young officer who immediately said, "I don't think you know me, sir. My name's Philip."

"Thank God you're here," I said, "but how did you get aboard?"

"Well," he grinned, "I came up to your quarterdeck brow, but there was a large sign that said, 'Keep Out. This Means YOU'. So I went back to the jetty and came aboard over the fo'c'sle."

Basin trials were carried out by the beginning of May and the Admiral-Superintendent inspected the ship on the 18th. It was all very leisurely. The charts came aboard on 30 May, and storing commenced.

Following her full-speed trials, *Sheffield* departed for the Mediterranean to apply herself to a month of drills and evolutions, damage-control exercises, gunnery and torpedo practice. Harkness took the cruiser into Malta's Grand Harbour on 17 July, easing her past the sunken floating dock and other wrecked hulls without aid to the innermost berth.

Malta was still recognizably the same Malta that the older hands had known when *Sheffield* had fought with Somerville's Force H. Much of the wartime rubble had been cleared and the Barracca Lift still climbed from the waterfront for a fare of one penny. Blue Label bottled beer had now been supplemented by Anchor and Hop Leaf Ales, but the Gut was still the point of convergence for all shore-going ratings in uniform and midshipmen in mufti. Jim Irish's lodging house still reeked of damp plaster and urine, and tea made from the island's desalinated water was always scummed. Passengers on the home-going troopship *Dilwara* shouted gleefully at ships proceeding eastward: 'You're going the wrong way!'

Three weeks of intensive working-up, including a four-days' course in Aid to the Civil Power, for the Marines, had resulted in a passably efficient warship when the CinC came aboard to give his approval, followed by Admiral Sir William Tennant, CinC designate, North American and West Indies Station and whose flagship *Sheffield* was subsequently to be. (In late 1941 Tennant, commanding the battlecruiser *Repulse*, had fought a brilliant but hopeless battle against Japanese air attacks in the South China Sea.)

At 0900 on Monday 12 August 1946, being in all respects ready for service, *Sheffield* slipped and proceeded on the first leg of her journey to her new station. Two days later she called at her first foreign port, Punta Delgrada, São Miguel in the Azores, and the Royal Marine's journal, *Globe & Laurel*, reported: 'We spent three days in the Azores, where the band beat the retreat – a ceremony that was so popular that it has been repeated at every port we have visited since.'

Everything, from now, was going to be different for Old Shiny. The younger H.O.s and the more recent graduates from shore training establishments knew no different, but the older men, who had spent the previous five or six years at sea were not impressed. During the war the Navy's peacetime rituals, perpetuated in the name of tradition and discredited by pettiness, had been abandoned in favour of fighting efficiency, and an indifferent officer class had been largely replaced by men who, in most cases, had come from a more attuned middle, and even working, class, who accepted that human dignity was the right of even the lowest ordinary seaman. Even before *Sheffield* had docked in Bermuda on 30 August there was a massive issue of hard soap, soft soap, Brasso, Blanco, buckets, scrubbers and squeegees. The writing was on the wall.

'I wish to stress', announced Vice-Admiral Sir Irvine Glennie, CinC, A&WI, after inspecting an immaculate Division, before church service, 'the importance of a return to the peacetime standard of smartness in the Royal Navy. Many countries in the Western hemisphere have seen little of the White Ensign during the war years, and a high standard of smartness will have a good effect on Britain's relations with these countries.'

Bungy Williams was a three-badger, greying and paunchy. He never exposed himself to messdeck gaze before Up Spirits at 1150 or after First Dog Watchmen at 1530, but could reliably be found playing Tombola in the Office Flat or watching *Snow White and the Seven Dwarfs* in the Starboard hangar. Holding court, he sniffed. 'Never mind the bleedin' armour, mate. Jes' look at our tiddley brightwork. If yer see anything that moves, salute it. If it don't move, paint it. If it's got a red face an' sez "Take 'ees card," every time he sees a dirty gash bucket, then salute it twice. It'll be the Commander.'

For the next three months – until Christmas – *Sheffield* would show the flag through the West Indies, in Nassau, Kingston, Port of Spain, Grenada, Barbados, Antigua, to New York to embark Vice-Admiral and Lady Tennant, and then back to Bermuda, where, on arrival, the local newspaper reported that 'When *Sheffield* docked at Malabar at 10 a.m. (23 October) she had the look of a schoolboy, scrubbed and polished for Sunday dinner about her. She was carrying a new chieftain who would guide her destiny through peaceful waters.' It was written by a Miss Virginia Russell, who, the crew decided, must be the paper's religious affairs correspondent.

Three weeks were spent in Bermuda's floating dock, partly for minor repairs to the rudder but rather more to exercise the dockyard's personnel, for whom the operation was a major undertaking. It was during this period that Stoker Woodhouse, disengaging some hoses, fell from the dock's first platform to the bottom, hitting every step of the wall on his way. Incredibly, he not only lived, but recovered in time to return to duty for the ship's next cruise. The incident proved that not only was Old Shiny a remarkably lucky ship with regard to casualties but also that stokers,

Above: After working up in the easy environment of a peacetime Mediterranean, *Sheffield* proceeds to the West Indies to fly the flag of Admiral Sir William Tennant, CinC North American and West Indies Fleet. 'Bill' Tennant had earlier fought a brilliant but hopeless battle in *Repulse*, against Japanese aircraft in late 1941.

as Bungy Williams said, were made of rubber, solid from the neck upwards.

On Sunday 22 December Captain Harkness relinquished command, relieved by Captain G. B. H. Fawkes, CBE. Although Harkness had commanded *Sheffield* for only thirteen months, of which only six had been sea-going, he had the satisfaction of knowing that he was handing over a warship he had worked up in all respects for service, and it was his persistence alone that had achieved the flagship's wooden quarterdeck.

Throughout 1947 *Sheffield* cruised, lotus-eating, from Bermuda to Jamaica, to Panama, Peru, Chile, the Falklands, Uruguay and the Argentine, Brazil again, Trinidad, then back to Bermuda. There were cocktail parties, beer-and-sandwich parties, banyan parties, yacht club parties and just booze-ups, then open days during which crawling hundreds of vociferous West Indians penetrated the most inaccessible areas of the ship to gaze agog at the gun breeches, shake their heads in the laundry, and marvel at the seamen's heads. Ashore, rum was 2*s*. 4*d*. (12p) per bottle.

With Captain Harkness, a hundred of the ship's company returned to the UK for demobilization, boasting of civilian affluence to come and patronizingly sympathetic towards those who must remain. Ten large rums-and-coke for thirty bob was all very well, mate, not to mention buxom black parties with rubber mouths at two quid, but give me nine-to-five, matie, a pint o' Courage's and the missis every night in the dark that yer jes' tell yerself is Betty Grable.

Captain Fawkes, inevitably dubbed 'Guy', ordered a suggestion box to be placed outside the Regulating Office. 'An almost unheard of thing,' wrote Chief E. A. Standen, perhaps not entirely approving, 'but although, at first, the large majority of suggestions submitted asked, "When are we going home?", the box remained, and played a big part in making a happy ship.'

A modest ship's magazine, the *Sheffield Salvo*, was being produced monthly, for internal distribution, covering sport, departmental news and views, poems, jokesy features and cartoons. Typical was a poem by 'Nauta', with apologies to Kipling.

IF you can rise with bugle in the morning,
   Scrub decks and go to breakfast with a smile
Then get fell in on time without a warning
   And carry on with work in naval style.
IF you can keep yourself way out of trouble,
   Your record sheet as pure as driven snow,
Can execute your orders at the double
   And not be caught with 'swede crashed' down below.
IF you can nip ashore right neat and natty
   And come off looking sober as a judge,
Can keep your tongue in cheek and not get ratty
   When the bloke slung in your billet just won't budge;
IF you can do all this and still keep smiling,
   Why then you'll be a sailor true, my son,

Be right up there on top line, smart and snappy –
   But, sonny boy, you'll be the only one.

In July *Sheffield* visited Halifax, Nova Scotia, and subsequently St. John's, Newfoundland, where she entertained a flock of weepie British war brides. The canteen committee had also organized a party for 110 orphan children, but an announcement by the local radio station, briefly stating that *Sheffield* was throwing a children's party, resulted in two thousand juveniles pouring aboard and a hurried revision of catering arrangements.

There now followed a slow cruise northward among the scattered and isolated coastal settlements, for many of which the sea was the only means of communication and ships few – Peter Arm, Arrege Bay and the Salmon River, Port Saunders, Forteau Bay and the River of Ponds. Entire communities filed aboard, many for medical or dental treatment, others to see the first film of their lives in the starboard hangar. Radio had hitherto provided them with their only knowledge of the outside world, and one old gentleman who had journeyed from the interior confessed that *Sheffield* was the first ship he had seen since the 1914–18 war.

Gaspé, New Brunswick, was next on the cruiser's itinerary, and then Quebec – where, in a sports meeting against the Canadian Army, *Sheffield*'s seamen won the 220 yards, the mile and the javelin, and the Marines won the tug-of-war, but lost, by a narrow margin, an all-day shooting match. In Montreal, during 27–28 August, more than 6,000 people swarmed over the ship. Joined by the escort sloop *Snipe, Sheffield* went onto renew old friendships, and finally to New York, where the honeymoon ended.

The ship had been warned of possible anti-British demonstrations on the part of Irish-Americans or Jews, or both – but either seemed nonsensical. Ireland had survived the war by courtesy of Britain despite Republican enthusiasm for German successes and de Valera's condolences to Berlin on the occasion of Hitler's death. With regard to the Jews, Britain was even now, in 1947, about to terminate her mandate held over Palestine since 1920, but was compelled to attempt some degree of control over the flood of Jewish refugees prematurely flooding into what they considered their promised land of Israel; they would not wait. The Jews who, only months earlier, by hundreds of thousands, had been herded uncomplainingly into concentration camps, had submitted meekly to death by gassing, starvation, brutality and horrific surgical experiment, were now suddenly a warrior race. They were, after all, faced by inoffensive lads from Ramsgate and Yeovil, King's Lynn and Dundee, very different from the SS. Jewish terrorist organizations, including the Stern Gang and Irgun Zvi Leumi, embarked on a campaign of assassination, kidnapping and hanging, bombing and arson. In September 1947 the United Nations recommended the partition of

Palestine, resented by both Arab and Jew, at each other's throats, while the British – many of whom were merely time-serving their eighteen months of National Service – wished only to be free of this stinking cess-pit of the Middle East.

Sheffield was moored at New York's Pier 54, and the New York Jews met her with the distribution of thousands of leaflets vilifying the Royal Navy, the British Government, and the British people.

'TO THE JEWISH PEOPLE OF NEW YORK:
After assisting the Nazis to slaughter six million Jews by banning the doors of Europe from the outside, the Pirates of the British Fleet have come to New York. After Sturma and Patrin, after their infamous crimes against Our People of the Exodus, His Majesty's Perfidious Navy has come to New York, to the greatest Jewish community on Earth to celebrate their bloody victories over refugees in our midst.

It is not coincidence that Bevin's Pirates chose this week that the UN begins its Palestine deliberations at Lake Success, to make their first official visit to New York.

We cry to all Jews to join our mass demonstrations. Give the Pirates a welcome they do not expect; show your scorn for these new disciples of Hitler.'

The Jewish-American ill will surprised the men of *Sheffield* and *Snipe*, a large proportion of whom had fought Naziism from 1939 to 1945, but they were more annoyed that, because of this malice, only sixteen children arrived for a party arranged for 18 September aboard *Sheffield* – although more than 500 adults jostled to attend a cocktail-party in the cruiser on the following day. Men ashore experienced minor harassment from Jewish demonstrators, but the New York police generally held the situation under control. The two British warships departed the Hudson at 1530 on the 22nd, not entirely unthankful, but during the Dog watches were overtaken by a signal from the Consul-General in New York; a communication from an anonymous but allegedly Jewish source warned that bombs had been planted in both *Sheffield* and *Snipe*. The ships began searches immediately, with nothing found, and it was evident that the alarm had been intended merely to generate consternation and to impose a great deal of unnecessary work on the British sailors.

The Annapolis Navy Academy in Chesapeake Bay, achieved on 30 September, proved a more cordial host. A Naval guard, colour party and Royal Marine band were landed to be paraded before Fleet Admiral Nimitz, and *Sheffield* was required to represent the Royal Navy against the United States Navy in a tug-of-war for the Friedlander Cup. The Americans (USS *New York*) had won the trophy in 1936, the Royal Navy (HMS *Apollo*) in 1937 and 1938, so another British win would mean permanent possession. Now, in 1947, and despite the years of war rationing, the Royals of Old Shiny pulled to defeat a team of bicep-rippling U.S. Navymen, and the Friedlander Cup was secure.

The U.S. Naval Base of Norfolk, Virginia, was the last on the American programme. *Snipe* had already detached, replaced by *Padstow Bay*, and all were relieved to regain the relative quiet of Bermuda. There was a limit to the number of Rye Highballs, Scotches on Rocks and Straight Bourbons that any gastric function could tolerate, and to Americans at leisure the merest five minutes deprived of something to drink, eat or chew was a penance.

It had been announced that HRH Princess Elizabeth was to marry a vaguely remembered Lieutenant Prince Philip Mountbatten, RN. India had achieved independence and was now to be partitioned. The last battleship built for the Royal Navy, *Vanguard*, had completed the Royal Tour of South Africa and was about to refit in Devonport, while cruiser after cruiser was being struck from the Admiralty's muster list – *Kent, Colombo, Emerald, Despatch, Delhi, Dauntless*. Brave *Achilles* had been sold to India, *Aurora* to China.

All of the remaining 45,000 Hostilities Only ratings in the Royal Navy were to be demobilized by March 1948; in *Sheffield* 40 of the 85 men of the Forecastle Division were HOs, with other ships similarly manned, which meant that after a reassignment of retained personnel, the West Indies Station must be reduced by one cruiser and two frigates. *Porlock Bay* left for the UK on 22 October, *Kenya* on 4 November – having exchanged a number of ratings with *Sheffield* in order to take home those highest on the list for demobilization – and *Padstow Bay* departed on the 18th. The men in the ships remaining – *Sheffield, Snipe, Sparrow, Moorpout* and the RFA *Gold Ranger* – resigned themselves to at least another season of exile.

Much had gone, leaving the Navy the poorer, such as canteen messing, Ally Sloper's Favourite Relish, parcels of comforts from the WVS, Canadian nutty and Sweet Caporal cigarettes, but there was still powdered egg, and a new monstrosity – dehydrated potato. Still, thank God, there remained the sailor's daily tot of rum, and absolutely nothing could ever deprive him of that. Everyone was stung by references in North American newspapers and radio programmes to the impoverishment of the UK. 'I was extremely annoyed', wrote the Midshipman Cremer, 'to learn in Canada that Britain was at her last gasp; she was down and out. We are continually being told how poor Britain is.'

The celebrations on the occasion of the wedding of HRH Princess Elizabeth and Prince Philip, and the pomp and ritual described over radio at breakfast-time on 20 November, did much to show the world that there was life in old Britain yet – 'but still the papers were filled with references to "the worn and patient wives and mothers", says Cremer, 'and "the shabby masses of Britain". They attributed the fainting of several people – inevitable in a crowd of a half-million people who had waited in the streets all night – to the "long years of food rationing".'

Yet, contrarily, those long years of food rationing, uninspiring but balanced, had resulted in a people healthier and fitter than ever before or likely to be again, and during the months to come the impoverished old country would still mount a massive airlift to help provision Berlin, establish a National Health Service, stage the Olympic Games and the Festival of Britain, successfully defeat a Communist campaign in Malaya when larger French and Dutch forces were being flung out of Indo-China and Indonesia, send land, sea and air forces second only to the Americans' to Korea, be the first to climb Mount Everest and the first to run a sub four-minute mile. Midshipman Cremer had little for which to apologize.

The year 1948 opened with a visit to Havana, where the younger officers were dismayed to discover that any rendezvous with a lady had to be closely chaperoned by an ugly aunt, an arrangement that tended to stultify any amorous initiative. The ratings were less dismayed. They did not rendezvous with that kind of lady. In New Orleans, during late January, the temperature fell to ten degrees below freezing, which must have been the only occasion on which the Louisianans saw overcoats worn by libertymen. On 23 February, comfortably moored in Boca Grande Bay, Colombia, *Sheffield* was ordered to proceed with despatch to Belize, British Honduras, reported to be under threat of invasion by neighbouring Guatamala.

There was a comic opera feeling about the whole thing; it wasn't really serious – but, waiting only to embark the Commander-in-Chief and his staff – *Sheffield* slipped, and Fawkes called for 30 knots. On passage, landing parties were detailed, briefed and equipped. Bombardment shells were fuzed, boats made ready and all Bofors guns prepared for landing.

Old Shiny crashed her anchor into the blue waters off

Above: British Honduras is under threat of invasion by neighbouring Guatamala, and *Sheffield* lands her Marines, led by the band, to parade through the streets of Belize, highly appreciated by a following army of small black boys.

Belize at 0944 on Friday, 27 February. Everything seemed tranquil, but Admiral Tennant and his staff were put ashore immediately to confer with the Governor. At 1315 the first of *Sheffield*'s Royal Marines landed, followed by the band and a headquarters unit. The local airfield was placed under guard, with two Bofors guns positioned, and then the Marines paraded through the streets of clapboard buildings and timber yards to boost public confidence, pouring with sweat in blue working rig and steel helmets. The people of Belize, totally unperturbed by Guatamala's posturings, were equally only mildly interested in *Sheffield*'s demonstration, although dozens of small black boys enjoyed marching behind the band. Across the border, Guatamala Radio was still claiming that they 'didn't care if *Sheffield* were at Belize or not', while in Belize the natives shrugged. Who cared about the stinking Guats?

On 1 March the cruiser *Devonshire*, now serving as a cadet training ship, arrived from Jamaica with the 2nd Battalion of the Gloucestershire Regiment, which was disembarked. The warlike noises from Guatamala ceased, but *Sheffield* remained off shore until 16 March, when she departed for Kingston.

The commission was beginning to approach its close when the fifth and final cruise commenced in late June, taking the ship to the principal ports on the western coasts of Canada and the USA. The welcome printed by the *San Francisco Chronicle* was in direct contrast to that expressed by the Jewish community of New York during the previous year.

'HMS *Sheffield*, 10,000 tons of veteran British fighting ship, is showing the flag in San Francisco Bay; that is to say, dispensing goodwill in the tradition of seafaring nations. We welcome the *Sheffield* and her men, because we like the kind of ship she is, and the kind of men they are. We are also grateful that the *Sheffield* can sail in boldly, and not creep in silently and painfully, as did her smaller sister, the *Orion*, one spring day of 1941.

Looking at the trim profile of the *Sheffield* we were reminded of the *Orion* and of the whole tense aura of those days before this country plunged into the most savage war of all time.

The *Orion*'s profile was not trim. We learned her story then, but couldn't tell the half of it. She had been evacuating British soldiers from Greece to North Africa when a lone plane caught her fair in the forward deck with a lone bomb. The bomb tore through several steel decks and exploded in the hold.

Huddled in the hold, crammed into every available cubic inch of space, were the Tommies, who had already taken enough hell during the battle for Greece. Their end was mercifully swift, and the painful role fell to the men of the *Orion* who survived, carrying the remains of the hundreds of dead to the quarterdeck, where the Chaplain muttered the service before they were rolled in canvas and dropped over the side.

All the heroism of war at sea is not fighting. The *Orion*,

hideously crippled, her useless forward guns bent vertical by the bomb's concussion, came half-way around the world at four or five knots, watchful every moment of the day or night lest she be overtaken by some enemy prowler and despatched for the sitting duck she was. She dragged herself into Mare Island Navy Yard and sent small boats out to sea to bury such of her dead as could not be dug out from behind her twisted plates except by yard machinery; and those who were left came ashore and relaxed for a time, and then went back to the war, which would not end for four more years . . .

All of which has only this to do with the visit of the *Sheffield*:

Whatever honor is done to *Sheffield* is not done to one ship or crew alone, but to the whole of the Royal Navy and all its men, living and dead – to the *Sheffield*, which fought her way all through; to the *Orion*, which lived to fight again, and to the mighty *Hood*, and those others, which went to the bottom with guns still blazing, to maintain a tradition and a principle. Without this senior, seagoing service of the British Empire, the face of the world would be vastly different. Without it, indeed, the United States could not have grown to its present stature.'

It was a generous, open-hearted compliment that compensated amply for the malevolence of New York's Pier 54.

During her first post-war commission, *Sheffield* had steamed 60,000 miles and visited fifty ports. More than 175,000 people visited the ship and 12,000 were entertained on board. Tea-parties were given for more than 2,000 children.

The cruiser arrived in Chatham on 5 November 1948, a date that might have been appreciated by Captain 'Guy' Fawkes's crew had they not been too concerned with Customs clearance, leave and travel warrants. It was damply

cold; a grey industrial haze hung over the Medway and the dockyard seemed shabbily neglected after the tall palms and white-washed buildings of Bermuda which dazed the eyes under bright sunshine.

The following week a baby son was born to Princess Elizabeth and the Duke of Edinburgh; he would be named Charles Philip Arthur George. Later in the month *Sheffield* paid off into dockyard hands, where she would remain, refitting, until March 1951.

Her crew dispersed, to courses for promotion, some into barracks and subsequently fresh ships, or to discharge from the service. Much happened during those twenty-eight months. In Britain, the sweet ration ended, was re-introduced, and then raised from 4 to 4½ ounces per week. The bacon ration was increased from 4 to 5 ounces. The West German Government abolished petrol rationing and of all other commodities except sugar; the British, still widely restricted, asked who the hell had won the war.

In Korea the 41st Royal Marine Commandos, the Glosters, Ulster Rifles, 5th Fusiliers, 8th Hussars, Royal Artillery and Royal Engineers were holding a sector of the United Nations battle line; the light fleet carriers *Theseus* and *Glory* operated off the peninsula's west coast, and *Ocean* was soon to depart from Rosyth. The Royal Navy's cruiser strength was being remorselessly slashed; as *Sheffield* lay empty and silent in Chatham the axe fell on *Frobisher*, *Orion*, *Ajax*, *Leander*, *Scylla*, *Arethusa*, *Norfolk* and *London*. Building programmes were cancelled.

Below: June 1946. After almost a year of refitting in the USA and at Portsmouth, England, *Sheffield* rejoins a peacetime Fleet, her warpaint removed. So, also, is her 'X' turret, aft, to allow space for additional light AA armament. Advanced electronics have been fitted, including target acquisition and air warning radar, barrage directors and height-finding systems. She is assessed to be good for another twenty years of peace-tempo service.

21

'Ingenious games and English tarts for all hands'

THE tempo had slowed. Captain Michael Everard assumed command in January 1951, and his ship was recommissioned in March, to be attached to the 2nd Cruiser Squadron of the Home Fleet. In May the cruiser, no longer young, was still able to work up to 28 knots in response to a distress signal from a storm-damaged trawler, and on the last day of that month came alongside Princess Stage, Liverpool, to embark King George and Queen Elizabeth for passage to Belfast. Here, however, cabin arrangements had to be hastily changed in order to accommodate Princess Margaret in place of the King. He had, two years before, undergone surgery to relieve an arterial obstruction; he was now to suffer the removal of a lung, and had only eight months to live. Aboard *Sheffield* the Queen hid her concern, asked Bandmaster Attfield to continue playing as the Royal Party watched the shipping in the Mersey fall astern, and later, in the wardroom, insisted on mixing cocktails for Everard and the commanding officers of *Battleaxe* and *Broadsword*, the attendant destroyers. She climbed to the bridge during the Middle Watch and, in the moonlight, took a cup of cocoa.

Consensus of opinion had it that *Sheffield*, refitted, would be despatched to the Far East. There was growing disillusion in Europe with regard to the Korean War and the Allies' support of Syngman Rhee's brutal and corrupt regime. The Americans had resorted to saturation bombing and napalm, a superb weapon against naked peasant flesh. President Truman had relieved seventy-year-old General Douglas MacArthur of his command of UN forces following his (MacArthur's) outspoken criticizms of American war policy. Meanwhile King Leopold of Belgium had abdicated and King Abdullah of Jordan had been assassinated.

At 1330 on 1 October 1951 *Sheffield* departed Portsmouth's North Corner Jetty bound for Bermuda, reappointed flagship of the America and West Indies Station.

The Royal Navy was now a two-tier service; there were those who wore four or five medal ribbons and those who wore none. RNVR officers and HO ratings had gone back to their office desks and shop-counters. There remained only long-service personnel, and there was a tacit freemasonry shared by those officers and men who had served the war years; it was a bond that could not be penetrated by the junior officers too young to have sniffed cordite smoke. It had become impossible for a smooth-cheeked though determined midshipman to tell his party of two-badged and beribboned ratings that, if this exercise were really a war situation, then, well, they'd better watch out. Their bland, musing eyes silenced him, and, later, his Divisional Officer chuckled, patted his head.

In Bermuda *Sheffield* hoisted the flag of Vice-Admiral Sir William Andrews, KBE, CB, DSO, Commander-in-Chief, and with *Snipe* and *Sparrow* joined up with the US Atlantic Fleet, to exercise until mid-November. In Baltimore, in addition to staging a children's party, the ship received 9,000 visitors and entertained 600 guests. Subsequently, returning to Bermuda in bad weather, a heavy sea crashed over the quarterdeck, and a search was begun for a seaman thought to have been carried over the side. Within minutes, however, the absentee was found sitting in a pool of water at the bottom of a hatch, shaken but unhurt.

Left: February 1951, in home waters again. HRH the Duchess of Kent is introduced to *Sheffield*'s 'Y' turret by Captain M. Everard.

Below: August, 1952. In San Diego, *Sheffield*'s Commodore John Inglis presents a 'genuine cutlass and spyglass' to a Cub Scout who had earlier written a request to the Admiralty, London, for the souvenirs. On the west coast, at this time, the British were highly regarded as America's staunchest friend . . .

Christmas was spent in Hamilton, where there were more visitors and another children's party. The ship's company were becoming adept at wiping juvenile noses, taking small boys to the 'John' and helping small girls to 'throw up'.

With the New Year – 1952 – began the Caribbean Spring Cruise, taking in Antigua, St. Lucia, Barbados, Granada, Port of Spain, Guairia, and finally Curaçao, Dutch West Indies, on 5 February. Here, at 0800 on the following day, news was received of the death of King George at Sandringham. An unassuming man, unexpectedly called to the throne in December 1936, his conscientious adherence to the strictest principles of constitutional monarchy, his quiet courage and constant devotion to his duty to his country under increasing physical handicaps had earned him an unusually affectionate place in the hearts of the people. He had been a good king, perhaps even a great one.

Sheffield's log recorded, in the briefest words, the duties carried out by a warship in a foreign port.

February 1952.

Wed. 6. 0800: Colours half-masted. Death of His Majesty King George VI.

a.m.: Moved to Prince Hendricks Wharf.

Th. 7. 0748: Divisions.

0800: Memorial service on quarterdeck.

Fri. 8. 1100: Proclamation of Her Majesty Queen Elizabeth II. Colours re-hoisted.

The log, unfortunately, did not tell that, as *Sheffield*'s ensign was lowered, so was that of every other vessel in harbour, nor of the hundreds of people, including children with simple posies of flowers, of many nationalities and of

every walk of life, who came shyly aboard to tell the British sailors that they, too, grieved for the quiet King who had never left Buckingham Palace but had shared with London's citizens every terrifying moment of the Blitzkrieg.

Two weeks later the cruiser anchored off Pigeon Island, which, Captain Everard said, 'appeared to be inhabited only by land crabs and a honeymoon couple, all of whom resented our intrusion', – and not least, one supposes, the flag-deck's telescopes. Within a further few days *Sheffield* received from Messrs. Forth's, England, the new letters for the rum tub, so that it now proclaimed 'The Queen, God Bless Her'. In London, the name *Formidable* was struck off the Navy's list of aircraft carriers; she was to die in Faslane. Peace talks in Korea had re-opened, but a settlement seemed as remote as ever. Fighting continued. Incredibly, in Pittsburgh, the slouching Jersey Joe Walcott had knocked out the world heavyweight champion, Ezzard Charles.

In early May Old Shiny turned northward for Canada, the St. Lawrence and Montreal. Here, about to berth on the up-stream side of a projecting quay with a current running at 7 knots, but with two tugs assisting, Everard was startled when the leading tug, fearful of girdling, suddenly cut her towline. Worse, the skipper of the second tug panicked and

followed suit, abandoning the cruiser at right angles to the current. 'I was very afraid', Everard confessed, 'that I was going to find myself responsible for a good deal of damage to Old Shiny. However, by going full ahead I got the ship into the back-wash of the current, and then full astern, and she just stopped perfectly alongside the quay. A very kindly, helpful lady was Shiny, on this and probably many other awkward occasions.'

In June Everard was appointed Captain of the Fleet on the staff of Admiral of the Fleet, the Earl Mountbatten of Burma, now Commander-in-Chief, Mediterranean. On 17 June Everard handed over *Sheffield* to Commodore John Inglis, KBE, CB, and was pulled ashore by his officers. Lower deck was cleared and Bungy Williams cheered, lifting his cap. Tot-time was only twenty minutes away and Dinger Bell owed him gulpers after last night's uckers.

Sheffield continued to steam her leisurely way through 1952, exercising with ships of both the US and Canadian Navies, then passing through the Panama Canal to San Francisco and subsequently Vancouver, enduring a continuous round of parties and receptions, parades, Aqua Follies, picnics, Guard and Band Retreats. In San Diego Commodore Inglis presented a 'genuine cutlass and spyglass' to a Cub Scout, Michael Hatcher, aged 10, who had

Right: In that same month, in Seattle, the cruiser throws a party for more than 1,000 local children, who swarm over the ship. The US Navy's Public Information Office issued an approving press release: '*Sheffield*'s Jack Tars rigged a carousel, a chute-slide, and many ingenious games for the children to play . . . and climaxed the party with English tarts, pop and ice cream for all hands.'

Left: At every port of call, in both North and South America, there is a request: for the Royal Navy's sunset ceremony; for a parade of the Royal Marines and a detachment of British seamen. In Vancouver on 20 August 1952; for the celebration of the Pacific National Exhibition . . .

Left: . . . in Lima, Peru, on 24 October 1952, for the national wreath-laying ceremony . . .

Left: . . . in Valparaiso, Chile, on 4 November 1952, to be reviewed by President Ibanez.

Right: And there's still spit and polish when returned to the UK. In February 1953 a detachment of *Sheffield*'s seamen re-visit the City of Sheffield, but none of these men had marched to Sheffield Wednesday's ground in 1937.

earlier written to the Admiralty in London, requesting the souvenirs. *Sheffield*'s party for 1,000 underprivileged children in Seattle was the subject of an approving Press release from the USN Public Information Office: '. . . *Sheffield*'s jack tars rigged a carousel, a chute-slide and many other ingenious games for the children to play . . . and climaxed the party with *English tarts*, pop and ice-cream for all hands'.

Americans, accustomed to their own 'dry' warships, were intrigued at being served alcohol aboard *Sheffield*. 'We had thought', wrote the *Los Angeles Times* representative, visiting the cruiser, 'to be offered grog or pink gin, but were introduced to a Royal Navy Martini, which apparently had no name, though 'Blimey' might be a good one.

This consists – and we got the ingredients carefully – of two bottles of gin, two bottles of French Vermouth and one bottle of Spanish Sherry mixed in a bucket (wooden) with about equal quantities of ice. When the Royal Navy mixes cocktails, the smallest measure is apparently the bottle, but we were assured that the same proportions will, in smaller amounts, produce an identical result – which in our case was an overwhelming interest, through glazed eyes, in Queen Elizabeth's warships.'

'After Acapulco, Mexico City, Callao and Valparaiso', says Inglis, 'the whirl of hospitality had reduced many to a state of semi-exhaustion' – and not least the fifty altruists who had donated blood to the Red Cross Blood Bank in San Francisco. In early November the ship steamed thankfully for Bermuda, where she secured on Thursday 20th, landed a Royal Guard and Colour Party and transferred the Queen's Colour and the flag of the Commander-in-Chief to the cruiser *Superb*. On Monday 24 *Sheffield* left for the UK, and after an uneventful voyage anchored in Spithead in time for Christmas leave. The commission had been an outstanding success, the crew had behaved everywhere with credit to their ship, their service and their country. It had often been said that a Royal Navy man-of-war was Britain's finest ambassador, and *Sheffield* had proved no exception.

But Old Shiny needed a rest before contemplating an uncertain future. During a chilling mid-December she moved from Spithead to North Corner Jetty, and finally into No. 3 Basin. The war was a fading, grey dream, but there were events of importance. *Mauritius* had lifted civilian employees of the Anglo-Iranian Oil Company out of Abadan, Europeans were being murdered by the Mau Mau in Kenya, and there was a Communist-inspired terrorist campaign in Malaya. The war in Korea, into which the United States had so precipitately drawn the United Nations, was continuing expensively, and during a single day off the west coast the British light fleet carrier *Ocean* had flown-off an incredible 123 bombing sorties against enemy shore installations. She would subsequently be awarded the Boyd Trophy in recognition of her pilots' outstanding flying performance.

22

'A pink-faced, beardless youth asking about Houston night-life'

IN DOCKYARDS, rivers and estuaries moored warships stagnated, transferred to the Reserve or awaited tugs to tow them to Faslane, Troon or Dalmuir. The last of the battleships, the virgin *Vanguard*, had been relegated to a training role at Portland. Manning problems continued. Almost weekly there was a fresh exodus of those experienced Chiefs, Petty Officers and two-badge leading rates who had completed their long-term engagements; Divisional officers in homecoming ships interviewed men approaching time-expiry, urging them to re-engage, but with little success. Increasing technical specialization, it was being said ruefully, meant that soon there would be few left in a ship who knew how to lower a boat manually, splice a wire rope or heave a lead when the depth-sounder failed. Bungy Williams shrugged. Having served his time, he was now to become a partner and shareholder of the Welfare State, paid if he worked and paid if he didn't, with free doctors, free glasses, false teeth, wigs and appliances various including contraceptives and aphrodisiacs. His Labour candidate had promised, and Bungy was going to apply for the bleedin' lot.

Sheffield had lost her CinC's flag and John Inglis his temporary rank of Commodore. He resumed command as Captain Inglis, taking the cruiser through her postdockyard trials at the end of March 1953. It was confidently anticipated that the ship would be assigned to the Korean war zone, probably working-up on passage, but first there must be the Coronation Fleet Review. The Royal Navy's contribution in 1953 would be pitifully thin by comparison with those of 1935 and 1937, when the Home Fleet alone could anchor seven operational battleships and three battle-cruisers in Spithead, but there were representatives of sixteen foreign navies and of the Commonwealth. For weeks agencies had been advertising steamer trips for the day, 15 June, at prices ranging from £7 to 12 guineas, which covered the rail fare from Waterloo and a buffet lunch. For the girls of Portsmouth, Gosport and Southsea it was to be the week of a lifetime; with Brazilians, Turks, Greeks, Thais, Italians and Frenchmen roaming the streets it was impossible to miss unless one was hare-lipped, had a club foot or was obese and over fifty. And train-loads of speculative, more professional ladies arrived from London, Bristol, Birmingham and all intermediate points, immediately obliging. No fool was more quickly parted from his money than a shore-going sailor, but the old law of supply and demand gratifyingly reduced the price of all night in the arms of a sweaty angel, even though the cost of Bed & Breakfast in Southsea soared from 30s. to 50s. in advance and leave the bathroom as you found it other people have to use it after you.

On Thursday 17 September Captain Inglis was relieved by Captain K. McN. Campbell-Walker. Anyone with a name like that, said Bungy Williams, must remember going down with Alice to Buckingham Palace, but, anyway, the appointment of a new commanding officer hardly suggested that the ship's retirement was imminent. It must surely be Korea this time. *Sheffield* had never travelled further east than Malta, and there had been some intriguing yarns circulating RNB about the liberty-going delights of Japan – like mixed-sex baths for starters, and being gently soaped all over by geisha girls. Incoming stores were watched for clues that pointed towards the Far East, but they were only the usual cotton waste, lube oil, electrical cable, split peas, haddock, slab cake and potatoes, and nobody claimed to have overheard the Paymaster-Commander telling the Chaplain the currency exchange rates for Japanese Yen, BAFS vouchers and US Scrip dollars. All conjecture was abruptly terminated on 6 October when, at Greenock, the ship embarked the Governor of Bermuda and his aide-de-camp, to sail on the following day for Bermuda.

This was to be *Sheffield*'s last commission in the West Indies, and to follow her cruises in detail, following closely the pattern of earlier years, would be tedious. From October 1953 until October 1954 the cruiser showed her flag along the entire length of the North-American seaboard from Mexico to Newfoundland. *Sheffield*'s Dental Officer, Surgeon Lieutenant-Commander J. d'O. Ruttledge, was flattered by the repeated requests from medical officers of the USN and RCN to visit him, until he discovered that they were principally interested in his surgery's Oralix X-ray equipment, superior to their own, and which was to be frequently requested for the examination of jaw fractures, broken fingers and noses. In Houston, Texas, *Sheffield* saluted the old battleship *Texas*, built before the First World War and now a maritime museum. The Royal Marine Band played *Deep in the Heart of Texas* as the cruiser departed, and Mary Frazer of *The Houston Press* wrote of the many things aboard Old Shiny that had impressed her . . .

'. . . a tiny chapel deep in the heart of a great ship, where a chaplain robed in the Queen's scarlet prays for far-away families, beneath a clock set at English time . . . men with such unmistakeably British faces, queued up by a barrel labelled "The Queen, God Bless Her" . . . a framed photo of the Duchess of Kent, marred by jagged shrapnel holes that date back to a bloody battle with the *Bismarck* in 1941 . . . a pink-faced, beardless youth asking about Houston nightlife, then adding, in Yorkshire accents, that he's only eligible for "Boys' Leave", since he's not yet seventeen and a half . . .

There was a clear, midnight blue sky, a shimmering quarter moon, and under this typical Texas canopy was a completely British show that had cocktail-partying Houston stock-still with awe and admiration. The show had a brass band and a Marine drill team that combined the precision of the Rockettes with the tradition of five centuries. And put such showmanship touches as a leopard skin vest and perpetual motion batons into a thrillingly serious military spectacle . . . it was the climax of a glittering display by the crack Royal Marines of *Sheffield* on 75th Street Docks. The damp eyes of Houstonians, many of them transplanted Britishers, following the playing of *God Save the Queen* and *The Star Spangled Banner*, were not caused by the brisk breezes . . .'

At Newport, Rhode Island, reported the *Globe & Laurel*, "Four thousand citizens watched our Tattoo. Our American Marine cousins must be mentioned; never before have we been as cordially treated. At every port from Houston, Texas, to Portland, Maine, there has been a US Marine officer on the jetty to meet us on arrival.'

Hospitality was similarly generous in Canada. Alongside in Montreal, the ship was visited by Chief Poking Fire and his family from a nearby Iroquois reservation, and Campbell-Walter (now Commodore) submitted to being dressed in feathers and blanket, given a tomahawk and smoking a pipe of peace. Both the Commodore and *Sheffield* were given Indian names, not recorded because nobody could spell them, and nobody wished to ask.

Returning southward via New York, there was no repetition of the anti-British demonstrations of 1947. The cruiser docked at the Cunard berth, Pier 90, from 15 to 22 September, to be overwhelmed with offers of tickets for Broadway productions, concerts, radio and television shows. HRH the Duchess of Kent and Princess Alexandra, visiting the city during this period, came aboard to inspect Divisions. Bermuda was regained on 1 October, and, transferring the Queen's Colour to *Superb* three weeks later, Old Shiny fired a 15-gun salute before sailing for Portsmouth. She anchored in Spithead on 26 October 1954 and on the same day moved into the dockyard, subsequently into No. 14 Dock for refitting.

When *Sheffield* emerged from the dock on the last day of January 1955 she had been in service for eighteen years, of which six were intensive war years. In 1954 *Devonshire*, retained as a sea-going weapons-testing vessel, had been scrapped, and now *Australia*, *Shropshire*, *Sussex* and *Argonaut* had been sentenced. *Phoebe* and *Sirius* would follow in 1956; several of these were younger than *Sheffield*. All work had been stopped on the half-built *Swiftsure* in Chatham, while strong rumour had it that the 'Colony'-class cruisers were next in line for the axe. They were all junior to Old Shiny, so what hope was there for her survival to the end of this decade?

In early 1955 *Sheffield* was a reconditioned but elderly cruiser with a new ship's company and a new commanding officer, Captain T. E. Podger, a new Commander and a strange First Lieutenant. A few Chiefs and Petty Officers and only those rare others who wore three badges on their left arms had any experience of sea warfare. Aggie Weston's, the Mission to Seamen and the Sally Ann had disappeared from Devonport, Portsmouth and Chatham. There was still a thin handful of men in the ship who could recall a pre-war docking in *Sheffield*'s home depot, *Pembroke*. They could still reminisce, if any of the teenage ODs cared to listen to an old lamp-swinger, of the welter of compressed airlines and temporary power leads that trailed through every messdeck and flat, filth everywhere and idling dockyard maties, the bulk purchase of rail tickets on Thursday for the following long weekend and the dash for the station by bus or cab. And there had been the old Empire where, during mid-week, sailors could whistle at high-kicking chorus girls or, if bored by a baritone rendering of 'Mandalay', could retire to the bar, still within earshot of the stage, roll a cigarette and drink Style & Winch ale. Nowadays they seemed to prefer duty-free 'tailor-mades', and nobody made up a prique from leaf tobacco. There were even a few who used after-shave, and went ashore for a 'styled' haircut. Ratings were marrying younger – they no longer had to wait until the age of 25 before qualifying for a marriage allowance – and many preferred a few hours of domesticity to pub-crawling and local womanizing. The Regulating Branch had been reinforced by the introduction of the Leading Patrolman, the only channel of promotion beyond the level of AB, said the knowing, for the illiterate and moronic. Ratings' uniforms could now incorporate officially approved zip fasteners, and plastic instead of canvas white caps; in barracks there was even a menu that allowed men a choice of fare. The Andrew just wasn't the soddin' Andrew any more, the old men said, but at least there was still a tot of rum every midday. If that was ever withdrawn, Nelson would turn in his grave.

Sheffield reached Gibraltar on 28 February 1955 and secured on 47/48 Berth. During a two-day stay both watches got ashore, but it was unseasonably cold, with rain in the air, and the palm trees sagged sadly. Gibraltar was an anti-climax; most of the shore-going facilities enjoyed by thousands of wartime sailors had long disappeared – there were no longer crowds of shore-going sailors with jingling pockets. The street names were still the same, but the Casablanca Bar on the Piazza – where so many blue-jackets had drunk to excess, sung, blasphemed, vomited over another's feet, reeled into the warm darkness – all this was now the Gibraltar Tourist Office behind dark-tinted glass, and the sporting ladies in Rosia Road and Flat Bastion Road has returned to Tangier, now middle-aged but very wealthy and you like something you've never had before, *Sheffield*, eh? All your Marines came here, every day. Upstairs, very cheap, very clean. But they had all gone.

By 10 March *Sheffield* was at sea to take part in Exercise Sea Lance, which was to accommodate the combined Home and Mediterranean Fleets. The deepening paucity of the Navy's resources was illustrated by the fact that a similar combined fleet exercise during the late thirties could call upon nine battleships and two carriers, a squadron of heavy cruisers and two of light (1CS, 2CS and 3CS), six flotillas of destroyers, twenty-eight submarines and four depot ships in addition to oilers and other auxiliaries. By 1955 Sea Lance, opening with a convoy escort and attack exercise, deployed two carriers, four light cruisers, seventeen assorted destroyers, three frigates, a minelayer and a tug. The convoy was led by the Royal Yacht *Britannia*, flying the flag of the Duke of Edinburgh, and consisted of one depot ship (*Tyne*), an RFA and five fleet oilers. This was Navy on the cheap.

Old Shiny, a component of the 'attacking enemy force', accompanied by *Jamica* and *Glasgow*, performed commendably despite having not yet worked up. On completion, the combined Fleets departed Gibraltar for Malta for the traditional and punishing few weeks of football, rowing, boxing, athletics, hockey, five-a-side rugby, boozing, brawling, brothelizing and morning-after hang-overs, Commander's Defaulters' musters on the quarterdeck and ten days stoppage of pay, but, by common consent, a bleedin' marvellous run. *Sheffield* remained in Grand Harbour to begin five weeks of gunnery drills and shoots, general drill, towing and refuelling at sea. She was still there in late April, berthed alongside Boat House Wharf in French creek, when orders were received from the Commander-in-Chief, Admiral Sir Guy Grantham, to slip and proceed with all speed for assist MFV72, hove-to with a disabled engine two miles off Lampedusa, which was 120 miles distant.

It was unfortunate that, in this rare moment of peacetime excitement, Captain Podger was ashore in Valletta, attending an investiture at which he was to be received into the Legion of Merit. *Sheffield* threw off her lines and made for the open sea without him, working up to 29 knots, course 245, with the glass falling and the sea getting untidy. It was positively nasty when, four hours later, the little, 50-ton MFV was sighted, rolling and plunging in a welter of spindrift, and *Sheffield*'s junior element were no longer jolly tars, but were praying for the ship to be stopped so that they could get off. The older badgemen sniffed and took double portions of macaroni cheese with sauté potatoes, talked loudly of catching a seagull with a piece of fat pork on a long string, or how the forward latrines were vomiting up their foul contents because of the sea's pressure from outside. It could go on for weeks and weeks. A man could get gangrenous piles, they said. They took another portion of macaroni cheese. Do you know what gangrenous piles look like . . .?

The sea was too heavy for the distressed vessel to be taken in tow, but *Sheffield* stood by her all night, and by dawn the MFV's motor mechanic had managed to coax his Kelvin diesel into producing an unsteady three knots, enabling the craft and six very sick crewmen to be escorted to Lampedusa. This done, *Sheffield* turned away for Malta, and was steaming through the Comino Channel at 25 knots when met by a helicopter carrying Captain Podger.

It was the only incident of the commission that, in earlier days, might have been considered worthy of mention in the log. Repainted Admiralty B55 light grey, the cruiser proceeded to Cannes in time for the 1955 Film Festival; there was not a starlet to be had for a sailor in a blue jean collar, nor were the ship's boats adequate for all those men with a few hundred francs who desired to at least walk ashore in the South of France. The Royal Marines' gunnery instructor said that he had seen Doris Day from a distance.

In Istanbul the brothels reeked asphyxiatingly of cheap perfume, the women demanded twenty Turkish pounds, settled for three, and breathed peppermint and onions. The British warships were to be the first to visit Alexandria for five years. In 1951 Egypt had denounced the treaty of 1936 which provided for British defence of the Suez Canal and there had followed a period of tension that, in early 1952, erupted into civil riots and a police mutiny. Mobs burned down several European clubs, Barclays Bank and Shepheards Hotel; a number of British lives were lost. The Royal Navy's Task Group 56.2 steamed off shore and troops stood by in Cyprus and Tobruk, but the riots were quelled by the Egyptian Army. In July 1952 a very fat King Farouk was ousted by General Mahomed Neguib.

Despite misgivings, however, the visit in early June 1955, by *Sheffield* and *Jamaica*, the destroyers *Duchess* and *Diana*, the CinC's despatch vessel *Surprise* and the RFA *Fort Duquesne*, was received without any unpleasantness. In Larnaca, Cyprus, the beer tasted like boiled liquorice, and its effect on the bowels suggested it probably was, but a locally distilled spirit, allegedly brandy, variously coloured and flavoured, was not only viciously potent and highly volatile, but, apparently, the best thing ever for cleaning tarnished brightwork – better, even, than Ally Sloper's Favourite Relish.

For the return to Malta the squadron was joined by HMIS *Delhi* (ex-HMNZS *Achilles*) and the Indian destroyers *Ganga*, *Gomati*, *Rana* and *Ranjit* (ex-*Chiddingford*, *Lamerton*, *Raider* and *Redoubt*) and on passage both *Sheffield* and *Delhi* were manoeuvred for the benefit of film crews making the film *Battle of the River Plate*. The film screened in *Sheffield*'s starboard hangar was *The Dambusters*, which most men managed to see twice. Captain Podger recalls that, 'during the passage we were mystified one evening by a mysterious flying object which passed across our front a few miles ahead, and which nobody could identify. While all glasses were trained upon it, our next astern, *Jamaica*, signalled: 'Don't look now but I think we are being shadowed by a flying saucer.' Later experience would suggest that the culprit was probably a big meteorological balloon that had lost most of its gas, but UFOs were then becoming fashionable things to see, and the next mail to the UK would carry many reports of a UFO sighting in position 36°06'N, 23°36'E. *Sheffield*'s log remains uncommittal.

Left: Following Exercise 'Sea Lance' in the western Mediterranean during March 1955, *Sheffield* anchors in Malta's Grand Harbour (left foreground). Beyond her are *Glasgow*, the depot ship *Tyne*, and the royal yacht *Britannia*. The destroyer *Decoy* lies in the right foreground.

Right: A young, but already curvacious, Diana Dors comes aboard in Venice – one of several British celebrities attending the Film Festival – and all hands clear lower deck.

July of 1955 was given largely to refurbishing the ship and to drinking Blue Label beer in Valletta, Floriana and Sliema, which was exchanged for vino plonk under the coloured pavement umbrellas of cafés in Livorno in early August. There had been a prolonged newspaper strike in the UK, but the BBC bulletins relayed by Malta Radio, and the *Times of Malta*, had told of Winston Churchill's retirement, Chelsea becoming Champions of the Football League, and heavyweight Don Cockell's decisive defeat by Rocky Marciano in San Francisco. The world's first atomic-powered submarine, USS *Nautilus*, was in service.

Many men took advantage of organized coach trips to Florence and Pisa, and a concerted effort was made by ninety ratings to push the leaning tower even further, but failed. There was another film festival in Venice during September, and *Sheffield* moored off St. Mark's Square to lend moral support to the British stars attending, who included Diana Dors, Jeanette Scott, Belinda Lee, Eunice Grayson, Jack Hawkins and James Robertson Justice. The ship's company's favourite was Diana Dors, for all the obvious reasons, and she responded by coming aboard 'in trousers fitting more tightly than is usual in the Navy . . . and looking every cubic inch Miss Soda Fountain 1955 . . .'

Old Shiny's age was beginning to show. The Engineer Commander reported that fatigue cracks had been discovered in the superheater headers, and that meant dockyard attention without delay, presumably in Malta, possibly the UK. It was a bolt from the blue, and the Admiralty's response was both cheering and ominous. *Sheffield*'s commission was to be curtailed and she would return to the UK immediately.

The possibility of yet another commission seemed remote; it was more probable that repairs would be considered a waste of time and money, that *Sheffield* would follow *Phoebe*, *Sirius* and *Royalist*, withdrawn from service, and *Nigeria* and *Diadem*, paid off for the last time.

The cruiser reached Malta on Sunday 11 September 1955, but only to disembark the CinC and his staff, who had taken passage from Venice. A two-day call at Gibraltar allowed each watch ashore to purchase gifts and souvenirs – the sailors' 'rabbits' – and on the 27th the ship anchored at Spithead.

Of the ten 'Town'-class cruisers built, four had been sunk by enemy action, but ten years after the war the survivors were still afloat and fit for service. The high standard of their pre-war construction meant that, although longer in the tooth than the wartime-built 'Dido' and 'Colony' classes, they were better investments for refit expenditure. Old Shiny's corsets were stronger-boned, and her men would have been delighted to hear of it.

Even so, money was short, and every year grew shorter. Despite all the nostalgia and old sailors' oaths, there was a good case for cutting away all old wood and building twenty-five new cruisers that embodied all the lessons of

the war and were installed with the newly developed rapid-firing 6-inch gun, the new twin 3-inch AA gun intended to replace Oerlikons and Bofors – both inadequate against Kamikaze attacks and guided missiles – and a new AA gun mounting which threatened to totally baffle the last of the parrot-teaching and bawling Gunners' Mates of Whale Island. The battleship, of course, was dead – or would be, literally, within forty-eight hours of another war starting. The Navy's light fleet carriers (infuriatingly to the diehards built to only merchant ship standards) had performed brilliantly whenever deployed and all could operate jet aircraft: the Hawker Sea Hawk, the de Havilland Sea Venom, Fairey Gannet, Westland Wyvern. All these aircraft were inferior to their counterparts flown by the USN, but it was a matter of money, a commodity of which the Americans seemed to possess more than the rest of the world combined. Meanwhile the British perfected the angled flight deck, the mirror landing aid and the steam catapult, all of which were gratefully snapped up by the USN.

During the whole of October and November 1955 *Sheffield* was nudged from berth to berth within the Portsmouth docks area, from Pitch House Jetty to Whale Island, then to South Railway Jetty and, on the same day, to 10 Berth in No. 3 Basin. Nobody seemed to want, or know what to do with, an elderly Chatham cruiser gathering grime. In early November she was moved to 'C' Lock, then returned to 10 Berth. Finally, on 4 January 1956 the ship was tied alongside the depot ship *Montclare* – but only for twenty-four hours. On the 5th, at 1000, four tugs took her in hand and eased her into the five-fathom channel and then slowly to meet the first sea-borne Spithead swell. There was a low-lying, dank mist that hid Ryde Pier and the Nab ahead and the entrance to Langstone to port, but the smell of salt sea after two months of rancid dockyard was sweet in the nostrils. It wasn't that there was much wrong with Portsmouth, exactly, despite the port's post-war shabbiness, empty berths and shrinking facilities. Officers had brought their wives to the Keppel Head and Solent Hotels, and there was a good rail service to London. Ratings were well accommodated in the Union Jack Club, close to Waterloo Station, and junior officers excellently received by the Goat Club in New Bond Street, although, perhaps understandably, most preferred to forage for themselves among the seductions of Soho, Southwark and South Wimbledon – which was only twelve minutes away on the District Line. Back in Portsmouth the younger men had eyed the stone lions outside the Guildhall, had never seen them rise and roar, but would, in due course, pass on the story. Most of them had never entered their home dockyard, Chatham – which, a handful of older hands had already offered, was nothing to warble about.

During the late forenoon of Wednesday 11 December, 1956 *Sheffield* arrived at the Outer Lock of Chatham Dockyard and that afternoon moved into No. 2 Basin to begin a Care & Maintenance refit that would continue until May 1957.

23

'Pyjamas are required on loan for Wrens sleeping on board'

SHEFFIELD had been docked for six months, with most of her AA armament removed, her foremast lowered and the bridge structure gutted in readiness for a reconstruction costing £1.5 million, when, in July, Gamal Abdel Nasser, the Egyptian president, announced the nationalization of the Suez Canal. Five months later the Israelis launched an attack on Egypt, and British and French forces had moved against key points in the Canal zone, taken Port Said, Port Fuad and Ismailia. Marshal Bulganin, the Soviet Prime Minister, had proposed that the US Sixth Fleet should join with Russian air and naval forces to stop the Middle East 'aggression'. Only a month earlier a revolt in Budapest against the Communist regime had been crushed by Russian tanks and machine-guns. For Britain the Suez venture proved an ill-advised and embarrassing fiasco; troops began withdrawing in the troopship *Dilwara* on 6 December, and a few weeks later Prime Minister Sir Anthony Eden would resign, ostensibly on the advice of his doctors.

There had never been the remotest possibility of *Sheffield* joining the Suez fracas. Of greater relevance to her C&M crew was Floyd Patterson's defeat of Archie Moore for the vacant world heavyweight title and the 16th Olympic Games that opened in Melbourne on 26 November.

Sheffield lay in Chatham's No. 2 Basin. On the first day of July 1957 the International Geophysical Year opened, and by that time the old cruiser had hoisted an ensign, which meant that somebody remembered she was there. At 0900 on Tuesday 7 May 1957 Captain L. P. (Paddy) Bourke, OBE, DSC, RD, RNZN, had assumed command. He was of Irish stock, born in Adelaide, Australia, but had entered New Zealand's Navy. Now he was to command a British ship.

Old Shiny's new foremast had been installed and subsequently festooned with a complexity of aerials, lights and bird-nest racks. All bathrooms except the officers' forward had been lined with a new, labour-saving material, Formica, and claims were being made to lockers as new drafts from *Pembroke* climbed aboard. On 1 July 1957 the ship's lower deck was cleared and the commissioning warrant from CinC Nore, Admiral Sir Frederick Parham, was read by Bourke to his assembled ship's company and a gathering of families and friends. The new chaplain, the Reverend E. Levinge, conducted the commissioning ser-

vice, and at 1500 *Sheffield* was once again a serving and fully manned warship of Her Majesty's Navy.

The ship was at Portland three weeks later to celebrate her own 21st birthday – 23 July – and to signal HRH the Duchess of Kent, Princess Marina:

'The Captain, officers and ship's company of HMS *Sheffield* with humble duty send their best wishes on the occasion of the ship's coming of age, twenty-one years after she was launched by Your Royal Highness.'

Princess Marina returned her thanks and congratulations. Messages of goodwill were also received from the builders, Vickers-Armstrong, the Lord Mayor and Master Cutler of the City of Sheffield, and, ever loyal, the Sheffield Sea Cadets. A month later, just twenty years after the first and only other occasion, *Sheffield* berthed in Immingham Dock to exchange courtesies with the City of Sheffield. It could be good for recruiting. This time, however, there would be no march behind a police band with the Petty Officers ensuring that nobody slipped away from the ranks en route. Cars were provided for Captain Bourke and several officers, a coach for fifty ratings, first for midday cocktails at the Town Hall and then a massive luncheon as guests of the Lord Mayor, Alderman A. Ballard. Afterwards, ratings were released for the afternoon; some sought an armchair, others strolled the city centre, but most accepted an invitation from the Yorkshire County Cricket Club to watch a few hours of the Yorkshire-Lancashire game, with access to unlimited beer, pork pies and sandwiches, and then the presentation, by Sheffield United, of football shirts for the ship's team. By now most of the men were glassy-eyed, but the City, determined to give the sailors a 'reet good time', was far from finished; the day was still young. The next trial was high tea at Barker's Pool – and only in Yorkshire is 'high tea' really understood to mean ham and cold chicken, haslet, cold roasted beef, green salad, mixed salad, pigs' trotters, salmon, roll-mop herrings, jellied eels, sausages, mountains of potatoes – new, creamed, coleslawed; trifles, sundaes, pickles, jellies, gateaux, crumpets, cheeses various . . .

The *Sheffield Telegraph*'s Gala at Farm Ground sorted out the men from the boys, and even the surviving men were too debilitated to take advantage of the dance at the City Hall, where the girls had not been specially selected by Employment Exchange officials and did not, as in Bungy

William's day, have their soddin' knees welded together. They knew all about the contraceptive pill, and even fifteen-year-old Sheffield lasses were readily available for experiment in those bushes at the other end of Eccleshall Road behind Pickford's. The girls' problem was that all the younger sailors who resembled Elvis Presley, earlier full of risqué nautical jokes and with caps flat-aback, were puking all the way to the coach rendezvous outside Victoria Station, while the older, steadier ones showed no enthusiasm for a tumble among nettles and damp shrubbery with a squealing teenager. Not after Acapulco and Valparaiso.

Back in Immingham some five thousand people had swarmed over the ship, followed by a further three thousand on the following day, including Sea Cadet contingents from Doncaster, Scunthorpe, Grimsby – and especially Sheffield, who presumed a special relationship. That evening, 6 August 1957, two hundred local VIPs were entertained by the Captain and, as their predecessors had, twenty years before, the Lord Mayor of Sheffield, Master Cutler, alderman and councillors stumbled over ring-bolts and gingerly negotiated steel ladders before qualifying for quarterdeck cocktails under bunting and coloured lights. Again, as before, four of the ship's company who were natives of Sheffield were presented, somewhat disinterestedly, although one of them, writer Harry Diver, was sufficiently diplomatic to tell the *Sheffield Telegraph*'s reporter: 'It has been my life's ambition to serve in her.' Perhaps the Master-at-Arms was within earshot.

Sheffield entered the Clyde to assemble for the NATO Exercise 'Strikeback' on Friday 13th, which may account for the fact that, subsequently, she was considered to have been 'sunk' by a submarine while attempting to force a passage through the Iceland-Faroes gap with *Gambia* and the 4th Destroyer Flotilla, USS *Essex* and USS *Iowa*. Fortunes improved in the second stage. With the destroyers *Agincourt* and *Daring*, Old Shiny was defending the carriers *Bulwark* and *Ark Royal* against a surface attack by *Apollo*, the Netherlands cruiser *De Zeven Provincien* and two Canadian Tribals. *Sheffield* won through.

Several ships had suffered a high incidence of Asian 'Flu, and *Sheffield*, with several cases on board, although they were isolated, was requested to keep her distance by the authorities of Bordeaux, an intended port of call. Bourke politely complied, disappointing the forward messes whose younger element, having recovered a degree of chauvinism after the Sheffield adventure, had been rehearsing *Embrasse-moi, ma chéri*, which would lead to a bit of French out of station. Bourke settled for Guernsey, which was a nice place for bracing walks, but the girls were distinctly superior; they spoke English and understood, which was a handicap.

November opened with Exercise Sharp Squall II, and *Sheffield* flying the flag of Rear-Admiral J. D. Luce and staff, which ended in Rosyth in mid-month, whereupon

Exercise Phoenix II commenced. 'If exercises are the bread and butter of a peacetime commission,' sighed Instructor Lieutenant-Commander R. E. B. Budgett wearily, 'then visits to foreign ports are the jam – but like jam they can sometimes be a little sticky.' Like Bremen, for instance, where Old Shiny secured alongside Europa Hafen on 28 November 1957 . . .

The war had ended only twelve years earlier, and 'the docks were of very modern construction, for which, the Captain of the Port explained, they had the RAF to thank for.' Ashore, however, there were restaurants and beer cellars the like of which Devonport, Portsmouth and Chatham had never known, and where nobody sang old Wehrmacht songs; the frauleins were less interested in a man's nationality than in the colour of his Deutschmarks. There was no suggestion of austerity. Shops were brim-filled with goods, anticipating Christmas, particularly ingenious mechanical toys that were far superior to their unimaginative British equivalents. It was very likely that the boring Mobo and Meccano toys made in England would last for ten years, but the sailors decided that the German (and, soon, Japanese) jumping, dancing, all-guns-firing products were better purchases, even if they failed after a month. Children were only small adults. Pleasure was made for now; ten years later could wait.

In Troon, Faslane and Inverkeithing the battleships *King George V*, *Duke of York*, *Anson* and *Howe* were being progressively reduced to unrecognizable scrap; the cruisers *Dido*, *Cleopatra*, *Glasgow* and *Liverpool* had been withdrawn from service in readiness for the same end. The first of the 'Towns', *Sheffield*'s men noted, had been sentenced. A new terminology was being introduced into wardrooms by the more recently joined junior officers, such as 'Guided Missile Destroyer' and 'Logistic Support Ships'. *Sheffield* moved to Farewell Jetty on the first day of 1958 to provision, slipped on the 22nd and a week later secured alongside Wharf 41, Gibraltar, ordered to take aboard the Commander-in-Chief, Mediterranean, Admiral Sir Charles Lambe, GCB CVO. Rain was falling on arrival, and continued to fall as the seamen in oilskins, in preparation for repainting, scrubbed the ship's side allowing the rain to wash off the soap. The Mediterranean Fleet, pattern 1958, entered harbour on 31 January – *Kenya*, *Ark Royal*, *Eagle* and a clutch of destroyers. *Sheffield*'s log records, in an astonished scrawl, that the CinC stumped aboard at six in the morning, just as the Marine bugler was licking his lips in readiness for blowing Reville and Men under Punishment. The messenger had just disappeared below to wet a kettle of tea, an' don't forget ter shake the Chief Cook in Two Mess, just inside on the right . . .

Malta was reached on 7 February. It was the week of the Munich air crash in which almost all of the talented Manchester United football team were killed, and the

Above: The last few months of 1957 saw *Sheffield* participating in several NATO exercises in northern waters. Above, she steams in company with the Royal Navy's last battleship, *Vanguard*, in a rising sea.

news had subdued the usual repartee at tot-time. On Sunday 9th Rear-Admiral Saltun of the Turkish Navy was piped aboard under the eyes of a crowded Barracca, and that same day *Sheffield* slipped, steaming sixty-two miles across to Tripoli, off which a 21-gun salute was fired to the President of Turkey in the TS *Gemlik*. Sea Hawks, Venoms and Gannets of the Fleet Air Arm executed a fly-past, and *Sheffield* increased to 24 knots as her company lined the rails to cheer 'whilst waving caps in a clockwise direction ('– and don't shout Hurrah; shout Hooray.)'

Grand Harbour was regained on the 21st, on which day, in Göteborg, the British heavyweight challenger, Joe Erskine, was knocked out by the European Champion, Ingemar Johansson. It looked like February was going to be a bad month. Spirits rose briefly when the Commander-in-Chief decided to relinquish his flagship and employ the despatch vessel *Surprise* for future sea-going, only to have Flag Officer Flotillas, Vice-Admiral Sir Robin Durnford Slater, immediately stake his claim to the vacated quarters in *Sheffield*.

Malta had changed, said the older hands – but old hands always do. The wartime rubble that had choked every Valletta street had been cleared and new buildings had risen everywhere, particularly hotels for tourists. Before, in Valletta, there had been the outmoded Phoenicia and not much else to approach European standards. Now, roads were congested with traffic and beaches were crowded; not even remote locations like Ramla Tal Qortin and Ghajn Tuffiema were too far for the madding crowd. Marina Wharf was still where it had always been, but Mary's Bar, the Dreadnought Bar and the Movement Inn were thronged with package holiday-makers from Birmingham and Leeds demanding rum-and-cokes and Campari-and-lemonades.

Fat Mary, who had always scratched a sweaty armpit as she made up a fried egg sandwich before cranking the gramophone, had retired. The Gut now accommodated cramped and airless cafés capable of serving only two or three dishes from a menu that offered fifty Mediterranean 'specialities' (all the others were 'off'), and tawdry souvenir shops.

From the level of Marino Pinto or Lascaris Wharf it was still possible to be hoisted to the Barracca by an alarmingly geriatric lift. Or one could always climb four hundred steps in a pounding sun, only to find oneself, utterly spent, in Floriana, or, finally, hire a decrepit gharri, hauled by an equally decrepit horse whose wheezing labour tore at the heart-strings of every animal-loving Englishman. From the City Gate Terminal the No. 6 green buses still skidded away to Sliema, the blue 80 to Rabat and Dingli. Someone named Mintoff was making rude noises, and water taken from island sources still made lousy tea.

Sheffield departed on Exercise 'Marjex' before first light on 3 March 1958 and the first news bulletins of the day announced the crossing of Antartica by Dr. Vivian Fuchs. Five days later the ship berthed alongside Molo di Ridosso, Bari, on the Adriatic above the heel of Italy. It had been here, on 8 December 1943, that the Luftwaffe had bombed crowded Allied shipping, and the American freighter *John Harvey* had been hit. Unknown to almost everyone in company she was loaded with drums of mustard gas, and the subsequent casualties among personnel afloat and ashore had been viciously heavy. Now, fifteen years later, the port had been extensively rebuilt, the people were friendly and the bars, which seemed never to close, too cheap for the Captain's peace of mind.

Split, Yugoslavia, was reached in rain and heavy winds which continued throughout a five-day stay and eventually turned to snow and sleet. In contrast with Italian Bari, the Communist location was austere, and shops, bars and cafés were few and expensive. The townspeople thawed slowly, but never relaxed beyond the stage of cautious agreeableness. They had never heard of Floyd Patterson or Henry Cooper, Marilyn Monroe or even Hancock's Half Hour, but *Sheffield*'s football team was beaten 6–3 by a very strong Split eleven on a rain-lashed, quagmire pitch, and the ship's party for children, provided with mountains of sticky buns, ice cream, fizzy drinks – not to mention the clowns and pirates – was an outstanding success.

There must be Yugoslavs today, middle-aged, who will still remember with a glow of pleasure the strange, laughing sailors, and jam doughnuts, pineapple chunks with pink custard, and Donald Duck films. The patch-eyed pirates chased and the children shrieked, ecstatically enjoying every moment; they took home bags of nutty crunch toffee, sausage rolls, Mars Bars, salted peanuts and potato crisps, fruit cake and squashed cream slices – and it was thus, by

such home-spun means that relationships were cemented and remained firm for decades – by Lower Deck matloes and not by high salaried turkey-cock diplomats and government emissaries. When Old Shiny departed Split on 16 March 1958 she left behind her thousands of Yugoslavs who had decided that perhaps there was something to be said for Democracy and the Western World. Perhaps. It was something to think about.

Bremen, Venice, Istambul, Haifa and a dozen other ports would be remembered for the quality of their booze or brothels, or, for the dilettante, their museums and old castles, but all would fondly recall 14 April 1958 for quite different reasons.

It all began at 0800, when *Sheffield* embarked three WRNS officers and twenty Wrens from RNAS Halfar, Malta, for a pleasant day at sea. To amuse the girls, huddled in the lee of the port director, the AA guns fired a few

Below: In Split, Yugoslavia, on 14 March 1958, Captain 'Paddy' Bourke, (right) commanding *Sheffield*, receives the Commander-in-Chief of the Yugoslav Navy, Admiral Mate Jerkovic, during a cruise of the Adriatic.

rounds at an aircraft-towed target, and a torpedo was fired and recovered. The Wrens seemed less than impressed, and more concerned that their hair was being mussed up by the wind, and it was chilly up there. Subsequently the guests, in twos and threes, were being introduced to the bridge and the director control tower, the engine-room, the galley and the wardroom ante-room. Then the ship found itself enveloped in fog.

Sheffield was edged into Marsaxlokk, but with visibility reduced to a few yards and now a nasty swell running, it was decided that the Wrens must remain on board for the night. To soothe the girls' apprehensions they were shown a film – *Moulin Rouge* with Jose Ferrer, at whom the ship's company might normally have been expected to bawl, 'Git orf yer bleedin' knees' but on this occasion remained politely mute. The Supply Department found twenty camp-beds and toiletry sundries; the only things missing were pyjamas.

'D'yer hear there? Twenty-three pairs of pyjamas are required, on loan for the night, by Wren personnel sleeping on board. Suitable garments should muster at the Regulating Office immediately.'

Within minutes an avalanche of pyjamas of every style, size and colour overwhelmed the Regulating Office and its duty RPO. 'When I get mine back', one donor promised, 'I'll never dhoby 'em again. I'll use 'em for pillow-cases.' Two garments were quite distinct from the others; they were of gauzy and translucent nylon, delicately coloured pink and blue respectively. They had obviously been purchased ashore for a wife or sweetheart, but were now gallantly surrendered. In the interest of fair play, ruled the Commander, David Williams, those offerings were reluctantly declined.

By dawn the fog had cleared; the Met. personnel would never satisfactorily explain why such thick fog had approached completely unexpectedly, but neither ship's company nor the twenty-three guests wished to complain. Where exactly the young ladies had spent the night was never established nor closely questioned. The WRNS Chief Officer, indeed, spent the night in the Admiral's bed, although *Sheffield*'s log records that Sir Charles Lambe had disembarked several days earlier at Parlatorio Wharf. All that can be said is that twenty-three Wrens were taken ashore looking like kittens that had just stolen the cream, confident that the Navy was a very silent service.

When *Sheffield* arrived off Limassol on 7 June, a considerable force was already mustered in Cyprus waters, including *Ark Royal*, under Rear-Admiral R. Alistair Ewing. After almost two years of rioting, arson and murder, incited by the Greek *Eoka*, Archbishop Makarios had been returned from deportation with a view to the establishment of an independent Cypriot republic, but the situation was still very fragile. This time, however, the Fleet was not concerned with Cypriot affairs but with the crisis in nearby Lebanon, where subversive Arab elements had become active, aided by Syria, and it was considered likely that troops would be flown into neighbour-

ing Jordan and British civilians evacuated from Tripoli.

Meanwhile, westward, a bloody and brutal war was being fought in Algeria, while distant Vietnam, following the defeat of the French at Dien Bien Phu, had been divided into a Communist North under Ho Chi Minh and a non-Communist South under Ngo Dinh Diem. Several hundred American military advisers were in South Vietnam, but it was small print stuff . . .

Eoka extremists were still active; there could be no general shore leave, and organized parties, for cricket, swimming from the beach or visits to archaeological sites, had to be watched over by soldiers with Sten guns. Every morning Old Shiny's bottom was inspected by her own shallow-water divers, and sacks of potatoes supplied by a Greek Cypriot contractor were subjected to inspection by a mine-detector before being lifted aboard. Captain Bourke considered the local liquor to be more dangerous than Colonel Grivas. Ashore, there were several near-incidents, usually involving groups of Greek youths, brave in numbers but always sickeningly abject when alone, who hurled obscenities and occasional missiles, from a safe distance. A cricket eleven from *Sheffield* were in the field against an REME team, near Famagusta, when they were ordered to stop play in mid-over and return to their ship immediately.

The sailors' cricket bags carried rather more than bats, stumps and keepers' pads, but the trouble with Cypriot pseudo-brandy was not just its alcoholic influence on the unsuspecting drinker but that its fumes escaped from the most remote of sanctuaries – even the Auxiliary W/T Office or the Paint Store forward – to tickle nostrils as far aft as the chapel and the officers' bathroom flat.

News had been received of the assassination of King Faisal II of Iraq and his family, with the country declared a republic. *Sheffield* weighed at 1812, immediately everyone had returned aboard, and by the following day, 16 July, was patrolling off Tripoli in readiness to lift off British nationals if their safety were threatened. To southward, *Eagle* was providing cover for the aircraft flying troops in to Jordan at King Hussein's request, and within four or five days the situation had been stabilized (although British troops would remain in Jordan until October.) By 28 June Old Shiny had returned to Cyprus, and off Akrotiri embarked forty men of 40 Commando who, after six months of operations against *Eoka* terrorists, were to be rested in Malta.

'The ship', wrote Commander C. C. H. Dunlop, 'seems to be bursting with bootnecks, but they are very welcome guests – the more so when our arrival at Malta was greeted by boat-loads of waving lovelies; their families had come to meet them. And so ended our time in the eastern Mediterranean, dull at times, but doubtless worthwhile in implementing the policies of H.M. Government.'

The R.M. Commandos, followed by Rear-Admiral Ewing and his staff, disembarked during the afternoon of Wednesday 30 July, leaving *Sheffield* strangely empty and free of the clatter of steel-tipped boots. The queues at the galley and the dry canteen were shorter, and, someone said, a bloke could have a bath without finding himself soaping someone else's leg.

In truth, with or without passengers, shipboard conditions were almost luxurious compared with those of fifteen years earlier. *Sheffield*'s complement was now down to about 650, of whom 181 were seamen, mustering as the Forecastle, Top and Quarterdeck Divisions and consisting of three Chief Petty Officers, eighteen Petty Officers, fifteen Leading Hands and 145 Junior Rates. Pay had improved substantially, and the wartime sailor would have been wide-eyed, disbelieving, could he now see the standard of catering. Corned beef, herrings-in, powdered egg, pot-mess and pea-doo – all had gone, and the word 'rations' would no longer be understood. There was now cafeteria messing. Commander David Williams, with tongue in cheek and with apologies to Lewis Carroll, mused accordingly . . .

Bucket and his winger were walking in the waist,
Discussing food at supper, its texture and its taste.
'D'you suppose', the winger said, 'that if I had two steaks,
    That someone else would go without and have to eat
      hash cakes?'
'Most likely,' said young Bucket, 'I've just had steak at
      supper;
    I'm working up my appetite by walking round the upper.
And when the Last Dogwatchman queue becomes a little
      slack,
    I'm joining up with them again to have another whack.'

It was now known that the final duty of *Sheffield*'s commission would be that of resident cruiser in the Persian Gulf before returning to the Mediterranean and subsequently the UK during early 1959. The Persian Gulf was regarded as probably the least comfortable of all foreign stations, but in this instance the period promised to be brief, and at least the ship would be proceeding beyond Port Said for the first time in her life.

Meanwhile, like any ageing lady who resorts to increasingly heavy cosmetics, *Sheffield* had painted her anchors white with disregard to Mediterranean Fleet orders, which ruled that warships should be uniformly grey. During the forenoon of 3 May, as she steamed past Admiralty House and Fort St. Angelo towards the open sea, a signal was received from Flag Officer Flotillas.

'Good luck to you all. I have never seen *Sheffield* looking so smart as she does today, but CF04 relevant.'

The anchors were repainted grey, and David Williams lamented.

'If seven men with seven pots painted for half a day,
Do you suppose', the Admiral said, 'that *Sheff* would be
      all grey?'
'I doubt it,' said the CSO, 'if *Sheffield* had her way.'
'It seems a shame,' the Admiral said, 'perpetuating whiting.

I think we'll reprint CFOs, and put it down in writing
That anchors shall be painted grey; it's far far less exciting.'
'I weep for you,' the Admiral said, 'I deeply sympathise.
White anchors must have memories and sentimental ties.'
The Commander held his handkerchief before his
      streaming eyes.
'O, *Sheffield*,' said the Admiral, 'I'm sure this caused you
      pain.
Shall we be trotting off once more?' But he was on his ain.
And this was scarcely odd because they were heading for
      Bahrein.'

A passage through the Suez Canal, the Red Sea and Arabian Sea hardly justifies comment. Hundreds of thousands of British servicemen had passed that way under far less comfortable circumstances than the crew of *Sheffield*. Old Shiny let go an anchor three cables off Bahrein's oiling jetty on 14 September 1958. *Newfoundland*, relieved, departed with almost indecent haste, leaving a parting gift to *Sheffield* of the all-purpose tender HMS *Jawada*, which had once been LCT4063, of 895 tons, built by Maclellan of Glasgow in 1943. She had been lent to the Qatar Petroleum Company by the Admiralty in 1952 on the understanding that she was maintained in an operational state. Whilst with the Company she had been manned by an Arab crew, operating as a general cargo carrier, and, if there had been any maintenance, it had been kept a secret; the crew quarters were indescribably filthy and stinking. The cruiser *Gambia*, first to reassume responsibility in August 1958, decided to do nothing with her. *Newfoundland*, next in possession, tinkered with the engines sufficiently for her to run to shore and return once every week, but left the crew quarters untouched and unentered. It remained to *Sheffield* to grasp the unsavoury nettle.

'She approached us out of the mist,' wrote Lieutenant C. R. Stansbury, 'that day we arrived in Bahrein; the full shock did not hit me until she was fairly close. I was standing on the quarterdeck, near to the Commander, and I distinctly felt the shudder of horror that shook him as he surveyed the *Jawada* from truck to waterline. He missed nothing – the rust and grime, the ropes' ends and the gash that littered her decks. Turning to me he said, "You realize what your first task is, Stansbury?" I replied, "Yes, sir – scrub out and repaint that ship." He nodded. "So get cracking." '

Shore-going in Bahrein, as Bungy Williams might have said, was bleedin' diabolical. To begin with, the town was several miles away from the ship's berth. It was a place of modest size, its buildings varying from featureless concrete monstrosities of Western design to flat-roofed Arab houses, ramshackle hovels and even tents. Shops were few, and offered very little worth buying. It was hot – *bloody* hot. The few women seen were closely swathed in shapeless black, with lower faces masked, so that it was impossible to distinguish between a nubile Bedouin maiden, hot for an English sailor, and a wizened and toothless grandmother infested with camel-fleas. On balance, even

Right and below: During her period in the Persian Gulf, *Sheffield* assisted the Army in a number of landing exercises, here shown re-embarking the 1st Battalion Royal Fusiliers from the island of Hallul in 1958. On boarding the cruiser, 'a little figure screamed at us, telling us to take off our bleeding boots because we were mucking up his deck'.

Bungy Williams would have conceded that it was better not to investigate. There were sheiks in pink Cadillacs, and Rolls-Royces with gold-plated accessories, discarded as scrap, it was said, as soon as the ash-trays were filled. Everything was crazily expensive. Worst of all, there was not a drop of booze to be had anywhere, on pain of flogging, so those of *Sheffield*'s company who made one visit never made a second, and warned off those who had not.

Meanwhile, in two days, Stansbury's party had washed down, scrubbed out and repainted *Jawad*, including the galley but not the Arab quarters, which would have to be gutted and rebuilt. Several tons of accumulated scrap – old pipes, ropes, oil drums, rotted canvas and miscellaneous garbage – were jettisoned from the tank deck, which in turn was red-leaded and painted. Below, three of the four Paxman diesel engines and their generators were firing, and a trickle of smoke was rising from the galley chimney.

A crew was left aboard to complete the reconditioning when *Sheffield* left Bahrein to exercise in the Gulf of Oman on 19 September. In four days *Jawada* was to be turned over to a maintenance party from the local frigates, and her scratch crew would not be sorry to be rid of her. Now, however, the Army asked if the vessel could co-operate in manoeuvres during which vehicles would be landed on Halul, recovered, and returned to Bahrein.

It all promised to be a bit of a lark for Stansbury and his party, weary of scouring and painting. In any case, it was always very necessary to show the Brown Jobs that the Royal Navy could do anything at any time.

Despite a degree of awkwardness in opening the bow door and lowering and raising the ramp (which necessitated Petty Officer Hill using one hand to close the main contactors with a broom handle and the other to operate the motor) and the immense vomit of choking back smoke from the engines when started (with twelve Army signalling batteries reinforcing the vessel's own) all went well until the crew saw the four vehicles to be loaded. Someone said he had seen a Laurel and Hardy film, just like this, and the end had been horrific. The vehicles were obviously the largest the Army could find; the smallest was a bull-dozer of more than twenty tons, and what would happen to *Jawada*'s rust-corroded deck under these deadweight monsters boggled the imagination. Worse, the vehicles were to be loaded by crane, and when the Arab crane-driver – receiving shouted instructions from five Army officers, six NCOs and a shrill scattering of Arab brethren – released the bull-dozer as it hovered four feet above the deck, all Navy personnel cringed with eyes closed. *Jawada* shuddered, but by the mercy of Allah, assisted by the high quality of Clydebank shipbuilding, the ravaged deck held firm. Two days later Stansbury (who had been mentally preparing his defence for a Court of Enquiry involving the sinking of one of HM Ships by a bull-dozer) and his equally grateful crew were taken off by the frigate *Loch Alvie*.

On 19 September, at the mouth of the Persian Gulf, *Sheffield* had spoken by light to *Melika*, a Panamanian-registered tanker of 32,000 tons, bound for Holland with a full load of oil. During the night *Melika* was struck amidships by the French *Ferdinand Gilibert*, proceeding into the Gulf in ballast. Both ships were badly damaged, there was a fire but no explosion, and a distress signal was broadcast.

By now, *Sheffield* was too far distant to be of assistance, but it was learned that the light fleet carrier *Bulwark* had reached the collision position, where she was joined by *Loch Killisport* and *Puma*. On arrival, however, there was no sign of *Melika*. She had disappeared, and it was thought very possible that she had already sunk. Despite a high sea running, *Loch Killisport* took *Ferdinand Gilibert* in tow, and turned towards Karachi.

Aircraft from *Bulwark*, however, now reported *Melika* thirty miles away, listing badly. The crew had abandoned her but had not closed down the engines, and the big tanker, unmanned, was pounding away on a steady course under her auto-pilot. *Bulwark*'s helicopters put a salvage crew aboard, and eventually the carrier took the crippled tanker under tow for the shelter of Muscat Bay.

And that was where *Sheffield* found her, leaning drunkenly to port with her tank deck almost awash, but still a valuable commodity. Bourke was ordered to assume responsibility for the salvage of *Melika* for the Admiralty, to act as salvage HQ ship for the daily arriving recovery experts, insurance assessors and shipping company representatives. The damaged ship's cargo was pumped partly into the RFA *Cedardale* and then *Melika*'s sister tanker *Kuwait*. Thus lightened, *Melika* rose to reveal her injury – a gash some seventy feet along her port side that denied any possibility of putting to sea. Meanwhile, Old Shiny's Supply Department personnel had the unenviable task of clearing out *Melika*'s cold storage which, without electrical power for a week, was now far from cold and reeking abominably.

On 30 September, thankfully, *Ceylon* arrived with steel from Malta, and *Sheffield* raised steam. There were no regrets at leaving Bahrein and the geriatric *Jawada*, or Muscat, where there had been no leave after sunset and no smoking in the streets at any time. Nobody disputed that the best view of any Arab port was over the stern when under way, and as Bungy Williams would undoubtedly have said, 'It it wasn't for the bleedin' oil, mate, the Arabs could soddin' stuff their Persian Gulf.'

Some weeks later it was heard that, following temporary repairs, *Melika* was coming through the Suez Canal with salvage tugs in attendance, but by that time Old Shiny was back in Grand Harbour and her crew were frantically buying their final souvenirs – ground bait and rabbits – in readiness for their return to the UK. She departed Malta on 20 December and at one minute before midnight on Monday 12 January 1959 her anchor crashed into the black waters of Spithead. Captain Bourke ordered 'Stop engines,' just as eight bells rang, and Old Shiny had faithfully completed her last commission.

24

'She lies mute and gunless . . . there are ghosts here'

AT 1125 on Tuesday 13 January the ship's company mustered by divisions on the upper deck, and twenty minutes later the bosuns' pipes were shrilling as the barge of CinC, Portsmouth, Admiral Sir Guy Grantham, came alongside the starboard ladder, bringing HRH the Princess Marina, Duchess of Kent, who had launched HMS *Sheffield* almost twenty-three years before. Addressing the men of 1959, the Duchess said: 'She was the first I launched for the Royal Navy, and so I have always had a special and very personal affection for her. I have followed her fortunes throughout the years with interest and pride . . . her name, *Sheffield*, brings to everyone's mind the qualities of toughness, resilience and endurance . . .'

Early that afternoon the cruiser weighed and proceeded into harbour to berth alongside Fountain Lake Jetty,

Right and below: Piped aboard, escorted by the CinC, Admiral Sir Guy Grantham, and welcomed by Captain Bourke, HRH the Princess Marina, Duchess of Kent, visits again the ship she had launched twenty-three years before – the first warship of her name. Twelve battle honours, under her proud crest, are engraved in brass and teak on her quarterdeck.

Portsmouth, where she would remain, unloading stores in preparation for going into reserve. The paying-off ceremony was carried out at noon on 24 June 1959, the ensign was lowered and the ship's company transferred to nearby *Vanguard*, flagship of the Reserve Fleet and NATO headquarters, herself only a year away from the breaker's yard.

Sheffield's silken Ensign and Union Flag, together with other mementoes and trophies, including the ship's bell, were handed over to the Lord Mayor of Sheffield for safe-keeping, but three years later a Town Hall officer, late Royal Navy, discovered the two flags dustily stowed and forgotten in a rank-smelling store-room. Lieutenant-Commander Richard Long, RNVR, retired, was very annoyed, and said so. In 1963 the flags were placed in Sheffield Cathedral. The service was attended by three sometime comanding officers of the warship - Captain A. W. Clarke, Vice-Admiral Sir John Inglis and Captain K. L. Harkness. Still later, in 1966, the flags were hung in the new Chapel of St. George by the Bishop of Sheffield in the company of HRH the Princess Margaret and the Archbishop of York.

For some years *Sheffield*, since her last commission, had been the headquarters ship of the Reserve Fleet at Portsmouth, but in this role was relieved by *Belfast* in 1966. Old Shiny, it was announced, was to be broken up. In January 1967 she was moved from her Portsmouth berth to Rosyth, and then, on 18 September 1967 taken in tow for her last voyage to Faslane. Before she left the Forth, however, a number of officers and men who had served in her held a final party on board. At the evening's end it was arranged that Mr. Thomas Bolton, who had been the first man to join *Sheffield* in 1936 should be the last to descend her gangway in 1967.

An attempt to raise a fund for the preservation of Old Shiny failed. As the scarred old cruiser lay alongside Clydeside at Faslane, the squat white towers of the new Polaris submarine base could be seen from her quarterdeck, and from across the wharf leered a vicious engine, built in Düsseldorf, Germany, that waited to hack *Sheffield*'s steel into neat pieces measuring five feet by two. On the forecastle two men, raincoated, were solemnly assessing. One knelt with a penknife, probing the deck-planks. 'It's not teak,' decided Max Wilkinson, Deputy Chairman of Shipbreaking Industries Limited. 'It's Borneo Berayah.' The other, General Manager George Fleming, nodded resignedly. 'Well, it'll make good garden seats.' Vandals had already stripped and ruined the wardroom and offic-ers' cabins; mahogany had been smashed, linoleum ripped up. Graffiti announced, 'Hibs Rule OK' and 'Up Celtic – Right Up'. The age of the simian had begun. The Sheffield *Morning Telegraph* of 30 October 1967 protested, and the journalist Peter Bloxham wrote that:

'. . . She lies mute and gunless now, this scarred old warrior that kept the name of *Sheffield* bright through twelve battles . . . all is silent and dankly dark below her

Below: June 1963. *Sheffield* is in reserve, justifying only small print in the Royal Navy's muster list, but a retired officer discovers her ensigns gathering dust in a Sheffield store-room. They are placed in the safe-keeping of Sheffield Cathedral by three of the cruiser's earlier commanding officers.

Right: The last sad journey, 18 September 1967. *Sheffield*, disarmed, is towed down-river from Rosyth, bound for the breaker's yard at Faslane, Gare Loch. There are no cheering crowds, no pipes or bugles calling

hands to attention, no ensigns whipping and snapping in the wind. Nobody cares. It's just one more old grey warrior going to her grave – and so many have gone before.

Bottom: Thirty years on. In 1969 a reunion of 'old Sheffields' brings together ex-Leading Stoker Fred Foulger (left), who had served in the ship for 11½ years from 1937, and ex-Chief Stoker Tom Boulton, first rating to join the ship on 6 June 1936 (to 1941) and by arrangement the last leave in July 1967 at Rosyth.

decks. A seaman's locker door hangs half open in the torch beam, disclosing a brash array of yesterday's pin-up girls. The tailor's shop still has its sign, the laundry its ironing boards. There are ghosts here.

On the bridge deck a smashed engine-room telegraph orders, hopefully, "Half Speed". On the deck are a long-discarded Bingo ticket and an emptied RN cigarettes carton. Nearby, a stained and trodden Wardroom luncheon voucher. The celebrated Firth-Vickers stainless steel deckrails, the City's gift and the first ever fitted in a warship, are progressively and rapidly disappearing . . .'

Old Shiny would completely cease to exist within the next six months, but Bloxham need not have lamented. A thousand tons of Sheffield's armour plate – special steel sold on its nickel analysis – would find its way back to Sheffield, while six thousand tons more of milder steel would reach Scottish steelworks. After that, some 700 tons of non-ferrous metals would live again in thousands of different ways. As the old cruiser died, deck by deck, so, alongside her, did the graceful and brave old passenger liner Queen of Bermuda, of Furness Withy.

Following a year of preparation, a once-only reunion of all who had served in Sheffield since her first commission was held aboard Belfast in Portsmouth on Friday 5 April 1968 by permission of the CinC, Admiral Sir John Frewer, KCB. Some 206 officers and men attended, among them five Admirals and twenty Captains RN, one Major-General and two Colonels RM. No fewer than five of the cruiser's commanding officers were present, and several ex-officers had travelled across the Atlantic. The Chief Host, Admiral N. E. H. Clarke (the first officer to board Sheffield in 1936) read to the assembly the message of greeting and affection earlier sent to HRH the Princess Marina, and the reply he had received.

Kensington Palace, W.8.
5 April, 1968.

I send to you, and through you to the officers and men assembled this evening, my warmest thanks for your kind message on the occasion of this Reunion.

I was greatly touched by your thought in recalling my connection with HMS Sheffield, an association of which I was very proud indeed. I therefore send you all my very best wishes for a thoroughly enjoyable and happy Reunion of those who served in this splendid ship.

MARINA.

HRH the Princess Marina, Duchess of Kent, died during the morning of 27 August 1968. A memorial service was held at Westminster on Friday 25 October. Sheffield – always 'her ship', was represented by Vice-Admiral Sir John Inglis, KBE, CB.

On 22 April 1969 a new public house, the Shiny Sheff, at the junction of Crimicar Lane and Sandygate Road, Sheffield, was opened by Vice-Admiral Sir John Inglis, KBE, CB on behalf of the owners, Tennant Brothers Ltd (later Whitbread Ltd) and was invited to 'open the starboard sea cock' in order to pull the pub's first pint. The original name-plate of HMS Sheffield, the cruiser's twelve battle honours and many other mementoes and photographs were displayed in the two bars – Portsmouth and Plymouth – while among the many ex-Sheffield guests was Ken Chambers, Deputy Chief of Sheffield Police CID, who had joined Old Shiny as a 16-year-old Signal Boy in 1941. 'The thing I remember most about those days', he said, 'is the tremendous comradeship. If you were broke and your mate had 3s.6d. – then you both had 1s.9d. That's just how it was.'

Left: October, and the wind blows chill around the cruiser at the Faslane breaker's jetty. She is tethered and toothless now, waiting for the humiliation of piecemeal acetylene dissection, but nothing can rob her of her proud record, a legacy for later ships of her name.

Nine months later, Thursday 15 January 1970, the first section of a new 'Sheffield' class (Type 42) destroyer was laid down in the Barrow-in-Furness yard of Vickers Ltd. The eventual class of fourteen vessels, each of 3,660 tons, would be equipped with the newly developed Sea Dart missile system, be capable of a nominal 30 knots and accommodate a complement of 280. The first of the new class, *Sheffield*, and the second of her name, was scheduled for full completion in 1974.

Within the eighteen months to follow, however, the detested President Milton Obote of Uganda had been overthrown and replaced by the popular and amiable soldier Idi Amin. American forces were progressively withdrawing from Vietnam, Cambodia and Laos; a Gallup poll had revealed that more than half of all Americans had no idea what the war had been about.

There was guerrilla warfare against Portuguese rule in Angola, Mozambique and Guinea, while Sheik Mujibur Rahman had declared that East Pakistan would henceforth be the independent state of Bangladesh. A delegation of Falkland Islanders was visiting Buenos Aires to participate in an agreement by which Argentina would provide an air service to replace the supply ship *Darwin*, which was being withdrawn. An air strip was being built at Port Stanley.

In Los Angeles, California, Charles Manson, also known as Jesus Christ, God, had been found guilty of the savage murder of seven people and sentenced to life imprisonment. Joe Frazier had retained the World Heavyweight Championship by defeating Cassius Clay over fifteen rounds. Arsenal had won the League and FA Cup double and Kevin Keegan had been transferred from Scunthorpe to Liverpool for £33,000. Agatha Christie's *The Mousetrap* was astonish-

ingly playing its 19th year, but even films like *The Sound of Music, Doctor Zhivago* and *Lawrence of Arabia* could not stay the closures of Odeons and Gaumonts in every High Street. Now television ruled.

Twenty-six years after Hiroshima there were no groups of destitute with faded medal ribbons begging for coppers. Most of the great names were no more; Alexander, Gort, Slim, Tedder, Somerville, Cunningham – all had gone. The trades unions were all-powerful, and the nineteen-sixties had been a decade of rising wages, consumer spending and easy credit.

At precisely 1230 on Thursday 10 June 1971 Her Majesty Queen Elizabeth stepped to the front of a platform hung with bunting and flowers, and announced: 'I name this ship *Sheffield*. May God bless her and all who sail in her.'

From the beginning the destroyer *Sheffield* and her class sisters had been designed down to the financial limitations imposed by a Labour government; every possible corner had been cut in order to economize. Minimal dimensions meant not only cramped messdecks, a short forecastle and thus poor sea-keeping, but also serious restrictions on the space available for weaponry and instrumentation. One twin Sea Dart missile system (for which there were only 22 missiles in a magazine equipped with a manually operated hoist) was supplemented by a single 4.5-inch gun and two 20mm Oerlikons. Any addition to armament could only have been achieved by removing the boats. Only one helicopter could be accommodated, while the radar equipment can only be described as obsolescent, too slow to track either supersonic or low-flying targets or to detect aircraft approaching over land. The Operations Room was badly designed, and the ability to assess, integrate and exploit incoming action information was extremely poor.

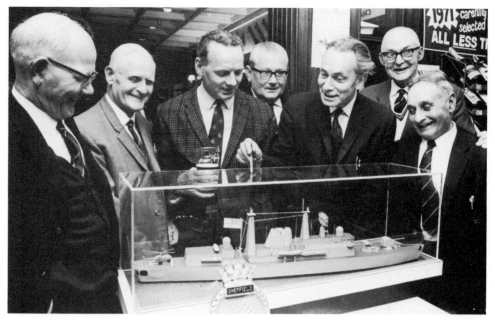

Right: And the final muster. On 16 June 1971 the last of the few (including Tom Boulton) gather around a model of the second *Sheffield*, launched only a few days earlier. Tragically, the new warship is destined to be destroyed by an Exocet missile, eleven years later.

Just after 1000 on Tuesday 4 May 1982 *Sheffield* was struck by a single Exocet anti-ship missile fired by an Argentine Super-Etendard aircraft – one of three that had been able to approach dangerously close before being identified as hostile. The missile, approaching from off the starboard bow, struck the warship on the starboard side amidships at lower deck level, penetrating the forward engine room and passing over the gas turbine finally to pierce the after bulkhead. *The 364-pound warhead did not detonate*, but flames, choking smoke and intense heat defeated all fire-fighting efforts with hopelessly inadequate equipment. Captain Sam Salt ordered his ship to be abandoned, her twenty-two Sea Dart missiles and some 120 4.5-inch shells unfired. Twenty men were dead and many more hideously burned. In only a few minutes the second *Sheffield* had suffered more casualties than Old Shiny had in twelve battles during the Second World War.

The destroyer's hulk remained afloat, smoking and waterlogged, for six days before sinking, a complete loss, while under tow.

The Royal Navy's contribution towards the recovery of the Falklands was a near miracle of improvisation when the service was left reeling as a result of the crippling Defence Review of 1981. The Admiralty would have been acutely embarrassed if the Argentines had delayed their enterprise for a further year or eighteen months; during 1982 ten Royal Naval destroyers were sold off, three frigates in 1983, two destroyers and three frigates disposed of in 1984 and six frigates in 1985. Replacements have averaged one vessel per year.

On 29 March 1984 the keels of two Type 22 frigates, *Sheffield* and *Coventry*, each of 4,100 tons and costing £150 million were laid down in Swan Hunter yards on the Tyne. Attending the ceremonies were Captains Sam Salt and David Hart-Dyke, whose destroyers similarly named had been lost during the Falklands operation. Two years later, on 26 March 1986, the third *Sheffield* was launched. She was commissioned and entered service in 1988, commanded by Captain Nicholas Barker, earlier commanding the ice patrol ship *Endurance*, which first signalled to the Admiralty warnings of the Argentinian occupation of the Falkland Islands in 1982.

The warship had taken 3½ years to build. Many of the shortcomings of her predecessor were corrected. The PVC electrical insulation that had been the cause of so much smoke and toxic fumes was replaced by a less volatile material, and although easy-to-clean acrylic was still employed in cabins and messdecks this was firmly secured to strength sections of the structure so that, under impact, it would not shatter into shrapnel-like fragments. Two missile systems were installed instead of one – surface-to-surface Exocet and anti-aircraft Seawolf – while three types of submarine detection sonar were fitted in addition to more highly sophisticated radar equipments and electronic jammers. There is accommodation for two Lynx or one Anglo–Italian EH101 anti-submarine helicopters.

Cotton underwear is now mandatory for the crew, as are horsehair mattresses and participation in survival courses. 'Anything that can burn has been eliminated as far as possible from the ship,' said Swan Hunter's joint managing director, Mr Alex Marsh.

Captain Barker added, 'We all feel very proud to be in this ship; she carries a fantastic name – the best-known in the Navy after *Ark Royal*. She's a 21st-century ship.'

Her fitting-out, sea trials and working-up routine completed, the third Old Shiny, ready in all respects, joined the Fleet at Portsmouth on 25 March 1988.

Bibliography

BOOKS

Bassett, Ronald. *Battle-Cruisers. A History, 1908–1948*. Macmillan, 1981

Bekker, Cajus. *Hitler's Naval War*. Macdonald & Jane, 1974

Berthold, Will. *Sink the Bismarck*. Longman, 1958

Broome, Captain J. *Make a Signal*. Putnam, 1955

Cain, T. J. (A. V. Selwood). *HMS Electra*. Frederick Muller, 1959

Campbell, Vice-Admiral Sir Ian. *The Kola Run*. Futura, 1975

Churchill, Winston S. *The Second World War*. Cassell, 1949–51

Connell, G. C. *Arctic Destroyers*. Kimber, 1982

— *Valiant Quartet*. Kimber, 1979

Costello, John and Hughes, Terry. *The Battle of the Atlantic*. Collins, 1977

Cresswell, John. *Sea Warfare*. Hamlyn, 1975

Cunningham, Sir Andrew. *A Sailor's Odyssey*. Hutchinson, 1951

Divine, A. D. *Destroyers' War*. John Murray, 1942

Edwards, Commander Kenneth. *Men of Action*.

Grenfell, Captain Russell. *The Bismarck Episode*. Faber, 1968

Haines, Gregory. *Destroyers at War*. Book Club Associates, 1982

Heckstall-Smith, Anthony. *The Fleet That Faced Both Ways*. Antony Blond, 1963

Hezlet, Vice-Admiral Sir Arthur. *Aircraft & Sea Power*. Peter Davies, 1970

Hurren, B. J. *The Swordfish Saga*.

James, Admiral Sir William. *The British Navy in the Second World War*.

Jameson, Rear-Admiral Sir William. *Ark Royal, 1939–1941*. Hart-Davis, 1957

Kennedy, Ludovic. *Menace. The Life and Death of the Tirpitz*. Sidgwick & Jackson, 1979

— *Pursuit. The Sinking of the Bismarck*. Collins, 1974

Lamb, Commander Charles. *To War in a Stringbag*. Bantam Books, 1980

Macintyre, Captain Donald. *Fighting Admiral*. Evans, 1961

Mars, Alistair. *British Submarines at War, 1939–1945*. Kimber, 1971

Mordal, Jacques. *25 Siècles de Guerre sur Mer*. Editions Robert Lafont, 1970

Nicoll, *The Supermarine Walrus*. Foulis.

Northcott, Maurice P. *Renown and Repulse*. Battle of Britain Prints, 1978

Ogden, Lieutenant-Commander M. *The Battle of North Cape*. Kimber, 1962

Pearce, Frank. *Last Call for HMS Edinburgh*. Collins, 1982

Pope, Dudley. *73 North. The Battle of the Barents Sea*. Weidenfeld & Nicholson, 1958

Porten, Edward Von der. *The German Navy in World War Two*. Arthur Barker, 1972

Raven, Alan. *Town Class Cruisers*.

Raven, Alan and Roberts, John. *County Class Cruisers*. RSV Publishing Inc, 1978

Bivouac Books, 1975

Roskill, Stephen. *Churchill and the Admirals*. Collins, 1977

— *Naval Policy Between the Wars*. Part II. Collins, 1976

— *The War at Sea*. Vol. I. HMSO, 1956–61

Rutter, Owen. *Ark Royal*.

Schofield, Brian. *Loss of the Bismarck*. Ian Allan, 1972

— *The Russian Convoys*. Batsford, 1964

Smith, Peter. *Hit First, Hit Hard*. William Kimber, 1976

Smith, P. C. and Dominy, J. R. *Cruisers in Action, 1939–1945*. Kimber, 1981

Snyder, Gerald S. *The Royal Oak Disaster*. Kimber, 1976

PUBLIC RECORD OFFICE

Adm 199/47-63 Convoy Reports

Adm 199/423 Western Approaches War Diary

Adm 199/575-78 HX and ON Convoys

Adm 199/1187-1188 Pursuit and Destruction of *Bismarck*

Adm 199/1931 Mediterranean Convoys

Adm 116/4351-4352 Boards of Enquiry: Loss of HMS *Hood*

Adm 223/36 Engagement and Destruction of *Scharnhorst*

DOCUMENTS, NEWSPAPERS, PERIODICALS

London Gazette Nos. 32281 (Action of Cape Spartivento), *38377* (Operations 'Excess', 'Substance' and 'Halberd'), and *38098* (Sinking of the *Bismarck*).

The logs of HMS *Sheffield*, August 1937 to September 1967.

The diaries of Midshipman L. Cobb and Midshipman D. H. Creme when in *Sheffield*.

The Times, Daily Telegraph, Daily Mail, Daily Mirror, News Chronicle, Sheffield Telegraph, Sheffield Star, Newcastle Journal, The Scotsman, Kirkwall Herald, Illustrated London News, Picture Post, Gibraltar Chronicle, Times of Malta, New York Daily News, Houston Press, Los

Angeles Times, Navy News, Globe & Laurel, Sheffield Salvo (ship's magazine).

ILLUSTRATIONS
Photographs were sent to Lieutenant-Commander H. Treseder during 1968 by very many men who had served in *Sheffield*, and some may have come from the Imperial War Museum, but no record of the origins of pictorial material seems to have survived Treseder's death. To all contributors, whoever they may be, the author extends acknowledgement and thanks.

One photograph, showing *Sheffield* in the Persian Gulf, was sent to the author at the last moment by Fire Officer Michael Sterling of Britoil (North Sea). He had been a National Serviceman during 1957–9, in the Royal Fusiliers, and had taken passage in 'Old Shiny'.

Index